Borrowed Tongues

LIFE WRITING SERIES

In the **Life Writing Series**, Wilfrid Laurier University Press publishes life writing and new life-writing criticism and theory in order to promote autobiographical accounts, diaries, letters, and testimonials written and/or told by women and men whose political, literary, or philosophical purposes are central to their lives. The Series features accounts written in English, or translated into English from French or the languages of the First Nations, or any of the languages of immigration to Canada.

From its inception, **Life Writing** has aimed to foreground the stories of those who may never have imagined themselves as writers or as people with lives worthy of being (re)told. Its readership has expanded to include scholars, youth, and avid general readers both in Canada and abroad. The Series hopes to continue its work as a leading publisher of life writing of all kinds, as an imprint that aims for both broad representation and scholarly excellence, and as a tool for both historical and autobiographical research.

As its mandate stipulates, the Series privileges those individuals and communities whose stories may not, under normal circumstances, find a welcoming home with a publisher. **Life Writing** also publishes original theoretical investigations about life writing, as long as they are not limited to one author or text.

Series Editor
Marlene Kadar
Humanities Division, York University

Manuscripts to be sent to
Lisa Quinn, Acquisitions Editor
Wilfrid Laurier University Press
75 University Avenue West
Waterloo, Ontario, Canada N2L 3C5

Borrowed Tongues
Life Writing, Migration, and Translation

Eva C. Karpinski

WILFRID LAURIER UNIVERSITY PRESS

Wilfrid Laurier University Press acknowledge the support of the Canada Council for the Arts for our publishing program. We acknowledge the financial support of the Government of Canada through the Canada Book Fund for our publishing activities.

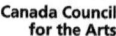  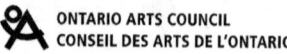

Library and Archives Canada Cataloguing in Publication

Karpinski, Eva C.
    Borrowed tongues : life writing, migration, and translation / Eva C. Karpinski.

(Life writing series)
Includes bibliographical references and index.
Issued also in electronic format.
ISBN 978-1-55458-357-7

    1. Canadian prose literature (English)—Minority authors—History and criticism. 2. American prose literature—Minority authors—History and criticism. 3. Women immigrants—Canada—Biography—History and criticism. 4. Women immigrants—United States—Biography—History and criticism. 5. Autobiography—Women authors—History and criticism. 6. Translating and interpreting—Philosophy.
I. Title. II. Series: Life writing series

PS8185.A88K37 2012   818'.50809920691   C2011-908616-6

Electronic monograph in PDF format.
Issued also in print format.
ISBN 978-1-55458-399-7

    1. Canadian prose literature (English)—Minority authors—History and criticism. 2. American prose literature—Minority authors—History and criticism. 3. Women immigrants—Canada—Biography—History and criticism. 4. Women immigrants—United States—Biography—History and criticism. 5. Autobiography—Women authors—History and criticism. 6. Translating and interpreting—Philosophy.
I. Title. II. Series: Life writing series (Online)

PS8185.A88K37 2012   818'.50809920691   C2011-908617-4

© 2012 Wilfrid Laurier University Press
Waterloo, Ontario, Canada
www.wlupress.ca

Cover design by Heng Wee Tan. Cover image: *1989*, by Daniel Karpinski. Text design by Angela Booth Malleau.

Every reasonable effort has been made to acquire permission for copyright material used in this text, and to acknowledge all such indebtedness accurately. Any errors and omissions called to the publisher's attention will be corrected in future printings.

No part of this publication may be reproduced, stored in a retrieval system, or transmitted, in any form or by any means, without the prior written consent of the publisher or a licence from the Canadian Copyright Licensing Agency (Access Copyright). For an Access Copyright licence, visit http://www.accesscopyright.ca or call toll free to 1-800-893-5777.

In Memory of Barbara Godard, 1941–2010

Contents

Introduction
Migrations of Theories: Autobiography and Translation   1

1   **Literacy Narratives:**
    Mary Antin and Laura Goodman Salverson   41

2   **Immigrant Crypto(auto)graphy:**
    Akemi Kikumura and Apolonja Maria Kojder   93

3   **Experimental Self-Translations:**
    Eva Hoffman and Smaro Kamboureli   129

4   **Translation as Allegorical Metafiction:**
    Marlene Nourbese Philip and Jamaica Kincaid   173

    Conclusion   223
    Notes   229
    Works Cited   245
    Index   263

Introduction

Migrations of Theories
Autobiography and Translation

"Why does everything have to be translation?" (anonymous)

Reading a library book, I pause at the comment scribbled in the margin by a previous borrower. Is the frustrated voice telling me that translation has become another critical cliché, a dead metaphor? Has the academic market been saturated with calls for translation? Or is this reader's reaction to be taken as a symptom of resistance to translation whose challenge entails a discomfort of stepping out of the familiar zones of self, language, history, and culture? I argue that despite the accelerated movements of people across the globe we have far from exhausted the possibilities of translation—learning to translate and learning from translation. The voice above reminds me that in addition to historically persisting inequalities, there are new conflicts and scattered hegemonies asserting themselves through globalization. From illegal immigrants, victims of human trafficking, farmers evicted by transnational corporations, to new cosmopolitan elites, both financial and intellectual, and mass consumers of globalized popular culture—translation (and often wilful mistranslation) has its place in the production of new hybridities, new linkages between the local, the national, and the global. In the landscape where migrancy and translation are inextricably linked, people affected by larger historical shifts, past and present, turn to life narrative as a means of translating their lived experiences into texts. This book hinges on translation as itself a migratory practice that transfers meaning from one signifying context to another and on translation as practised by migrants in their life narratives.[1] Why do they often feel, or are told by others, that they are living and writing in "borrowed tongues"?

The idea of a borrowed tongue—of living, communicating, and working in a language that is not one's mother tongue or mother's tongue—has been constantly present in autobiographical narratives written in English by American and Canadian immigrant women who are the subjects of my study. The metaphor of borrowed tongues refers primarily to writing literally in a second language or a language which is perceived as not one's own, a language "on loan" by migrants, immigrants, or various displaced subjects. For indigenous and postcolonial subjects, writing in borrowed tongues often means using the language of colonial oppression and domination while at the same time trying to challenge cultural imperialism and the dominance of standard English through the use of various local "englishes." But amid the pronouncements that in a postcolonial, globalized culture there are no longer "pure originals" as regional and national identities are remade in a constant flow of "borrowing and lending across porous cultural boundaries" (Lionnet, *Postcolonial* 15), there lurks a more sinister meaning of "borrowing" linked to economic dependence. After all, the creation of those vibrant diasporic and migrant cultures and identities is frequently one of the material consequences of poverty and debt incurred by the countries forced into a discursive regime of neoliberal economies. Likewise, writing in borrowed tongues may refer to any discursive activity—complicitous or otherwise—that involves engagement with dominant ideologies of gender, class, and racialization, the imposition of normative (hetero)sexuality, and the hegemonic constructions of religion, ethnicity, and citizenship. Life in a borrowed tongue can also describe a general mode of being in the world for women writing under the conditions of patriarchy and using the master's tools—man-made languages and male-dominated discourses—to dismantle the master's house, to borrow Audre Lorde's memorable phrase. In particular, writing as an immigrant woman in the genre of autobiography means writing both in a borrowed tongue and in a borrowed genre—grappling with a legacy of (or indebtedness to?) inherited models of androcentric or mainstream autobiographical representation. Focus on language and translation in immigrant women's narratives makes these texts suitable vehicles for the task of feminist rewriting and remaking of the "mastercode" of autobiography into new sub-genres of what I prefer to call life writing.[2]

Since borrowing and debt are as ubiquitous as translation, and it is tempting to see them as synonymous, in this book I examine different attitudes to translation as a form of working in a borrowed tongue. All chapters are organized around a few general questions: What mutualities and affinities exist between life writing and translation? How is life writing staged and performed as a project of translation in particular texts? What is the relationship between languages and identities they are capable of constructing and articulating? How does the writer's choice of translation strategies correspond to her understanding of social and symbolic power invested in languages at a particular historical moment? What can the underlying philosophical and ethical paradigms of translation located in each text reveal about the writer's conceptions of subjectivity, alterity, and genre? How do the translator's choices correlate with her politics and ideology? My goal is to supply theoretical insights into individual narratives, place different articulations of immigrant subjectivities in a comparative perspective, and develop sub-generic categories capturing prevailing themes and methods of immigrant women's life writing. The underlying premise of my approach is a belief that autobiography studies can benefit from "borrowing" concepts and theories from translation studies so as to enrich and expand our reading of life writing.

Introducing Translation

> How many people live today in a language that is not their own? (Gilles Deleuze and Félix Guattari, "What Is a Minor Literature?")

A poststructuralist answer to the question posed in the epigraph would be: Everyone. "Living in a language that is not one's own" addresses two kinds of linguistic displacement: the subject's universal displacement from language and the translating (and translated) migrant's displacement from the host language, both of which resonate with the scope of this study.[3] In my discussion of immigrant women's life writing I rely on poststructuralist approaches to translation, language, and subjectivity that allow me to deploy these concepts as heterogeneous, decentred, and non-unitary. Consequently, when I use Roman Jakobson's classic paradigm of translation to map out different practices of linguistic and cultural translation, I can do so only with a qualification that language and culture are not stable entities with fixed boundaries but rather categories that are already plural and divided within, leaking and contaminated, open to flux and fusion. Jakobson's definition of three types of translation—*interlingual*, or translation proper, between the signs of two different languages; *intralingual*, between the signs of the same language; and *intersemiotic*, between linguistic and non-linguistic signs—has been criticized by Jacques Derrida as monolingual, presuming in each case "the existence of one language and of one translation in the literal sense, that is, as the passage from one language into another." As Derrida further reminds us, there is no unity of the linguistic system; there is no purity in language; rather, "there are in one linguistic system, perhaps several languages and tongues" (*The Ear* 100).[4] In this sense, translation processes are at work in every text inasmuch as every language is foreign to itself and can never be one. Translation is thus a function of meaning making. If translation can be defined as "the transport of a semantic content into another signifying form" (Derrida, *The Ear* 120), writing in general can be viewed as translative. Kathy Mezei voices this hermeneutic sentiment, describing writing "as always a translating—the translation of thoughts, images, concepts, silence into words" (9). One can detect here the tensions between different philosophical and linguistic traditions: the Platonic one that posits translation as a link between thought and language, and the Aristotelian one that tends to focus on translation proper. As a result of "the process of disciplinary hybridization" (Simon, *Gender* ix), translation studies today has left behind narrow Eurocentric definitions of translation as a univocal and unidirectional transfer of meaning from the source language to the target language, both of which are viewed as already polyvocal and hybrid. At the same time there has been a widespread recognition of the plurality of translational practices going beyond the linguistic model.[5]

In the chapters that follow I examine different strategies chosen by different writers for dealing with the problems of borrowing and translation and a range of positionalities employed in response to "borrowed" tongues and discourses that traverse their narratives. Translation, more specifically its forms and models, provides a structural pattern to my contextualized close readings that focus on language practices grounded in concrete social, historical, and cultural situations.[6] In each text I trace the movements of translation described by Jakobson, as well as multidirectional translations that occur at the interfaces of different systems. I attend to the material traces of translation proper as a linguistic transfer between a source language and a target language, where each language is already seen as plural within. I look at passages that are identified as translated and try to find evidence of the untranslatable and unassimilable difference in them. In terms of intralingual translation (within the same system of signs), I pay attention to negotiations and mediations in English of multiple constructions of subjectivity, through different intersecting codes of gender, race, class, sexuality, ethnicity, religion, and age—often conflicting or contradictory, filtered through the autobiographical subject's experiences in non-English-speaking cultures. In each narrative, I analyze cultural translations that make possible contestation of discourses of assimilation, citizenship, nationalism, and diaspora. I study intersemiotic translation (between two different systems of signs) in the relationship between subjectivity and genre as a search for a form capable of accommodating specific gendered, racialized, and class experiences of the writing subject that exceed the traditional "norms" of masculinist genre. Through the problematics of accent, I also show how different authors "translate" between speech and writing. Moreover, I analyze the material, historical, and geopolitical conditions of the texts' production and consumption as these conditions determine to a large extent the shape of each text. I ask how these conditions "translate" into a possibility of a specific kind of life writing and how they permit or hinder different constructions of migrant subjectivities. Both language and translation operate in the material world as commodities, granting their users a privileged or marginalized status in the structure of social power relations, including those of the institutions of literary production and reception, access to publishing, and dissemination in the global marketplace.

All this signals that I foreground translation in a double sense—as a linguistic and as a philosophical phenomenon—while also pointing out its political and ethical implications. Part of my intention is to engage in current debates in translation studies concerning what many translation scholars find to be the annoying habit of "borrowing" the term translation and extending the boundaries of its usage. The two competing approaches identified above are known as a narrow and a broad view of translation. The narrow view, corresponding with Jakobson's translation proper, is defended by such theorists as Theo Hermans, who criticizes Jakobson for including intralingual and intersemiotic translations in the umbrella category of translation and argues that it is necessary to arrest a free semiosis of the sign "translation" in which "one semiotic entity is transformed into another" (44). Hermans's views are opposed by André Lefevere, who challenges the idea that linguistic codes play a primary or fundamental role in translation.[7] Generally speaking, broad approaches to translation are supported by different perspectives: poststructuralist, feminist, phenomenological, and postcolonial, on which I draw in my readings. In poststructuralist terms, all texts and subjects are viewed as always-already translated, so translation is part of any inscription of meaning. Feminist translation presents itself as a form of cultural production of gendered discourse that critiques and revisions patriarchal languages. In the context of phenomenology, translatability is treated as a hermeneutic property of discourse, a necessary condition for the production of meaning. Finally, in postcolonial studies, translation is often used as synonymous with colonial technologies of domination. In particular, Eric Cheyfitz's comments seem pertinent to my discussion. Analyzing the role of translation in the history of Anglo-American imperialism, he returns translation to its etymological roots and rhetorical function as *translatio*, the figure of metaphor. The intertwining of translation and metaphor is expressed through their common grounding "in the desire of what names itself the *domestic* to dominate what it simultaneously distinguishes as the *foreign*—in the desire of what imagines itself as the *literal* or, crucially, the *proper*, to bring what it formulates as the figurative under control." Since I agree with Cheyfitz's point that "the proper rarely imagines its own figurative status" (Cheyfitz xii), my own inclusive tendency is to combine the best of both approaches. While I consistently try to pay attention to language transfer and interference, justified by my choice of authors who are bilingual or translingual,[8] I am also open to broader applications of translation as a route to uncovering complex relations between language and the social and symbolic realms.

How Is Life Writing a Project in Translation?

> This is how we are, this is how we exist, scattered and confounded, and called to what? Well … to translation! There is a post-Babel, defined by "the translator's task." (Paul Ricoeur, *On Translation* 19)

To unpack the complex question of the affinities between autobiography and translation, I turn to deconstruction, as well as to feminist, postcolonial, and cultural studies theories, all of which have contributed to a radical reconceptualization of both terms. Historically, autobiography as the writing of one's own life and translation as the rendering of another's text into a new language have been assigned a marginal status in literary studies. Both have been seen as forms of processing what is "already written" rather than as "creative" activities in their own right. As "derivative" or "imitative" forms, translation and autobiography have occupied a similar supplementary space in the hierarchically ordered literary institutions that have always privileged originality. Formalist criticism did not consider autobiography to be "literary" in the same sense as "creative" works were literary, and even within the hierarchy of "literary" versus "autobiographical" narratives, ethnic or immigrant autobiography was further marginalized as "aesthetically poor."[9] One of the most important insights of deconstruction is a recognition that systems such as language, culture, or philosophy operate on the oppositional logic of the supplement, suppressing what they consider secondary or supplementary, but what is nevertheless necessary for them to achieve a semblance of identity and completeness. In the case of translation, the original appears as a "totalized self-presence" only by defining itself against translation "that it has banished to its 'outside'" and labelled as derivative (Davis 35). Translation shares this structure of supplementarity with immigrant subjects, immigrant identities, and immigrant languages, all of which are designated as the "outside" or "margin."

The philosophical and political rethinking of autobiography and translation is related to the postmodern anti-essentialist shifting of such categories as subjectivity and language, which are no longer viewed as stable elements in the process of linguistic and cultural meaning transfer. Both translation and autobiography have ceased to be perceived as sites of mimetic reproduction of meaning or identity, "mirroring" their respective sources in reality, but rather have to be considered in terms of their active participation in the production of difference through language. The decentring of the universal subject, together with the deconstruction of the humanist, binary notions of translation and self-representation, has led to challenging the concepts of authorship and originality on which these cultural practices have traditionally rested. From the poststructuralist perspective, neither the "original" nor the "author" can serve as a guarantor of meaning or truth because "texts" and "subjects" are not originary and unified, but always already derivative and heterogeneous, themselves constructed at the intersections of multiple languages and codes. Theorized as isomorphic, the text and the self each is a system of relations rather than a self-identical presence, understood as processes rather than products. Both textuality and subjectivity are posited as effects of what Jacques Derrida calls *différance*, that is, of the continuous movement of difference and deferral in language, which destabilizes the work of signification and signature, making meaning plural and not reducible to the intentions of its presumed "originators" or signatories. Moreover, recontextualized through reading, texts and selves are vulnerable to further transformations and reframings and consequently must be seen as performative rather than reflective.

Like performance, autobiography and translation are thought to "supplant" the "original," which—whether as the autobiographer's "self" or the "source text"—is seen as already plural, located in a grid of intersecting discourses and unsaturable contexts, and open to the possibility of multiple repetitions and citations. Sidonie Smith has adapted Judith Butler's theory of gender performativity for autobiographical performativity as a process of subject constitution through available discursive resources. "The history of an autobiographical subject is the history of recitations of the self," much the same as "the life as lived experientially is itself performative" (Smith, "Performativity" 21). The effect of stability and substance of the self, as well as of narrative coherence and meaning of a life, is produced through re-enactment or repetition of cultural scripts, "among them the culturally pervasive discourses of identity and truthtelling that inform historically specific modes, contexts, and receptions of autobiographical narrating" (Smith, "Performativity" 18). Autobiography is performative in Butler's sense of performativity as the power of discourse to produce effects of solidity, interiority, and depth through iteration (18).[10] The intelligibility of individual autobiographical performances depends on the audience's ability to recognize and process the norms and patterns of self-construction. This departure from the idea of autobiography as a product of self-expression has been echoed in translation studies by a shift away from understanding translation as a transfer of pre-existing meaning. Derrida in "Des Tours de Babel," his rereading of the myth of Babel and of Walter Benjamin's influential essay "The Task of the Translator," makes an opening toward "the performative dimension" of translation, rejecting the "representative or reproductive" relation between the original and translation (180). According to Benjamin, translation is transformative rather than imitative in that it makes the target language "grow" at the same time as it ensures survival of the original by making a foreign text perform new meanings in the target culture. What translation communicates is "the kinship of languages" longing to converge into the ideal "pure language." For Derrida, too, language and translation neither reproduce nor communicate the meaning of the original. What they communicate is not the content but the need to communicate. The meaning of language is communication: a performative gesture of receptiveness, opening to the "foreign" or Other. What is at stake from the beginning in his interpretation of the translated myth of Babel is the type of language contract involved in translation: the double bind of the unity of language and the multiplicity of tongues, the impossibility and the necessity of translation, of translatability and untranslatability (185).

Derrida's theory here moves away from traditional discussions of fidelity and infidelity to the original toward contemplation of the performative nature of translation. However, rejecting speculative notions of translatability versus untranslatability as a final impasse, or aporia, of translation and working from the model of translation as a craft, Paul Ricoeur in his essays *On Translation* also arrives at a performative paradigm, recasting faithfulness and betrayal as indispensable "practical alternatives" in the exercise of translation (14). In fact, the "passage" of translation, its productive work, consists precisely in translating the untranslatable by generating "equivalence without adequacy" (7). His view of translation as construction of commensurability entails betrayal as the condition of possibility of translation, whose risks must include "creative betrayal of the original [and] equally creative appropriation by the reception language" (37). He thus proposes to accept the limits of translation as a philosophy of in-between, without absolutes. Paradoxically, by accepting a definition of translation as "equivalence without identity" we remain faithful to language's rhetoricity and its propensity for disseminating meanings. Ricoeur's reconceptualizing of the problem of fidelity and betrayal can be compared to Barbara Godard's reformulation of the same challenge in terms of "the ethical constraint of 'fidelity' to *two* languages" ("Introduction" 18), which puts the translator in a different relationship to the source and target texts, de-emphasizing her mastery and control for the sake of creative, dialogic intercession that honours the generative powers of both languages.

Interestingly, self-representation, like translation, has also been framed in terms of fidelity to the "real" and "authenticity" of expression. It has a lot to do with the fact that both translation and autobiography are produced under the sign of the proper name, making them indexical genres that point to something "real" other than themselves. The proper name metonymically identified with the "author" or the "original" traditionally functions as a transcendental signified, the untranslatable "presence" or the outside referent that arrests the process of supplementation. But translation can be replaced by retranslation just as life narratives are open to retellings and rewritings. Also, as Derrida shows in interpreting the meaning of "Babel" as both the name of God and the word "confusion," the proper name can be translated into a common noun. Names can be changed, and signatures can be forged. A signature on the contract in both autobiography and translation has an institutional, legal significance, a reminder of property or copyright laws under which they both operate. How strong is the power of the proper name as a guarantor of "authenticity" can be seen in situations of exposed fraud or forgery, which only intensify the binding force of the contract. One can recall the recent controversy around *A Million Little Pieces*, James Frey's "fake" memoir, whose readers demanded "a thousand little refunds" when the hoax was discovered. This incident has prompted revisiting the terms of what Philippe Lejeune calls the autobiographical pact, sealed by the signature of the proper name as a mark of "an unquestionable world-beyond-the-text, referring to a real person," and has confirmed that "[e]xceptions and breaches of trust only emphasize the general credence on the type of social contract" (11).

The function of the proper name in both autobiography and translation is not only ideological, as an instrument for producing and maintaining distinct subjects, but also genealogical, linked to transmission and continuity. According to Derrida, the scene of translation is inscribed "within a scene of inheritance and in a space which is precisely that of the genealogy of proper names, of the family, the law, indebtedness" (*The Ear* 104). Earlier, in his essay on Babel, Derrida reflects on Benjamin's view of the translator "as an indebted subject, obligated by a duty, already in the position of heir, entered as survivor in a genealogy, as survivor or agent of sur-vival'"("Des Tours" 179). Following Benjamin, Derrida posits a double sense of "sur-vival" (*sur-vivre*), namely that of "afterlife" and "living on," spanning two temporalities of translation: past oriented and future oriented, and corresponding with the genealogical and invigorating functions of translation.[11] This relation of survival is common to both translation and autobiography, as simultaneous attempts to commemorate and to inscribe something new and "unique" in the inherited system of language. While the text's "afterlife" is a promise of its collective remembrance (Brodzki, *Can These* 156), it also lives on through the possibility of its future rereadings.

Deconstruction is not always perceived as politically viable, and in fact its claims have often been excessively distorted.[12] Still, I argue that for the subject who is posited as a "supplement" deconstruction opens the possibility of empowerment and change through decentring and unravelling hegemonic meanings. Feminist, postcolonial, and cultural studies theories have politicized the concept of translation in both a literal and a metaphorical sense, relating it to the entire problematic of the power to represent. For example, from the mid-1980s, the Canadian feminist bilingual journal *Tessera* has showcased translation "both as literal practice and as metaphor for how women [and, one might add, other minoritized subjects] are situated vis-à-vis the dominant culture" (Godard, *Collaboration* 13). Both translation and autobiography have undergone scrutiny as gendered and racialized concepts, implicated in the production and maintaining of ideologically charged, hierarchical oppositions between original/copy, active/passive, male/female, and self/other. Feminist translation studies claims that such oppositional thinking justifies a dominant tendency to feminize and devalue the figure of the translator, while for feminist autobiography critics such rigid binarism is linked to the hegemony of the (white) masculine subject. Similarly, postcolonial theories draw attention both to the exclusionary character of Western autobiographical practices in their constructions of the writing subject and to the historical role of translation in perpetuating colonialism.

At the same time, translation and autobiography have been adopted and revamped by cultural studies as sites where cultural identities, individual and collective, are negotiated and produced when people strategically align themselves with and/or are forced into the existing regimes of difference. Taking the cultural turn, translation has become reconceived as part of the process of cultural representation and interchange, an interactive textual practice of transcoding and constructing meanings and selves cross-culturally. Embracing a plurality of translational practices as linguistic and cultural performances means abandoning both linguistic relativism (seeing language as culturally specific, basically untranslatable) and linguistic universalism (seeing language as capable of representing some transcendent human truth). It also means the end of a theory of translation as equivalence, grounded in a poetics of transparency that Barbara Godard, one of the pioneers of feminist translation studies, characterizes as "the way in which certain cultural traces and also certain self-reflexive elements are eliminated from the text so that the translated text is deprived of its foundation in events" and its performative status ("Theorizing Feminist" 47). In practice, feminist translations have been used to counteract the erasure of the translation effect and to flaunt the translator's presence as a gendered, racialized, and cultured being who leaves her signature on the work (Godard, *Collaboration*, 50). By bringing to the forefront the movement of its production, translation not only draws attention to the constraints of language and other semiotic practices, but also restores visibility to the figure of the translator and opens up a "third space" between the extremes of pure difference and universal sameness, both of which render translation useless and both of which delegitimize the subject of difference into either absolute otherness or complete denial of specificity.

Flaunting the cultural and ideological underpinnings of translation reveals mechanisms of suppression and domination, of exclusion and inclusion, of appropriation and unequal access to self-representation that operate through specific linguistic practices—the processes which Gayatri Spivak defines as "the staging of language as the production of agency" ("The Politics" 189). She also posits the politics of translation as epistemologically enabling in trying to rethink the binding problem of identity (the obligation of identity), of how boundaries are drawn within, around, and between the selves, and to envision other possibilities, of letting go of boundaries. Language is where the self loses its boundaries but also where it is constituted. Metaphorically speaking, translation can be adopted as a paradigm for transgressive or "border" writing by women, migrants, and other marginalized groups, who experience "the difficulty of access to language, [or] a sense of exclusion from the codes of the powerful," and therefore call themselves "translated beings" (Simon, *Gender* 136), becoming "supplements" in a double sense: additional (secondary) and supplanting (alternative).

As a "borderline" activity, translation can be turned into new modes of cultural production, or is indeed incessantly at work in the process of culturing, as the title of Spivak's more recent essay "Translation as Culture" indicates. This idea is present in Homi Bhabha's understanding of global culture from the postcolonial perspective as a category of translation, which involves precisely "borderline" transformations of cultural identities in migrant or minority discourses.[13] Such ways of viewing translation as a productive (and sometimes violent) space of the border mark a departure from traditional vertical models in which sense or ideas "trickle down" from the original (as a source of profound meaning) to translation (as an interpretation toward depth). The collapse of the hierarchy of "originary" and "secondary" languages and cultures is best captured by the image of translation as a transversal movement across surfaces that reveals unexpected linkages and genealogies, reflecting both postmodern fascination with different modalities of movement and mobility and the reality of global displacement of people that produces various migrant hybridities and located hybridities (Spivak, "Translation as Culture" 16). Barbara Godard explores the ethico-political implications of this shift from verticality to the horizontal in-between-ness by looking at indigenous Canadian resistant practices of translation as telling the story across, connecting translation with performance of testimony against colonialism by staging the encounter of "your word *against* mine" ("Writing between Cultures" 87).

The Law of the Genre

> The question of gender, then, cannot be explored mainly through the compulsory lumping together of all male-authored texts, on one side, and all female-authored texts on the other. Instead, I think the question can usefully be enjoined at a more specific level, at the level of each text's engagement with the available discourses of truth and identity and the ways in which self-representation is constitutively shaped through proximity to those discourses' definition of authority ... Generalizations about gender and genre in autobiography naturalize how men, women, and the activity of writing an autobiography are bound together within the changing philosophies of the self and history. (Leigh Gilmore, *Autobiographics* 12–13)

My study of different forms of self-representation performed under the conditions of patriarchy and migrancy includes three interconnected theoretical directions, focusing on translator as an autobiographer, translator as a female writer, and translator as a producer of cultural identities. The first area revisits the law of genre, exploring how inherited forms of autobiography get "translated" into sub-genres of life writing to accommodate texts and experiences which would have been "barred from consideration as 'autobiography'" (Gilmore, "The Mark" 11). The second area addresses the question of man-made language, or the name of the Father, by focusing on women's writing, and especially French and Quebec *écriture au féminin* or feminist discourse, as well as gendered diasporic shifts from standard English (the language of the "master") to non-standard "englishes" (mother tongues). Finally, the third locates the possibility of creating new names and genealogies in life writing by minoritized subjects, a process which often involves complex transfers and ruptures of meaning between languages and cultures.[14]

As the history of women's use of the genre shows, women have consistently attempted to rewrite and remake autobiography, by "translating" the traditional project of autobiography into new forms and theories of self-representation. Since the early 1980s, feminist criticism of autobiography has developed strategies to challenge the patriarchal law of genre, including a direct critique of male-identified autobiographical presumptions and conventions; an identification and analysis of women's specific practices; and an insistence on redefinition and expansion of the genre so as to make it more inclusive.[15] In her collection which inaugurated a wave of autobiography studies by women in the 1980s, Estelle Jelinek distances herself from the male-defined tradition of autobiography by claiming that emphasis on personal lives, interest in others, and fragmentariness—as opposed to public lives, individualism, and linearity and coherence in male-authored texts—constitute characteristic marks of the female autobiographical tradition.[16] Nancy K. Miller's influential theories of female authorship and the difference that "changing the subject" makes in the production and reception of writing coincided in the year 1988 with the publication of the next two important collections, one edited by Bella Brodzki and Celeste Schenck, and the other by Shari Benstock. While Brodzki and Schenck's feminist agenda consists mostly in filling historical gaps and gender omissions in the study of autobiography, Benstock observes in her opening essay that the very requirements of the genre—"a drive toward unity, identity, sameness"—are put into question by the limits of gender, what she calls "the fissures of women's discontinuity" (20). For Susan Stanford Friedman, who pursues the ideas formulated in Mary Mason's landmark essay,[17] women's autobiographical forms are not only individualistic but also collective. This "relational" aspect of women's self-representation makes the humanist models of autobiography unsuitable for "women, minorities, and many non-Western peoples" (Friedman 34). As Sidonie Smith shows, these subjects systematically dismantle such "certitudes" of traditional autobiography as "chronological time, individuality, developmental selfhood, myths of origins, the fixedness of identity, bodily wholeness, the transparencies of referentiality, the will to knowledge, the unified self" (*Subjectivity* 184). Following similar transitions in feminist theory, feminist autobiography studies in the 1990s moves from emphasis on differences *between* women and men toward differences *among* women. In particular, Françoise Lionnet's *Autobiographical Voices: Race, Gender, Self-Portraiture* expands the theory of women's autobiography beyond the unifying perspective of gender by foregrounding the importance of racial, cultural, and economic differences and exposing the genre as not only masculinist but also Eurocentric. The project of "de-colonizing the subject" of autobiography gains a strong impetus in the collection by the same title edited by Sidonie Smith and Julia Watson. Similarly, Leigh Gilmore in *Autobiographics* questions the limits of gender as a category of analysis and offers a postmodern meta-critical examination of feminist theories of autobiographical production. The 1990s witnessed the bourgeoning of the field that reached new levels of theoretical and methodological sophistication, and achieved an increasingly interdisciplinary scope largely due to the work of female autobiography scholars. Indeed, as Julie Rak contends, "feminist autobiography criticism has had the most impact on the study of auto/biography as a field" (14). Exemplary in this respect is Sidonie Smith's monumental contribution, often in collaboration with Julia Watson, spanning such areas as the poetics of autobiography, theories of subjectivity and autobiographical performativity, the politics of gender and genre, the uses and applications of autobiography, and the histories of women's criticism and practice of autobiography.

Women's self-insertion into the theory and practice of autobiography operates according to Derrida's deconstruction of "the law of genre" as "a principle of contamination, a law of impurity, a parasitical economy ... a sort of participation without belonging" ("The Law" 227) that also follows the logic of the supplement, bringing out to the forefront what has been marginalized. The feminist claim that the personal is political has led to radical uses of life writing as a form of theory making by such writers as Audre Lorde, bell hooks, Gloria Anzaldua, and Adrienne Rich (Huff 6), who treat personal experience as a basis of insight into social, political, cultural, and economic power dynamics. Following a decade of such practices, Nancy Miller's "personal criticism" advocates bringing the critic's own autobiographical experience into her analysis of other texts. The "purity" of the genre is constantly being undermined by the existence of what Caren Kaplan calls "outlaw" genres such as testimonios and other forms of autobiography as counter-discourse including women's journals and diaries, theorized by Helen Buss, and autoethnography, defined by Françoise Lionnet. Other sub-generic examples that might be added to this category of writing viewed as "outlaw" or "resistant" include collaborative narratives, oral histories, told-to narratives, prison memoirs, culinary autobiography, trauma narratives of incest, Holocaust, and other accounts of survival and catastrophic events.[18] The context of autobiography has been widened to include women; ethnic and racialized subjects; working classes; people with disabilities, chronic illnesses, and addictions; and gay, lesbian, trans, and queer writers—the silenced or "scandalous" Others of traditional Western autobiography. However, the idealism of feminist scholars who often align life writing by minoritized subjects with progressive politics needs to be treated with caution. As Gillian Whitlock's reading of several Middle-Eastern and Afghan texts shows, such life narratives are "soft weapons" because they can be easily co-opted into propaganda (3); hence, she calls for including analyses of commodification into autobiographical criticism.

The robustness and vitality of feminist autobiography studies are visible not only in its response to non-canonical genres excluded from "literary history," but also its adaptability to constant change in the conditions of production and consumption of life narratives, as well as its ability to keep pace with emergent visual and textual cultures of autobiography such as comics, graffiti, zines, internet blogs, and social networking, as well as a practice of reading at the visual/textual interfaces. As a result, very few feminist critics are happy with the generic label "autobiography." Frustration with boundary setting has led to perennial attempts at creating new labels, from Benstock's periphrastic "autobiographical writing," or Culley's "women's personal literature of the self," to Stanton's "autogynography" and "female autograph," Lionnet's *"métissage"* and "autoethnography," Gilmore's "autobiographics," Gonzalez's "autotopography," Brooke-Rose's "bifography," Mintz's "auto/body/graphy," Whitlock's "autobiography in transit," as well as such Canadian coinages as Brossard's *"fiction-théorique,"* Gagnon's *"autographie,"* Marlatt's "fictionalysis," Kadar's "life writing," and Perrault's "autography."[19]

In particular, Marlene Kadar's early reconceptualizing of life writing translates different kinds of autobiographical practices into completely new terms and subverts the genre to the point where it loses any claims to clearly demarcated specificity. Her project is tantamount to "a gradual reworking of the idea of the self in writing," by detaching the *autos* (the I, the self) of autobiography and spreading it "more evenly and in greater variety in life writing of all sorts, including intricate, percipient contemporary poetics" (Kadar, "Whose Life" 155). This is a revolutionary, political gesture, motivated by Kadar's desire to unsettle traditional hierarchies of objective/subjective, fiction/non-fiction, or high culture/low culture, which have selectively validated and valorized different kinds of literature. Life writing is conceived as a continuum of narrative—fictional, non-fictional, and metafictional—from the original androcentric genre (including both biography and autobiography), to feminist rewritings of the genre (still steeped in dualisms), to what Kadar calls "a critical practice" of reading, which brings the reader's subjectivity into the process, inviting the reader to respond to subject-positions constructed for him/her by the text ("Coming to Terms" 10). In its most radical version, life writing is "a way of looking at all texts" (Kadar, "Introduction" x), or even beyond the text, at images and fragments, as in Kadar's recent approach to the poetics of the fragment in *Tracing the Autobiographical*. Because of the ease with which it can cross genres and disciplines, blend them and create new forms, life writing is "the playground for new relationships both within and without the text, and most important, it is the site of new language and new grammars, sometimes blended non-white languages, including

Native-Canadian, African-American styles and dialects" (Kadar, "Whose Life" 152–53). As an anti-hegemonic counter-discourse by various "undesirable" or "unruly" subjects, life writing can be irreverent of boundaries, working the border, and border crossing.

A writer who bridges theoretical reflection with the practice of experimental life writing is Daphne Marlatt, one of the co-editors of *Tessera*. If for Kadar life writing culminates "in its combination of feminism and narrative, fictional and non-fictional, in what has come to be known as *l'écriture au féminin*" ("Whose Life" 158), Marlatt might well illustrate its principles. She also provides a transition from life writing as translation between genres to life writing as a search for the woman-identified "interlanguage," a language in-between meanings, which takes leave of the patriarchal "androlect."[20] Challenged to resist the bias of the inherited forms of language and subjectivity, which she associates with the "white, heterosexual, middle-class, monological, probably Christian and usually male [subject]" ("Self-Representation" 205), Marlatt elaborates her own position regarding a theory and practice of life writing. She introduces the notion of "fictionalysis," which contests the territorial confinements and demarcations of writing and life, of truth and artifice, of language and the body. Fictionalysis, defined as "a self-analysis that plays fictively with the primary images of one's life," allows Marlatt to foreground her non-hierarchical and anti-dualist stance. Through anamnesis and imagination, Marlatt's own texts uncover "that territory where fact and fiction coincide" ("Self-Representation" 204). As she explains, one's life does not comprise only "facts" but also "the phantom limb" of memory (often theorized as temporal translation),[21] as well as what she calls "the imaginary"—a residue of the subject's desire, dreams, imagination, and projections. The reality of the phantom limb and of the imaginary is the reality of the body, of its pleasure and pain, of remembering bodily sensations. Performing a kind of intersemiotic translation, Marlatt's writing stages "an exchange between the text and the body gendered as female." The translating process works bidirectionally since the body "also writes, speaks, gestures, signs, sighs, and sings back. The body translates" (Banting 152). This tradition of writing the body goes back to the 1970s, to Hélène Cixous's *écriture féminine*, a translative practice that would allow women to forge connections between the body, subjectivity, and language. This new "insurgent" writing is "working (in) the in-between," seizing the peripheral, borderline territory as the territory of women (Cixous, "The Laugh" 254). In the words of feminist translator Marlene Wildeman, women's writing of the body is transgressive or "intrinsically *inédite*, that is, different from what has been written before, since only yesterday women were obliged to subject their writing to masculinist literary standards" (36).

At the same time, Marlatt's texts emphasize the ethical prerogatives of life writing as inseparable from the question "How do you represent others?" ("Self-Representation" 202). According to her, women's analysis of their lives, of "the repressed, suppressed ... [and] the power dynamics at play," inevitably leads to "a beginning realization of the whole cloth of ourselves in connection with so many others" ("Self-Representation" 203). These realizations become "real-other-i-zations" that can potentially be conducive to feminist empowerment and the constitution of the political subject:

> Autobiography has come to be called "life-writing" which i take to mean writing for your life and as such it suggests the way in which the many small real-other-i-zations can bring the unwritten, unrecognized, ahistoric ground of a life into being as a recognizable power or agency. ("Self-Representation" 206)

Writing, in Marlatt's terms, is a political and translative process. Its innovative and experimental character lies not only in confounding the boundaries of language and genre, but also in a total re-visioning of life writing as an ethical project of "self writing life" rather than "the life of the self" ("Self-Representation" 205).

Is the Language Male?

> How hard it is for us to *think* we can choose to become writers, much less *feel* and *believe* that we can. What have we to contribute, to give? Our own expectations condition us. Does not our class, our culture as well as the white man tell us writing is not for women such as us? The white man speaks: *Perhaps if you scrape the dark off your face. Maybe if you bleach your bones. Stop speaking in tongues, stop writing left-handed. Don't cultivate your coloured skins nor tongues of fire if you want to make it in a right-handed world.* (Gloria Anzaldua, "Speaking in Tongues: A Letter to the Third World Women Writers" 166)

Second-wave feminist writers from diverse backgrounds have pointed out that translation could be women's mode of being in the world. In addition to Cixous, Luce Irigaray provides a compelling argument in support of this position, declaring that "woman does not have access to language, except through recourse to 'masculine' systems of representation which disappropriate her from her relation to herself and to other women" (85). A slightly different line of reasoning could be opened by linking gender and translation through "lessons of femininity acquired during adolescence," which are like moving into a new culture and a new language (Hirsch, "Pictures" 74).[22] Accordingly, Adrienne Rich admits that, for her, life "under the naming and image-making power of a dominant [male] culture" has demanded "a constant footwork of imagination, a kind of perpetual translation" (175). Echoing Dale Spender's idea of women's foreignness to a "man-made language" by which they are "colonized," Susanne de Lotbinière-Harwood interprets every woman as at least bilingual: "I am a translation because I am a woman" (95). Following Barbara Godard's notion of feminist translation as a rewriting in the feminine, Lotbinière-Harwood attributes to feminist practices of translation

> the intention of recasting women's role in language, changing her [sic] place from phallocentric object of discourse to gynocentric subject/producer of discourse. Making the female body a generative locus of speech means to inaugurate women's linguistic agency as speakers and writers. (150–51)

Furthermore, Godard's work of theorizing feminist discourse as translation draws attention to its emancipatory potential in subverting the monologism of dominant culture. Elaborating on Madeleine Gagnon's comments, she views women's writing as polyglossia:

> Confronted with a plurality of discourses, the mixture of levels of language within one national culture or heteroglossia, wherein their language is marginal with respect to the dominant discourse, women writers figure this metaphorically in terms of polyglossia or the copresence of several "foreign" languages. (Godard, "Theorizing Feminist" 45)

The polyvocal, dialogic, intertextual feminist discourse is translation in a double sense of "transformation" and "performance," both transforming the dominant language and performing or "translating" the female body, turning "a muted discourse" of gesturality into words (46). As in the aesthetics of parody, through ironic repetition with a difference, women's "miming" of the dominant language destabilizes it, transforms its meaning, and extends its usage.

Although these kinds of feminist discourses, focusing on multiplicity of languages within the female subject and pursuing the utopian possibilities of *écriture au féminin*, have played an important role in challenging the "man/dated" discourse, their potential to mobilize multiple subjects under the hegemonic signifier "woman" remains limited unless we adopt an integrative feminist perspective so as to view gender as intersecting with multiple axes of difference, including access to literacy warranted by the subject's social location. Not all women are identically positioned in relation to the "master" tongue, and a degree of distance and proximity to the "centre" of power bears on the possibilities of agency and self-representation. Historical developments of feminist theory show that feminism has undergone a series of creative crises whenever its hegemonic language has been called into question by those who perceived it as a foreign tongue. Not surprisingly, the oppressed speakers often rely on the dynamics of translation as a figure of possible transformation of cultures of monolanguage. Following Cherríe Moraga, many lesbians of colour have symbolically positioned themselves as translators, inventing the lesbian "idiom" in order to express a non-heterosexist economy of desire and sexual pleasure (117). At the same time, feminist Chicana writers such as Moraga, Gloria Anzaldua, and Norma Alarcon have reclaimed La Malinche—Cortez's legendary interpreter—as a powerful symbol of transgressive, multiple-coded identities. Whether vilified as traitor of Mexican indigenous cultures or as collaborator of conquistadores, La Malinche is primarily a survivor of both nationalism and imperialism, two controlling patriarchal regimes.

We cannot forget that while retaining its hermeneutic usefulness as a trope revealing the problematics of mastery and resistance, translation not only is a tool of economic and cultural power brokers but it is also adopted daily as a vital strategy for survival by thousands of various "supplementary" subjects. Those who literally live in translation are displaced, marginal people, refugees, migrants and immigrants, subjects of external and internal colonization, diasporic subjects, subjects of intersecting racial, gendered, sexual, ethnic, or religious oppression. The life writing texts I am specifically interested in as instances of symbolic and material translation belong to a category that can be called ethnic/immigrant life writing.[23] Like any namings, the terms "ethnic" and "immigrant" are highly contested and carry echoes of multiple inscriptions of meaning. As Carole Boyce Davies says, such terms "have power only when one accepts the constraints of dominating societies or when one chooses tactical reappropriation for resistance" (14). Viewed from a transnational and translational perspective, proliferation of "nations" and "ethnicities" can be recognized as part of an effort of a nation-state to contain and bind difference and multiplicity within its borders, or, alternately, as a counter-response to the homogenizing forces of globalization. The dangers of containment, control, and commodification present in liberal pluralist societies that officially embrace multiculturalism and cultural diversity are well summarized in Trinh Minh-ha's words:

> Authorized marginality means that the production of "difference" can be supervised, hence recuperated, neutralized and depoliticized. Unless they "force" their entry, therefore, marginalized "interpreters" are permitted into the Establishment only so long as the difference they offer proves to be locatable and evaluable within the ruling norms. ("An Acoustic Journey" 8–9)

Nevertheless, the cross-cultural narratives in the pages to follow, exploring the tensions between the contingencies of migrant displacement and the linguistic displacement, illustrate how women writers positioned as subjects of difference not only resist but also try to change the dominant norms.

Borrowed Tongues or Mother Tongues?

> We had grown up in a compulsory language system, but, as if to strip us of all language, we were constantly reminded that this language did not belong to us. Depriving us of Chinese or Malay or Hindi, British teachers reminded us nonetheless that English was only on loan, a borrowed tongue which we could only garble. (Shirley Geok-lin Lim, *Among the White Moon Faces* 121)

In Derrida's terms, the gift of tongues, sowing confusion among people, is a *pharmakon*: both a poison and a cure ("Des Tours" 167). While the myth of Babel is the origin of mother tongues, "of the multiplicity of idioms," the confounding of the tongues is also the beginning of a diaspora, a dispersal of people over the face of the earth. Spanning the axis between "mother tongue" and "borrowed tongue," translation for a migrant encodes the tensions between the two and can be experienced through metaphors of movement and displacement, as exile from one or the other, tinted with nostalgia for either language, or as exile from both, the mother tongue and the borrowed tongue. In the latter case, the migrant as a translingual subject unsettles the priority of either language. This experience is akin to the experience of the "foreignness" of any language, of its structural otherness. However, the key question is to distinguish between these two kinds of displacement without collapsing them into a universal condition of the subject of language that occludes the very real differences in privilege and oppression accorded by social categories occupied by migrants.[24]

Terms such as "ethnicity," "immigrancy," and "race" have been undergoing repeated translations of their own. As different critics have pointed out, multicultural emphasis on "ethnicity" constructed as a condition shared by everyone has often been used to diffuse issues of racial discrimination and inequality. Canadian critic Arun Mukherjee criticizes the interchangeable usage of the terms "ethnic," "racial minority," and "immigrant"—a common government practice that leads to denying "the specific oppression that racial minority women experience in Canadian society" (6). Instead, she proposes a distinction between such categories as "ethnic minority women" and "racial minority and Aboriginal women," rejecting the concept of "visible minority" as having negative undertones. Mukherjee's views concur with Sneja Gunew's reading of race as a constructed category imposed from without, in contrast to ethnicity, which is often a "self-chosen appellation" (Gunew 9). According to Gunew, this explains why race is more often associated with group identity, while ethnicity—even though related to group belonging—is frequently embraced as part of individual identity. However, race can also be raised to the status of "self-identified" category and embraced strategically "as a way of signaling … determination to resist assimilation and to pursue cultural difference and autonomy" (Gunew 9–10). Contemporary advocates of a realistic conception of identity such as Paula Moya underscore this dynamic relationship between ascriptive and subjective identities. Ascriptive identities, also called "imposed identities" or "social categories," are historical and collective and "generally operate through the logic of visibility," like race and gender (Moya 97). Subjective identity, or simply subjectivity, "refers to our individual sense of self, our interior existence, our lived experience of being a more-or-less coherent self across time" (Moya 98). Although it may feel "internal," subjectivity is shaped by the experience of social recognition; it is relational because it includes our sense of self in relation to others and to our various identifications. People neither are wholly determined by social categories through which they are identified, nor can they be totally free from them. There is a close connection between how society is organized, what social categories are available, and what subjectivities are possible in a particular historical time, place, and situation.[25]

Possibilities of different identifications and disidentifications accorded by ethnicity, immigrancy, and racialization would not be complete without consideration of the concepts of diaspora and exile, which, according to Shirley Geok-lin Lim, complement the notions and histories of immigration ("Immigration" 269). All the above categories can be mobilized in ethnic or immigrant life writing so as to further make problematic the concepts of nation and citizenship. Viewed etymologically, the basic terms "emigration" and "immigration," giving precedence to either the "source" or the "target" country, relate to traditional models of translation with which they share a binary structure used to support and maintain boundaries between two separate entities, in this case two nation-states.[26] In global capitalist postmodernity (Whitlock), as these boundaries become untenable, we see a shift to different forms of diasporic migrancy that are less territorially bound and can challenge the episteme of the nation-state. Ien Ang recognizes the opportunities present in diasporas:

> Since diasporas are fundamentally and inevitably transnational in their scope, always linking the local and the global, the here and the there, past and present, they have the potential to unsettle essentialist and totalizing conceptions of 'national culture' or 'national identity' and to disrupt their presumption of static roots in geography and history. (558)

Diaspora, however, is itself a highly contested term, another example of an imagined community often constructed for political ends as "a coherent unit of analysis" from a position of marginality (Roberts 188). According to Paul Gilroy, diasporas are created by the non-voluntary international scattering of peoples, "whether as the result of war, oppression, poverty, enslavement or the search for better economic and social opportunities, with the inevitable opening of their culture to new influences and pressures" (304). While immigration and exile often remain articulated within the discourses of nation and nationalism, diaspora "denotes a condition of being deprived of the affiliation of nation," characterized by fragmentation, provisionality, and exigency of history, language, and place (Geok-lin Lim, "Immigration" 297). Where immigration is associated with historical amnesia, diasporic and exilic imaginations are often haunted and obsessed with the past. To this category Geok-lin Lim assigns "minor literatures," defined by Deleuze and Guattari as those "which a minority constructs within a major language" (59), as well as literature written from the transnational and the ex-colonial or postcolonial positions.

Under the conditions of postcoloniality, "colonization" or "autocolonization" of the female subject is more than simply a trope of patriarchal symbolic violence, to use Pierre Bourdieu's term. The ethnic, immigrant, or diasporic subject is constituted through the lived legacy and reality of imperialism. She is literally a translator, possessed of what W.E.B. Du Bois calls "double [or better yet, multiple] consciousness," in that her survival often depends on her simultaneous mastery of several codes of both dominant and colonized languages and cultures. As a result, her writing is infused with ambivalence, growing

> out of the tension between the abrogation of the received English which speaks from the centre, and the act of appropriation which brings it under the influence of a vernacular tongue, the complex of speech habits which characterize the local language, or even the evolving and distinguishing local english [*sic*] of a monolingual society trying to establish its link with place. (Ashcroft et al. 39)

Ironically, as a side effect of persistent efforts to impose English as the imperial language, a "standard" version of the metropolitan language has proliferated into diverse variants and demotic varieties of English. Through those "englishes," the formerly colonized question the authority and dominance of English as well as white supremacy in the material and the symbolic spheres. On the other hand, as the centre-periphery model of "resistance" is disappearing from theory, with post-colonies passing into nations and settler colonies confronted with indigeneity, the problem of diffusion from one cultural centre is replaced by visions of polycentric global dissemination.

By taking up life writing as a project in translation, an immigrant woman makes a leap of faith in "translatability" and constructs her difference as transmissible, making it accessible to her readers from "mainstream" and ethnic communities alike and creating a new subject-position for other women like her. At the same time, however, she foregrounds the asymmetry between the two (or more) cultures and languages by forcing her experiences into the regime of monolingual standardization. According to sociolinguist Rosina Lippi-Green, a transition to mainstream language and culture is associated with formal education systems, upward mobility, success in institutional settings, and "looking beyond the primary networks of family and community for behavioural models and value orientations" (59).[27] The choice of target language determines from the beginning the type of textual authority the writing subject can assume and the type of readers she can reach. Writing in English, either as the language of symbolic empowerment for many immigrants, or as the language of historical oppression for many indigenous and postcolonial subjects, already "disarticulates" the original, and therefore exposes violence inherent in the act of translation. Gloria Anzaldua expresses a radical awareness of this asymmetry:

> Until I can take pride in my language, I cannot take pride in myself. Until I can accept as legitimate Chicano Texas Spanish, Tex-Mex and all the other languages I speak, I cannot accept the legitimacy of myself. Until I am free to write bilingually and to switch codes without having always to translate, while I still have to speak English or Spanish when I would rather speak Spanglish, and as long as I have to accommodate the English speakers rather than having them accommodate me, my tongue will be illegitimate. (*Borderlands* 59)

Against the forcible assignment of grammatical correctness (English or Spanish but not "Spanglish"), she chooses self-reflexive linguistic mobility, replacing locations and categories with languages. She moves from the confinement of space to the translative use of language as cutting across territories, creating fluid demarcations and connectivities, and working against compartmentalization of identities. Translation here acquires a more material status as a survival strategy for women who adapt these languages for their own usage. Therefore, self-representation within a culture that is colonized in a plural sense of symbolic domination through discourses of heteropatriarchy, capitalism, and imperialism, "often involves techniques and languages 'borrowed' from the colonizer" (Niranjana 166). As mentioned earlier, such "master" discourses and "metropolitan" (mostly European) languages are usually gendered as masculine, in contrast to diverse "mother" tongues of marginalized cultures.

Consequently, the project of translation such as ethnic/immigrant life writing can be extremely conservative, reinforcing the symbolic domination of mainstream culture (as a piece of cultural anthropology; a dream of crossing over to the mainstream; a dramatized struggle for control of the metropolitan language); or it can be rich in subversive potential (as when the translator acknowledges her borderline, "hybrid," multiple positionality across languages and turns it into the source of literary, cultural, and subjective redefinition); or it can be, paradoxically, both conservative and subversive. Thus, in the specific situation of ethnic/immigrant self-representation, the practice of translation can be complicit or reclaimed as one more strategy of resistance, rereading and rewriting dominant cultural scripts. Migrant subjectivities, like translation, comprise genealogical and generative functions. On the one hand, they commemorate both the losses and inheritance of migration, encrypting, entombing, and enshrining individual and cultural memory. On the other hand, they are capable of performing difference in creative, invigorating, and unruly ways, through ingesting, assimilating, and combining plural elements. As they cross borders, they also confound separations and challenge fixities imposed by dominant social forces. However, I am far from idealizing migrancy and translation as always potentially progressive. They can be turned into productive sites sparking new languages, subjectivities, and ideologies, enacting and legitimizing new oppositional knowledges and identities. But they can equally become quite reactionary, aligning themselves with power and tending toward fossilization, appropriation, and relativism. In this sense, immigrant women's life writing must be seen as a contradictory site of linguistic and cultural legitimation, governed by mechanisms of complicity and resistance, conflict and containment, commodification and subversion of immigrant subjectivities.

The Subject in/of Language

> From one day to another, from one page to the other, writing changes languages. I have thought certain mysteries in the French language that I cannot think in English. This loss and this gain are in writing too. I have drawn the **H**. You will have recognized it depending on which language you are immersed in. This is what writing is: **I** one language, **I** another language, and between the two, the line that makes them vibrate; writing forms a passageway between two shores. (Hélène Cixous, *Three Steps on the Ladder of Writing*)

Cixous's passage captures the in-between-ness of the subject in/of language and the performative nature of the relationship between them. This vignette or parable plays itself out at the interface of the visual and the textual as the letter H, the subject's signature, is constructed as a sign. But it also illustrates a reiterative nature of the subject—one "I" added to another "I"—while it draws attention to the materiality of language which is composed of a fixed number of letters forming visible marks on the page. Cixous alludes to multiple translations involved in the process of becoming the subject through self-representation, as if echoing Benveniste's thesis that "the basis of subjectivity is in the exercise of language" (226). The subject's dependence on language situates her in discourse and opens her up to the workings of various ideologies. This discursive marking is described by Sidonie Smith from the perspective of the body in autobiography:

> subjectivity is the elaborate residue of the border politics of the body since bodies locate us topographically, temporally, socioculturally as well as linguistically in a series of transcodings along multiple axes of meaning. And so, to ask once again, What does skin have to do with autobiography and autobiography with skin? Much I think—as the body of the text, the body of the narrator, the body of the narrated I, the cultural body, and the body politic all merge in skins and skeins of meaning. ("Identity's Body" 267)

Smith's emphasis on the body serves as a reminder that although subjectivities are produced discursively, they are also phenomenologically experienced, lived as embodiment on the cusp of the physical and the cultural. A screen onto which various social meanings are inscribed, a script to be decoded, and also an active instrument of translation—the body is all three at the same time.

As already noted, translation in a wider sense involves more than a language transfer in that it also requires a transposition of an entire system of cultural, political, and historical meanings. This tendency to see language as embedded in culture allows us to consider as translations even texts written in English but originating in other than English-speaking cultures—such as immigrant cultures or diasporic cultures (Dingwaney and Maier 4). Women's life writing produced from such locations has contributed richly to the development of contemporary theories of subjectivity. Written from a position of displacement and deterritorialization, such texts can potentially transform the way subjectivities are thought and conceptualized in feminist theory in at least three aspects. First, these narratives offer performances of identity that open up some "unthinkable" subject-positions which can be described as translative, transnational, border-crossing, migratory, diasporic, and multiple. Some well-known conceptual labels for such non-unitary, fluid subjectivities include a mestiza, a nomad, a world traveller, a cyborg, or a hybrid self. Feeding directly into feminist theory, they have a certain utopian potential, opening up toward future possibilities. Their performances often constitute disruptive inscriptions of self, pushing against existing definitions and boundaries, embracing heterogeneity and a plurality of positions.

Second, this kind of writing provides specific articulations of difference, confirming the main methodological tenets of multicultural and transnational feminisms, namely the need for an intersectional feminist perspective that would be able to account for multiple and often conflicting locations of the subject. The interlocking of specific markers of difference with language privilege in immigrant women's life writing enables or renders difficult the possibility of particular constructions of subjectivity and agency and determines what subject positions are considered thinkable and "translatable" at this particular historical moment. Since the status of the writer's language and her access to publishing often decide what kinds of subjectivities are constructed and circulated, the analysis of power differentials within and without the immediate text and contexts of self-representation cannot be ignored. It can be helpful to understand the autobiographical subject's frequently fractured and contradictory, temporary and situation-specific loyalties and identifications.

Third, such narratives force us to move beyond the dualisms that still haunt contemporary feminisms, especially when we focus on difference. Translation-based approaches allow us to move beyond the binary logic of the "original" and the "translated self" and instead speak of the interstitial, in-between spaces of the two-way transformation where both source and target are affected. Assimilative models traditionally applied to immigrant women's life writing, like binary models of translation rejected by current theory, are insufficient to describe the multi-layered inscriptions of immigrant women's subjectivity. Consequently, the binaries such as white/other or Western/other cannot be uncritically assumed, but rather in each case the subject's differences have to be carefully historicized and contextualized through thick description. Such narratives invite us to perform a difficult balancing act: we need to mobilize the "third space" of translation between or among the categories. But we also need to understand who invokes or dismisses a category and why. When are categories self-identified and when are they imposed from without? When do we need categories and when not? Who gains and who loses when a category is dropped or embraced? It may also mean that we need to abandon the automatic connection made between marginality and disenfranchisement on the one hand, and progressive and/or subversive tendencies on the other, a romanticizing connection, one might add, that is sometimes made in feminist thought. If we examine linguistic and semiotic practices of translation at interfaces of various codes and discourses that traverse immigrant women's life writing, including discourses of assimilation, literacy, citizenship, ethnicity, nationalism, multiculturalism, and diaspora, we will be able to discover much more complex negotiations of identity than the binary ones. Such narratives are often sites of ideological contestation over meanings inherent in conservative assimilationist, liberal-pluralist, separatist, or progressive feminist and anti-racist rhetoric.

Translation and Alterity

> Language is for the other, coming from the other, *the* coming of the other.
> (Jacques Derrida, *Monolingualism of the Other; or, The Prosthesis of Origin* 68)

Translation establishes the mode of connection and exchange between self and other and is thus inextricably linked to the experience of alterity. When translation is used as a figure of relation to alterity in immigrant women's life writing (including alterity *within* the self), as a way of overcoming the impasse of separations between self and others, it can point us toward an anti-ethnocentric ethics which will open itself to otherness and offer the possibility of forming alliances across languages, races, and cultures, without cancelling difference through the rhetoric of "same but different." Reviewing several contemporary theories of translation formulated by Homi Bhabha, Tejaswini Niranjana, Rey Chow, Jacques Derrida, Gayatri Spivak, and Paul Ricoeur, one can draw parallels between their theoretical models of translation and attitudes to alterity adopted by autobiographers. The comparison can be further extended to the corresponding models of reading and interpretation which emerge from these theories. What reader-positions do we assume when approaching these texts? What concrete reading strategies do we employ in dealing with them? What fault lines in our thinking about alterity are revealed by various translation theories applied to our own readings and interpretations? This critical strategy concretizes the idea of translation as reading which, we are reminded, can be "for connection, invasion or exploitation" (C.B. Davies 23).

While warning the critic/translator against assuming invasive, colonizing postures in relation to the texts, Carole Boyce Davies at the same time stresses the importance of recognizing how power and dominance work in the texts themselves. In the case of ethnic/immigrant women's life writing, it is necessary to identify those repressive/oppressive cultural practices that may constrain the subject's self-representation and may account for what can be voiced and what remains muted. One of the persistent features of discourses of marginality is what might be called a "fallacy of voice." Phrases such as "giving voice to the silenced," "coming to voice," "breaking out of voicelessness" are repeatedly used, suggesting that voice is usually positively valorized over silence. However, in ethnic/immigrant women's life writing, it is equally important to look for the traces of chosen or culturally imposed silencing, to attend to those silences and analyze them. In both reading and translation, it may be beneficial to "demythologize the power of the tongue," associated with "phallic mastery" (C.B. Davies 160). The anxiety or struggle over language—in whose language to write?—is a common topos in feminist and postcolonial theories of translation that has to be deconstructed in the context of both the discursive dominance of English and the frequent heterosexist silencing of ethnic/immigrant women.

These two problems are exactly what seems to plague Homi Bhabha's theory, which is otherwise useful in reconceptualizing the relations of transnationality and emergent types of subjectivity they give rise to. Focusing on migrants and minorities in Western metropolitan spaces—figures whose "liminal" experience he sees as a translational phenomenon—Bhabha develops his concept of a supplementary "third space" of hybridization. The migrant culture occupies this space of translation at the interstices, in the "in-between," and as such it can dramatize the effect of excess, "the stubborn chunks" which do not lend themselves to translation ("How Newness" 224). He is interested precisely in this "'foreign' element that reveals the interstitial ... that has to be engaged in creating the conditions through which 'newness comes into the world'" ("How Newness" 227). Bhabha sees the performance of cultural translation (the staging of cultural difference) as potentially "blasphemous" and thus capable of desacralizing the assumptions of cultural supremacy. However, in his construction of the subject of cultural difference, he tends to ignore gender differentials. He also fails to examine power dynamics between languages within the interstitial spaces of hybridity and ignores the fact that pockets of liminality can exist right at the centre while the marginalized can be quite assimilated. According to Sherry Simon, Bhabha's own writing style, while promoting intellectual hybridity, "seems to convey implicit assent to the dominance of the English language" (*Gender* 153).[28] In addition to these important lessons, what a reader/translator of ethnic/immigrant women's life writing can also learn from Bhabha is that it is often tempting "to see the discourses of the minority as symptoms of the postmodern condition" ("How Newness" 230).

Despite some ethical objections to the deployment of metaphors of hybridity and hybridization as evidence of a continuing grip of colonial and racist categories on our imagination, such categories get re-translated and further politicized as "a potentially oppositional, subversive or democratic space between legal categories of national identities" and the informal as well as cumulative affiliations across national borders (Joseph and Fink 14). These "new hybrid identities" are related, on the one hand, to the growth of cultural diasporas (generating pan-identities such as West Indian, Anglophone, or South Asian) and, on the other hand, to the articulation of transnational political identities (such as feminists, women of colour, Third World women, minorities, refugees, migrants, illegal workers or, more recently, "terrorists"). In Bhabha's terms, they all point to hybridity as an expression of a transnational "third-space" of multiple and often contradictory affiliations. A slightly different take on Bhabha's "third space of hybridity" is given by Ien Ang, who defines the politics of diaspora by insisting on keeping "a creative tension between where you're from and where you're at" (64), where the mobile subject escapes containment by slipping out of any category.

Writing from a predominantly postcolonial perspective, informed by poststructuralist theory, Tejaswini Niranjana describes translation as an imperialist tool, reinforcing "hegemonic versions of the colonized" in such discourses as philosophy, historiography, education, missionary writings, or travel writing (3). The knowledge produced by Western orientalists appropriates "the power to represent the Oriental, to translate and explain his (and her) thoughts and acts not only to Europeans and Americans but also to the Orientals themselves" (11), who thus participate in autocolonization. However, Niranjana also wants to reclaim the notion of translation by deconstructing it and reinscribing its potential as a strategy of resistance, especially in the hands of colonial subjects. Her study seeks "to describe the economies within which the sign of translation circulates ... to probe the absence, lack, or repression of an awareness of asymmetry and historicity in several kinds of writing on translation" (9). In what way can her insights be useful in looking at ethnic/immigrant women's life writing? She inevitably provokes questions about the conditions of possibility for ethnic/immigrant (self) translation and whose interests it serves. Very often such texts duplicate assimilationist rhetoric through normative success stories of crossing from margin to centre, modelled on traditional types of "conversion narratives." A dominant culture encourages such narratives as a voluntary "tribute" to itself in that they ultimately inscribe the very possibility of "translation" as part of cultural hegemony. The subject of ethnic/immigrant life writing is caught up in relations of power, and unless she elaborates strategies of resistance, she may run the risk of losing herself in translation through language and techniques "borrowed" from the dominant culture, or through commodification of her "difference" by liberal discourses of plurality. Commenting on Niranjana's theory, Rey Chow notes that the term "translation" is not only given here many confusing analogies (a "problematic," a "philosopheme," a "field," an "act of resistance," a "transactional reading," or a "hybrid"), but is also valorized as "good" or "bad," depending on who is the translator. Ultimately, the status of translation remains ambivalent, empty, and idealist (Chow, *Primitive* 190). However, Niranjana's warnings should be recognized as valid, especially when dealing with cases of cultural co-optation.

In Rey Chow's own attempt to reconceptualize attitudes to alterity within the framework of ethnography and cultural translation, she advances a bold notion of translation as "a process in which the 'native' should let the foreign affect, or infect, itself, and vice versa" (*Primitive* 189). This is not exactly a new notion as we may recall earlier theories of translation as cannibalism, popularized in the 1960s mostly by the Brazilian poet Haraldo De Campos, where "ingestion" of the foreign is supposed to revitalize the native. Chow's purpose is to create an anti-ethnocentric theory of translation that does not reproduce the ontological hierarchy of languages and cultures, but assumes their absolute co-temporality and coevalness. Her concepts are most useful for the project of reading ethnic/immigrant women's life writing when she develops a critique of Eurocentric tendencies to orientalize, or to exhibit attraction to what she calls "primitive passions." She argues that current critical obsession with "subjectivizing" the subaltern, the native, or the ethnic woman is no less compatible with imperialism than the traditional orientalist "objectifying" gaze. "The reinvention of subjectivity" as a "cure" to imperialist distortions of "other" identities in feminist and postcolonial criticism ("Where Have" 127), together with calls for "thick" description to invoke "history," "context," and "specificities" can be seen as a new form of a plunder of cultures. It "easily becomes complicitous with the dominant discourse, which achieves hegemony precisely by its capacity to convert, recode, make transparent, and thus represent even those experiences that resist it with a stubborn opacity" ("Where Have" 133).

Among the most influential theories, Derrida's philosophy articulated in "Des Tours de Babel" is important for the critique of liberal-humanist concepts of translation, grounded in the order of mimesis, identity, and truth. It prepares the ground for new humanism based on the recognition of the possibility of remaking "the affinity among the languages." In the essay he raises several points that might enrich readings of ethnic/immigrant life writing. He addresses the issue of the asymmetry of languages and, by extension, cultures spanned by translation: "One should never pass over in silence the question of the tongue in which the question of the tongue is raised and into which a discourse on translation is translated" (166). What translation often obscures is "the effect of plurality" or, in terms of postcolonial theory, of hybridity of the text which may be "written in several languages at the same time" (171). Quoting from Benjamin's "The Task of the Translator," he points to the presence of Mallarmé's French in Benjamin's German. The same "contract" to hide difference occurs within one idiom: to maintain its singularity it must suppress the "remainder"—"the multiplicity of tongues must be absolutely dominated" (185). The labour of translation is to challenge the regime of monolanguage and the law of identity, of the same that feeds off its supplement (the foreign). When God confounds the languages, "he ruptures the rational transparency but interrupts also the colonial violence or the linguistic imperialism [of a universal language]. He destines [people] to translation" (174). This simultaneous multiplicity of idioms is both a promise of democratization and a good metaphor for subjectivities produced by ethnic/immigrant life writing. Derrida's reading of Benjamin's theory of translation as the possibility of "alliance and a promise" (202) focuses on translation's ability to reveal a kinship, affinity among the languages (as the condition of its own possibility). Translation promises "the reconciliation of languages" (200), their "symbolic complementarity" (201). "Owing to translation, in other words to this linguistic supplementarity by which one language gives to another what it lacks ... this crossing of languages assures the growth of languages" (202). Translating these ideas into the language of ethnic/immigrant life writing offers the possibility of asserting this symbolic kinship and viewing such narratives in terms of an ethical project.[29]

The problem of translation as an ethical project is given further elaboration in Gayatri Spivak's essay "The Politics of Translation." She has a double stake in translation, both as a translator of Derrida and Mahasweta Devi, and as a poststructuralist, postcolonial critic. She thus deals with both, the practice of the craft and the theoretical implications of translation understood in a narrow sense of interlinguistic process, as well as more broadly, as cultural translation. On the postcolonial map, translation appears as a possible form of neocolonialism: giving *voice* to the other *in* English. Unlike Bhabha, Spivak is concerned with the asymmetries between languages, what she calls "the law of the strongest," since she claims that "you cannot translate from a position of monolinguist superiority" (195). In positing the translator as an ethical agent, she envisions the possibility of the "ethical" meaning of translation—enabling its extension into the "political" meaning—in its ability to defer otherness or "absolute alterity" (181). This is reminiscent of Benjamin mediated by Derrida. However, for Spivak, the ethical aspect of translation is exceeded by the erotic aspect because ethics, in its Western, Kantian version, means "turning the other into something like the self." Translation as a loss of boundaries, "the most intimate act of reading," identified with "surrender," is more erotic than ethical (183). In contrast to male theorists, Spivak defines the task of the translator in gendered terms, demanding respect for the rhetoricity of texts written especially by subaltern women, who are often reduced to sociological specimens in translation. For her, translation means "a simple miming of the responsibility to the trace of the other in the self" (179). Any critic of ethnic/immigrant women's life writing, even when involved in "sympathetic reading as translation" (197), must heed Spivak's warning against "the old anthropological supposition ... that every person from a culture is nothing but a whole example of that culture" (192). When she additionally challenges feminist translators to learn other languages, one can grasp the importance of her concepts for feminism. Through her thinking about translation and language, Spivak arrives at the necessity of problematizing the signifier "woman." It is a truly materialist way of activating the rhetoricity of the sign "woman," attesting not only to the limits of gender as an autonomous category of analysis, but also exposing the often-ignored role that differential language privilege plays in creating and maintaining hierarchies among women. In her later essay "Translation as Culture" she makes an even stronger claim for translation as "transfer from one to another" and "the ethical being-for" which defines what it means to be human (21). "Hearing-to-respond" is the founding task of translation understood as "a listening with care and patience, in the normality of the other, enough to notice that the other has silently made that effort" (22).

A similar call to acknowledge the irreducibility of the other to the self can be found in Paul Ricoeur's philosophy of translation. He goes back to the interpretation of the myth of Babel in Benjamin's essay that was subsequently used by Derrida and offers a more optimistic and pragmatic version, reading Babel as "the non-judgemental acknowledgement of an original separation" (18). The plurality of languages and the diversity of people must be accepted as "the solid fact" of life (11). Translation exists because of this simple fact of heterogeneity. Ricoeur rebuffs Benjamin for his eschatological approach, proposing instead "to take on the 'translator's task' without intoxication and in all sobriety" (16) as a precondition of communication. Translation is possible when we accept its limits. Resistance to translation is associated with ethnocentrism and cultural hegemony; it is an expression of "the mother tongue's nervousness" around its borders and its identity (4). The act of translation is necessarily dialogic, and the translator who recognizes the absolute otherness of the other can find happiness in the experience of "linguistic hospitality ... where the pleasure of dwelling in the other's language is balanced by the pleasure of receiving the foreign word at home, in one's own welcoming house" (10). Despite its benevolent intentions, Ricoeur's rhetoric of hospitality is saturated with uncritical assumptions of privilege and might not be appreciated by those who are homeless. Still, his concept of "equivalence without adequacy" contains the injunction to avoid forcing the other into the regime of sameness. The ethical challenge of translation would then lie in the question of how to practise linguistic hospitality.

From "Ethnics" to "Ethics"

> Writing and reading are not separate, reading is part of writing. A real reader is a writer. A real reader is already on the way to writing. (Hélène Cixous, *Three Steps on the Ladder of Writing* 21)

Both immigrant women's life writing and translation are concerned with the politics and ethics of linguistic and cultural transfer—the very proximity of the terms "ethnic" and "ethics" provoking a slip from "ethnics in translation" to "ethics of translation." As modes of reading, of a life or of a text, life writing and translation both require heightened self-reflexivity and are always about ethical choices as they are confronted with heterogeneous selves and texts, with conflicting intentionalities, with multiplicity of interpretations. Any choice made by the writing subject has to be seen as implicated in power dynamics, an assertion of the violence of closure. Derrida uses the example of *pharmakon*, translatable as both "remedy" and "poison," to illustrate the reductiveness of any decision made by a translator who is faced with the interpretive difficulty of translation arresting the play of rhetoricity. Work on translation makes us realize that attention to both rhetoric and ethics should be integral to any critical approach to the text. Both exceed the autonomy of the subject and direct us toward the other. Rhetoric puts language at the centre of reflection while ethics sends us back to examine issues of identity and difference and our relationship to alterity. Rhetoric and ethics are bound together and cannot be detached from any discursive activity or exempted from any critic's self-reflexive scrutiny. After all, language as discourse, with its underlying cognitive structures for making connections and/or separations between self and other, can be both the most enabling and the most constricting factor in communication. In this sense, Emmanuel Levinas's two-pronged definition of the term rhetoric—as "the art that is supposed to enable us to master language" and as "the knowledge of certain 'figures' of the *said*," of rules and structures of intelligibility that "belong" to language (135)—already signals the ethical significance of rhetoric as "a modality of the approach to the other person" through language. Levinas warns that in language we can forget a fellow human being in the eloquence of our rhetoric or, alternately, we can cultivate "a non-indifference to the other person" (142).

My concern with the ethics of reading and writing echoes Julia Kristeva's search in *Desire in Language* for a theory that would challenge monological approaches espoused not only by rationalist philosophy, but also by literary and cultural discourses of identity and representation. My approach to life writing is informed by a simultaneous pursuit and understanding of both "the rhetoric of ethics" and "the ethics of rhetoric." I take these two phrases to mean recognizing and reading different patterns that encode attitudes to otherness in the text while at the same time maintaining a respect for that text/person who invites me to experience what Levinas calls "proximity to one's neighbor," the proximity that allows the other text/person to remain "totally other" and in relation to which the effects of my own rhetoric, of my own use of language are to be measured (142–43).

Choosing translation as a terrain where attitudes to otherness can be fruitfully explored allows me to return to the question of ethics throughout this study. Translation-based approaches discussed above can be productive in our attempts to restructure models of encounters between self and other, which not only form the basis of the ethical in narratives written by/about ethnic and immigrant subjects, but also structure our own critical responses to such texts. Needless to say, encounters with otherness occur as well in the situation of reading and interpreting texts. In fact, following Levinas, Geoffrey Bennington reminds us that "reading-as-inheritance is not only itself an ethical relation, but ... it can be taken to *exemplify* the ethical relation as asymmetrical relation to an unmasterable and unassimilable other" (67). The critical vocabulary related to the problematics of the subject that I use in the following sections preserves the tensions between what I call hermeneutic humanism (seeing texts as endowed with traces of personhood) and discursive constructivism (seeing texts as traversed by a multiplicity of discourses) as two theoretical bases from which different understandings of writing and subjectivity can be triangulated. These are my phenomenological and linguistic horizons that always remind me of the ethical requirement to respect the unknowable.

Reading life writing through the conceptual framework of translation provides evidence to reinforce the need for an ethical call to attend carefully to language as a primary site where subjects are "fixed" and where categories and boundaries are constituted, boundaries to our thinking that have a concrete, material bearing on the lives of many people. Consequently, the meaning of borrowed tongues must be challenged in the end. The concepts of "mother tongue," or first language, and "borrowed tongue," or second language, are proven to be inadequate. Ultimately, the texts I analyze unsettle any claims of the law of the "proper" in more than one sense—engaging the questions of "property" and "propriety," that is, language ownership and linguistic correctness, in politicized ways. All these meanings of the "proper," linked to property rights, proper name, proper meaning, but also purity, are related to reasserting "hegemonic boundaries that repress difference" (Davis 45). What Derrida calls "the appropriative madness" (*Monolingualism* 24) translated itself into modernity's obsession with drawing boundaries, classifications, hierarchies, and exclusions, generating fantasies of belonging, propriety, and order that serve to justify "nationalist aggressions and monoculturalist homo-hegemony" (*Monolingualism* 64). The reading of immigrant life writing can lead to demystification of such dangerous illusions.

The Architectonics of the Book

> Whereas the wall braces while concealing (it is *in front of* the original), the arcade supports while letting light pass and the original show." (Jacques Derrida, "Des Tours de Babel" 187–88)

In the following chapters I analyze multi-practices of translation and deployment of different strategies of translation in individual narratives as symptomatic of different possibilities of constructing subjectivity, alterity, and textuality on the continuum of choices between heterogeneity and homogeneity, pluralism and ethnocentrism, multilingualism (or bilingualism) and monolingualism, dialogism and monologism. There is a progression from more conventional to more experimental auto/biographical texts which, taken collectively, inscribe a rich generic legacy, from immigrant success story and conversion narrative to confessions and *Künstlerroman*, oral history and autoethnography, *Bildungsroman*, the Canadian long poem, travel writing, and ethnic autobiography. They explore and play with different possibilities of situating the autobiographical "I" that is always already divided, caught up in a complex web of linkages connecting the writing subject, or the narrating "I"; the subject of writing, or the narrative "I"; and the historical subject, or the biological "I."[30] These speaking positions are by no means to be treated as consecutive, but rather as distributive positions entangled in overlapping temporalities, geographies, and modalities of the personal pronouns of discourse.

In chapter 1, "Literacy Narratives: Mary Antin and Laura Goodman Salverson," I focus on two early twentieth-century immigrant life narratives as examples of modernist translation suspended between a tendency to foreignize or to domesticate the source text into the target culture. Although they both exhibit a predominantly assimilatory thrust, constructing empowerment through acquisition of cultural literacy in the "borrowed" tongue, they still find subversive ways to resist dominant structures of representation and genre and challenge the symbolic power of mainstream culture. Under the surface rhetoric of assimilation, Antin's *The Promised Land* and Salverson's *Confessions* perform negotiations of identity through complex and multiple dis/identifications, revealing translation's ambivalent status in the processes of immigrant adaptation and transmission of cultural memory, illustrative of genealogical and generative functions of translation.

In chapter 2, "Immigrant Crypto(auto)graphy: Akemi Kikumura and Apolonja Maria Kojder," I continue exploring the genealogical functions of translation as intergenerational passage between mothers and daughters that ensures the sur-vival of memory. I use Derrida's vocabulary of gift and debt to analyze the economy of the bond between mothers and daughters as similar to that between the original and translation. Central to my argument is the figure of the crypt referring to life writing as a form of preservation or burying the presence of the other. Translating their mothers' lives in an auto(bio)ethnographic manner, these writers exemplify ethical and methodological problems inherent in any form of mediated recovery of "herstories," that is, accounts of women's experiences occluded by the official monolithic History.

In chapter 3, "Experimental Self-translations: Eva Hoffman and Smaro Kamboureli," I examine two life writing texts which situate themselves theoretically and/or performatively in relation to the postmodern. Hoffman and Kamboureli produce narratives that are language-conscious, experimental, and deconstructive. Both writers symbolically reject their immigrant parents in search of new linguistic and cultural affiliations. They both also voice their distrust of translation, viewing it as a product rather than a process. Hoffman's case against translation is based on her recognition of a failure of translation to recapture the "essence" of the original, hence her nostalgia-driven focus on the untranslatable and on what is lost in translation. Kamboureli, on the other hand, repudiates the possibility of translation and perceives its danger in a movement toward closure, blocking the endless proliferation of difference and heterogeneity.

In the last chapter I look at "Translation as Allegorical Metafiction" in Marlene Nourbese Philip's *Looking for Livingstone* and Jamaica Kincaid's *The Autobiography of My Mother*. Both texts replace vertical models of translation as power imposition with horizontal models of creolization and creative borrowing. Philip's narrative literally and symbolically juxtaposes standard English and the Caribbean demotic in the context of diasporic histories of racism, slavery, and colonization. As anti-ethnographic, self-reflexive parody of travel writing, her text re-turns the colonial heteropatriarchal gaze. Kincaid's multi-layered allegorical counter-discourse brings together several themes discussed previously, including an unsettling of the autobiographical contract through the mother–daughter relationship and the economy of debt, as well as a dramatization of the postcolonial trauma of historical, familial, and linguistic ruptures. Most important, however, her narrative models translation as an ethical obligation to the other that puts into question traditional Western assumptions of identity and property rights to the story.

In the concluding chapter I suggest some epistemological lessons that can be learned from reading immigrant women's narratives. I explore the possibility of using translation and life writing in feminist theory as models for feminists to develop complex understandings of identity and agency as produced at interfaces of diverse discourses. How can current theories of translation and life writing be useful to feminists across disciplines? I offer suggestions about how these theories can help us rethink the ways we approach difference, in the context of globalization and under the conditions of neoliberal white supremacy that is paralleled by the supremacy of English as a privileged language in transnational migrations of theories and capital.

Cutting across different types of translation practices identified in particular texts are thematic continuities, such as the issue of genealogy: from "mother" to "mother tongues" and "generic matrices." Quite frequently for women, generic reinventions take the form of "borrowed memories," referring to the possibility of narrating the self through the stories of others, most importantly through the mother's story. The writers' genealogical preoccupations are seen from a number of shifting perspectives exemplified by first- and second-generation immigrant children (Antin and Salverson), first-generation immigrant mothers mediated through the voices of their daughters (Kikumura and Kojder), grown-up daughters distanced from their immigrant parents (Hoffman and Kamboureli), a "motherless" writer struggling with the abusive father tongue (Philip), and a daughter impersonating her mother (Kincaid). Another related motif running through these narratives is the problem of debt and gift, in the sense of indebtedness and inheritance of language, proper name, and genre. My discourse analysis is also thematically focused on the motif of trauma and the challenges that the consequent loss and mourning pose to translation. The selected texts are interrelated through the haunting of memory, individual and collective, including anti-Semitic pogroms, involuntary exile, internment camps, forced deportations to Siberia, the Holocaust, ethnic and nationalist oppression, the Middle Passage and slavery, colonialism and death. As a result, there is evidence of non-translation, of muted discourses, silences, and omissions in all discussed texts, which supports the need to respect the limits of translatability rather than accepting the violence of translation aimed at appropriation or homogenizing of difference.

Chapter 1

Literacy Narratives
Mary Antin and Laura Goodman Salverson

> For some strange reason, I still use my old tattered Hungarian–English dictionary which I bought in Winnipeg in the summer of 1957....The book became a symbol of freedom to me when I bought it on that hot summer day many years ago. This dictionary has helped me to speak English. This dictionary has helped me to write. And I have many things in my mind to write about. As I put them down on paper, I still use my faithful dictionary. (Ibolya Grossman, *An Ordinary Woman in Extraordinary Times*)

Locating Early Paradigms of Immigrant Women's Life Writing

Homage to a dictionary—in immigrant families an object of everyday use elevated to the status of an heirloom—is a poignant image of writing an immigrant life as translation. This image is a visual reminder of the power of literacy to bestow significance on a seemingly ordinary existence. However, by pointing to the freedom gained through translation, this passage attests that language transfer is only the first, or fundamental, level of exchange in the traffic between a minoritized source culture and a dominating receptor culture. For immigrant women writing in English, two-way cultural translation "takes place whenever an alien experience is internalized and rewritten in the culture where that experience is received" (Carbonell 81). And since no culture is monolithic, we must expand this binary model to account for multi-level translations that each subject is called on to perform *within* different cultures she inhabits. In this chapter, I examine the role of translation in the context of linguistic and cultural pressure for assimilation and the bearing of various translation practices upon the formation of immigrant subjectivities in two early texts, Mary Antin's *The Promised Land: The Autobiography of a Russian Immigrant* (1912) and Laura Goodman Salverson's *Confessions of an Immigrant's Daughter* (1939). These two texts have a special symbolic, historical, and heuristic value for my project. First, Antin and Salverson symbolically demarcate my field of inquiry in terms of location and generation, as an American and a Canadian writer, respectively, representative of first- and second-generation immigrant authors. Furthermore, they allow me to historicize the genre of immigrant women's life writing, taking us back to the beginning of the twentieth century when the autobiographical tradition was still largely male-defined. Antin and Salverson also send us back to the rhetoric of assimilation that dominated discussions about immigration early in the century, before the turn to multiculturalism in the 1960s revitalized ethnic literatures. Theorizing today's discourses of multiculturalism against the background of these early narratives, we can fully realize the persistence and continuity of assimilationist patterns of immigrant acculturation. Finally, as paradigmatic examples, *The Promised Land* and *Confessions* embody (although not necessarily exhaust) different possible approaches to translation in immigrant women's life writing, ranging from monolingual and monocultural, to bilingual, bicultural, polyvocal, and multicultural, or any combination thereof.

Translation theorists such as Antoine Berman or Paul Ricoeur often quote Franz Rosenzweig's famous adage that to translate "is to serve two masters" (Berman 3). The source text, the author, and the source language are the "first master" whereas the translated text, the public, and the target language are the "second master." If in the process of translating emphasis is put on the source, we have the case of what after Friedrich Schleiermacher is called "leading the reader to the author." Among the risks involved in this approach to translation is that of producing an unintelligibile text, or, alternately, of "robbing" the source culture of its "proper" content. If translation is moving in the opposite direction, in Schleiermacher's words, we speak of "leading the author to the reader." It may result in "a conventional adaptation of the foreign work" (Berman 4), which constitutes another form of "betrayal" of the source culture through a denial and suppression of cultural specificity. This "test of the foreign," which according to Berman is at the heart of translation, creates an impossible quandary:

> Every culture resists translation, even if it has an essential need for it. The very aim of translation—to open up in writing a certain relation with the Other, to fertilize what is one's Own through the mediation

of what is Foreign—is diametrically opposed to the ethnocentric structure of every culture, that species of narcissism by which every society wants to be a pure and unadulterated Whole. There is a tinge of violence of cross-breeding in translation. (4)

Translation is divided between the reductionist aim of cultural appropriation and the ethical aim of conjoining or bringing together described by Berman as "the essence of translation," which is "to be an opening, a dialogue, a cross-breeding, a decentering" (4). However, the situation of immigrant translators is even more complicated in that we must attend to unequal power dynamics at work and ask: Where is the centre? How is the centre shifting? Consequently, Berman's two forms of resistance that Paul Ricoeur summarizes as "that of the text to be translated and that of the translation's language of reception" (8) do not cover a full spectrum of problems encountered by the translator, who constantly hovers between the poles of ethnocentrism and hospitality apparent in both the source and the target cultures.

Although both Antin's *The Promised Land* and Salverson's *Confessions* illustrate amply the kinds of resistance to translation discussed by Berman and Ricoeur, their challenges as immigrant autobiographers can also be captured accurately through Derrida's description of his own predicament as a French Maghrebian Jew:

> Where then *are we*? Where do we find ourselves? With whom can we still *identify* in order to affirm our own identity and to tell ourselves our own history? First of all, to whom do we recount it? One would have to construct oneself, one would have to be able to *invent oneself* without a model and without an assured addressee. This addressee can, of course, only ever be presumed, in all situations of the world. (*Monolingualism* 55)

Derrida's words illuminate my reading of Antin's and Salverson's life narratives in this chapter, revealing the in-between-ness of their location, the instability of their belonging to either the community of "origin" or the mainstream culture, and the divided loyalties to self and audience. Their texts can be fruitfully considered through a dialectic of foreignizing and domesticating, that is, through Schleiermacher's notions of bringing the reader to the foreign source and bringing the foreign source to the reader, which can be seen as compatible with the conflicting goals of cultural pluralism and assimilation. Moreover, as immigrant women ostensibly engaged in a public act of "confession," they are both interesting insofar as they cross-culturally translate the received codes of gender, sexuality, family, and the body.

Antin's and Salverson's texts belong among what Janet Eldred and Peter Mortensen call "literacy narratives," that is, texts which foreground issues of language acquisition and literacy and which may include explicit images of schooling and teaching. For Mary Soliday, "literacy narratives become sites of self-translation where writers can articulate the meanings and the consequences of this passage between language-worlds" (511). Antin, along with her father and a score of other immigrants, embraces "the literacy myth" derived from the "assumption that better literacy necessarily leads to economic development, cultural progress, and individual improvement" (Eldred and Mortensen 512). For Antin and Salverson, writing their autobiography in English seems to be the ultimate test of arriving; the book's publication marks the apex of the literacy narrative, and the book itself, a physical object, becomes a metaphor of literacy. However, such texts may both challenge and affirm culturally scripted ideas about literacy, extending the concept to include not only writing, but also reading and translation as skills necessary to cross over languages and cultures. The epistemological utility of immigrant literacy narratives lies in the fact that, openly or surreptitiously, they often legitimize alternative forms of knowledge, including those in languages other than English. Antin and Salverson had fathers who were scholars and intellectuals in their respective ethnic communities and passed on high standards of learning to their daughters.

For years, both autobiographies discussed here have generally been regarded as evidence of their authors' successful assimilation. *The Promised Land* was considered a classic text in the discourse of American "civic" religion in urban classrooms during the twenties and thirties (Proefriedt 78). And even when emphasis on assimilation was replaced by multiculturalism in American political and cultural life, when Antin's text has been reclaimed for the Jewish American canon of ethnic writing as "a profoundly Jewish book" (Tuerk, 33), its perception as purveyor of assimilation could be accommodated under the popular rubric of "double identity" or hyphenated identity. However, the "double life" thesis is often cast in simplistic binary terms, leaving no space for ambiguity. I suggest that when the perspective of translation is applied to the question of assimilation, that is, if we keep the tensions between foreignizing and domesticating in both texts, we will be able to locate much more complex negotiations of literacy and identity, including also the autobiographer's positioning vis-à-vis the generic matrix of autobiography. As a result, the very concepts of translation and literacy may have to be recognized as ambivalent and constrained by power structures that determine their content.

Placing *The Promised Land* and *Confessions* side by side as "prototypical" models of immigrant women's self-translation helps to visualize the differences between first-generation and second-generation immigrant narratives. First-generation narrators are those literal migrants, like Antin, whose experience of displacement is not only linguistic and cultural, but also geographic, whereas second-generation narrators, like Salverson, typify the condition of immigrant daughters who have been brought up in immigrant communities. Where Antin's narrative gives first-hand account of life in the Pale, the crossing, and settlement in the new land, Salverson reconstructs in a fictionalized manner her family's pre-immigration past, the history of their crossing, and economic conditions of immigrant life, presenting it in a highly stylized literary form. Nevertheless, immigrant parents in both first- and second-generation narratives make similar sacrifices, investing all their hopes in children whose career as published autobiographers constitutes proof of successful reterritorialization. At the same time, a common focus on children and literacy in both narratives has repercussions on the way immigrants are perceived as infantilized—as "the youngest of America's children" (PL 286) to be educated in "this pleasant nursery of America" (PL 143). Their narratives can thus easily be domesticated into the dominant culture's paternalistic constructions of immigrant "others."

However, both writers demonstrate contrasting attitudes to their families' experience of migration. For Antin, there is no homeland left behind; her family migration is given biblical proportions as an escape from Egypt in search of the Promised Land. Salverson proffers visions of an idealized past in the old country, seeing the present as exile. She makes it clear that theirs was a migration forced by "economic pressure, and nothing else" (C 76). Contrary to Antin's optimism and success,[1] Salverson's narrative grows out of "disenchantment and frustration" (C 6), from a sense of failure despite awards and recognition meted out to her. Although both texts are structured around the motif of the quest, Salverson's quest is dressed in a different kind of romantic rhetoric as a voyage through rough seas, duplicating her Viking ancestors' coming through the storms. There is a hidden paradox though, in that each author takes her respective celebratory or critical stance in response to the value the host culture places on her ethnicity. Salverson can afford to extol the virtues of her "racial" superiority in view of the preferential treatment that Canada's immigration laws had given to Nordic immigrants, as opposed to rampant anti-Semitism exhibited in North America until the end of the Second World War.[2]

Finally, one more difference between the two works concerns the question of the place of immigrant writing in relation to national literature and the rhetoric of citizenship and nationhood. Unlike Salverson, whose one major antecedent in Canada is Frederick Philip Grove's *A Search for America* (1927) and, possibly, Martha Ostenso's earlier semi-autobiographical novel *Wild Geese* (1925), Antin's autobiography must be situated in direct relation to two powerful traditions in American writing, namely the tradition of American spiritual autobiography and the tradition of Jewish American autobiography.[3] Both these traditions are characterized as pre-eminently suited to the expression of American selfhood and the inquiry into what it means to be an American (Couser 13–14). Consequently, Antin's project is framed from the start by the national context, including that of ethnic American literature. On the other hand, Salverson's autobiography introduces a different type of the writing subject in Canada, namely, an immigrant woman writer as oppositional figure, giving a new "ethnic" meaning to the tradition initiated by nineteenth-century British pioneer women writers such as Susanna Moodie or Catharine Parr Traill, who struggled to forge radically new identities in the prevailing context of Anglo-conformity.

Mary Antin's *The Promised Land*

> No, "th," "th," put your tongue against the roof of your mouth,
> lean slightly against the back of the top teeth, then bring your
> bottom teeth up to barely touch your tongue and breath out, and
> you should feel the tongue vibrating, "th," "th," look in the mirror,
> that's better
> And with distance traveled, as part of it
>> How often when it rains here does it rain there?
>> One gives over to a language and then
>> What is given, given over? (Myung Mi Kim, "Into Such Assembly")

Antin's arrival in the US in 1894 at the age of thirteen coincided with what American historians define as the second great wave of migration, from the 1880s to the 1920s, which brought immigrants from southern and eastern Europe: peasants or uneducated urban people from Italy, Greece, the Slavic countries, and a distinct group of Jews from Eastern European shtetls. Unlike the first wave of immigrants who came mostly from northwestern Europe, of British, Irish, German, and Scandinavian extraction, these "huddled masses" of the second wave faced an increasing hostility and anti-immigrant backlash, the sentiments supported by eugenics theories of racial and ethnic superiority and by xenophobic nativist trends.[4] With the closing of the American frontier and the government debate about the need to reduce immigrant quotas, Antin's autobiography clearly carries a political mandate to swing public opinion in favour of immigrants and to counter her readers' prejudices, especially anti-Semitic stereotypes. "Speaking for the Jews," she testifies "to the noble dreams and high ideals that may be hidden beneath the greasy caftan of the immigrant" (PL 157). She positions herself as a translator and apologist on behalf of thousands of poor immigrants, victims of oppression, who are greeted with suspicion and lack of sympathy in their new land. Her mission is to facilitate the communication between the Russian Jew and the American reader, both of whom need to learn "a common language" (PL 144–45). Interestingly, she is ahead of her time in her understanding of the supplementary status of the Jewish people and her stipulation that the official history, preoccupied with "the lives of the great," is incomplete without "the lives of the humble" (PL 72). The historical Antin continued to advocate for open immigration policies as a public speaker campaigning for the Progressive movement and published a pamphlet called *They Who Knock at Our Gates* (1914). Ironically, the success of *The Promised Land* as a model immigrant autobiography and its canonical status in American literature have been dictated less by the book's pro-immigration stance than by its supposedly unconditional praise of the American Dream.[5]

Although *The Promised Land* opens in the tradition of conversion narratives, with Antin's introductory pronouncement of the birth of her American self and her wish to put the past behind, almost half of the narrative is devoted to detailed recollections of early childhood, spent mostly in Polotzk, a small Jewish town in the Russian Pale of settlement. Consequently, her narrative should more accurately be recast in terms of Jewish diasporic experience, with immigration to the New World as its final stage. The text reveals significant differences in how diasporic identities are negotiated in Russia and in America. The Jews in the Pale reject and actively resist assimilation as a sign of bondage, embracing their condition of *goluth*—exile (PL 178). In contrast, the choice of Americanization is presented as an act of free will, a form of reclamation of agency, boldly stated in Antin's declaration that "naturalization, with us Russian Jews, may mean more than the adoption of the immigrant by America. It may mean the adoption of America by the immigrant" (PL 179). For Jews in the Pale, as well as for Russian Jewish immigrants, America represents the challenge of modernity, a clash of times and values. Emerging from "the Middle Ages" of life in the Pale, the diasporic Jew in the New World is initiated into modern discourses of citizenship, nationalism, and patriotism. If the transition from the Russian to the American diaspora encompasses two temporalities, mythical and historical, immigration enacts the movement from myth to history through a symbolic juxtaposition of the founding narratives of both peoples. The biblical story of Exodus is situated outside of history, unlike the story of the American Revolution, which is more "real" to Antin. While Jewish tradition is viewed as "a glorious myth, a belief in which had the effect of cutting [her] off from the actual world," state belonging and patriotic pride are seen in terms of positive transformation from "a people without a country" (PL 178) to "the citizen in the making" (PL 283).

Despite Antin's ostensible preoccupation with "the process of becoming an American" (PL 259), and despite her declared intention to show "what a real thing is this American freedom" (PL 281), the "autoethnographic" first part of the book (which, ironically, records the story of resisting assimilation in the Russian diaspora) plays an important framing role in relation to the "American" part. An attempt to carry over this immigrant "baggage" of the past is specific to the genealogical function of translation. It provides a safeguard against a complete obliteration of transplanted identities and defies the naive image of a marginal subject yearning to be assimilated into the mainstream (George 79). However, the inclusion of such ethnographic or folkloric elements in Antin's—and as we shall see later in Salverson's—narrative can also be looked at as a form of cultural brokerage in response to the readers' expectations. Sau-Ling Cynthia Wong observes that "what gets retrieved and presented as memory may be colored by what the autobiographer feels to be attractive to Anglo readers." As ethnographic translations, these texts are "subtly 'sponsored'" (Wong 158). Although Antin apparently acts as a "native informant," her writing carries traits of diasporic double-coding, containing an implicit warning to the American audience too eager to read her text as an unequivocal expression of "the [immigrant] cult of gratitude" (Holte 31).[6] We find numerous signals that we are in the presence of discourse that is also subversive, inscribing difference, transgressive, cautionary, and resistant in relation to its publicly voiced stance.[7] Even the construction of Jewish medievalism as a foil to the New World's progress loses its propaganda appeal, considering that medievalism was both enforced and voluntarily adopted by the Jews. What is more, in a twist of rhetoric, she actually redirects the charge of medievalism to the Russian Gentiles as perpetrators of "mediaeval injustice to Jews" (PL 90). Nevertheless, Antin has her own agenda, signalled in the text and in her copious correspondence with Ellery Sedgwick, her editor at the *Atlantic Monthly*, where *The Promised Land* was serialized before coming out as a book. She wants to be a historian of both the Jewish life in the Pale and the Jewish immigrant experience. Regarding the first task, she compares it to "being called to the 'bima' (pulpit) to read the Torah" and prays that "no error will pass [her] lips" (Salz 46). Yet, what seems to be motivated by respect for Jewish heritage is also a gender subversion of the religious ritual that excluded women from that function. Whether proselytizing on behalf of Jewish immigrants or exuding her youthful admiration for America, she preserves her right to independent thinking and individualism and refuses to surrender to any form of orthodoxy, religious or nationalistic.

Despite later accusations of becoming a traitor to Judaism, not an uncommon turn of events for a cultural translator,[8] Antin emphasizes the fact that she remains Jewish, calling herself "the spokesman [*sic*] of the 'luckless sons of Abraham'" (PL 183). At the same time, she unabashedly claims the label "American," so much so that some alarmed American-born citizens saw it necessary to launch alternative terms such as "native Americans" or "real Americans" (Sollors, "Introduction" xxxvii). This privileging of Americanization in response to Antin's autobiography has led to the thesis of radical discontinuity between the pre-immigration self and the New World self.[9] However, the text resists this notion by encoding pre-existing divisions within the subject and symbolically displaying diasporic strategies of survival, suggesting correspondences between exile and immigration in the continued experience of poverty, prejudice, and marginality. Different meanings of survival in both parts are exemplified by the symmetrical placement of the tsar's portrait occupying a place of honour in her father's house, and the eulogy of George Washington, declaimed "with a foreign accent, but with plenty of enthusiasm" (PL 163). Similarly, the titles in the Table of Contents rewrite American history in terms of Jewish tradition, simultaneously playing on the universalist motif of the immigrant "bible." Antin appears to be translating both ways, applying her newly acquired language to the task of retelling her past through American rhetoric, and vice versa, conflating the Jewish dream of deliverance from exile, of finding "The Promised Land," with the American Dream. The text is set up as a pedagogical allegory: in the process of Americanization the young are teaching the old, Antin teaching her parents, the New World teaching the Old World. But she also anticipates the possibility of cultural interchange, with the New World learning from the old, in the manner analogous to the readers' "learning" from the immigrant author.

Speaking with a forked tongue, Antin in her use of language strikes an uneasy balance between the foreign and the domestic elements, refusing to yield to her editor's pressure to make her text completely transparent to American readers. As her letters to Sedgwick show, she had to fight for inclusion and retention of a number of Yiddish and Hebrew words that he wanted to cut out from the publication. Such "untranslated" and "untranslatable" content is most tangible in the ethnographic first part, where she foregrounds translation directly in the narrative through reminders that the filter of English has been inserted between the reader and the absent "original" in Yiddish, Hebrew, or Russian. At the beginning, foreign words are avoided, but they gradually become more intrusive, especially in discussions of religion and schooling. She uses different strategies to highlight the non-English linguistic substratum of the text, sometimes providing immediate translations of Yiddish words in the text. At other times, she gives an untranslated term in italics (for example, *zimblers*), to be looked up in the Glossary appended to the text, complete with the Key to Pronunciation. Sidonie Smith comments on the ambivalent status of the glossary, which both effects "a standardization ... a denial of the otherness of language" while also paradoxically disrupting the monolingualism of the text, "insisting on the foreignness of the language, even if that place of foreignness, that place of necessary translation, is marginalized at the back of the text" ("Cheesecake" 129). A common strategy in ethnic literature, the glossary retains its double-edged function as a tool used to establish the author's authority as translator while at the same time foregrounding the presence of the untranslatable chunks that can only be explicated through definitions and approximations.

As Werner Sollors notes, Antin's approach is not systematic but selective, and she leaves out such lexical items as "Pale," "Hebrew," or "skull-cap" from her glossary ("Introduction" xxi–xxii). In many places translation appears without the original but is signalled to be a translation of "the mongrel phrase" from "a mixture of Hebrew and Russian" ("Mayst thou have gold and silver in thy bosom," PL 57). Still in other places, the foreign term is first left untranslated and then explained elsewhere in the text (such is the case of a *kiddush* cup, for example). She draws attention to the process of translation even through deliberate withdrawal of translation. An example of such withholding of translation is Antin's mention of the uncle who gave her "the name of 'Zukrochene Flum', which [she is] not going to translate, because it is uncomplimentary" (PL 55). The narrative also conveys the polyglossia and the polyphonia of the author's world: she recalls her "father ... singing our favorite songs, sometimes Hebrew, sometimes Yiddish, sometimes Russian, or some of the songs without words for which the Hasidim were famous" (PL 61). The text is saturated with acoustic memories of the voices of people around her, with recollections of people screaming, laughing, singing, cursing, and saying their prayers. One of the most memorable scenes is the farewell at the station, where she recalls "a confounding *babel* of voices" (PL 134; emphasis mine), an uncanny image that marks this particular moment from the past as an opening to her future life in translation. Such muted linguistic polyphony is consistent with Derrida's point about frequent erasure of "the effect of plurality" in translation ("Des Tours" 171), a tendency which Antin's text strongly tries to resist.

In the transitional chapter called "The Exodus," a record of the crossing, Antin literally inserts a translated text as a bridge between the two worlds. She "copies" fragments from a genuine letter to her uncle, including a detailed account of her transatlantic journey, which her father "induced [her] to translate" from Yiddish into English (PL 134). She admits to being in possession of "the oily, smelly original" of the letter that she had sent in duplicate after accidentally spilling kerosene on her writing table (PL 134). The passages in petite font are in fact slightly edited excerpts from her previously published pamphlet called *From Plotzk to Boston* (1899), introduced by Israel Zangwill as "the thing" written by Antin in Yiddish, supposedly at the age of eleven, and translated when "she was thirteen" (7).[10] Visually marked off and identified as translated, these elements flaunt the grounding of this part of the text in unfamiliar linguistic and cultural sources, both authenticating her role as a cultural mediator and bringing the audience to the "foreign" source. This strategy illustrates well Antin's double-pronged approach to translation, which is assumed to be an indispensable tool of assimilation and which paradoxically can also be turned into a prominent tool of resistance. Comparing the 1899 pamphlet with the passages reprinted in the autobiography, Sollors notices some significant changes she made, toning down the Jewish idiomatic expression and reorienting the text from a Jewish audience to a presumably Gentile audience ("Introduction" xx). However, the insertion of this heterogeneous material under the sign of translation shows the push and pull of Antin's domesticating and foreignizing tendencies. It suggests both her distancing from the "original," visible in the choices that facilitate access for her American readers, and her simultaneous refusal of a "transparent" narrative that would require her to cover up the presence of translation.

The difficulty of Antin's strategic uses of translation is compounded by the fact that according to her recollections, translation used to be an integral part of her life back in the Pale, and already there it was tainted with ambivalence. Growing up in the European diaspora entailed exposure to several languages. Even within the Jewish tradition, translation was a basis of education that actually consisted in moving back and forth between Hebrew and Yiddish, or Yiddish and Russian. When she started her schooling with a rebbe, she was taught to read and translate passages in Hebrew. She gives detailed accounts of how translation formed a basis of religious instruction and served to maintain gender privilege. Only boys were allowed to be fully literate and "to translate as well as pronounce Hebrew" (PL 112), whereas girls had to memorize specially prepared translated versions of prayers. Kathryn Hellerstein compares this exclusion of women to exile from "the *loshn-koydsh*, the Sacred Tongue" of Hebrew and Aramaic. Most women had access only to the Yiddish vernacular in which they read "the large body of devotional literature—supplicatory prayers, translations-adaptations of the Bible, and sermons" (Hellerstein 65). The ability to translate was tied to social class and status attained through learning, as in the case of Antin's aunt Hode, who was admired for speaking Russian "like a Gentile" (PL 45). An interesting instance of politicizing translation can be found in Antin's descriptions of forced assimilation of Jews in the Pale. The text constructs a cautionary allegory of the "original" that always resists "translation," recounting stories of Jewish conscripts in the tsar's army. These "soldiers of Nicholas" had their bodies, memories, and names—all traces of origin—taken away from them through forced baptism and conversion, but they kept their Jewishness intact by still saying their prayers secretly in Hebrew. Consequently, the sense given to translation is often contradictory: from celebrating the self "made over" in translation to identifying translation with snatching and substituting, as in another cautionary story about "the Evil

One," whose "pet amusement ... was the translating of human babies into his lair, leaving one of his own brats in the cradle" (PL 56). This nursery tale, circulated in the Pale, offers a vivid metaphor for fear of translation as assimilation.

There are numerous examples in the text exposing performative dimensions of literacy and translation as forms of repetitive mimicry without depth, similar to re-enactment of cultural scripts in the process of assimilation. In once such performance Antin learns to chant the Psalms in Hebrew without understanding a word; in another, she pretends to read the *humesh* (The Books of Pentateuch), enjoying the illusion of pure sound, beyond translation, created by her voice of "an unconscious impostor" (PL 92). In both cases, the body seems to be a translating instrument, although it is only mimicking and miming the prescribed words or rituals. As we know from Judith Butler's theory, this performativity extends to what might be called "gender literacy," which enables the female subject to perform socially approved versions of feminine behaviour. A good example of deconstruction of this type of performance is the Jewish women's celebration of the "feast of tears," a traditional lamentation on the anniversary of the fall of the Temple. Antin reports that suddenly, all women in the circle burst out laughing, breaking the illusion of authenticity through this eruption of self-conscious play. Such performances of femininity, in the sense of re-enactment of cultural scripts of gender through imitation and repetition, are a kind of gender mimicry producing the effects of "naturalness." However, if gender and literacy can be mimicked or performed, they can automatically be laid bare as mere surface effects rather than essences. Performance thus proves itself to be a potentially dangerous tool of transgression and deconstruction, especially when we suspect that the anti-essentialist spirit of performance may also have "infected" Antin's entire production of her immigrant self. A disclosure of her transgressions from the beginning constructs her image as a rebel, "the child with the staring eyes" (PL 101), always questioning, demonstrating her nonconformity, curiosity, or disobedience. Where the historical Antin presumptuously steps up to the "bima," her textual counterpart dares to compare herself to King David, who rose to prominence from humble beginnings (PL 92). Similarly, she challenges the rebbe with her endless questions and even puts God to a test, deliberately trespassing against a religious taboo by carrying a handkerchief on a sabbath. This incident mirrors her father's breaking of the sabbath prohibition against labour and reveals her alignment with her father, another "doubter."

However, Antin also has another role model in her great-aunt Hode, an unconventional woman rebelling against patriarchal norms. Even though Antin occasionally opts to perform conformity—when she manufactures tears to look like other girls, or lets her cousin beat her at lotto in keeping with the convention of manliness—her ambivalence in relation to Jewishness and the Judaic tradition is largely correlated to gender politics. As she bitterly confesses, "it was not much to be a girl" in the Pale (PL 29). Despite some evidence of less repressive attitudes to the body, supplied by her memories of bathing naked in the river, she offers a plain denunciation of women's oppression in the Pale, comparing their fate to that of treadmill horses. Unlike her sister Fetchke, young Maschke has been lucky to escape the tyranny of the orthodox family model. The sacrifice of her sister is an obsessive motif for Antin, who seems to be haunted by the conflicted emotions of gratitude, guilt, and pity. In America, as earlier in the Pale, Fetchke, renamed Frieda, is a "little housewife," sent to earn money as a seamstress as soon as she is of legal age to be put to work. The importance of Fetchke/Frieda to the story has rarely been noticed even though Antin's autobiography can be treated as an exorcism of her guilt over Frieda, her alter ego, personifying the fate that the younger sister has happily avoided. Together they form a double configuration of immigrant women, with Mary as a precocious child saved by her exceptionality, and Frieda as an embodiment of a more typical immigrant story. One singular, exceptional Mary speaks for a multitude of immigrant Friedas. Antin blames "a social tyranny" as responsible for her sister's deprivation (PL 198), turning her into a tragic figure impersonating "a sense of loss and a woman's acquiescence in her fate" (PL 158).

Curiously, Antin's performances of femininity seem to be cued to the expectations of her new cultural context. While she displays rebelliousness against women's lot in the Pale, acceptable to her American readers, she seems to be generally oblivious to gender inequalities in America and reproduces gender stereotypes rather uncritically, talking about "stupid little girls and inattentive little boys" (PL 201), or listing proper occupations for girls (to "sew, cook, dance, and play games") and for boys (to "hammer and paste, mend chairs, debate, and govern a toy republic," PL 214). At the same time, she must pay the price for this denial by being forced to suppress her own sexuality.[11] According to Magdalena Zaborowska, "the lower-class female immigrant, like the female slave, can be seen as the most oppressed alien in the land that has always been mythologized in terms of a woman's body" (47). Consequently, the immigrant woman feels compelled to renounce her sexuality, "defying the traditional roles prescribed for females by her own ethnic group and [modifying] the roles defined by the host culture she longs to enter" (Zaborowska 48).[12] As a result of such gender dissimulation, Antin as autobiographer has been accused of emulating masculinist models of "isolate individualism" reinforced by her education and her reading of Horatio Alger and boys' adventure fiction (Zierler 5). Obviously, her selective attention accorded to the woman question must be viewed through the prism of her overwhelmingly negative experiences of gender politics in the Pale. By contrast, identifying with America's gender conservatism, she views it as "the fulfillment of my country's promise to women. A long girlhood, a free choice in marriage, and a brimful womanhood are the precious rights of an American woman" (PL 218). It is precisely this kind of "liberation" that her older sister Frieda missed. In what may look like puzzling inconsistency, the historical Antin was opposed to women's suffrage and in her letters often bemoaned her failure at domesticity.[13]

For young Antin, transplanted into the New World of educational opportunity, it may have been expedient to hide evidence of her maturity in order to prolong her child-prodigy image and to ensure continued support from her American sponsors. She started school in 1894 in Chelsea, where she was soon recognized as gifted and attracted the attention of teachers and philanthropists. Still, she consistently ascribes part of her educational success to her ancestry and family: "I was Jew enough to have an aptitude for language in general, and to bend my mind earnestly to my task; I was Antin enough to read each lesson with my heart, which gave me an inkling of what was coming next" (PL 163). As the main terrain of assimilationist practices, American schools were also sites of discrimination against Jewish children, punishing them for refusal to recite "The Lord's Prayer." This strict enforcement of hegemonic values reveals sinister aspects of literacy that encouraged absorbing anti-Semitic or anti-immigrant attitudes. Similar to her experiences in the Pale, in her Chelsea school the method of teaching "foreigners" to read was based on translation harnessed in the service of assimilation of immigrant children, who were encouraged "to find out how the common world looked, smelled, and tasted in the strange speech ... [and were allowed to] help each other out with a word in our own tongue" (PL 163–64). In the chapter called "Initiation," which is also a tribute to her teacher Miss Dillingham, who was instrumental in getting Antin's school essay published, Antin makes "public declaration" of her love for English, describing how she acquired the language word by word and how she struggled with correct phonetics. Using a rhetoric of conquest, she claims English as her own, calling it "this beautiful language in which I think" (PL 164). In an oblique way, she signals that she does not feel less entitled to the use of English than her fellow Americans, whose exclusive property rights to the language are challenged by her reminder that it belonged to "Englishmen" before they became Americans (PL 164).

While the story of Antin's acquisition of literacy in English is used as an example of "what the Russian Jew can do with an adopted language" (PL 166), it also shows that the ability to translate, to move from one language to another, constitutes a mark of adaptability and flexibility necessary for survival in America, much the same as it did earlier in the Pale. She proudly describes herself as "quick enough to fix meanings to new words" (PL 125). Similarly, her mother, whose work sustained the family both before and after emigration, makes rapid progress in English, giving "her whole attention to the dark mysteries of language" (PL 155). As a storekeeper, she could serve her New World customers without any sense of linguistic dispossession. By contrast, her father, who could not secure a job in the United States, "was hindered by a natural inability to acquire the English language ... and his pronunciation remains extremely foreign to this day" (PL 161). The issue of foreign accent comes up again and again, in an incident with a rude boy mocking Antin's pronunciation, or later on, when she says that one form of polite reaction to her accent was asking her if she was French. Through her attempt to write verses in the style of Longfellow, she manages to displace the problem of "accent" as an indelible trace of the body's nonconformity, to "accent" as a rhythmical pattern of versification that can be imitated in writing. In the end, she announces with pride: "I learned at least to think in English without an accent" (PL 282). Since the policing of accent can be associated with the policy of bounded expression and "authoritative discourse" that demands "unconditional allegiance" (Wasson 181), Antin's self-consciousness about her accent reflects rather ironically on the limits of American "freedom" granted to newcomers like her.

Although she benefited from the American system of education, Antin's text inscribes covert resistance to assimilation equated with a full translation of the foreign subject into the American context. Besides, such complete domestication is impossible, given the pervasive ethnocentrism of American culture. Therefore, she employs a whole range of foreignizing strategies that subvert and deconstruct the project of assimilation through literacy. She registers a continuous, gradual process of expansion rather than a sharp caesura between the Old and the New Worlds, showing that the process of intellectual growth does not start with emigration and is broader than Americanization. She draws upon a rich tradition of respect for scholarship that flourished among Jews in the Pale, where the desire for learning cut across social hierarchies. Scholarship was literally linked to "religious ardour" since the predominant form of knowledge was religious. After the initial period of religious education with a rebbe, she comments on the first day of school with a secular teacher as the event that opened "a view of a large new world" (PL 94), introducing her to Yiddish and Russian, and a little arithmetic. How valued education was—often acquired at the cost of sacrifice and physical pain—can be seen in the example of her father whom the grandmother used to carry to heder in the snow. Her father, who brought the ideal of liberal education from his travels, hoped that for his children learning would be "the one means of redemption" (PL 62) that would offer happiness and social mobility. In fact, his "religion" of education—a mutated form of his religious education in the Pale—is his greatest asset in the New World, where it can be taken as a guarantee of immigrant assimilability. His worship of knowledge explains Antin's hyperbolic statement that her father, "by the simple act of delivering [his children's] school certificates to [the teacher] ... took possession of America" (PL 162). Unfortunately, the father, formerly destined to be a Hebrew scholar, is a schlemiel, "unable to provide even bread and shelter" for his family, whom he drags from one slum tenement to another (PL 159). It is sadly ironic that he was the one who instilled in Antin enthusiasm about "the boasted freedom of the New World ... the right to reside, travel, and work wherever he pleased ... freedom to speak his thoughts" (PL 160). Characteristically, she is trying to locate the reasons for his failure inside rather than outside, blaming his lack of success on "some fault of hand or mind or temperament" (PL 160).

The myth of liberal education, ostensibly endorsed in *The Promised Land*, is continuously deconstructed through different meanings assigned to literacy. Antin subtly undermines the dominant notions of school literacy by acknowledging such alternative forms of home literacy as letter writing in Yiddish and reading Yiddish newspapers to which her father subscribed. She validates knowledge and experience acquired from non-conventional or non-institutional sources when she claims that her "education was not entirely in the hands of persons who had licenses to teach. My sister's fat baby taught me things" (PL 264). Both in the Russian and the American diasporas, choices between assimilation and separation hinged on access to language and education. She employs metaphors of hunger to speak of her educational deprivation in both contexts. Her hunger for learning is reflected in her attitude to books; she devours all kinds of storybooks and poems, including serialized romances in Russian periodicals while staying at her uncle's place in Vitebsk. She firmly believes that books cannot be quite useless, even the worst ones. To the immigrant child living in the slums, the library opens "the door of paradise" (PL 201). However, the motif of hunger, first introduced as a metaphorical frame for the dream of education, soon becomes literalized in America, where she frequently suffers from real, physical hunger. Ironically, then, "hunger" represents a mark of an ideal student. It is never quite possible for the ambitious, poor, immigrant student to separate the two meanings, as her rhetorical question clearly implies: "Was all my life to be a hunger and a questioning?" (PL 260). This potent metaphor inevitably forces us to expand the frame to include also the economic realities of the immigrant dream of success. The double meaning of "hunger" implicates education as a class privilege. Four years after landing in Boston, ready to enter the Latin School upon her graduation from grammar school, she is keenly aware of her inferior class status: "Until then I had gone to school with my equals ... Now ... my schoolmates were socially so far superior to me that my poverty became conspicuous" (PL 230).[14] She often has to go without breakfast, struggling "to stand up and recite Latin declensions without trembling from hunger" (PL 231).

Part of Antin's reaction to her circumstances is to sublimate her dispossession into a spiritual hunger, which also signals a different way of "undoing" hegemonic concepts of knowledge. The superiority of a spiritual quest reveals "the emptiness of knowledge" and "facts" which can feed the head but are mere "crumbs" for the soul. Taken to the extreme, her revised concept of literacy includes the possibility of living "without knowing everything" and even trying "to be happy in a world full of riddles" (PL 261). Her quest culminates in her experience of the Hale House Natural History Club, which is a catalyst for a further expansion of her sense of self, beyond her identification with being "a daughter of Israel" (PL 76) and an American citizen. Characteristically, she discloses that as a naturalist, she was less attracted by the study of facts than by the glimpse of "the grand principles underlying the facts" (PL 258). The collegial atmosphere of the Club and exposure to natural history exemplify for her genuine equality emancipating her from the slums (PL 283). Her embrace of nature provides a more expansive temporal and humanist perspective, capable of displacing the narrowly nationalist focus on Americanization, which often prevailed in the reception of her work:

> Vastly as my mind had stretched to embrace the idea of a great country, when I exchanged Polotzk for America, it was no such enlargement as I now experienced, when in place of the measurable earth, with its paltry tale of historic centuries, I was given the illimitable universe to contemplate, with the numberless aeons of infinite time. (PL 258)

Recontextualized through her passion for natural history, the "promised land" of the title takes on a broader significance, becoming the promised land of evolution. Tying America to the evolutionary narrative is a gesture that can be read as simultaneously aggrandizing and humbling. The last image of the book encapsulates the symbolic conundrum of Antin's position as she has just returned from the Club's field trip to the seashore. We leave her—or she leaves us—poised at the threshold, between the past and the future, between the sea and the library where she wants to be instituted as author.

The Club's empiricism resonates with Antin's sensuous affectation, with her tendency to use her body as a medium of knowledge and to learn "by the prick of life on [her] skin" rather than relying on "borrowed experience":

> I am a thinking animal. Things are as important to me as ideas. I imbibe wisdom through every pore of my body ... The earth was my mother, the earth is my teacher. I am a dutiful pupil: I listen ever with my ear close to her lips. It seems to me I do not know a single thing that I did not learn, more or less directly, through the corporal senses. As long as I have my body, I need not despair of salvation. (PL 108–9)

But her empiricism still situates her story within the context of the Western metanarrative of science and progress, articulated through her obsession with individual success as a step in what she calls "the progress of the race" (PL 108). Significantly, the sections devoted to her American education reflect a basic premise found in the American system of education, namely "that the body is private and untouchable while the mind is public and open to manipulation" (Eldred and Mortensen 532). In her reflections on geography, she voices a "distrust of the map as a representation of the earth" (PL 173), insisting that she needs a "*sense* of the facts for which the symbols stood" (PL 173; emphasis mine). "Symbol" is juxtaposed with "sense"—where the meaning of "sense" is always double, semantic and sensory, or sensual as well as abstract and symbolic. Words become symbols detached from their "sense" when she writes geography papers, repeating the words without knowing their meaning. Somehow, this practice, at which she excels, is reminiscent of the Jewish tradition of chanting in Hebrew, which was an altogether mystical-sensory rather than mystical-intellectual experience, as the meaning of words remained mysterious and inaccessible. Disconnect between mind and body applies differently to the American system of education, touching on the deeply hidden larger contradictions within American society. Antin deplores the fact that "the City Fathers provide soap and water for the slums, in the form of excellent schools, kindergartens, and branch libraries. And there they stop … They cleanse and discipline the children's minds, but their bodies they pitch into the gutter" (PL 225). A social critique of the neglect of the body in education is mollified by idealistic constructions of the body as "the nursery of the soul; the instrument of our moral development; the secret chart of our devious progress from worm to man" (PL 225). However, Antin's rhetoric inadvertently reveals that such ideology of privileging mind over body is consistent with the neglect of the body in a capitalist democracy, where drastic economic inequalities are masked by lofty ideals.

Within an overriding framework of the narrative of Americanization, the signifier "America" is inflected with contradictory meanings and emotions. Counter-discourses of poverty and Jewish ethnic pride compete with discourses of assimilation, citizenship, and freedom. "America" is introduced as a protagonist when Antin shows her family preparing for emigration. The traditional Passover greeting, "May we be next year in Jerusalem," is replaced by "Next year in America!" The rhetoric of dream, vision, promise, inspiration, elation, and triumph informs her account of the critical first years of immigration: "I thought it miracle enough that I, Mashke, the granddaughter of Raphael the Russian, born to a humble destiny, should be at home in an American metropolis, be free to fashion my own life, and should dream my dreams in English phrases" (PL 156). Formerly referring to herself as "Mashke," she easily slides into her new name, "Mary Antin," excited by the novelty of having to use her surname. The episode describing a substitution of American names for the family's "impossible Hebrew names" (PL 149) highlights the doubleness of translation. On the one hand, the domestication of their foreign-sounding names represents a symbolic violence of assimilation, while on the other hand, replacing one proper name with another deconstructs the solidity of any concept of ethnic "self." The subject is de-essentialized, mobile, travelling from one culture to another. The most patriotic chapter, called "My Country," focuses on the making of an American and the opportunities America could offer an immigrant child. She expresses her sense of entitlement as a "citizen" by symbolically claiming her place next to George Washington, "a Fellow Citizen" (PL 177). However, insofar as the discourse of citizenship is prominent in her narrative, it is also inadvertently deconstructed. There is a superb irony in her identification with George Washington, showing either her immigrant chutzpah or a real measure of her dispossession.

Antin's exposé of life in the slums further contributes to the subversion of the rhetoric of assimilation. Although poverty figures large in her accounts of life in both diasporas, she introduces the theme of slums in the chapter ironically called "The Promised Land," recounting her first contact with America. The experience of the slums, by her own admission, has helped her become who she is. However, the not so hidden intention to raise awareness and possibly help the poor is entangled in contradictions because Antin never really questions the system responsible for their dispossession. Rather, she conceives of her mission in terms of dominant "maternal" sentiments of middle-class female social reformers of the time, preaching salvation through platitudes: "Not a child in the slums is born to be lost. They are all born to be saved" (PL 254). Her attitude to poverty stems from her belief that the discourse of "private disadvantage" can be overcome by "public opportunity" (PL 281). She downplays poverty as "a superficial, temporary matter" (PL 233) and remains surprisingly unshaken by the contrasts experienced while moving between the world of the poor and the world of her rich sponsors and "friends." In terms of her philosophy of opportunity, America has a lot to offer to immigrants, "but opportunities must be used, must be grasped, held, squeezed dry" (PL 276). Herself a recipient of the Morgan Chapel's charity, which provided free entertainment, music, and moral uplift, she nevertheless distrusts missionaries. However, she unhesitatingly speaks in the "borrowed" language of the Christian temperance movement, comparing the moral disintegration of immigrant families in the process of Americanization to "the cross that the first and second generations must bear" (PL 213). She advocates sanitation as a cure for social evils: "it will take a powerful broom and an ocean of soapsuds to clean it out" (PL 224). Acting as a "sociologist" of poverty for the reader, an insider/outsider whose success is supposed to secure a distanced, objective view on her past, she throws in her observations about "the improvidence" or "the follies of the poor" (PL 217). Yet, she admits to "moments of depression, when [her] whole being protested against the life of the slum" (PL 233). Her saving grace may be her inability to cling to negatives (PL 123), which also accounts for a philosophically optimistic economy of loss that informs her narrative. When back in the Pale the family loses all its possessions, Antin concedes that "nothing was lost out of the world by the transfer" (PL 118). Only death and spiritual loss matter; she is "indifferent" to material loss and fully "alive" to what she has (PL 123). Likewise, translation, in a literal sense of transfer, does not necessarily imply loss; there is inevitably a remainder. Whatever is left, whatever persists, can be fruitfully mobilized to counteract a sense of loss.

Antin compensates for poverty with a sense of her own destiny and her boundless faith in the future. Her self-awareness is developed already in the pre-immigration stage of her life: "a super-feeling, the sense that it was I, Mashke, *I myself*, that was moving and acting in the midst of unusual events" (PL 133). She never doubts her exceptionality, calling herself "the intelligent immigrant child" (PL 157) who can make the best of American institutions. She remains grounded throughout in her consciousness of the unique elements in her character and individual history, convinced that she has been "pursuing a single adventure since the beginning of the world" (PL 232).[15] All the while she is also documenting countless acts of generosity and friendships that have sustained her. Seemingly acknowledging and repaying her debt to all influential sponsors from Boston's high society, her narrative is truly a tribute to ordinary people like her own father or Mr. Rosenblum, a grocer who helped her family. She is grateful to her father who would "borrow, beg, go without, run in debt—anything to secure for a promising child the fulfillment of the promise" (PL 276). There are implicit ironies in the contrast between her rich American friends' interest in Antin and the support she received from people of her own class. One telling example is an anecdote about Dr. Hale's good advice to her never to study before breakfast, revealing his total ignorance of the fact that she can hardly even afford breakfast. Her recipe for this kind of "democratic friendship" is a subversive exercise of "citizen rights," which consists in writing letters to prominent public figures such as a senator and declaring her patriotic zeal (PL 269). Apart from other subtle subversions, such as de-emphasizing the system by stressing her Russian Jewish background, her sense of belonging or entitlement is limited to the intellectual not the material sphere. The ultimate cost of her admission is to suppress or downplay the truth about the material conditions of her life. As a result, the term "citizen" in the phrase "a citizen of the slum" is displaced and shown to be relative, similar to the word "freedom." In America, "free" is what you can get for free: space, education, books, and citizenship, albeit only citizenship of the slums.

Although Antin's rhetoric of the American dream has been interpreted as part of her self-delusion or self-deception (Proefriedt 80), it might equally well be construed as evidence of her calculatedness or even cynicism. Immigrant displays of loyalty and gratitude, especially coming from a child of the slums, undoubtedly had a great appeal for the American mainstream audience. She is tokenized, and the comments made at her graduation by a member of the School Board reveal the contract behind this type of immigrant autobiography: her "phenomenal career might serve as an illustration of what the American system of free education and the European immigrant could make of each other" (PL 221). Of course, the obvious racist undertones of this statement are lost on Antin, who fails to notice that the same system was not doing much for American Indian or African American children. Rather she seems to overlook completely the complexities of American race politics. Relating a court resolution of a clash between herself and a "wool-headed" and "hulky colored" boy, whom her father got arrested for bullying, she comments: "We were all free, and all treated equally, just as it said in the Constitution! The evil-doer was actually punished, and not the victim" (PL 203–4). This naive perception of equality has to be seen in light of Antin's experiences in the Pale, where a Jew had no chance of getting a fair hearing in the court of justice. However, the meaning of "equality" must have been completely different for African Americans living under Jim Crow laws, when the formula "separate but equal" sanctioned race segregation in the majority of American states. In a similar vein, she also uncritically fantasizes about being a boy and teasing "Chinky Chinaman" in his laundry (PL 204). What such incidents show is that as long as they benefit from their unexamined white privilege, the oppressed white immigrants are not necessarily sensitive to the oppression of racialized others. Antin's narrative unveils by accident the aporias of assimilatory discourse: When there are gender, class, and race divisions in a stratified society, which part does one assimilate to? Her autobiography verifies that in the early twentieth century the project of nation building and nationalism becomes increasingly racialized, pushing for assimilation of European immigrants whose second-generation children could lose any traces of otherness and claim their "rightful" place in American society while Native American and other racialized people remained firmly fixed in the place of radical difference. From this "melting pot" of various European ethnicities emerges the ideological package of whiteness as an invisible hegemonic category that ironically contrasts with the invisibility of "visible minorities" in the grand narratives of Americanization.

When Antin confesses that she likes "everything that was a little risky" (PL 86), it is tempting to ask: What exactly does she risk in writing *The Promised Land*? In her Introduction, she rather self-consciously positions herself in relation to autobiographical conventions, referring to "a proper autobiography" as a "death-bed confession" of the subject (PL 2). Although it is hard to believe that she is prepared to "die" (except symbolically), her autobiography flaunts its generic affinities with confession, raising interesting questions that echo those asked by Derrida quoted at the beginning of this chapter: Who does Antin identify with? To whom is she telling her story? From a poststructuralist perspective, confession is a ritualized discourse producing the truth of the subject, unfolding in the presence of the authority that requires and judges the confession. The agency of deciding which "truth" will be accepted rests with the one who listens, the one to whom the subject is confessing. It raises the question of the audience, of "the ear of the other" as the text's destination, which is a question to which I will return in every chapter, with every reading of life writing. Derrida speaks of this "borrowed ear" as necessary for autobiography to take place as, in fact, part of "the structure of textuality in general (*The Ear* 51). Passing through the ear of the other, the *autos* of the autobiographical subject is displaced into the *otos* of "otobiography," reminding us that the "self" is "performed and performing—not at the moment when [the confession] apparently takes place, but only later, when ears will have managed to receive the message" (*The Ear* 50). Antin's text exhibits a strong awareness of the presence of the deciphering ears that are not always sympathetic and receptive to her message. Her direct appeals to the reader, as well as her private correspondence with Sedgwick, show that she was trying to offset the anti-immigrant sentiments and was self-consciously bound on promoting Jewish culture. This hostile, presumably Gentile reader is directly addressed as "my American friend," "you" who cast "the looks of suspicion" and shrink with "repugnance" at the foreigner's touch; "'the

Jew peddler!' you say, and dismiss him from your premises" (PL 144). She urges her fellow American citizens to respect "the Jew peddler" because "he may have something to communicate to you, when you two shall have learned a common language" (PL 144–45). Thus the autobiographical act presented to the audience is implicitly understood as a negotiation of a common language, a process of translation, which is simultaneously an extension of the possibility of "democratic friendship" in spite of inequalities. Antin realizes that her readership is unprepared for the history she is bringing to them and that she is dealing with a great deal of prejudice and anti-Semitic stereotypes. Responding to Sedgwick's feedback on another instalment of her narrative, she observes: "what you and others have said does give me some idea of the figures my poor Jewish people make when standing detached from their overwhelming history, in the sight of a world that knows them but little" (Salz 50). We might say today that having done her market research, she is literally ready to launch a new type of American subject: the assimilable Jewish immigrant.

However, her mediation exceeds the program of domesticating a foreign culture into the host society. She communicates a clear sense of accountability to multiple audiences when, within one paragraph, she turns to "you born Americans" and to "you ... my comrades in adoption" (PL 175). She is not only "speaking for the Jews" (PL 157), but also speaking to the Jews, demanding from her American readers a reciprocal recognition of how America appears in the eyes of the immigrant (PL 145). Her correspondence with Sedgwick repeatedly shows how important it was for her to include the Jewish material and to expand the Russian part of her story. But it also shows a fear of failing her Jewish readers. Inscribing their history, she agonizes over the speedy editing process in a letter to Sedgwick, written on August 9, 1911:

> This haste makes my conscience sore. Jewish readers will reproach me for leaving out some of the most characteristic things in the picture of the Pale—the inner Jewish things. Neither did I use to the full the opportunity afforded one by Chap. I to answer certain popular criticisms of the Jew. (Salz 58)

Addressing her audience through the bonds of community and kinship, she considers the autobiographer's role as bearing witness and speaking "for thousands" (PL 195). In a sense, she seems to have translated the traditional autobiographical formula for presenting individual life in the aura of the universal, into a more politicized formula of witnessing that is explicitly declared to be her mission. A rationale for her project to speak for the humble multitudes is that "the humble are apt to live inarticulate and die unheard" (PL 72). At the same time, her model for the genre is derived from biographical entries in the encyclopedia, which inspire her hope that one day she will deserve her own entry. Yet, despite her unabashed celebration of the self, combining the American ethos of self-improvement and the Horatio Algerian formula of success story, and despite her conviction that she is destined "to soar above [the mire of the slum]" (PL 279), she vows never to forget where she came from.

Using the slums as an autobiographical subject matter is a risk that she can dismiss by saying, "It was not what a thing was that made it interesting, but what I was able to draw out of it" (PL 271). But she takes further risks, playing with the generic conventions of truth telling in autobiography. Enacting a kind of performative paradox, she asks: "What proof [does the reader have] that I am not lying on every page of this chronicle, if, by my own confession, my childhood was spent in a maze of lies and dreams?" (PL 108). In keeping with the tradition of confessional literature, she makes public admission of her "lies" and childhood "depravity" but reassures "the noble reader" that in America she has made a "conversion to veracity" (PL 108).[16] However, lying and withholding knowledge are recognized as survival strategies against the oppressive and dehumanizing conditions of living in the Pale, where a dual conscience allowed for cheating the authorities while behaving honourably toward other Jews. Her disclosures of past trespasses, combined with self-analysis and introspection, produce a desired effect of "honesty." Her self-reflexivity is evident in the use of personal pronouns, shifting from the first to the third person, referring to the latter as a "fraud," and then returning "to the honest first person" only to confess: "I *was* something of a fraud" (PL 101). Pondering her name printed under her essay published in the paper, she is struck by its materiality and experiences a dizzying moment of defamiliarization: "what relation did it all have to *me*, who was alone there with Miss Dillingham, and the printed page between us?" (PL 160). This splitting of the pronouns of discourse, attesting to their instability, seems to be consistent not only with multiple transformations of subjectivity traced in the text, but also with the inscriptions of distance between the historical subject, the autobiographical narrator, and the autobiographical subject.[17]

Given the tenacity of the untranslatable, whether in the form of accented speech or lexical and cultural items that refuse to be domesticated, we might return in the end to Ricoeur's concept of translation as equivalence without adequacy, which preserves the difference between the source and the target text while remaining open to dialogue and communication. This renunciation of absolute fidelity or truth makes it possible for Antin's narrative to "live ... the impossibility ... of serving two masters: the author and the reader" (Ricoeur 8). An excellent example of her aiming for non-identical equivalence is the way she deals with childhood memories. In the chapter "I Remember" she ponders the difficulty to distinguish between her "genuine recollections" and memories planted in her head by relatives (PL 65). However, when told that the "deep-red dahlias" she remembered from Polotzk were in fact poppies, she insists on the value of personal truth over facts:

> I have so long believed in them, that if I try to see *poppies* in those red masses over the wall, the whole garden crumbles away, and leaves me a gray blank. I have nothing against poppies. It is only that my illusion is more real to me than reality. And so do we often build our world on an error, and cry out that the universe is falling to pieces, if any one but lift a finger to replace the error by truth. (PL 66)

For her, memory is not a rational process; the rules of recollection are affective rather than rational, and memories are "constructed" according to the emotional truth of the "I" who remembers, who pieces together fragments from the past. If memory "translates" the past experience into the present moment of writing, we must accept the temporal and spatial non-identity of these two moments and the necessary failure of any attempt to collapse them into each other in some idealized moment of "recovery."

Such a "failure" to recapture the sensory truth of the "real" thing is documented by the famous passage about the Polotzk cheesecake which Antin's mother used to bake.[18] The taste remembered by the body is like "the phantom dish" of memory that can only ever be an approximation of the "original" although it does not seem less real (PL 75). Memories of eating and drinking, the taste of cherries or strawberries, activate the chain of associations, linking tongue-taste-language-speech. The fact that "the flavor of ripe strawberries on [her] tongue" (PL 76) triggers a sense of self and grounds her in her unique history may help us to understand the role of the topos of ethnic food in immigrant literature. Not only does there occur a reversal of the stylistic cliché of knowledge as nourishment, with food now becoming a source of knowledge as the tongue "remembers" both tastes and languages, but the metaphor of the tongue—like the memories of food discussed earlier—connects language and the body through a metonymic substitution of the material for the abstract in Antin's proclamation: "The tongue am I of those who lived before me, as those that are to come will be the voice of my unspoken thoughts" (PL 169). What is more, food in ethnic literature is so important perhaps because it reterritorializes the tongue doubly deterritorialized through foreign sound: "The mouth, tongue, and teeth find their primitive territoriality in food. In giving themselves over to the articulation of sounds, the mouth, tongue, and teeth deterritorialize" (Deleuze and Guattari 19). How the taste of food brings back memories, momentarily reterritorializing and overcoming the subject's displacement, can be seen when, tasting the strawberries, she becomes "a child again" (PL 75). In a parallel scene, eating ham, "forbidden food" for a Jew, becomes synonymous with ingesting America and transporting her into the territoriality of "a genuine American household" (PL 196). There are further reterritorializations, into distant histories and even mythical pasts, enacted through the archaeology of taste, when she expects "to extract from my pudding the flavor of manna which I ate in the desert" (PL 76). Just as she can discover the taste of biblical manna buried in a dish of porridge, so Hebrew and her other diasporic languages are encrypted in the language palimpsest of *The Promised Land*.

In *The Ear of the Other*, Derrida discusses autobiography as a debt of which the subject must acquit herself. It is "an acknowledgement of a debt incurred toward 'myself'" (*The Ear* 14), a debt that comes with a gift of life, "my life" that one wants to tell oneself. Reading Antin's autobiography, one gets a sense of her being "fully alive" to everything she has received and aware of her obligation toward herself and others—her family, teachers, and sponsors—who have offered her "gifts of love and service" (PL 170). She gives credit to them, talking even about her talent as a gift recognized by others. But the meaning of indebtedness that informs her narrative is not always voiced directly. We would have to look again into her correspondence to understand fully how it defines her relationship with the text. Describing to Sedgwick her connection with the book, she reprimands herself for forgetting that "it is less my possession than a solemn trust. It is the fruit of my life, and my life was a gift from many givers. I must see that I render a sufficient account to them" (Salz 54). Discharging her debts, to herself and to her native and adopted communities, she rewrites the meaning of property through the economy of the gift, relinquishing a fiction of the authority of a sovereign self in autobiography and showing in turn how this self is "authored" and authorized through a network of relationality to others.

Laura Goodman Salverson's *Confessions of an Immigrant's Daughter*

> The worst shock of my ethnicity was a combination of religion, class, and economy. Oh, there was no doubt that I was white, northern European, capable of assimilating without a hitch and without a shudder, despite being female, near-sighted, and not particularly healthy ... I was what my now-colleagues disparagingly refer to as "poor white," well, not quite "trash," but certainly dirt-on-the-hands-working-class. And the glance that still skips past that instant of ethnic crisis has been burned into the back of my neck, spiralled into a repudiated narrative that cannot be told without my becoming ludicrously sodden with its poverty and clumsiness, its disdain and its dismissals. (Aritha van Herk, "The Ethnic Gasp")

Published more than a quarter-century later than *The Promised Land*, a Canadian autobiography by Laura Goodman Salverson covers the years between 1890, when she was born, and 1923, when her first novel, *The Viking Heart*, came out. Similar to Antin, in "a movement of retrospection" that characterizes modernity (Berman 2), Salverson's grown-up narrator looks backward on her younger persona, revisiting her childhood, adolescence, and youth, spent mostly in Winnipeg and Duluth. She also leaves out the part of the story that covers her more mature years, as if publicity gained after 1923 required more reticence about her private life. Although extremely popular in the 1920s and 1930s, and a double recipient of the Governor General's Award, Salverson's work has been either temporarily forgotten or largely misunderstood.[19] For years she has been dismissed from the Anglo-Canadian mainstream as too marginal, classified at best as a prairie writer, or similarly excluded from the canons of ethnic writing due to her perceived Anglo-conformity, assimilation, and the fact that she wrote in English. Critics interested in ethnicity have found fault with her for being either too Icelandic or too Anglo-Canadian.[20] Only recently Daisy Neijmann has made attempts to recover her for the Western Icelandic tradition while several feminist critics have tried to recuperate her for different traditions of women's writing in Canada.[21] The "daughter" in the title of *Confessions of an Immigrant's Daughter* suggests that it is a self-consciously gendered narrative, inviting us to question its ostensibly proclaimed continuity with the male-defined Augustian and Rousseauistic traditions of "confessions" based on the assumptions of personal autonomy, distinctiveness, and coherence.[22] It is important to see in what ways Salverson's text upholds and/or departs from this tradition and to recognize the complexity of her conflicted inscriptions of gender, ethnic identity, and class, as well as her positioning in relation to the literary genre and language, as barriers against which she constantly pushes. As previously, we will have to ask: What "truth" of the subject is constructed through this public act of confession? For whose ears is it destined? And what happens to a division between public and private life that confession in a seemingly contradictory way both maintains and subverts?

Elaborating on the problem of reception of the text marked as "foreign" by an audience in another culture, Lawrence Venuti speaks of the communication gap that often induces the translator to use domesticating strategies. A domesticating translation increases the appeal of the foreign text to a target audience, "reducing the foreign text to what domestic constituencies have in common, a dialect, a cultural discourse, an ideology" ("Translation" 482). Its goal is to produce a translated text that is immediately intelligible to the receiving readership and that can be easily consumed in the cultural marketplace. However, the readability of translation is linked to the effect of transparency achieved at the expense of the translator's visibility. As Barbara Godard writes, a poetics of transparency (which has been associated with ethnocentric, domesticating translation) is based on the assumption of a direct transposition of meaning from one language to another, without revealing the translator's "manipulative work ... of reading and (re)writing" ("Theorizing" 47). Salverson's strategies seem to be consistent with this description of ethnocentric translation that valorizes transparent discourse and aims for fluency, removing or hiding a "remainder" of linguistic and cultural differences. She establishes an interpretive community with her audience by means of stylistic and narrative choices that would be recognizable to readers who are familiar with the conventions of turn-of-the-century Canadian literature, ranging from popular romantic fiction, with its combination of melodrama and history, to sketches of reality and sentimentalist writing on the land and nature. At the same time, her adoption of the *Künstlerroman* formula is consonant with the Oscar Wilde-like aphoristic dictum that life imitates art far more than art imitates life. In Schleiermacher's politicized terms, such domestication constitutes submission to dominant values in the target culture: "Submission assumes an ideology of assimilation at work in the translation process, locating the same in a cultural other, domesticating the linguistic and cultural difference of the foreign text" (Venuti, "Genealogies" 146).

Yet, as Venuti argues, even foreignizing translation, which is a concept linked to resistance, is never free from ethnocentrism implicit in the translator's interpretive choices of what constitutes the foreign. His discussion of the effect of transparency as contributing to the invisibility of the translator finds its corresponding problematic in immigrant women's life writing when it confronts the dilemma of foregrounding difference by refusing transparency or, alternately, choosing protective silence and invisibility. Transparency in their narratives takes on a double and contradictory meaning as it pertains to smoothing strategies of domestication or to revealing secrets. Using "transparent" discourse that masks or suppresses linguistic and cultural traces of otherness in the source culture does not have to be viewed solely from the perspective of domination. Paradoxically, it may become a resistant strategy of chosen invisibility in the hands of the subject who wishes to protect her secrets. Consequently, the dialectic of foreignizing and domesticating needs to be carefully contextualized, to keep in sight the pressure points of the messy ideologies of gender, body, and ethnicity, which can skew the translator's decision to reveal or to conceal herself in her work.

It has become a kind of critical commonplace to speak of duality or dualisms informing Salverson's writing, often classified in oppositional terms such as ethnic/mainstream, male/female, matter/memory (or matter/God), body/dream, materialism/intellectualism, motherhood/creative writing, embodiment/spirituality, pragmatism/idealism, the past/the present, Canadian/Icelandic, American/Canadian, or romantic/naturalistic.[23] The central symbolic embodiment of such contradictions in her narrative is the mother-father dyad. Her parents arrived in Manitoba three years before her birth. Her father was afflicted with a "wanderlust" and relocated his family several times, trying to avoid economic insecurity and deprivation. As a child, Laura identifies with her father's adventurous spirit, utopian impulse, and idealistic outlook, against her mother's pragmatic femininity. He personifies "the power to dream" against the drab circumstances (C 293). However, after a series of aborted moves between Canada and the United States, the evocation of "papa's dream" becomes more problematic. He gradually fades away from her account, and the last glimpse we get of him is that of a broken man. She never openly blames him for the family's misery, although his responsibility is strongly implied. By contrast, Salverson's mother, ministering mainly to the needs of the body, such as hunger and comfort—but also to the need for a story—is associated with fertility and resourcefulness. It is through her mother's drudgery and her frequent pregnancies and miscarriages that Salverson gets her first intimations of women's oppression and a sense of being defeated by "the arbitrary fates" (C 211). As a result, she initially rejects identification with her mother, whom she sees as an enforcer of proper gender socialization.

Determined not to repeat her mother's fate, Salverson stages herself as a rebel against patriarchy. Having learned early about the "predestined handicap" of her sex (C 70), she rejects one identity available to her, refusing to "be a girl to sew a fine seam and rock a little cradle!" (C 23). Little Laura "detested everything sweet" (C 15), and on several occasions she manifests her dislike of eggs that her mother repeatedly offers her as nutrition. She is fascinated with any form of subversion of conventional gender roles, from acting like a tomboy, to disliking dolls, and comparing Icelandic and Canadian attitudes to the body and sexuality. Her rebellious behaviour is clearly directed against her mother's efforts to socialize her to be like a nice girl, "seen not heard" (C 15)—in conformity with a traditional prohibition against women's speech. Still, her ambivalence towards women, situated on the scale from deep empathy to internalized sexist stereotypes, is discernible throughout, with diatribes against boring domesticity and romantic fantasies about beautiful, exotic women coexisting side by side in her narrative.

Despite her early disidentification, she is aware of her similarities to her mother, whom she describes as "helplessly inarticulate," silenced, incapable of finding words, in contrast to her father's "floods of glowing eloquence" (C 69). Ironically, Salverson admits to the same inarticulateness in the sphere of intimacy and emotion, which hinders her communication with her mother. Like her mother, she often has no words to express "her innermost sensibility" (C 69), and like her mother, she often refuses to explain herself (C 317). With years, Salverson—not without regret—moves to embrace her mother's world: "The more sleep I lost about it, the more certain I grew that papa must be right—and mama, too, up to a point" (C 230). Moreover, despite her primary characterization of her parents as different, she also foregrounds their commonalities: pride in their Icelandic heritage, respect for learning, sense of humour, love of storytelling, and compassion for human suffering. As a result, any attempt to resolve her ambivalent attitude to her parents and, by implication, to other binaries detectable in her work, seems counterproductive as the autobiographical subject refuses to draw a clear-cut boundary between apparently antithetical constructs, oscillating instead between various female-identified and male-identified positions.

Salverson's sense of collective identity, that is, her identification with "women," is inextricably bound up with her ethnic self-awareness and derived from her analysis of class and gender injustice. She exposes the inhumanity of sweatshop labour as affecting both immigrant men and women, by showing her father's overwork and exhaustion, yet she feels particular affinity with other women: "Whirling the old machine, I thought of the millions of women committed to this sort of thing, world without end. To drudgery, and pinching, and those niggardly economies that stifle the spirit and slay all hope" (C 291). Bitterly, she sees herself as part of a class of women who are economically and sexually disadvantaged: "For girls like us the dice were loaded from the start" (C 323). A victim of harassment by her boss in the garment industry, she angrily distances herself from those who self-righteously complain about "sin and degradation and decadence," in a world that lacks social consciousness and fails to make provisions for vulnerable women (C 372). Her idealism is constantly challenged by her nascent feminist consciousness, the latter inspired to a large degree by the powerful influence of her aunt Haldora, with whom Salverson boarded during her stay in Duluth. An early activist for women's reproductive rights and a midwife, Haldora offered illegal abortions and adoption services to destitute women under the guise of her "maternity hospital." Her Icelandic brand of pragmatic and non-judgmental feminism contrasts sharply with the dominant Anglo versions of "maternal" feminism of the time, directed mainly at the "improvement" of immigrants and lower classes. Although both Antin and Salverson exhibit similar compassion for the plight of the poor, where Antin seems to echo the sentiments of the temperance movement, Salverson definitely shows more skepticism and bitterness about the movement's condescension toward immigrant women.[24] Her curiosity about women's lives and their fates leads her to record histories of brave, ordinary, or unhappy women, including two full chapters of "pathetic" cases from her aunt Haldora's clinic. Two powerful images in her narrative epitomize women's lot: one is the Pieta, showing her mother as a newly arrived immigrant mourning her dead baby, while the other is a haunting picture of Joan of Arc's death at the stake, a symbol of women's suffering through the ages.

Predictably, approaching Salverson from a gendered perspective alone, critics like Barbara Powell and Helen Buss have ended in re-enacting the Oedipal scenario of mother-daughter split, for which they condemn Salverson herself. Buss observes that *Confessions* "speaks most loudly in the doubled discourse of female autobiography in which the maternal pre-text erupts through the gaps of the patriarchally defined surface text" (*Mapping* 171). Furthermore, she views Salverson's text as a failed attempt to inscribe female subjectivity and describes her as ultimately "hostile to the female." Similarly, Powell refers to Salverson as "Her father's 'own true son'" (78), focusing selectively on male-identified aspects of her philosophy of life writing. However, rather than reproducing the male-female dichotomy, a more accurate interpretation of her narrative would suggest that her discourse is not just "doubly" coded, but contains multiple, contradictory, and partial inscriptions of meaning, transposing the elaborate politics of the body located "topographically, temporally, socioculturally as well as linguistically" (Smith, "Identity's" 267). What these critics seem to struggle with is, to use Buss's words, Salverson's "refusal of the 'egg' of womanhood" (*Mapping* 175). They identify the painful split in her sense of herself as a woman and a writer, but they fail to notice that the sign "woman" in Salverson can be read in multiple ways: as socially available scripts of femininity ("gender roles"); as the phenomenologically experienced "female body"; and also as the possibility of an "authentic" or "real" self. Her wavering attitude to womanhood tends to be viewed as symptomatic of her horror of biological femaleness rather than as rebellion against constraining gender roles. There might be several reasons why feminist readers have criticized Salverson for her alleged "betrayal" of her sex. On the one hand, the imposition of the simplistic Freudian pattern reproducing her supposed identification with her father against her maternal identification must inevitably lead to reductive and distorted conclusions regarding her autobiography. On the other hand, reading feminist criticism, we are often in the presence of a bias that motherhood and femininity must be celebrated, not denigrated, which is characteristic of the modern middle-class "celebratory" feminist sensibility, not necessarily compatible with Salverson's view of femininity, determined largely by her proletarian experiences. From the vantage point of her working-class background, Salverson foregrounds the disadvantages of being female and poor, extensively documenting women's suffering and oppression. Needless to say, for impoverished women, the prospect of a new baby can be an unsentimental reminder of economic hardship and powerlessness, more so than simply another delightful miracle of life.

Rather than "disarticulating" Salverson's experience of the body, I think it is much more productive to see her as writing despite the constraints of the genre, societal structures, and discourses of femininity available at her time. In this sense, she is writing under a constant threat of voicelessness, symbolized by her recovery from diphtheria, which almost took her voice. As Salverson's narrative demonstrates in a compelling way, history happens to the body: to the immigrant body; to her mother's undernourished, coffee-drenched, pregnant body. She translates the experience of female embodiment into words conveying powerful sensory images of hunger, pain, illness, death, birth, cold, smell, taste, and other bodily sensations. And although we cannot deny that it is mostly a censored translation, as in her case writing *from* the body literally means *away from* the trap of biological essentialism, she nevertheless captures the material reality of inhabiting a body marked as female, ethnic, and proletarian. Focusing on whether she is more her father's than her mother's daughter, that is, privileging gender as a category of analysis, obscures the multiplicity, mobility, and fragmentation of Salverson's constructions of self. Rather than collapsing her dualisms, I suggest that we view them as a source of indeterminacy and productive tensions involved in being a woman writer, equipped with her immigrant and class baggage, who has also been culturally conditioned to find writing and mothering incompatible. Her narrative is interesting precisely because it dramatizes the impossibility of being "completely one thing or another"—neither fish nor fowl (C 232). In this context, the introduction of a transversal perspective of translation is a welcome methodological move in reading her work, traditionally viewed as entangled in dualisms. Neither the maternal—whether as "mother," "mother tongue," or "generic matrix"—nor the paternal values alone offer subject positions that Salverson could fill unproblematically. Exploring the possibility of translating in the world split by dichotomies, her text presents itself as resisting an easy totalization. Its reading is enmeshed in a complex politics of location that involves the author's and the reader's shifting positioning vis-à-vis discourses of ethnicity, gender, class, nationality, and sexuality, including even the preferred "type" of feminism.

Translation operates on many levels in *Confessions*, including linguistic translation from Icelandic into English, disguised by means of fictionalization used in Part One, and cultural translation, which she ambitiously undertakes to convey information about Icelandic customs, history, politics, economy, climate, geography, and national character of the Icelanders. Moreover, Salverson uses translation as a metaphor for the writing process, which for her consists in turning "human experience" into "mind-stuff" (C 144). Translation is a transcendental faculty that allows those who have "eyes to see" to read "a fascinating epic" of the past incarnated in matter. A writer translates this vision into words, turning "pictures" into stories. In her romantic interpretation, translation is extolled as a life principle itself, where "humanity" can be deciphered as "a sort of living hieroglyphics" embodying "the strange forces" that make people act in certain ways (C 401). This extended meaning of translation resembles a traditional metaphysical notion of speech as translation: "*speaking* is *translating*—from an *angelic language* into a *human language*, that is to say, transposing *thoughts* into *names—images* into *signs*" (Berman 14). Interestingly, Antoine Berman links this romantic, speculative theory of translation to the monologic, modernist theory of literature as "intransitive" (18). Salverson's text partakes of this modernist tradition, by downplaying the historical and linguistic difference while monumentalizing the mythical dimension of the source culture. As we shall see, universalizing as a strategy that underdetermines translation seems to be consistent with her overall tendency to naturalize translation in her narrative and to domesticate the foreign into the target culture.

By Salverson's own admission, the opening chapter—a fictionalized account of her family's journey to Winnipeg after a failed attempt to raise sheep in Dakota—is conceived as "a symbolic introduction" (C 407). She adopts here clearly recognizable techniques of fictionalization, such as a distancing use of the third person, descriptions steeped in figurative language, as well as dialogue and characterization. Fictionalization—as a strategy that flaunts literariness and relies on familiar conventions of storytelling—typifies her attitude to translation. It renders the discourse transparent in order to conceal the reality of the other language encrypted in the text, creating the effect that Derrida, after Benjamin, describes as the wall of the sentence that "braces while concealing" ("Des Tours" 188). We hear the voices of the grown-ups—father and mother—whose speech is given in English although they have foreign-sounding names, Lars and Borga. We do not know what language they speak before the intervention of translation. The narrator's father's "warm, pleasant voice" is contrasted with "the savage tongues of this dark land, itself the voice of wilderness for which her mother had no heart" (C 11). A thousand "savage tongues" that "lash the silence of the night" turn out to be the sounds of wolves encircling the family carriage, ominously projecting the immigrants' linguistic and cultural alienation in the New World. Later, we hear a conversation in a foreign language—still unidentified—which is immediately translated into English. The family to whose house they are travelling, the Ericsons, within the same paragraph becomes anglicized as Mr. and Mrs. Anderson. There are scattered markers of foreignness in this chapter in the form of references to "Troll-karls and Troll-skessur" of Norse tales. The image of the Ericsons' monkey, furious because "no one understood him, no matter how hard he talked" (C 16), returns to the motif of linguistic displacement. Whenever foreign words or phrases are used, English translation is provided. However, the language is identified as Icelandic for the first time on page twenty—far enough not to halt the reader's smooth naturalization of the text.

The fact that the narrative perspective is doubly voiced seems to underscore the effects of translation in the first part of Salverson's narrative. The "innocent-eye" focalization of the child narrator who has no knowledge of English coexists with the "mature voice" of the autobiographical subject as an accomplished writer of books in English. The first perspective is fictionalized, with elements of local colour used to enhance the ethnic character of the community, so that translation—although constantly present—is rendered almost invisible. Salverson weaves in allusions to Icelandic stories such as the legend of the Hidden People and retells Norse sagas told by her mother who—like Antin's mother—acts here as an agent of traditional ethnicity. Chapter Six, which describes her mother's genealogy, is a hidden translation where only the presence of proper names signals the existence of the source text. Still, even names, including Salverson's own, can be naturalized. Although she uses the anglicized "Goodman," she occasionally gives variations of the original Icelandic name "Gudmund," which means "God's gift to the bride" (Stich, "Introduction" xvi). Her father's name appears as "Lars Gudman" (C 41) or, alternately, as "Lars Gudmundson" (C 147). The invisible "original" buried in the folds of her narrative corresponds to the role of ancestors in her life, the ancestors whose "ghostly court" (C 49) represents a kind of internalized moral conscience. These "translated" chunks encrypted in her narrative—usually based on recollection of orally transmitted Icelandic folklore from her childhood—undergo a significant degree of fictionalization, similar to the opening part.

While the effects of linguistic translation are erased through the poetics of transparency, the work of cultural translation is openly paraded in the text, with the intention of pacifying whatever fears British Canadians might have had regarding the influx of foreigners from Iceland. Salverson readily assumes the role of a tour guide through her ancestral culture to provide a rich ethnographic background for her English-speaking readers. Her domesticating stance as a translator of her people's experience into the Canadian idiom is motivated ideologically, and her efforts must be viewed against Canada's immigration policy, which at that time targeted the Scandinavian nations. K.P. Stich situates Salverson's book in the climate of prevalent anti-immigrant sentiments and concerns about "the ethnic inferiority and moral looseness allegedly accompanying the 'strangers within our gates' against whom Rudyard Kipling, among others, warned Canadians in 1908 and again in 1910" ("Introduction" vi).[25] As ultimate authority to legitimize her flattering portrait of her people, Salverson invokes Lord Dufferin, who "first drew attention to the Icelanders as possible settlers for Canada ... [and] had found the people interesting and admirable." It is to him that Salverson attributes the idea of cultural enrichment of the host culture central to her narrative, namely his belief that "in Canada, the qualities he had marked and admired might take root and contribute to the cultural life of the dominion" (C 76). In fact, her discourse of ethnic and cultural superiority feeds directly into mainstream hierarchical constructions of immigrant aliens segregated according to origins. Terrence Craig goes so far as to maintain that she was "trying to establish Icelanders and other Scandinavians in the same superior category as Britons, if not in fact superior to that 'type' of Briton found in Western Canada" (Craig 91). There is an interesting paradox in her position. Seen as a fervent ethnic traditionalist protesting against assimilation, she nevertheless exhibits very strong tendencies to domesticate and bring her culture to the centre by claiming kinship with the English Canadians. In particular, her novel *The Viking Heart* actually reminds the readers of existing blood ties between Iceland and England, where one can find "the fair descendants of the old Vikings" (111).

Unfortunately, Canada's abhorrent treatment of immigrants as a source of cheap labour disappoints Salverson, who accuses the Canadian government of deliberately misleading newcomers like her parents. They were consigned to "the fly-ridden marshlands of Manitoba" (C 13) and had to pay "the high cost ... for the rights of citizenship in the new country" (C 79), receiving little kindness for their pain and suffering. As a result, her mother staunchly refused to assimilate "with a people whose sensibilities she doubted" (C 82). Throughout, Salverson constructs a comparative portrait of Icelanders and North Americans, the latter associated with such traits as materialism, greed, ignorance, and snobbery (C 83). Drawing on portraits of other immigrants and histories of waves of immigration, she meticulously documents hard economic conditions, providing detailed calculations of the cost of living such as prices of food and shelter and the wage scale for piecework. Surprisingly, such critical comments did not jeopardize the book's eventual publication in Canada. It is impossible to decide if Salverson speaks to her readers through her identification as a fellow Canadian, an Icelander, or an Icelandic Canadian. Simply, the question of Canadian identity does not seem to carry so much resonance yet and is obviously not of primary importance to immigrants like her parents at this formative historical moment. The situation was obviously different in the United States, where a greater assimilationist pressure demanded instant declarations of loyalty of immigrant children like Antin, and where the whole nation-building project was well under way at the beginning of the century. Therefore, while Antin stresses the prospects of adaptability and suitability of Jewish immigrants for life in the US, Salverson insists on the intrinsic value of the Icelandic character that might provide a desired improvement to the Canadian stock. However, the nascent nationalist consciousness is already rising, and she admits that several years before publishing her autobiography she was hoping that *The Viking Heart*, where she glorifies the nation through the theme of immigrant sacrifice, would deliver the much-anticipated "Canadian product" and become a "great Canadian novel" (C 400).

The question of negotiating a national identity is further complicated by the fact that Salverson spent most of her adolescence and youth in Duluth, Minnesota. As Stich reminds us, the move "was typical of the times. About half a million people left Canada for the United States between 1882 and 1891 alone" (ix). To immigrants in Canada, the United States appeared as "a much more progressive country" (C 91). According to Salverson's aunt and mentor Haldora, who herself had settled in the States,

> Canada wasn't much of a country anyhow. So far as she had been able to make out, not even the English thought of it in favourable light. It was nothing but the hapless hunting ground for misbegotten upstarts who dreamt of easy fortunes with which to dazzle other fools back home. Now, in the United States it was altogether different. Even the stupidest foreigner quickly perceived that his ultimate success depended upon a whole-hearted acceptance of American ideals and American citizenship. In other words ... the United States was a self-respectful country—not just the tail-hair of the British Bulldog! (C 172)

There are multiple layers of irony in this passage. The fact that an immigrant is chastising Canadians for lack of interest in their "national destiny" suggests that necomers may have a strong investment in the host country's patriotism, thus showing their willingness to be co-opted by the powerful rhetoric of nationalism. At the same time, what we have learned about her parents' subsequent failure to find a fortune in Mississippi puts the viability the American Dream into question. The family's wanderings from the North to the South dramatize "the futility of any geographic quest for the promised land in North America" (Stich x). Revealing her pro-socialist sympathies and proto-feminist sensibility, Salverson implicates white Anglo-Canadian and American capitalism, imperialism, and patriarchy in the inhuman exploitation of immigrants, degradation of the oppressed races, as well as the subordination of women.

Salverson and Antin adopt two different approaches to retelling life in the slums. Although both recognize the need for reforms, Antin idealizes democracy and has trust in charity, whereas socialist-leaning Salverson does not shy from drastic documentary and naturalistic detail. Antin's strategy resembles what Salverson dismisses as the way of "the Sacred Monkeys, seeing no evil, hearing no evil, speaking no evil" (C 258). However, in both texts, there is a submerged narrative of a troubled relationship between non-English-speaking European immigrants and racially oppressed groups such as African Americans and indigenous people in the adopted country. Salverson repeats anecdotes stereotyping "Indians" and also uncritically accepts Southern racist discourse during the family's brief stay in Mississippi. In one scene she quotes the sheriff, who dismisses an Icelandic woman's concern about an apparent murder as merely a "half-breed squabble" (C 164). Such instances document the process that has characteristically passed unnoticed in official histories of immigration, namely the fact that immigrants are conditioned to assimilate mainstream racism. In some cases, this conditioning is facilitated by the attitudes of class superiority imported by many white immigrants from the old country, or by the absorption of white middle-class norms trickling down to those who aspire to social mobility. In the above episode, the figure embodying the authority of the law, the sheriff, imparts the knowledge of the Natives' inferiority to newcomers. The same scene shows how racism, sexism, and ethnic prejudice are in fact interlocked as the sheriff's attitude clearly reveals his disdain for the poor immigrant woman, too. Settler colonial racism sometimes takes the form of exoticizing, as in the tales of "Indians" unexpectedly helping immigrants, while at other times the racist attitude manifests itself in the form of erasure, as in Salverson's appropriation of the Canadian prairie as "the unpeopled plain," where she projects a natural link to her Icelandic ancestors (C 359).[26]

Her language contains traces of both critical reflection on race relations in the new country and blatant paternalistic stereotyping, evidenced in her description of the Métis people in Selkirk (C 156):

> The country was full of restless half-breeds—homeless malcontents who had been undertaken by the evil fate that good Father Lacombe had laboured so long to avert. A new way of life had robbed them of the only livelihood for which their restless souls were fitted. The day of the buffalo hunt and the river brigade was gone; Father Lacombe's attempt to settle "his children" on the land had failed. Now they were derelicts, debauched by the white man's whiskey, enfeebled by the white man's disease, drifting aimlessly before the deepening storm. These unhappy vagrants were not by nature vicious, but continued drunkenness made them quarrelsome and their pastimes, more often than not, were wildly orgiastic.

In such textual moments, she appears as an heir to the legacy of white settler colonies, built upon a Eurocentric fallacy of the uninhabited, virgin land, which served to mask the ethnocide of indigenous peoples. Moreover, not only are immigrants complicit in the erasure of the Native people; multi-ethnic immigrant communities internalize prejudice in relation to each other. Salverson recounts numerous examples of ethnic stereotyping and taunting. At school she befriends a Polish girl, Katie Pepolenski, who is an outcast because she plays with little "savages," as Native kids are referred to. Laura herself socializes mostly with the Swedes, Norwegians, and Germans—all of them, incidentally, together with the Icelanders, ranked high in the racist hierarchy of immigration quotas. How formerly oppressed groups are transformed into oppressors of others is well illustrated by young Laura's unfortunate love affair with an Irishman, an ethnocentric snob who models Anglo-superiority.

For Salverson, the issue of ethnic identity is inseparable from her perception of social class. The fact that she builds her apology for Icelandic immigrants based on contrasts between their supposed idealism and the host country's materialism, the Icelandic greatness of spirit and intellect as opposed to North American meanness and bigotry, can be better understood in the light of incongruity between her mother's aristocratic background and the family's proletarian status in Canada. In claiming Icelandic "superiority," she uses class as a compensatory, escapist construct. Similarly, in seeking grounds for identification with Canada, she chooses a "noble" form of relating to her adopted country through her sense of close ties to the land, which she describes as "cast in titanic mould" (C 83). She develops this motif further as her love of the prairie, which can be seen as equivalent of Antin's love for the ocean. However, if Salverson through her mother's heritage positions herself on the side of "nobility," at the same time, through her father, she often shows solidarity with the oppressed, "the humble of the earth" (C 394) with whom she gradually identifies. Her father is presented as capable of genuine compassion for the underclass and gets involved in helping new immigrants, visiting their sheds and offering them assistance. One more time we see that the maternal and paternal symbolism is insufficient to accommodate the complex intersection of gender, class, and ethnicity that decides what identification is thrust upon or embraced by Salverson at any particular moment. Her conflicts and contradictions are irreducible to simple binaries. While she becomes more attuned to the issue of gender oppression in both the English Canadian and Icelandic worlds, she also aligns her loyalties with her immigrant worker father, against the Anglo-dominated capitalist establishment.

Similarly, any association of literacy in her native tongue with the mother is simplistic as her father is an accomplished writer in Icelandic. Thus her initiation into English literacy coincides with her increasing identification with her "muted" mother and her pragmatic-feminist aunt, as well as her growing critical awareness of her father's faults. Salverson's father was well known in the community as a contributor to Icelandic journals. Talking about her home education, received in Icelandic, she reports the pleasure of rhythm and musical sound the language had given her. However, she refuses to learn to read from the Icelandic Bible and has to be bribed with an adventure story. Later, though, she accepts the English Bible as her primer. This division seems to have profoundly affected not only her literary style and language, but also her gender identity, polarized between the Anglo–North American puritanism and the Icelandic anti-conventionalism, as well as her attitude to religion which she simultaneously rejects as an instrument of oppression and embraces as a source of idealistic Christian beliefs. It is a good example of how the choice of language determines what kinds of subjectivities can be articulated through it. The English New Testament that Salverson has ingested contains misogynist depictions of women whereas her mother's Norse tales supply images of strong, powerful women.

Interestingly, Canada "gives" Salverson no English due to a relative absence of pressure for assimilation in the multi-ethnic west. According to K.P. Stich, immigrant ethnocentrism "has been easier to maintain in Canada than in the United States because of our long-standing support of multiculturalism" (xi). At the turn of the twentieth century, school districts in Manitoba respected language rights of such non-British minorities as French, German, Icelandic, Polish, and Ukrainian. The publication of foreign-language newspapers in the Prairies was unparalleled in the rest of Canada. Salverson was initiated into school literacy in English at the age of ten, when the family moved to Duluth. Her account of language acquisition is extremely succinct, with only one paragraph describing her wrestling with English as a new language. Recalling similar sentiments voiced by Antin, this paragraph is sealed with a proprietary declaration: "I made up my mind that this language was my own—that I would struggle with its capricious parts as patiently as papa wooed his Icelandic phrases." Actually, while learning English, she relies on translation, "memorizing a host of … words, fixing their sound in my ear and translating them back to their Icelandic equivalent" (C 195). She recounts two watershed moments intensely experienced in a sequence: the first day of school, which introduces her to English, and the first visit to the library, which introduces her to the world of books. The initiation into the library is presented in far more detail, as an "erotic" moment, filled with "rapture," "thrill," and strange sensations inside her body. The librarian's seductive voice invites her to the place where she meets her destiny as a future writer, or "a maker of books" (C 237). These experiences determine her lifelong passion for learning which, however, she was not always free to pursue. Her acquisition of literacy is from the beginning hampered by lack of gender and class privilege as well as by poor health. She despairs whenever a new illness removes her from school, and often hides her headaches to be able to stay at school. She has to share her time between studying and domestic duties and is forced to give up her ambition to go to Normal School. Unlike Antin, who received a lot of support from her relatives to continue her education, Salverson cannot escape being sent to work, first into domestic service and then to a sweatshop. Even as a grown-up, she found her persistent attempts at self-improvement constantly stalled by her financial needs and her efforts to "conform to the time-honoured duties of women," which bring her "nothing but endless work and disillusionment" (C 395).

However, comparing Antin's memories of her schoolteachers to those recalled by Salverson, one is surprised by Salverson's irreverent irony. There are no mentors, no inspiring "friends"; rather, she mercilessly mocks the teachers' role in the process of assimilation of immigrant children and demystifies the patriotic content of American curricula as "myths." Her sacrilegious humour, especially her parody of the glorious achievements of the Pilgrim Fathers, is obviously addressed to British and Canadian readers. Her narrative here appears to be double-voiced, reflecting her complicated national loyalties: the voice of the young child exults in her sudden mastery of English, but the mature narrator can politicize the context in which education is offered. Exposed to American school propaganda, young Laura quickly unlearns her ethnic ways and wants to become "an unspotted American" (C 245). What prevents her from total rejection of her roots is the peculiar "joy" she still derives from Nordic sagas. No matter that Salverson speaks sarcastically about Canadian attitudes to immigrants or that she is openly critical of the US melting-pot ideology—for the most part of her narrative she remains Canadian-identified. Navigating between Icelandic, American, and Canadian cultures, she eventually dismisses Americanness and opts for Canadianness, which she finds less threatening to the Icelandic part of her identity. The idea of multi-ethnic integration is more attractive to her than American-style assimilation, notwithstanding her Anglo-conformity through the choice of English. Consequently, "coming home" to Canada, she expresses disappointment with the Icelandic community's assimilating fast to "Canadian commonplaces" (C 357). She justifies her choice of Canada as a country where she must live: "I supposed I wanted to feel rooted somewhere, to feel that, other things failing, I had at least some sort of spiritual home" (C 375). Unlike Antin, who in similar circumstances manages to displace her material dispossession into enthusiastic idealism, Salverson does not hide her bitterness that Canada is not much of a material home to her.

A common topos of spiritual autobiography adopted by immigrant autobiographers, the topos of (re)birth, with which Antin opens her *Promised Land*, obsessively appears also in Salverson's imagery. The vocabulary of birth and birthing, returning in several literal and metaphorical scenes, represents potential eruptions into discourse of the body whose physicality has been excised from language. The rhetoric of birth relates to translation through genealogy and through the body it produces. For Barbara Godard, feminist discourse as translation seeks to break the patriarchal taboo on women's articulation of their embodied subjectivities and to invent a "notation" for "what has been hitherto 'unheard of,'" through a performative process understood as transformance of the body into language ("Theorizing" 46). We have seen a strong self-censoring grip of the mind-body split on women's writing already in Antin's narrative, in the severing of the linguistic and corporeal experiences, when she is struggling with the seemingly incompatible etymologies of "sense" as intellectual and sensory perception. Daphne Marlatt lines up more of similarly coupled etymologies that show hidden links with the body's physicality: "to utter and outer (give birth again); a part of speech and a part of the body; pregnant with meaning" ("musing" 46). Both Godard and Marlatt view the relationship between language and the body on the model of translation, as mutually effecting each other, with the body "birthing" its language, but also with language incorporating and bearing across the non-verbal experiences of the body. Salverson talks about real births that she witnesses in her aunt's hospital, which she chronicles as evidence against the ideology of motherhood. However, her preference for metaphorical births hints at her discomfort with the body which harbours "shameful" secrets of femininity.

The first such birth in the opening scene, showing the family riding through the dark prairie toward the lights ahead, marks Salverson's birth as "a predestined rebel ... [a] rebel who is myself" (C 17). The pronoun shift from "her" to "myself" signifies a symbolic coming to self-consciousness, her arrival at the "I," which also coincides with the birth of memory. Her second birth, the actual physical birth on December 9, 1890, takes place nine chapters into the book (C 120). The reversed order of these two births, one out of her mother's body, the other out of the darkness of the prairie—a preverbal state of undifferentiated identity—implies a hierarchical ordering of the mind over the body and her leaning toward literature as a transcendent form of existence. Accordingly, her third "birth" occurs through literacy, and its scene is the library. She writes her name on a library card and comes "into being" through letters

> that looked like tiny eggs strung on a wobbly string. But it made sense. That was the important thing. *Laura Goodman, Ramsey Street.* For the first time in my life, the funny characters had infinite meaning. They stared up at me from the face of the card, and seemed to say: Now you have really come into being. This is yourself, this string of wobbly ovals. This is your passport into the world of men. (C 298)

Apart from the unintended irony in "the world of men"—as indeed "the world of women" is far removed from the world of letters in Salverson's experience—there is a curious return of the "egg." It is no longer the "egg" of reproduction that little Laura rebelled against, but the "egg" transformed into oval shapes of letters. In a sense, it is a fit image of a transition from the maternal to the symbolic, or of the possibility of turning one into the other. At last, there is the "birth of an author" in the final chapter. Her account of how *The Viking Heart* was written shows what price she had to pay for trying to combine the traditional role of wife and mother with that of creative writer.

The connection between eggs and letters is parallel to that between food and language. Salverson gives detailed accounts of food (her mother's pancakes and pots of coffee; exact recipes for immigrant dishes). The description of her mother's pancakes is reminiscent of Antin's praise of the Polotzk cheesecake:

> These pancakes, made with flour and water, one egg and a dash of nutmeg, were, like the knitting, a source of joy and pride to mamma. They were thin as tissue paper and must be fried on a special griddle—to touch which for lesser purposes was a heinous crime in our house. They were greaseless, sprinkled with sugar, rolled into golden sheaves, and eaten red hot. They were justly famous, for after thirty years of prayerful attempt to create anything like them I acknowledge utter defeat! (C 169)

What this passage hides but what the reader already knows is that as a child she hated anything that was sweet, and particularly sugar and eggs. So is this elusive pancake yet another retrospective idealization of her roots? Or a reflection of the taste for cooking that Salverson developed later as an adult? I have previously mentioned how important food is in immigrant narratives of assimilation when discussing Antin. Salverson's mother's sarcastic words explain the material significance of food for starving bodies: "food couldn't be so extremely important, since most of the human race had to get by on so little of it!" (C 170). Echoing Kristeva, Sneja Gunew advances a thesis that connects food to the mother tongue and links assimilation to "the digestive models from which the term derives" (13). Foreign words "are feared because unlike food they cannot be assimilated," and as such they "emphasize the split within subjectivity" (17). Interestingly, unlike Antin, for whom food reterritorializes the tongue, for Salverson, one of the functions of domesticating translation is to neutralize this indigestible element that will not be assimilated.

References and associations between food, taste, tongue, voice, and writing are also consistent with the fact that her narrative is structured like a *Künstlerroman* of "the artist as a young (wo)man" whose readings, formative influences, and mental exercises in the writer's craft culminate in the "birth of an author" at the end of the book. She mentions that as a child she "formed the odious habit of eating paper," until she was told by her mother that the cowhide on the wall was from the dead cow that had eaten paper (C 17). The cowhide is an apt metaphor for life writing as having your skin turned inside out, suggesting that the punishment for "eating paper," that is, writing, is death. Similarly, the symbolic loss of voice through diphtheria, announced by the doctor's "prophecy" that she will live but her voice may be lost and she may not speak, is in a sense fulfilled by Salverson's "loss" of Icelandic and her adoption of English as her new voice. In fact, she recalls that upon hearing the doctor's words, she was determined not to lose her voice: "I had to have a voice to go on telling Uncle Jonathan my little stories " (C 31). The motif of the search for voice is also present in her ambition to write a book in English, that "greatest language in the whole world!" (238). Salverson's choice of English is supported by her recognition of power differentials between languages.[27] Icelandic is the language of home literacy, coded as marginal and ineffectual, incapable of improving her father's social position despite his erudition and literary fame, whereas English, the language of dominant culture, carries a promise of agency: of respectability and belonging, and, hopefully, of monetary rewards.

Salverson has yet another ambition that reveals how gender politics affects her ambivalence about femininity: she wants to distinguish herself from the crowd of women who even in art "reflect men, ape men, say what the smart man expects the smart woman to say" (C 378). In a way, she capitalizes on her ethnic difference to avoid the trappings of banality to which she feels condemned by her gender and embarks on a mission to translate her undervalued immigrant culture and her own experiences into the language invested with power. Her translation has to remain by necessity invisible since she attributes the highest value to "original writing," considering translation as only of secondary order (C 358). She harnesses her dream of becoming a writer to the idealistic goals of building "temples" for "the Human Spirit" (C 363), as well as to more practical ones of justifying her "race" in the eyes of British Canada while at the same time exposing the system that forces any immigrant group to pay a high price "for its place in the national life of the country of its adoption" (C 405). In the end, she invokes the ideology of cultural enrichment of the host culture, presenting her work to the Canadian audience as "some fair burnt offering to lay upon the altar of her New Country, out of the love of a small, passionate heart" (C 414). It is important to note that the concept of "enrichment" overlaps with conventional Eurocentric discourses of comparative literature, premised in the idea of increasing the cultural and intellectual capital of the nation through assimilation of "foreign" content, and as such it must be seen as oriented toward homogenizing rather than pluralizing.[28]

In the 1948 "Author's Foreword," Salverson identifies the differences between her book and traditional autobiography, referring to the "United Kingdom reviews, which, almost without exception, found the book a singular departure from the usual autobiography." She not only perceives her own work as "a more subjective and therefore more sensitive record" of the past, but also describes herself as "the immigrant who had the temerity to value his [sic] own traditions and dared to dream of justifying those traditions to the enrichment of his adopted country" (C 5). Significantly, the enrichment agenda is absent from Antin's text, which gestures towards "a common language" and mutual rapprochement. In Salverson's case, the ambition to enrich the host culture by introducing the values of her ethnic tradition was questioned by her own community:

> The Icelandic people were so indignant that I should have played fast and loose with their landscape, shrinking it, so to speak, until the volcano came to the sea, that the story itself had no merit. That I have tried, to the best of my ability, to represent those spiritual qualities of the people themselves, which must commend them to their Canadian brethern, was completely discounted. (C 408)

Ironically, while she "translates" Icelandic ethnic pride, trying to convince Canadians that Icelandic nationalism can easily be converted into Canadian nationalism, she is scorned by her community as a "traitor" who has failed to provide a literal translation, opting instead for a literary one. From La Malinche to Antin and Salverson, the culpability of translation, contained in the Italian adage *"traduttore, traditore"* (translator, traitor), is assumed to be a constant, with different inflections given to "betrayal," from the letter of the "original" to secrets of an ethnic community revealed to a dominant culture. As suggested by the political subtext of Salverson's narrative and her pro-nationalistic identification with great Icelandic poets, translation can be tied to nationalism. According to Mary N. Layoun, translation "simultaneously vacates and depends on operative notions of nation, state, language, and culture" (287) and can be used to construct and sustain the boundaries around these national concepts. This dual process is visible in Antin, whose ancestors and contemporaries in the Pale resisted Russian nationalism from which they were excluded as Jews, but whose nationalism in America appears to be a matter of successful adaptation and another survival strategy. At the same time, Salverson's domesticating approach to translation presents a distinct but related problem of the sacrifice and distortion of the source culture. By formulating an ethnic identity that is acceptable to the target culture, the translator engages in rewriting and manipulation through which the source culture is "homogenized and domesticated, the polyphony of its existence obliterated, and a unified, monolithic view of that culture is created as truly legitimate" (Sengupta 160).

Concluding Remarks

Although both Antin and Salverson start with the premise of assimilability and select what is acceptable to the dominant culture, their narratives show different possibilities of inscribing immigrant subjectivity through translation. Despite Salverson's claims to relativism and fluidity, or even solipsism, her biological, cultural, ethnic, racial, and linguistic essentialism has interesting repercussions for her text. Her voice appears to be more monologic than Antin's even though—paradoxically—Salverson peppers her narrative with Icelandic words and phrases more generously than Antin resorts to Yiddish. Part of the problem is undoubtedly related to the contrast between Salverson's dedication to becoming a serious novelist and Antin's commitment to journalism and public speaking. Two important influences on Salverson's style, Icelandic sagas and the Bible from which she had first learned English, can explain her predilection for high style and heavy rhetoric, a tendency to monumentalize her narrative into epic dimensions, creating at times an affected manner and a sense of verbal self-indulgence. Recounting her struggle for literacy, she regretfully observes that her fondness for "scriptural passages that rolled like grandest organ music" was not appreciated by people around her, whose speech and mental images were not coloured by "a poetic phrase" (C 293). Even where the text seems to be working against her essentialism, splintering into what she calls "subjective interludes," mixing up naturalistic and lyrical, mundane and sublime registers, or introducing a patchwork of loosely tied vignettes and portraits, the hovering presence of Salverson as a stylist crafting out an aesthetically controlled artifact is unmistakable. On the other hand, Antin, who has often been identified with essentialist constructions of Americanness, on closer scrutiny reveals herself to be more of a pluralist for whom translation is truly an interstitial process where languages are free to float, allowing for polyvocal, hybridized, protean articulations of immigrant subjectivity. Salverson's goal of enrichment based on appropriation of the source culture leads to coexistence of values in the context of Anglo conformity and, ultimately, to reasserting the supremacy of the dominant language and culture. By contrast, Antin's construction of the source culture in terms of radical foreignness is counterbalanced by her insistence on maintaining a dialogic contract with her readers. Her postulated total remaking of the self does not lead to the repression of unassimilable elements which keep resurfacing in the narrative in the form of her accent, her unabashed pride in her genealogy, or her sensory memories. Still, no matter whether the prevailing trend in their translation is to domesticate or to foreignize, we can see that both texts offer possibilities of subversive reading.

If confessions imply "emphasis on inner truth rather than the outer truth of historicity that one associates with memoirs" (Stich, "Introduction" xiv), both Antin and Salverson are compelled to modify this generic convention under the pressure of received gender codes shared by their target audiences. They withdraw a lot of personal information from the male-defined autobiographical space that could not accommodate women's experiences as sexual agents although these subject positions were open to Augustine and Rousseau. As Sylvia Molloy claims, female autobiographers are often forced to become self-censors, mapping out silences that point to the untellable (27). For Salverson, the corset of culturally sanctioned, traditional femininity is tied to biology as destiny; yet she manages to convey the horror and fascination with the "monstrous" female body as it is experienced by a woman trapped in a sexist culture. Antin comes a little closer to articulating her enjoyment of the body, albeit the body marked as pre-puberty and ethnic. Still, at the end of her narrative, she refuses "to cross the line of discretion" (PL 359), leaving the details of her personal life to the imagination (PL 360). As a result, in these female-authored confessions, the "inner" truth of the subject is highly constrained and must be masked by carefully controlled performances of the feminine norm, acceptable to their new cultures that viewed the writers' ethnicity with suspicion. In both texts there occurs a moment of looking in the mirror as a *mise en scène* of the autobiographical act. In both cases, the mirror returns an image of a woman writer struggling to find her voice, entrapped by poverty, isolation, and the "handicap" of her gender, trying to write "in a strange, new language … in the face of … the cold indifference of an alien people," determined to show that "what you want, you can do, no matter what the odds against you!" (C 413–14). Definitely, what sets apart these immigrant women's life writing from autobiography written by their male counterparts, both mainstream and ethnic, is how the women's gender complicates the material conditions of the text's production, making of Salverson a part-time writer for whom "the physical act of leaving the house" does not necessarily mean freedom (C 412). How fragmented her life was can be seen when she draws a picture of herself composing a lofty poem while ... frying bacon. Not surprisingly, she suffered from constant headaches and depression as well as a daunting sense of inadequacy. Similarly, for Antin to be able to devote herself to writing, another woman, her sister Frieda, had to sacrifice herself on the altar of domestic duty.

Borrowing from the masculinist model of confessions and reinscribing it with a gender and ethnic difference, Antin and Salverson resort to oral traditions of storytelling. They "hybridize" the genre by incorporating elements of the memoir and inserting heterogeneous materials such as self-contained mini-narratives, vignettes, and sketches. Rather than focusing solely on interiority, they additionally emphasize historical and ethnographic components of the narrative. As a result, their texts are also brimming with "tales" of others, speaking for a collectivity of immigrants. However, if we juxtapose their translation strategies so as to gauge their respective attitudes to alterity, we can see that in Salverson's naturalizing, target-language-oriented approach, alterity is replaced by sameness through the imposition of idealized equivalence that disarticulates the source while making the work of translation invisible. Antin, who exhibits a strong source-text orientation and a preference for foreignizing strategies, manages to mobilize the creative possibilities of difference. In her approach to alterity, the source is not hierarchically absorbed into the target, but instead they find a way to coexist in the productive "middle" ground of translation. In the end, though, what is at stake in these narratives is a successful translation of the migrant into the citizen. Does that explain the blindness to ethnocentrism and racism that they have also assimilated? As early immigrant prototypes invested in acquiring national identities, texts like Antin's and Salverson's remind us of the imperviousness of cultural imperialism and the violence of representation and point to the necessity and need to open up new subject positions for women of different backgrounds who will want to undertake the task of writing their lives.

Chapter 2

Immigrant Crypto(auto)graphy
Akemi Kikumura and Apolonja Maria Kojder

> Anthropology is, of course, the act of translating one language and culture into another. (Kamala Visweswaran, *Fictions of Feminist Ethnography*)

Matrilineal Narratives and Ethnographic Translation

Once it passes through the ear of the other, ethnic autobiography finds itself in a Babelian double-bind: translate me, do not translate me. The reception of Antin's and Salverson's confessions by their respective communities confirms what we have earlier identified as resistance of the source culture to the work of translation undertaken by immigrant subjects. As we have seen, this kind of problem is further compounded by the self-serving behaviour of the target culture, which may exhibit a tendency to swallow up and assimilate the immigrant other for its own enrichment, or to lock up the unassimilable other in a position of romanticized or demonized difference. All these moments of ethnocentric resistance show that there is but a thin line separating borrowing from appropriation, and that in working with borrowed tongues one risks being accused of stealing. Derrida acknowledges that this "gesture of appropriation" is part of the power dynamics in every translation (*The Ear* 156). However, nowhere are the links between power and translation more pronounced than in postcolonial studies' interrogation of linguistic and cultural translations performed by Western anthropologists and ethnographers.[1] Talal Asad, in particular, expresses concern that linguistic imbalance and social inequalities may drive an unskilful translator to "simplify in the direction of his [or her] own 'strong' language" ("The Concept" 158). Furthermore, as Maria Tymoczko observes, the greater the perceived distance between the source language and culture and the receiving language and culture, the more this tendency to simplify increases ("Post-colonial" 23). Similar anxieties about power-knowledge differentials have plagued the field of feminist oral history, a genre that until recently has been marginalized in mainstream autobiography studies. Like anthropology and sociology, women's oral history relies on collecting, transcribing, editing, framing, and interpreting oral narratives that often reach the audience in the form of texts produced "by" the scholar (Gluck and Patai 2). There is a huge potential for distortion and appropriation when assumptions of unproblematic transparency of access to language, subjectivity, and history are applied to such narratives and when the intersubjective and interdiscursive dimensions of their production are ignored.

The politics of authorship and representation gets even more complicated when the scholar has a filial or genealogical obligation towards her subject, as is the case of the two texts studied in this chapter. Akemi Kikumura, the author of *Through Harsh Winters: The Life of a Japanese Immigrant Woman* (1981), and Apolonja Maria Kojder, the author of "A Mother's Legacy," which constitutes the core section of *Marynia Don't Cry: Memoirs of Two Polish-Canadian Families* (1995), are both immigrant daughters and academics—an anthropologist and a historian, respectively—who tap and repackage their mothers' life stories. The former refers to her mother's narrative as "the life history" while the latter chooses "memoir" as her generic designation, both terms foregrounding their common interest in history.[2] These two narratives fit the agenda of feminist oral history as attempts to "repossess our matrimony" (Buss, *Repossessing* 86), that is, to recuperate our mothers' and foremothers' stories. Unlike the narratives in the previous chapter that focused on immigrant children, the texts of multicultural oral history examined here focus on the experiences of mothers, all of them first-generation immigrants. Two daughters-translators facilitate the reception of their mothers' life stories into the target culture in which they are both well established as cultural brokers. Consequently, in both cases we are dealing with translation from a "weaker" to a "stronger" language (Asad, "A Comment" 330). The question that arises is: How do the daughters' translations practise "linguistic hospitality" on behalf of the dominant language?

In this chapter, I refer to the type of writing produced by Kikumura and Kojder as "crypto(auto)graphy," playing on the Derridean sense of autobiography as writing from the crypt, that is, writing from the scene of loss and mourning, and writing beyond the subject (*The Ear* 57–59). Working from the concept of the crypt formulated by French psychoanalysts Nicolas Abraham and Maria Torok, Derrida describes the crypt as "the limit-position of the living dead" (*The Ear* 55). While in successful mourning the lost object is introjected and assimilated into the self, in "failed" mourning, as in melancholy, the loss is not worked through:

> The dead object is incorporated in [the crypt]—the term "incorporated" signaling precisely that one has failed to digest and assimilate it totally, so that it remains there, forming a pocket in the mourning body. The incorporated dead, which one has not really managed to take upon oneself, continues to lodge there like something other and to ventrilocate through the "living." The living dead … is the one who is enclosed in the crypt. (*The Ear* 57–58)

The problematics of the crypt "as a foreign body included through incorporation in the Self" (Derrida, "*Fors*" xxx) and its "ghost effect" of heterogeneity offer an important re-elaboration of the Freudian theories of mourning and melancholy. However, I am less interested here in unpacking the psychoanalytic meaning of the crypt than in exploiting its tropological and topological potential for figuring translation. For Derrida, a crypt—as words "in (the) place of an other"—always gestures towards something that was before and implies the interconnectedness of place, death, and writing ("*Fors*" xii–xiii). The crypt preserves, conserves, and hides, but it does not simply separate the inside from the outside. Rather, the cryptic safe contains "an outcast outside inside the inside" ("*Fors*" xiv). The "dizzying topology" of the crypt that troubles the boundary between the inside and the outside can be borrowed to describe the complex relationship between the source text and its translation: "the inside as the outside of the outside, or of the inside; the outside as the inside of the inside, or of the outside" ("*Fors*" xix). But as we have already learned from the story of Babel, the total "con-fusion" between the original and translation is not possible.[3] Moreover, the two types of interiorization related to mourning and encrypting might be seen as corresponding to different types of translation which can also be oriented toward assimilating the other so it is no longer "other" in becoming an enlargement of the self; or, written in place of another, translation can be oriented toward preserving and keeping the other as a living dead, thus foregrounding its relationship to inheritance and debt.

Similar to what we have seen in Antin's and Salverson's narratives, one of the central issues in the texts analyzed in this chapter is the issue of debt or indebtedness. A mother's gift of the story, enshrined and en-crypted in the daughter's narrative, becomes a debt to ancestors that is buried in the textual crypt. Significantly, for Hélène Cixous, "the birth of the scene of writing" is associated with death while writing itself is seen as "the attempt to unerase, to unearth, to find the primitive picture again, ours, the one that frightens us" (*Three Steps* 9). Cixous believes that the gift of writing comes from the dead, not only in the writer's personal experience of loss, but also in a more general sense of tradition or inheritance, simply what is passed on to us as writing. In this context, affinities of life writing and translation with "memorialization, redemption, and loss become a rich source of allegorical possibility" (Russell xviii). Obsessed with the proper name and signature, autobiography is thanatography, writing for the dead: "every name is the name of someone dead, or of a living someone whom it can do without. If the destination of one's own writing is names or if one writes in order to call up names, then one writes also for the dead" (Derrida, *The Ear* 53). Like Derrida, Paul de Man chooses the rhetorical figure of *prosopopeia*, meaning "the fiction of the voice-from-beyond-the-grave" (77), to define autobiographical discourse. In the specific case of multicultural oral histories or "as told" narratives, what I call "crypto(auto)graphy" doubles this general meaning of autobiography as writing "beyond the grave" to include life writing that hides the autobiographical self below and beyond the mediations and facilitations of the translating narrative voice. The "auto"—the truncated "author" or the subject—is encrypted in the text or "buried" under complex and multiple layering of voices in the intersubjective space of the narrative. Survival, then, is literally at stake in this type of writing where, much as in *testimonios* and trauma narratives, memory literally re-members, that is, restores form to bodies and selves that had been shattered or disappeared.

Referring to Benjamin's notion of translation's "afterlife" or "living on" (*Überleben* or *Fortleben*), Derrida explains that the translation contract between the original and the translating text is based on this double sense of sur-vival.[4] The translator is a subject "who finds him/herself immediately indebted by the existence of the original, who must submit to its law and who is duty-bound to do something for the original" (*The Ear* 122). The translator's task is then to respond to the demand for survival that comes from the original text. Thus a traditional view of translation as indebted to the original is here reversed, or better yet, the bond between the two is seen as "reciprocal claim and debt" (Brodzki, *Can These* 112). The contract between the original text and translation is not just about communication and reception of meaning, but about the process of their mutual growth. At the same time as it transforms the translating language, translation also "augments and modifies the original, which, insofar as it is living on, never ceases to be transformed and to grow" (Derrida, *The Ear* 122). As the original needs translation to ensure its "afterlife" and the possibility of continuing growth, we can speak of the genealogical function of translation involved in the intergenerational, matrilineal transmission of memory in Kikumura's and Kojder's narratives. However, translation in these matrilineal texts, in which the daughters inscribe their genealogical and symbolic legacy, can function both as a guarantee of survival of cultural memory, but also, ironically, as an instrument complicit in hiding the debt. Types of translation and attitudes to translation become symptomatic of the economy of debt and gift, operating in each text. The question whether the mothers' stories turned into the daughters' "capital" are stolen and appropriated, or borrowed and dutifully repaid, points to ethical and political consequences of the daughters' respective choices.

Each narrative discussed in this chapter represents different modalities and functions of translation, reflecting a different tangle of voices. At the centre of Kikumura's text is a seventy-page translated transcript of her mother's memoir surrounded by the elaborate editorial apparatus compiled by the researcher-daughter-translator. There are clear signals as to whose voice we hear and, occasionally, whether there are differences between the Japanese and English versions. By contrast, Kojder's maternal narrative utilizes her mother's memories, recasting them in the voice of a third-person narrator-translator, eventually shifting to the first-person point of view of the researcher herself. As intersubjective narratives, these texts need to be considered in terms of collaborative authorship and multiple mediations, a feature that sets them apart from Antin's and Salverson's narratives, which to a large degree suppress their intersubjective dimension in keeping with the liberal paradigm of individualism. In addition to production, the intersubjective aspect can also be seen as a function of the process of reading, where the presence of translation and editorial practices within the text mirrors the readers' engagement with the text on the "outside." Translation, then, underscores the fact that intersubjectivity in a life writing text involves other subjects as "an integral part of consciousness, events, and the production of a narrative" (Cosslett et al. 4).[5] Consequently, emphasis on the truth-value of oral history has to be counterweighed by attention to self-reflexivity manifest in the processes of telling, transcribing, translating, retelling, and editing of oral history narratives.

Moreover, oral history, together with other related ethnographic genres such as autoethnography, bioethnography,[6] "as told" narrative, or *testimonio*, is usually employed as a vehicle of narrativization of collective history and cultural memory rather than simply an instance of individual remembering. Self-representation in such texts is strongly tied up with representations of the collective past, invoking "an imbrication of history and memory" (Russell 279). This connection between personal biographical facts and historical facts that, according to Paul Eakin, is "presumed to ground the truth of a life in [any] autobiography" (141), seems to be heightened in the case of autoethnographic narratives. There is a general consensus among critics that autobiography becomes ethnographic when the writer "understands his or her personal history as implicated in larger social formations and historical processes" (Russell 276). Accordingly, the two matrilineal narratives frame the mothers as both ordinary and representative, embodying a particular story of displacement and migration, caught up with specific social and historical circumstances, and affiliated with particular communities and traditions. In this sense, these texts effectively perform the feminist work of politicizing the personal, helping readers to understand "how life stories of 'ordinary' women allow them to operate politically within a context whose structure affords them few direct expressions of power" (Weisser 252).

The reality of immigrant women's restricted access to a second language, writing, and publishing has a direct bearing on methodological constraints of multicultural oral histories. What gets published is usually written in English, with some acknowledged or unacknowledged editorial assistance. Oral histories and some anthologized life writing pieces are mostly translated. Whenever we read in prefaces that editors (or sometimes translators) of immigrant women's life writing feel compelled to revise the vocabulary and syntax, that is, that "grammar was corrected" (Warren 4) or "the peculiar language and expressions used by the women" were replaced (Makabe vii), we are reminded of the erasure of other languages performed by this kind of translation and editorial practice. A related sanitizing procedure, transcription from tapes, effectively removes from recorded voices traces of orality such as accent, dialect, or non-auditory cues. Other possible transformations of the source text by translators-editors may include rationalization, qualitative or quantitative impoverishment, homogenization, destruction of rhythms and underlying networks of meaning, destruction or exoticization of vernacular terms, effacement of overlays of languages, functioning of inadequate literary, social, or historical horizons (Berman 233). Broadly speaking, these various forms of using translation as a means of forcing immigrant "others" into the regime of "standard English" disguise the failure of liberal multiculturalism in the monolingual context of the US and English Canada. In the editorial climate which often encourages assimilationist rhetoric of liberal pluralism, as well as a tendency to parade the book itself as evidence of the author's successful acculturation, we constantly need to ask ourselves: Whose stories are brought to our attention and why? What forms of ethnic/immigrant identity merit translation and receive support from American and Canadian academic, literary, and cultural institutions? And what role can translation have in addressing the problem of authority and domination of one group over the other in a multi-ethnic, patriarchal society? Questions like these serve as a reminder that in reading life writing we cannot ignore larger issues of politically implicated sponsorship and agendas.

Akemi Kikumura's *Through Harsh Winters: The Life of a Japanese Immigrant Woman*

> When I moved out of my mother's house, shaky and determined, I began to fashion some different relationship to this country of our sojourn. I began to seek some more fruitful return than simple bitterness from this place of my mother's exile, whose streets I came to learn better than my mother had ever learned them. But thanks to what she did know and could teach me, I survived in them better than I could have imagined. (Audre Lorde, *Zami: A New Spelling of My Name*)

In light of the linguistic and cultural competency required of the translator as a migrant moving between the source and the target contexts, it is often second-generation immigrants, or children of immigrants, who are truly transitional and mobile, and therefore well suited to carry out the translator's task. Published in 1981 by the cultural anthropologist and writer Akemi Kikumura, *Through Harsh Winters* echoes two larger generic developments of its time: a rise in the number and popularity of ethnic autobiographies in the United States, including the postwar narratives written by Japanese American women,[7] and a widespread use, from the 1970s onwards, of the genre of "life-story" within the institutional framework of the social sciences. Similar to most authors of Japanese American autobiographies, Kikumura is a Nisei (second-generation), forty years younger than her mother whose life history she records and translates in order "to tell a story about an Issei woman's experience in America" (ix). Signalling a move from an individual life history to a collective life story, she declares her "respect and admiration" for all women of her mother's generation, for whom the process of acculturation—the theme Kikumura pursues in her research—was very slow because of language barrier, gender constrictions, isolation, and racism. The Asian American critic Sheng-mei Ma takes a rather cynical view of the practice of children marketing their parents' stories, a practice he sees as typical of Asian American literature, where first-generation stories are rarely told first-hand. When such stories are told by children or grandchildren, "there exists a tense triangular relationship: Asian American raconteurs and the American market actively woo each other in appropriating alien(s') stories, the surest sign of ethnicity, as commodity" (11).[8] I would argue that Kikumura's book defies a potential threat of commodification and, compared with the two autobiographies studied in the previous chapter and with Kojder's memoir discussed later, it demonstrates that narratives of racialized difference are much more effective in rupturing the dominant discourses of citizenship and nation through historicized inscriptions of the trauma of racism.

Kikumura identifies her text as an ethnographic genre of "the life history," which—like the life story—"is determined by an oral situation of communication, specified by an interview recorded on tape" (Chanfrault-Duchet 62). Indeed, the tape recorder reappears in her narrative as a tool and symbol of her trade, from its first mention, when she stands before her mother's relatives in Japan as an anthropologist ready for fieldwork, to the final disclosure of how the text originated over the five years of shared meals during which she listened and recorded her mother's life history (107). She has divided the book into three parts. Part One, a short personal essay, recounts the author's trip to Japan to learn more about her mother's past and to meet her family. Ostensibly, the official reason for her visit is to collect research data, but she also manages to re-establish family ties broken off by her mother's departure fifty-five years earlier. Part Two, "The Life History," told in her mother's translated voice, forms the main body of the text. The narrator, Michiko Tanaka, was born at the beginning of the twentieth century, during the Meiji period. She recalls chronologically the events of her childhood, marriage, hardships of immigration, the war, and the following years, concluding with an overly didactic chapter summarizing her life lessons. Finally, the third part of the book includes the author's Epilogue and the academic flanking apparatus (notes, appendices, bibliography, and even a scholarly essay on the Japanese American family and methodology). In addition to the above parts, there are the usual editorial frames, including the Preface, Acknowledgements, and Dedication based on a Japanese proverb from which the title has been taken: "Through harsh winters follow springs." Kikumura's translation is framed as research belonging in a specialized thematic or field series and situated, moreover, in the male academic network since, apart from gratitude to her mother, she extends her thanks mainly to male mentors.

The daughter's presentation of the mother's life history reads like a first-person voice-over, "a common feature of autoethnography," according to Catherine Russell (277). Kikumura consistently flaunts translation in all parts of the book. Early on, she explains in the Preface: "In the process of translating my mother's account, I have tried to remain as faithful as possible to her actual words in order to convey to the reader the flavor of her speech and to capture a better understanding of the individual" (x). The "I" of "The Life History" belongs to Kikumura's mother, creating the illusion of the subject speaking in English. This part begins with the editor's note: "The following history is my mother's, the memories she chose to tell me about her past life. The interviews were tape recorded in Japanese; I have translated it [*sic*] and made a few rearrangements to bring disconnected anecdotes together. But the story is my mother's" (15). Her insistence on the factual character of the narrative has to do less with the conventions of autobiographical truth telling than with the ethics protocols of qualitative research. On the editorial page, she tells the reader that names of people and places have been changed. Paradoxically, hiding the real name of the narrator contributes to a greater "realism" of the story. A pseudonym, a false name masks the "reality" of a person who must be protected from exposure and shame. Again, in Methodology, Kikumura stresses that the data collected from her family members have been presented in the participants' "own words" and the accuracy of the translation has been checked by academic and family consultants:

> I translated from Japanese into English the data collected from my mother and from her family in Hiroshima. When there were doubts as to the accuracy of translation, Dr. Hiroshi Wagatsuma, Professor at the University of Tsukuba and Visiting Professor in the Department

> of Anthropology, University of California at Los Angeles, or members of the family were consulted. (142–43)

By invoking the official academic authority and the private, familial sources of authentication, she simultaneously upholds and slightly challenges mechanisms of legitimation expected to be found in minoritized discourses presented for mainstream consumption.

From the beginning, the author places herself in a position of a competent learner whose "ear" is a passageway for translation. She foregrounds the image of translator as "listener"—learning through listening, always present on the sidelines—already in Part One, where she reminisces that as the youngest child, excluded from family discussions, she "sat in the most inconspicuous spot of the room and listened" (1). Later, as a grown-up woman, she went to Japan to listen and learn. In the section including her translation of the mother's narrative, she does not hide her presence, interjecting translator's comments and editorial asides. Her translation retains a lot of Japanese words and sentences—memorable phrases, proverbs, and sayings—always providing an English equivalent. Japanese words and expressions average two to three words per page. She explains them parenthetically or in notes. She also uses Japanese names in transcription and translates some phrases literally to retain the idiomatic imagery (as in "He was a living Buddha," 29). The vocabulary range is mostly concentrated in the areas of food, religion, and ethnic relations. The number and frequency of Japanese words are lowest in the last part of the mother's story, after Papa's death, when the mother lives on her own in the city.

Furthermore, Kikumura's notes offer a kind of running commentary on translation, both linguistic and cultural. The author foregrounds nontransparency of access to Japanese language and culture, keeping a Western reader at a respectful distance rather than giving her a sense of false mastery. For example, she explains a custom but refuses to rationalize it, simply saying, "it is not clear why" (109). Similarly, she signals words "which cannot be translated into a single word in Western languages" (111). The notes not only direct us to the presence of the untranslatable and give dictionary-like definitions of terms, but also engage in descriptive contextualizing of religious traditions, customary forms of address, historical background on life in Japan and immigration history, and even glosses on Japanese character traits. As Rosemary Marangoly George observes, any immigrant text written in English and intended for the Western audience "is expected to *and does* constantly 'translate' itself by dexterously and continuously explaining the local allusions, practices, and cultures that are incorporated into the narrative" (72). However, Kikumura's comments manage to sustain a balance between helpful assistance and defamiliarization, carefully avoiding commodification of her subject.

As already suggested, the work of cultural translation is particularly strong in the third part of the book, including Notes and Appendices. Generally, the editor here speaks in a sympathetic but detached, disembodied, objective, well-informed, expert voice of the cultural translator and researcher who only sporadically strikes a familial note when mentioning "Papa" and "Mama." Working from within the conventions of scholarly discourse, the annotations and essays focus on the history of Japanese immigration to the United States and discuss generational differences in Japanese American families. Most important, however, Kikumura places the American and Japanese families in a comparative perspective, finding "the compatibility of the Japanese culture and the value system of the American middle class" (121). Yet she rejects a simplistic view of acculturation, referring to studies on the Japanese family that indicate that acculturation is a patchwork phenomenon rather than a linear process (127). A historical outline of traditional models of Japanese society and family that have influenced the Issei generation stresses the centrality of the concept of *ie*—family, household, house—as "the primary unit of social organization" (124). The Confucian values that were adopted as the foundation of moral education included "respect, obedience, and filial piety to parents and ancestors (especially toward father)" (125) and emphasized the importance of "fulfilling the appropriate obligation, duty, and loyalty owed to others in each situation" (123). Her own narrative enacts precisely this virtue of being filial by placing the mother at the centre while also paying respects to the father. In the end, the effects of her two-way translation between American and Japanese cultures are potentially subversive. American readers experience defamiliarization of American culture viewed through the eyes of a cultural "outsider." However, what emerges as a side effect of an ostentatiously ethnographic project of introducing the culture of "strangers" to the mainstream is a critical vision of America plagued by racism, nativism, and ethnocentrism.

The way translation functions in the narrative depends to a significant degree on successful legitimization of Kikumura's role as native informant and her voice as translator and academic. Part One illustrates the author's acceptance by her mother's family in Japan; they are her "informers," initiating her into the status of an "insider." But in Methodology, she questions the illusory nature of any supposedly "informed" perspective, viewing herself rather as both an outsider and an insider. As an anthropologist and a Japanese American, she reveals her personal investment in research to "promote a greater understanding of Asians in America" (137). While she endorses the advantages of the insider perspective, claiming that "group membership provides special insight into matters (otherwise obscure to others) based on one's knowledge of the language and one's intuitive sensitivity and empathy and understanding of the culture and its people" (139), she simultaneously problematizes this assumed facility of access. She is aware that "in many cases, even an insider can be an outsider, depending on the definition used by the participant" (140). For example, her mother regards as "outsiders" any people from outside the family, no matter if they are Japanese or not, believing it is a "shame" to expose your problems to others. Again, readers are warned to avoid stabilizing categories and encouraged to view them as shifting rather than monolithic.

The insider/outsider vantage point entails a greater ease at code switching that occurs on many levels and involves manoeuvres from the familial to the professional and even jargonistic. Scholarly jargon appears especially in the Notes and Appendices, in such phrases as "behavioral and ideational structures," "modification in the symbolic structure," or "sociocentricity." In fact, switching codes in the Epilogue, which bridges the mother's story with the daughter's apparatus, becomes a symbolic moment of separation of the layers of voices blended through translation—the mother's testimonial voice and the daughter's professional voice—parallel to switching cultural contexts. At one point Kikumura suddenly turns to the audience, explaining: "The avoidance of shame because of failure is a reason why so many Issei like Mama did not return to their homeland: The Tanakas kept postponing their return" (86). Shifting to third person in reference to her own parents might be seen as a form of emotional containment. Rather than dealing with the emotive and affective aspects of her mother's painful story, she resorts to generalizing its use-value for her research. She also reminisces about learning in childhood to adapt communication styles to different situations: with *nihonjins* (Japanese), children's behaviour could not be too loud and pushy while with *hakujins* (whites), it had to be more aggressive, assertive, and individualistic (98). Children were also taught to respect silence and not to talk back. When she ponders how status- and role-consciousness are built into the Japanese language itself (123), one can suspect that by means of skilful linguistic and cultural code switching the daughter practises her parents' survival strategies in the academic world.

It is instructive to relate Kikumura's observations regarding cultural differences to the practice of autobiographical writing. According to Ann Rayson, the very genre of autobiography is "incompatible with Japanese behavioral codes and traditions" (132). Although the traditional Western autobiography extolling individualism and self-sufficiency conflicts with the Confucian tradition, which emphasizes interdependence and reliance on others, the values embraced by this tradition are congenial to what early feminist critics of autobiography such as Susan Stanford Friedman, following Nancy Chodorow's theories of female socialization, label as a self-in-relation, and what Kikumura calls collectivity-orientation and "other-directed" definition of situations (122). Another difference concerns the use of silence "as a safe or neutral response to an embarrassing or ambiguous question," recognized as one of the manifestations of *enryo* [reserve, constraint] adopted by the Japanese in America toward whites. She says that in contrast to the Americans' reliance on verbal communication, "the Japanese use more forms of silent, nonverbal communication in interpersonal relations—gestures and physical proximity" (128). Accordingly, as mentioned earlier in the Introduction, attention to a muted discourse, to what cannot be said or has been omitted, is one of the interpretive strategies that must be applied in reading immigrant women's life writing.

It is precisely this importance attached to the relational, interpersonal aspects of life that generates a central metaphor in Kikumura's oral history project. Referring to the dependence on parents, in particular on the mother, she recalls that "for Issei and Nisei alike, one never really breaks away from the mother as she continues to remain solidly internalized in the superego throughout life" (130). This self-reflexive image applies also to the narrative that tells of the mother "solidly" internalized in her daughter's work. There is more evidence of intersubjective exchanges in the text as the author inserts other heterogeneous materials such as letters or conversations with her sisters Keiko and Yoko. Similarly, she incorporates her reflection on "the reciprocal reactivity of researcher to participant and participant to researcher" (143–44). Because the reactivity increases when "the researcher is intimately involved in the participant's life," she admits that she "began to record not only the events of the interview situation itself and the specific, present-day events in the participant's life, but also [her] feelings, reactions, and events in [her] life which would have direct bearing on the life of [her] family" (146). Obviously, she is concerned about the effects of her life writing project on the family. She has already noticed that different family members have differing perceptions of the mother, and that some view her as "strong and loving" while others as "weak and dependent" (146). Under the pressure of the majority, the latter may revise their image. The ironic contrast between narrative disclosure and the cultural value placed on discretion is quite striking. However, the author rejects the possibility that her perusal of the mother's story might be construed as betrayal, claiming that her "mother was pleased with the possibility that her life history may be read by others" (140–41). As a result, Kikumura is convinced that her book has fulfilled the function of "filial piety" by drawing the family closer together.

Comparing the parents' self-perceptions and the children's perceptions of their parents, one discovers contradictions and ambivalences revealing not only differences within and between individual attitudes, but also the fault lines of the cultural translation of gender. The mother's self-disclosure is gradual, adding to and sharpening the reader's understanding of what she had said before. Michiko conveys "things from the Meiji Era," emphasizing a woman's passivity, obedience, and subservience to her husband. She had been abused and ignored by Papa, who never let her learn English. The parents constantly fought over money. The mother admits that only her low self-esteem kept her at her husband's side (37). She even had suicidal thoughts, but she "summoned [her] courage—only small people took their lives" (46). Mama's life was focused on work and her thirteen children, including ten daughters and three sons. In a typically self-incriminating manner, she blames herself for the death of her two sons during the period of hardships, in the years 1930–42.

Still, the narrative reveals women's agency despite the order of obedience. The mother does not hide that she had used her husband to go to America in 1923. Noting that he would come home with a waitress after a three-day absence (36), she plays down his manhood: "with women, he just drank and sang. He never had sexual relations with them. Of this I am absolutely sure" (37). She also reveals her secret love for another man and is frank about the body and sexuality, describing her frequent pregnancies, births, and miscarriages, and even her self-induced abortion. She takes pride in her work ethic and her ability to endure pain without a sound. She describes her husband and herself as good workers and is proud of her accomplishments and her ability to help others (70). As the narrative catches up with the "present tense" of telling ("Today is February 25, 1978"), the only note of disillusionment in the mother's voice reflects the generation gap existing in immigrant families: her daughters are divorced and her son Kenji is estranged from her. The daughter's assessment of her mother's life remains contradictory. On the one hand, she views this life as "dominated and determined by men" and "conditioned on subservience to the male" (103), while on the other hand she praises her mother for finding "a way to fulfill both new and old role expectations" (103).

"Mama" and "Papa" are signifiers that resist the daughter's interpretation. Like the mother, the author's father emerges from the narrative as a figure of ambivalence. Papa had a miserable childhood; his own father immigrated to San Francisco but lost a lot of money by gambling. When Papa also became addicted to gambling, the mother was helpless and fatalistic about it: "A woman can do nothing when her own husband gambles. You can't make things go the way you want. The Issei men all gambled" (34). When she was thirty-one, with eight children, her husband was dismissed for forfeiting other workers' pay. However, despite extreme poverty, they refused to go on welfare because Papa "thought it was *haji* [shame] to do such a thing" (43). During prohibition, he was arrested and sent to prison for bribing a federal agent. Ironically, in prison he could study and became fluent in English. He was academically gifted but never before had a chance to get a formal education. The year Papa spent in prison was the easiest one for Mama, who received money from the government (49). Yet, despite all the hardships and humiliations experienced during her marriage, the mother justifies Papa after his death in 1953, saying that she "became a fine, disciplined person because of Papa" (63). When she lived on her own in Los Angeles, working in a hotel and enjoying more independence, she rejected all potential marriage suitors (69). She concludes the narrative proper by reiterating the importance of intersubjective goals over individual happiness: "The secret of success is to get along with others, to combine energies. Together with nature, together with each other's strength, we survive" (72).

The mother's attitude is consistent with the Confucian ethics that "emphasized duty, obedience, filial piety, ancestor worship, and *bushido*— the way of the warrior, which began in the fourteenth century and stressed *giri* (indebtedness)" (123). The motifs of debt and gift are interwoven in different parts of the book and seem to be internalized by both the mother and the daughter. In the mother's narrative, the principle of *on*—a duty to repay a debt and to show gratitude for a gift—occupies a central place. In particular, gratitude to one's parents, "a fusion of bestowed benefit and incurred debt" (87), is seen as a lifelong obligation. Kikumura's mother is tortured by a sense of being ungrateful and "unfilial" to her own parents.

Her self-accusations and expressions of guilt, remorse, and shame stem as much from the Issei cultural tradition as from humiliations of immigrant experience that had prevented her from ever returning to see her family in Japan. Like Antin, whose writing was motivated by both hardships and gratitude, the mother also documents acts of generosity. She acknowledges her debt to the family's benefactor and employer, Yamada-san, and records all the names of people who sent her money offerings after her husband's death.

Akemi Kikumura inherits her mother's debt and repays it through her book. Moreover, she actually manages to erase her mother's debt of gratitude to her Japanese relatives by exposing gender discrimination as the reason for the mother's exclusion from inheritance. There is also a literal debt buried in the family history: the money appropriated from her parents by the paternal grandfather. Paradoxically, in the daughter's case, the old law of primogeniture that was operative in Japan before the Second World War, works to her advantage. Legally, she has no entitlement to the money her father's family owes her father, but morally, she has a right to it. Through primogeniture, they owe her nothing; however, she claims her rights by "taking back" from them—taking their story and writing about it. Ironically, although the daughter is excluded from sharing the material wealth with the family's male successors, her maternal "capital" is the story. In the Epilogue, it becomes clear that yet another exchange of gifts has taken place between mother and daughter. Mama's willingness to give her life history, to share her roots, and to facilitate Kikumura's trip to Japan constitutes a repayment of debts. After all, the mother describes herself as "*giri gatai* [a person who has a sense of duty, gratitude]" (47). According to her, "happiness will not come to you unless you repay the debts you owe to others. You must not forget the *on* that you owe to people" (89). At the same time, the mother views the daughter as an emissary who has "now paved the way for everyone in America to come" (86). In this sense, the genealogical work of translation in Kikumura's text helps to erect a bridge between the present and the past, but also between the mother and her estranged relatives. A conversation between mother and daughter about the daughter's trip to Japan suggests a vicarious re-presenting of the experience for the mother. The trip to Japan has brought the author and her mother "even closer together … America was a rite of passage from youth, innocence, and the protection of home to adulthood, suffering, and understanding of life … Mama's life history was a testimony to that experience" (107).

The economy of gift and debt, with its continuous flows and exchanges, requires constant strategizing on the part of women negotiating their agendas through the narrative. The mother's agenda is to justify her choices in life and to pass on the cultural legacy of her youth to her children. Her final gift is to proffer some traditional wisdom and advice to her daughters: to show a happy face, not anger; look beautiful, have good manners, smile—make people like you; make others happy; help one another and be grateful; improve yourself; instill gratitude in your children; use "righteous discipline"; praise and punish, but praise more. Running through her comments on health, religion, and ethics as well as her teaching about "one true *hotoke* [Buddha]" (79) is the theme of suffering, related to the Buddhist belief that "the harsher the winter, the fresher the spring" (106–7). Mama is convinced that important lessons in life are learned through suffering. Her last words are a touching request for a prayer, perhaps hinting at the possibility that she is trying to convert her Western-educated daughter, the "you" of her address. Part of Mama's agenda might also be to repair a rift between herself and one of her daughters, Naomi. While describing Naomi's wedding (for which the daughter had to pay from her own savings), the other daughter, Kikumura, in turn manages to insert her own agenda by extracting a lot of ethnographic information.

The mother's refusal or inability to return to Japan points to the role of shame as an underlying motive for the narrative and its subsequent omissions and understatements. What Kikumura describes as the "shame of returning to their homeland as someone who didn't succeed" (4)—the same shame masking the mother's real name under a pseudonym—was an experience common to many Issei. The fear of losing face explains why Mama doesn't want her parents to know how poor her family is. The narrative exposes painful family secrets: Papa's gambling, marital betrayals, rejection by grandparents, children's anger, and other dramas of estrangement. Still, there are meaningful omissions and silences that can be considered either shameful or strategic, adopted by both mother and daughter so as not to antagonize readers. The most conspicuous example concerns a rather unusual restraint in the treatment of the war years (1942–44). The forcible relocation of Japanese Americans as enemy aliens is related with reticence: "We traveled [to Arkansas] by train with the shades drawn down. It was better that way because quite a few Japanese people were killed by Americans before we were interned" (51). The mother's experience of internment camps is barely elaborated and surprisingly brushed away for the sake of assertion of her loyalty to her new homeland: "There were two factions in camp; one who said they would stay in America, and another who said they wanted to return to Japan. About half returned to Japan. I didn't want to return to Japan. America was my home. I know I made the right decision" (53). Under the circumstances, it is impossible not to ask: What has inspired her words? Is it her passivity? Shame? Fear of losing face? Or is it a retroactive correction, accurate from the point of view of the time of reminiscence rather than of experience itself? Can it also be considered in terms of debt, her "debt" to the country where after all she has survived and raised her children? Or is it a public sentiment that she has internalized?[9] In the Epilogue, the mother's life history seems to come full circle, in the ironic reversal of her dreams: if America was a dream of her youth, Japan is her dream now—a dream that she thinks unattainable because of her acute sense of shame.

Similarly, the encrypting of the crucial years 1945–46 remains to be puzzling. During these years the United States dropped the A-bombs on Japan. It was the time when Akemi Kikumura was born. Is her birth omitted because she does not want such personal details to diminish her stature and seriousness as a researcher of her family history, addressed to a presumably male-dominated academic environment? Or is her self-effacement simply part of the chosen adherence to academic objectivity? Kikumura also decided to stop the life history narrative "approximately 20 years before the actual time of data collection" (147). A withdrawal of information that might be too personal in relation to her as a researcher seems consistent with the principle of showing a "good face" to the outside world. But there is one more issue buried in the narrative that refuses to go away. The afterlife of the Japanese national trauma is curiously left unexplored. How is Kikumura's relationship with her Japanese relatives affected by the fact of the atomic bomb (the *pica* in Japanese)? For someone whose text reveals multiple and fractured identifications, loyalties, and attachments to such labels as Japanese, Japanese American, and American, she is quite uneasy with the topic. She views the Japanese family members as happier and more "fortunate" (8) than her immigrant mother who had experienced extreme poverty and abuse. However, only thirty years separate Kikumura's visit to Japan from the tragedy of Hiroshima. Silences of the survivors—survivors of the relocation and of the atomic bomb—create ghostly effects of haunting in her narrative.

As Marita Sturken observes, official history has an ambivalent attitude to survivors, who as the living dead "often disrupt the closure of a particular history" (5). Trauma survivors testify through their very presence to the body's importance to memory, to the materiality of memory. Embodying personal memory, survivors participate in the processes of inscribing, producing, and giving meaning to cultural memory understood as "a field of cultural negotiation through which different stories vie for a place in history" (Sturken 1). Thus survivors stand at the intersection of memory and history, where different narratives are legitimized so as to produce concepts of the nation and Americanness, especially in the event of great public traumas. To paraphrase Cathy Caruth's words, the traumatized text "carries on impossible history within [itself]," becoming itself "the symptom of a history that [it] cannot entirely possess" (5). Kikumura's narrative shows traces of the author's awareness of the powerful impact that the mere presence of survivors of historical traumas can have on readers. Consequently, she employs a number of strategies that the Japanese American critic Traise Yamamoto calls "masking." Discussing Nisei women's autobiography, Yamamoto claims that these texts adopt a non-threatening stance in order to avoid "overt conflict with those readers whom [the author] desire[s] to educate" (105). Survivors are careful to present their accounts in a selective and guarded manner so that they can reach "a potentially defensive and hostile white American audience" (Yamamoto 106). Tonal and narrative masking—whether through the use of ungrudging, reasonable voice, euphemisms, or omissions—gives their stories credibility and preserves a sense of dignity. The force of the question "Who is American?" resonates loudly in survivors' narratives: "These autobiographies self-consciously redefine the idea of home/land and their own relationship to it, mediated as it is by external and internalized racism" (Yamamoto 110).

The experience of many racialized groups of immigrants suggests that race politics and hard work are related. For Japanese Americans, in addition to being a means of success, the work ethic was also "a means by which an individual could maintain his/her self-concept as a virtuous person" (88). Kikumura provides an end-commentary, but also background information on the history and forms of anti-Asian racism in the United States. She clearly defines the setting: "the place—California, the hub of anti-Japanese sentiment; the time—prior to and shortly after World War II, at the height of racism, suspicion, and segregation between the races, and restriction of civil rights and liberties" (100). The racist aspects of the American Dream are mostly revealed through the figure of Papa, who quickly realized that there were hardly any Japanese counterparts to the Horatio Alger story such as George Shima, the Issei "Potato King," who created an agricultural empire out of unwanted land. And especially after the passage of the 1913 and 1920 Alien Land Laws, which essentially prohibited the Issei from owning or leasing land, his prospects as a successful farmer were dismal. Maybe by gambling he could make that one "big score" so that he could return to Japan a rich and proud man? (91–92)

Kikumura exonerates her father by questioning and challenging American democracy and citizenship. Consequently, in those parts of the narrative focalized through her the father appears to be a much more tragic figure than in her mother's account:

Coming to America, living as a minority, and facing racial prejudice and discrimination for the first time, he knew how difficult it would be for his children who had not experienced the security and knowledge of a country where they were of the majority ... He knew [the importance of pride] as long as one remained physically identifiable: "During my lifetime I hope that I can convince you, that as long as you look Japanese, you are going to be Japanese. No one is going to say, 'Oh look, there goes an American.' And you may never see Japan, but everybody is going to say, 'There's that Japanese girl.'" (93)

A sense of exclusion from citizenship and from the definition of the nation compels the father to try hard "to fight the inevitable process of Americanization" (100). However, she shows a double-sided effect of ethnic pride as a useful mechanism of coping with racism, but also a cause for alienation. Papa would believe in "the superiority of Japanese morals, values, and intelligence" while saying "that America had relegated the Japanese Americans to a second-class status" (93). As a result, he equipped his children with other survival strategies such as suspicion of the outside world and concealment of one's real emotions. Showing "a 'good face' as a representative of the Japanese in general insured greater acceptance by the majority society" (96). Kikumura observes how both parents had adapted their behaviour to the surrounding culture and how the mother, despite her marital problems, shared her husband's frustrations related to discrimination. Such solidarity of the oppressed serves as a reminder that like many other women of colour, Japanese women experienced sexism in their own communities, but they shared the experience of racism with

Japanese men. At the end of his life, the father admits that without the mother he "could have never made it" (98).

In relating the parents' joint experiences the text offers a submerged counter-narrative to the American Dream and its propaganda of success: "That the concentration-camp experience was recalled as a happy, carefree time without the worry of supporting her children only helps to illustrate life's adversities for the Issei woman in America" (107). Kikumura avoids a tendency to privilege one moment, namely, the internment, as the most disruptive and confusing experience for Japanese Americans, instead drawing attention to the continuous history of racism and exclusion experienced by the Issei also in the pre-war years. The discourse of Americanness is problematized throughout the narrative, both by mother and daughter. Significantly, the Epilogue gives the last word to the mother, who—after fifty-seven years in the country—wants to become an American citizen even though she realizes that she is "still considered a foreigner" (108). The final sentence reflects her hard-earned citizenship right in a simple and direct way: "On May 15, 1980, Michiko Tanaka became an American citizen." The silences enveloping this statement are symbolic of individual and collective triumphs over adversity, suggesting that citizenship may be a topos that reflects a political subtext of immigrant women's life writing. However, an important difference between Kikumura's text and the narratives discussed earlier is the contrast between the experience of anti-Asian racism versus unacknowledged white privilege through assimilation.

Ultimately, her narrative is open to two competing though coexisting readings. While it offers a didactic, critical corrective to the American Dream, it also qualifies, through the presence of normalizing strategies, for what David Palumbo-Liu calls "model minority discourse," defined as "an ideological construct not coextensive with the texts themselves, but rather designating a mode of apprehending, decoding, recoding, and producing Asian American narratives" (396). As the product of a particular mode of reading and subject construction, model minority discourse addresses potentially explosive issues of racism, sexism, and class differences in ways acceptable to a liberal audience. Such texts usually participate in the rhetoric of depoliticized self-healing that suppresses material differences and sees change as the function of individual adjustments required of ethnic subjects. To the dominant group, model minority discourse offers a sign of possible recovery from racism; to other immigrants, it represents patterns of assimilation that other groups ought to imitate.

According to Palumbo-Liu, Asian American literature has been exploited as model minority discourse in order to affirm dominant ideologies of the self and of success, popularizing the liberal notion that racial minorities can only blame themselves for their alienation in America (400). The dominant function of model minority discourse is to reproduce specific minority subject positions within the hegemonic order, reinforcing the dominant culture's normative expectations of conformity and a larger ideology of individualism. Against these expectations, Kikumura rehistoricizes and creates a counter-discourse to the narratives of America as an egalitarian democracy. She reveals race as "a powerful and negative signifier" that, together with gender, class, and other signifiers of difference, pushes against "the universalities of the modern state" such as citizenship, property rights, democracy, and nationalism (Palumbo-Liu 393). Witness narratives produced by racialized subjects retelling traumatic events such as the relocation force us to recognize the demand for a less monolithic, more inclusive image of the nation and remind us that "'America' is always in process itself" (Palumbo-Liu 389).

Apolonja Maria Kojder's *Marynia, Don't Cry*

> You a mortal, you a woman, who does not want to be small in any sense of the word. You a poet, you a feminist, who seeks beauty in and beyond the ordinariness of the everyday life. (Nellie Wong, "In Search of the Self as Hero")

Like *Through Harsh Winters*, *Marynia, Don't Cry* (1995) belongs to the category of second-generation narratives of immigration. Apolonja Maria Kojder is a child of Polish immigrants, born three weeks after their arrival in Canada, who sees herself as "a symbol of their new beginnings, a new chapter in their lives" (132). In the light of the tragic history that Kojder's parents and other Poles had suffered before and during the Second World War, it is understandable that they were hoping for a better future in Canada. Coming from the eastern regions of Poland, not only had they lived through extreme poverty and hardships in the years immediately preceding the war, but also as soon as the war started and the Red Army crossed the Polish border from the east, they were deported from the occupied territories by the Soviets to remote regions of Siberia and Kazakhstan. According to historian Norman Davies, in the years 1939–40, the number of Poles sent to *lagiers* (concentration camps), to hard labour, or to penal exile reached about one and a half million, almost half of whom died (451). The exact numbers will never be known, but the horrific trauma of their experiences, including "instances of derangement, frostbite, starvation, infanticide, even cannibalism" (N. Davies 449) has been slowly brought to light through survivors' memoirs.[10] Kojder's oral history, focused on interactions between history and individual biography, inscribes the heroic into the ordinary by intermingling "lofty" discourses of patriotic destiny with the "ordinary" women's accounts of their participation in these tragic historical events. Her life writing, then, offering a female perspective on this tragedy, displaces a predominantly male point of view privileged by the publishing industry. Ironically, the Canadian publisher's concern with a conventional requirement of "gender balance" resituates her narrative in the normative frame of male heroic individualism by placing it side by side with another Polish Canadian memoir dedicated to male experience of immigration.[11]

Kojder's text is a personalized memoir written by the granddaughter of the woman whose name—Marynia—appears in the title of the volume which contains these two stories. Subtitled "A Mother's Legacy," it is a woman-centred narrative which gives testimony to female resilience, ingenuity, and strength exhibited under adverse circumstances. Going back to the 1920s, the story depicts the family's struggle with poverty, deportation, and life in the Siberian labour camp; the exodus of Polish civilians out of Russia; the trail of the Polish army through the Middle East; the transport of Polish orphans to India and then to Britain; and, finally, immigration to Canada. The life stories of three generations of women—the author's great-grandmother, grandmother, and mother—reflect the old familiar pattern of gender politics experienced by Eastern European women who had to fend for themselves and manage on their own while their fathers and husbands had been swept away by war or emigrated to a foreign land. Kojder celebrates strong female bonds, especially those between mothers and daughters in successive generations. The mother–daughter couple in her family archive becomes a symbol of continuity, providing her with the wealth of positive role models of determined, spirited, and hard-working women. In a proto-feminist manner, Kojder's "foremothers," as she calls them, question prevailing gender norms and traditions of their society. For example, her great-grandmother and grandmother both reject a folk custom of "capping" (putting a kerchief on the bride's head during the wedding ceremony) as degrading to women, and both remain skeptical about the Catholic Church, whose attitude to women they find insulting. The measure of the grandmother's independence can be seen when she gives her daughter away in marriage without paternal consent. The same grandmother abandons her estranged husband after she joins him in Canada, choosing to live with her daughter, to whom she offers unflinching support. The Kojder women are thus represented as capable of matrilineal solidarity in challenging male dominance.

Nor surprisingly, the ideological focus of Kojder's narrative is survival of the family as a unit sustained by women's work and solidarity. She offers a heroic narrative of gender, focused on women's strength in the family and the importance of women's community. The Kojder women have all been helping each other through hardships endured in rural Poland between the wars, during the deportation to Siberia in 1940, and in exile. They have promoted the idea of a female support system and demonstrated amazing creativity in devising new survival skills, which for them constituted the most immediately available form of self-actualization. The women's stories abound in details of unusual home remedies and most unexpected edibles. And although it may occasionally seem that the narrative reinforces too much the traditional stereotypical image of women as nurturers, one must remember that for these women the immediate enemy was hunger and disease and that securing food for their needy families was an absolute priority, a matter of life and death. Both Kojder's grandmother and mother were so disgruntled and disillusioned with life in Poland that instead of returning to their homeland after the liberation, they chose to go to Canada, where Kojder's grandfather had been an immigrant since 1925.[12] Their ordeals supply a necessary corrective to unreflexive nationalism among Polish immigrants who in reaction to the Communist regime have often idealized pre-war Poland, despite its oppressive system of classes and ranks. In this sense, the narrative fills a significant gap in the history of Polish immigration in Canada. Although one can find numerous examples of middle-class or even working-class migrant accounts, there are hardly any records of immigration seen from the perspective of impoverished female farm workers, perhaps because theirs has been predominantly an oral culture. Kojder's story is exceptional in granting them a position of subjects in history.[13] After all, to recall Regenia Gagnier's observation from her study of working-class autobiography, working women's non-individualism, their alignment with home and family, was "the least conducive to the constitution of writing subjects" (265). As we shall see, Kojder's mother, Helena, has beaten the odds to become a writing subject; however, her textual agency has ultimately been erased.

Kojder's text can be read as an example of "crypto-translation," that is, translation hiding its traces in the text, pretending not to be a translation at all. Describing the crypt, Derrida says that its "grounds [*lieux*] are so disposed as to disguise and to hide: something, always a body in some way. But also to disguise the act of hiding and to hide the disguise: the crypt hides as it holds" ("*Fors*" xiv). As a "crypto-translation," the text literalizes the metaphor of translation as an invisible, transparent practice while, at the same time, by virtue of linguistic incorporation of other texts, it functions as a symbolic crypt for the voices buried in it. The cryptic character of Kojder's translation is covered up by her attempts to achieve transparency by erasing the effects of translation, that is, eradicating "the mark each translator, as a gendered individual, leaves on the work" (von Flotow 35), and by hiding the effect of hiding. For a larger part of her story, Kojder adopts the convention of third-person omniscient, objective, disembodied narrative voice. Like Salverson, she uses fictionalization by means of the third-person narrative voice in the first part of the text, smoothing out or eliminating any sutures that might raise the reader's suspicion of translation at work. This pseudo-fictionalizing stance, in her case, can be linked to the tradition of romanticism frequently displayed in ethnographic narrativizing of the experiences of the ethnic others. She never acknowledges her mediation, even when quoting direct speech or documents reproduced in her text, such as letters, telegrams, and—primarily—the motto which serves as a leitmotif running through her text: "Marynia, don't cry. As long as I'm alive I'll help you. And maybe you'll survive because nobody will bother you. And later your children will help you." This unavowed or disavowed translation, grounded in a poetics of transparency, makes the text appear as if it originated in English. In Kojder's narrative, for the most part, we do not know if anyone is translating, whose voice we are hearing, who remembers, and how these memories are tied to language.

There are, inevitably, textual moments when it is possible to locate a breakdown of the unproblematized transparency and when the presence of the buried "original" haunts the narrative. A crisis of the poetics of transparency is enacted both on the level of language and on that of subjectivity. The text signals its subdued plurivocality, pointing to the languages reverberating behind the official façade of English. We are told that characters speak in Polish, that Ukrainian children sing in Ukrainian, that Russian soldiers speak in Russian, that Helena, the mother, has to learn Gujarati during her stay in India. These "foreign" languages, including Persian, leave their traces in the fabric of language, "contaminating" the target text which gestures at the possibility of giving itself over to several other languages. The most obvious examples of the material that is untranslatable or left untranslated are proper names and idiomatic language, which resist transfer. Excluding approximations of single words that are occasionally offered, the only instance in the text when linguistic translation is staged on the page, right before our eyes, is a doggerel whose Polish and English versions are reproduced side by side:

Martwią się ludzie że się nie buduję [dom]	People are worried that I'm not building [a house]
Mam teścia w Kanadzie	I've got a father-in-law in Canada
To się nie torbuję	So I'm not worried
Mam teścia w Kanadzie	I've got a father-in-law in Canada
to się nie torbuję	So I'm not worried
Bo na każde Święta	Because on every holiday
Dolary sortuję	I'm sorting dollars (33)

The "original" here consists of rhyming couplets, strongly marked as peasant speech, which has been completely lost in translation. This example bears witness not only to a failure of linguistic equivalence, but also to the limits of cultural transfer since the literalizing translation cannot convey class, ethnic, regional, and stylistic differences manifest in spoken language. Paradoxically, this type of word-for-word translation, associated by Benjamin with literality (*Wörtlichkeit*), pierces the wall of transparency, becoming an arcade that "supports while letting light pass and the original show" (Derrida, "Des Tours" 188).

The crisis of transparency is announced differently by a break in the narrative voice that occurs close to the end of the text. In a most surprising gesture, Kojder situates herself in the story. This eruption of subjectivity initiated by the sudden appearance of the narrative "I" displaces the convention of scholarly/ethnographic narrative objectivity on which the text has relied so far. As she inserts herself into the text, Kojder's memory takes over, symbolically reaffirming the fact that "personal aspects always affect the production of texts, translations and scholarly work" (von Flotow 39), even while they remain invisible. There are significant stylistic differences between the two parts, between the third-person objective and the more personal tone. In the second part, the "I" regresses into the "innocent-eye" vision, recalling her childhood memories and reminiscences. Her voice often sounds naive and childlike when she summarizes some of the stories recounted earlier and stresses their formative effect on her. We can see a corresponding linguistic "regression" into the language of the narrator's childhood in the frequency of Polish words used in the text. In part one, over a hundred pages long, only nine Polish words appear, whereas in part two, condensed to a little more than twenty pages, the density of Polish usage increases dramatically to over forty words. Interestingly, a semantic analysis of Polish lexical items also suggests different thematic registers that dominate the two parts, with emphasis shifting from money/possessions/food in part one to family/cultural tradition/food in part two. Food seems to be a constant marker of ethnicity here, as it has been in the previously discussed narratives, showing the importance of specific foods and rituals around food preparation as metaphors for the "ingestion" of national and cultural identities.

In fact, the brief autobiographical "coda" coinciding with part two exhibits many clichés of immigrant genres as narratives of literacy and acculturation that we have already encountered in Antin's and Salverson's autobiographies. We find here Kojder's recollections of language acquisition, the experience of bilingualism, the praise of hard work, a record of rejection and disappointment, and a testimony to the importance of stories and the family history. She also speaks of the immigrant child's experience of a characteristic split between the reality of school, coded in English, and the reality of home, coded in Polish. She says that as a child she was furious when her mother tried to speak English at home. At this point one can recognize the hidden logic correlating Kojder's refusal to mix the reality of English with that of Polish in her childhood and her textual resistance to flaunting the effects of translation in her book. Her reliance on transparent discourse helps to maintain the illusion of clear-cut boundaries between the two cultures and to deflect her fear of contamination of one language by the other.

In the second part, too, Kojder reveals that as a result of her taking courses in women's studies at university, she actually managed to persuade her mother to write down the family history, which was supposed to help Kojder in preparing her assignments and, presumably, the book we are reading. However, she drops the subject of her mother's memoirs after the comment: "And so she began the task of writing her memoirs" (131). The actual memoirs never materialize and are never more referenced in Kojder's narrative, and we are left with many questions: How has she used her mother's memoirs in this book? Has she "robbed" her mother of her speech, or has she "usurped" the source text in the name of women's self-assertiveness so characteristic of her family? Why has she given up translation and opted instead for a stylized "reconstruction" of oral history? Everything seems to suggest that the story of the book's production repeats the recurrent thematic motif in the text: with her mother's memoirs as a literary source, it is Kojder's turn now to tap the matrilineal support system that has existed in her family for generations.

What remains hidden in the narrative is the image of the mother's manuscript that could be its hypothetical source, or its missing "origin." This image echoes Derrida's use of the figure of the crypt in theorizing autobiography and translation as writing in (the) place of another, also linked by their common investment in genealogy and the proper name. Commenting on the paradox of the proper name or the signature, he notes that "It's always the same thing, but each time it's different; each time it's a different history to which one must pay close attention" (*The Ear* 85). The inscription of the proper name problematizes the relation between inside and outside in autobiography and translation, framing the text from the inside, or bringing the outside inside the inside, folding into an internal pocket of externality like the crypt. But Kojder's narrative is a crypt not only because it is holding the supposedly "original" manuscript, which is only seemingly ingested and assimilated while in fact remaining "buried" in translation, hidden in the textual vault of language. Her text is also the crypt holding the living dead because it performs the work of mourning, listing the names of family members who had been killed or died during the war. In a sense, then, the book is the crypt of memory, just as the author's name is forever bound in a genealogical chain to her little sister, Apolonja, who died in Siberia. The proper name "Apolonja Maria Kojder" is a symbolic crypt for her buried other through whom she receives the privilege of life. Consequently, the dissemination of the proper name(s) is not just the way of dispersing the subject in the text, of losing one's name, but it can also be a way to celebrate the subject through monumentalization, erecting a monument in language as a practice of memorializing. Referring back to Derrida's terms, translation/autobiography is situated between life and death, survival and the crypt, death of self through writing and the possibility of "eternal return." As a narrative that buries while also preserving a trace of the other, Kojder's crypto-translation ensures the afterlife for the "original" confined to its textual crypt and the living on for the dead, thus doubling the motif of survival that dominates on the thematic plane.

Interestingly, in translation studies, the genealogical function of translation in providing the link between the living and the dead has been noticed in its historical connection to hagiographic commemoration.

According to Talal Asad, "in ecclesiastical usage ... the removal of a saint's remains, or his relics, from an original site to another is also known as translation" ("A Comment" 325). The narratives relating the events of such relocation of the bones were also called translations, once again reaffirming translation's ambivalent status as both representation and performance (as Kojder's narrative performs also the function of memorializing). As Asad further explains, "The transfer of relics involved the retention of something essential despite the change of location. What was transferred was not merely a relic but the power inherent in it" (325–26). In the metaphor of translation as the crypt, the relics of cultural memory are carried over and preserved in the "con-fusion" of the past and the present (similar to that between the outside and the inside of textuality), so that the past informs the present and the dead authorize the living to invoke a particular tradition and the shared values, histories, and standards. In Bella Brodzki's discussion of translation as a figure for processes of intergenerational and intercultural transmission, inspired by her reading of Benjamin, she underscores the reciprocity of the relationship between the original and its translation and the similarity of this model to the mother–daughter relationship: "Although the translation owes its existence to the original, [the original] also gains something, becomes more than itself by virtue of its being translated; both need each other to fill in spaces that would otherwise remain in the realm of images, unarticulated and unsignified" (*Can These* 124). The acceptance of this mutual bond potentially ameliorates the suspicion of appropriation directed at Kojder's narrative. It also creates the possibility of refiguring the crypt as not so much a tomb as a tunnel, according to a more archaic definition (Dawson 4), and hence, the possibility of viewing her translation not in terms of incorporation or appropriation but as a tunnel or a passage that opens a connection to the (m)other whose survival it signs.

However, what "survives" in the telling are not just women's experiences. Toward the end of her narrative, Kojder speaks in the name of her dead father, who is transformed into a symbolic figure aligned with Polishness, nationalism, and patriotic values. With this turn to the male figure, the text takes on a new urgency demanding not only public recognition of the silenced chapter of Polish history, namely, the forgotten fact of mass deportations of Polish civilians to the Soviet Union and their forced labour during the Second World War, but also historical retribution for the crimes committed against Polish people by the Soviets. In particular, a powerful signifier of national martyrology, the Katyn massacre of over

4,000 Polish officers in 1940, is mobilized as part of the tragic metanarrative of Polish heroism and victimization. The memoir concludes with her father's favourite quotation of a line from a famous poem by the Polish national bard Adam Mickiewicz (hopelessly mistranslated in her rendering).[14] Given the presence of so many powerful mother figures, such a conclusion to Kojder's narrative can only weaken its professed feminist allegiances, especially in the end, when another charged image, of her father persistently writing letters to the Red Cross from Siberia, is substituted in place of an image which we expect but which never materializes: the image of her mother writing. Leaving the last word to the father—both as a figure of genealogy and symbolic-cultural continuity—she reinscribes her "maternal" narrative in the context of Polish patriarchal culture, with its male-identified romantic ideology and the tradition of secular martyrology. Her translation, in the sense of cultural transfer of gender ideology bound to ethnicity, reveals reverence due to the mother, but gives the final say to the father. Ironically, it is an accurate formula of traditional Polish gender politics, which Kojder's own narrative repeatedly interrogates in its "maternal" sections.

Much like her positioning as the autobiographical subject suspended between the values embodied by her dead father and the living experience of the women in her family, conveyed through her mother's oral history, her text is uncomfortable with its own generic conventions. Similar to Kikumura's, Kojder's narrative is intended to legitimize and enhance her academic credentials, so she addresses herself to both academic and general readers. The issue of academic viability might partly explain the presence of several self-imposed narrative and stylistic constraints, including her preference for a domesticating, transparent type of translation. However, as we have seen, there are moments when the text puts into question the effect of transparency, such as the break in the narrative voice, which signals her readiness to abandon the scholarly corset of ethnocultural history and to assume a more personal, confessional posture. Such practice can also be seen as gendered, inasmuch as third-person objectivity can be coded as the voice of an ostensibly gender-neutral academic, whereas the first-person voice that breaks through it is clearly identified as female. Consequently, Kojder's translation in the end symbolizes the persistent presence of patriarchal forms and values in women's discourses, which opens up her text to the risks of misrecognition and co-optation for conservative ends. Derrida links such risk of "contamination and detour" to the function of the proper name:

> To the extent to which it can immediately become common and drift off course toward a system of relations where it functions as a common name or mark, [the proper name] can send the address of course. The address is always delivered over to a kind of chance ... There are, then, aleatory or chance elements at work in every kind of message, every type of letter, all mail, if you will. (*The Ear* 108)

In relation to reading and reception of Kojder's narrative, the missed address can be seen clearly in what returns filtered through the receiving ear of the other. One reviewer for the Polish immigrant press misses the implicit critique of the nation as a system stratified by class in pre-war Poland and describes her story as "a model of a patriotic outlook on Polish matters" (Wegierski 520). A selective reading of her text can also support a perception of Poland's unrecognized martyrdom, which is a sentiment shared by most of the conservative Polish Canadian press:

> It seems that in Canada today, virtually every minority group is stridently crying about its past suffering and victimization, in order to assert its moral superiority over the majority and obtain appropriate entitlements and redress. Among the hidden casualties of society consumed by victimology are those persons and nations that actually did suffer incredibly in the past, but whose histories are, for whatever reason, considered inappropriate or irrelevant to current public debate. (Wegierski 519)

A long time has passed since the days of Antin and Salverson, but in the above words we can see a reinvention of white supremacy in successive generations of immigrants as whiteness, threatened by the multicultural politics of recognition, insinuates reverse racism as a cause of its alleged marginalization.

The reason why Kojder's text yields itself to such appropriation might be related to the type of immigrant subjectivity constructed on the threshold between languages and cultures, which spans multiple contradictions in the coexistence of ethnic difference and assimilation, of polyvocality and univocality, of feminist and patriarchal ideologies, of the speaker as academic and child. The fact that she privileges a transparent or "fluent" translation over dialogic possibilities finds its meta-textual parallel in the positive valorization of acculturation as erasure of difference, as a linear progression from the pre-emigration to post-emigration self, which has been the *telos* of traditional immigrant autobiography, contested by several writers discussed earlier in this volume, including Kikumura. One can go even further and see Kojder's translation not only as an allegory of immigrant acculturation, but also an allegory of the situation of translation in Anglo-American culture at large, where, according to Lawrence Venuti, "translation has for so long remained discursively concealed and culturally marginalized, supporting a process of assimilating rather than living difference" (*Rethinking* 9). This persistent tendency bears directly on the imbalance in applying foreignizing and domesticating strategies in translations of immigrant women's life writing, the problem I have already signalled earlier. It seems that consumer preference for domestication of the "foreign" influences the publishers' selection of specific texts that meet the expectations of transparency and can be more easily commercialized in the contemporary cultural marketplace.

The issue of domesticating translation brings us back to the question of institutional determinations of Kojder's narrative and a larger context of production and reception of immigrant women's life writing. As already mentioned, she works as an academic and under the institutional and discursive constraints of the genre of "ethnic (auto)biography" published by the Multicultural History Society of Ontario (MHSO) as part of "Ethnocultural Voices Series," whose declared mandate is to showcase "representative" voices from different communities, thus reinforcing the idea of distinct and essentialized ethnic identities.[15] As a promoter of crosscultural translation, MHSO has done much to record and circulate ethnic/immigrant experiences and histories. According to the 1994 book catalogue, the Society's mission reflects Canada's Multiculturalism Act through its rhetoric of "appreciation" of Ontario's ethnic diversity and increased "knowledge and understanding of its unique multiracial, multilingual heritage." As Marlene Kadar observes in her writing about Ibolya Grossman's book published in the same series, the publisher is mostly interested in texts that serve the political needs of the MHSO by giving "evidence of the multicultural history of the democratic nation of Canada" ("The Discourse" 121). In this sense, Kojder's translation is clearly sponsored under the national agenda to celebrate a plurality of ethnic experiences as a form of indirect tribute to Canada's liberal management of diversity. The assumption of transparent translatability behind such domesticating translations constitutes an inhospitable imposition of monolingualism and a denial of the possibility of a social contract, which for Derrida "can only take place in translation, that is, only if it is *simultaneously* uttered in both my tongue and the other's. If it takes place in only one tongue, whether it be mine or the other's, there is no contract possible" (*The Ear* 125). The intergenerational and cross-cultural transmission performed through translation requires that we agree to the necessary existence of what he calls "a Babelian situation" that dooms the translator to staying in the middle, between total translatability and total untranslatability, striving to achieve Ricoeur's "equivalence without identity." Without totalizing in either direction of sameness or difference, it might then be possible to continue the productive work of translation as *différance* that can accept undecidability and the eternal return of the remainder or the supplement.

Concluding Remarks

The narratives produced by Kojder and Kikumura, two immigrant daughters as academics, perform an important institutional function also by virtue of participating in the production of academic knowledge, which is a specific type of mediation linked to cultural transmission, according to the following description provided by Trinh Minh-ha:

> Whether you translate one language into another language, whether you narrate in your own words what you have understood from the other person, or whether you use this person ... to serve the direction of your [work], you are dealing with cultural translation. (*Framer* 129)

In addition to linguistic transfers from Japanese and Polish into English, these narratives include a complex range of activities that are all part of cultural translation, corresponding to the continuum of discourses deployed in each text that work both ways, affecting both the source and the target cultures. Among a vast array of functions of cultural translation, we can name the subjective-genealogical function of translation as inscription of gendered subjectivity in the family and social history. There is the symbolic-ritualistic function of translation, where the book is an offering to the (dead) ancestors, and where it also performs the memorializing function. It is also possible to recognize the cultural-ethnographic function of documenting the life of a remote culture for the benefit of another culture, including also a transition from orality to print. Similarly, we have the historical-revisionist function of translation as changing official records of history, based on the experience of marginalized and oppressed groups such as first-generation immigrant women of colour or immigrant women of peasant classes. Finally, translation in these two texts has the political-ideological function of recasting women's experiences from patriarchal to feminist terms, or from silence to voice.

Like Antin's and Salverson's confessions, the matrilineal autoethnographies written by Kikumura and Kojder can be said to "elicit the unspoken (and perhaps unspeakable) private story" (Cosslett et al. 4), harbouring and sometimes extracting secrets about female embodiment and sexuality, family shame, and racial traumas. Secrets are at the centre of immigrant autobiography, according to Aritha Van Herk, who dismisses the covert story as the official, taboo version of "the great fiction of immigration" ("Writing" 184). In reading the two narratives in this chapter, I have tried to show to what degree each author does or does not acknowledge her debt to the mother and acquit herself of the duty to practise linguistic hospitality in translation. As explained above, the translation contract, symbolized by the heterogeneity of the crypt as writing in place of another, requires recognition without mastery of the difference of languages and preservation of the other's difference. Consequently, we cannot take for granted the assumption that daughters, especially feminist daughters, can restore subjectivity to the mother, by including her biography within their autoethnographies. Such assumption has been contested by autobiography critics:

> While daughters' accounts of their mothers' lives are clearly an important part of *their* subjectivities, the mothers are often denied full subjectivity. To posit the mother–daughter relationship so centrally to women's life-stories as "dialogic" is not to deny that it is also power-inscribed, with the two parties struggling for control and self-actualization. Yet whether, and how, the mother's subjectivity emerges varies in autobiographical practice and is more or less enabled by particular cultural practices. (Cosslett et al. 4)

For the daughters who become linguistic and cultural translators of their mothers' life histories, the meaning of the translator's signature undermines the primacy of the supposed "originator" buried in the story, at the same time "emphasizing the fragility of the relationship between name and work, between subjectivity and writing—fragility which [can be situated] at the heart of all creativity" (Simon, "Translating" 64). In the idealized version, the translator's signature can be read as an endorsement of an ethical contract between self and other, based on respect, non-aggression, and attentiveness. As we have seen, the encrypted story, even if it is not exactly hospitable to otherness, as in Kojder's case, nevertheless preserves the relation to the place of the other and invites a rethinking of responsibility to the other.

The (m)others from these narratives can be taken as figurations of the subject of multicultural history, or of "the ethnic as envisaged by multiculturalism." The frame—serial and/or editorial—can turn each woman more into a *sujet* or topic of the narratives of others than into the subject of her own discourse. She is "the product of the 'multicultural' mosaic, therefore invisible ... a character exiled in the story that contains [her]" (Kamboureli, "Of Black Angels" 18–19). There is, however, resistance to this objectification, in the form of strategies that destabilize the very notion of authenticity. One such form of resistance is through photography, which serves as a reminder of the uniqueness of each generalized multicultural subject. In particular, when the editor's authority is all-too-powerfully asserted, photographs tempt a reader to move beyond the text, giving a sort of compensatory "reality" to the muted subject. It may be seen as symptomatic that in Kikumura's narrative there are no photographs, except an unidentified one on the cover, whereas in Kojder's text photographic documentation is provided. Although photographs are always "framed" from a particular angle of vision and mediated through different conventions of seeing, still they can be isolated from the text in which they are embedded and treated as a relatively separate discourse of images, perhaps a site of possible counter-discourse.

Perhaps more than the previously discussed narratives, the genre of feminist oral history literalizes Derrida's definition of "otobiography," which I explained earlier as autobiography that needs the reader's ear in order to come to life. Shirley Neuman offers a critique of one particular danger of "otobiography" which, she says, is signed not by the author but by the "ear of the other [that] says me to me and constitutes the *autos* of my autobiography." Neuman sounds a cautionary note in relation to practitioners of oral history, warning that "when the self exists only in the ear of the other, and when that ear is deaf or uncomprehending or unwilling to listen, the *bios*/life disappears; something, or someone, is being snuffed out" (*Reading* 215–16). One casualty of such misapprehension is the lost possibility of more complex insight into constructions of ethnicity and race. This type of ethnographic life writing often exemplifies what Gayatri Spivak calls "a conventionally sanctioned carelessness about ethnic identities, which has rather little to do with the obvious 'fact' that all identities are irreducibly hybrid, inevitably instituted by the representation of performance as statement" (*Critique* 155). Comparing the experiences of eastern European and Japanese immigrants to North America articulated through ethnographic life writing, we notice some parallels. Feminized and relegated to a less desirable category at the turn of the century, Eastern Europeans have a past history of discrimination that lingers on, for example, in the form of "Polack jokes." Racialization, however, is much more tangible in the case of Japanese, who experienced years of straightforward anti-Asian racism, discrimination, and demonizing, which today have given way to the concept of "model minority" and proofs of assimilability. What these texts remind us of is that despite attempts to treat ethnic and racial identity as constant, their constructions prove to be historically contingent and unstable.

In summary, the texts written by Kikumura and Kojder illustrate the dangers inherent in such ethnographic practices where collective identities clash with the researcher's self, and attempted objectivity frequently verges on objectification. It is imperative that translators/ethnographers heed the injunction against creating the illusion of unilateral and unproblematic authority by disclosing their own locations, mediations, and power privileges. We always return to the same questions: In whose name are such translations made? Who benefits from such inscriptions? What institutional demands and calls do they respond to? The violence of representation often speaks through silences—things withdrawn voluntarily, by the subject herself, or suppressed by the translator. In this context, the concept of "shaming"—at work in Japanese life writing—points to continuous extortions of autobiographical discourse. In response to such public constraints, the choice of the genre of memoir or oral history, both of which de-emphasize the self and focus on the relations to the community and the social world, can be seen as yet another strategy of self-concealment. Such instances remind us that the proximity of autobiography and confession, discussed in the previous chapter, reflects the close connection between subjectivity and subjection, already exemplified by the concept of the disciplined subject of "confession" (forced or voluntary), which is a price for acquiring the self.

Chapter 3

Experimental Self-Translations
Eva Hoffman and Smaro Kamboureli

> We cannot write in any other way – without slamming the door, without cutting the ties. (Hélène Cixous, *Three Steps on the Ladder of Writing*)

Writing at a Loss: Postmodern Diasporic Narratives

In traditional European theories of translation there has persisted for a long time a certain negative valuing of translation perceived either as a "betrayal" of the original or its inferior "copy." Postcolonial translation studies theorists have even pointed out that the hierarchy between the original and its translation can be seen as modelled on the relationship between Europe and its colonies (Bassnett and Trivedi 4). Such depreciation has given rise to the myth that something is always lost in translation. Consequently, it is not surprising that the language of "loss" has been used to articulate a vision of translation as exile, or a fall from origin—the narrative situated squarely within Western metaphysical thought. Ganesh Devy illustrates this tragic view of the post-Babelian situation by quoting J. Hillis Miller's description of translation as "the wandering existence of a text in perpetual exile" (182). Undoubtedly, part of the explanation for such negative valorizing lies in the fact that, as we have seen, translation poses a challenge to ethnocentrism of every language and culture. After all, one of the "losses" that can be attributed to translation is the loss of the reassuring safety of monolingualism and the anxiety ensuing from the recognition that my language is only one among many. Paul Ricoeur associates this kind of linguistic ethnocentrism with resistance to translation demonstrated on the side of the language of reception, which may refuse hospitality to the "foreign" as a threat to its identity. On the side of the source language, a similar resistance takes the form of presumption of non-translatability and the presence of untranslatable elements that inhibit the translator's task. Remembering this insurmountable difference between the source and the target languages, between the self and the "foreign," leads to recognition that something is lost. The ever-present sense of loss expresses itself, for example, in the ceaseless urge to retranslate the works of "the great classics of global culture" such as the Bible or Shakespeare (Ricoeur 7). Ricoeur suggests that we need to pass through the work of mourning in order to "give up the ideal of the perfect translation" (8), let go of a loss, and accept the limits of translation as equivalence without adequacy. We have seen different types of resistance to translation and its potential losses in the previously discussed texts, through the writers' preference for foreignizing or domesticating approaches and their choices of transparency or stubborn untranslatability. But the problem of the limits of translation is what directly preoccupies Eva Hoffman and Smaro Kamboureli in their life writing narratives which I want to read in this chapter.

Before I turn my attention to these texts, I want to go back for a moment to the concept of *pharmakon*, which Derrida uses to address differently similar questions of translation's limits and losses. *Pharmakon* is one of those words which exist in every language and which test the limits of translation because they mean "two things at the same time and … therefore cannot be translated without an essential loss. Whether one translates *pharmakon* as 'poison' or 'remedy,' whether one comes down on the side of sickness or health, life or death, the undecidability is going to be lost" (*The Ear* 120). This case can help us understand the hyperbolic statement about translation that he makes in *Monolingualism of the Other*: "In a sense, nothing is untranslatable; but *in another sense*, everything is untranslatable; translation is another name for the impossible" (56–57). Similar to Ricoeur, he claims that translation in a loose sense of approximation is possible once we renounce the "economic equivalence." However, such translation—which of necessity involves one choice among many, a poison or a remedy—puts a closure to the textual play and indeterminacy, to which the "original" or the source text is always open, and fails "to restore the singular event of the original" (56).

In most general terms, the difference between the narratives discussed in the previous chapter and the ones examined in the following pages can be captured by referring to Caroline Brettell's distinction between "a life-focused story that treats a life as a window on the objective facts of historical and ethnographic events" and "a story-focused life story that emphasizes the subjective experience of the narrator and the form of the narrative itself" (225). In contrast to the autoethnographic translations produced by Kikumura and Kojder, which follow the logic of exemplarity in their testimonial use of the situation of the historical subject, in Eva Hoffman's *Lost in Translation* (1989) and Smaro Kamboureli's *in the second person* (1985) the narrative "I" as well as the narrating "I" is multiply split and highly self-conscious of its own discursive practices, focusing attention on the processes of writing. These self-reflexive narratives offer postmodern versions of the literacy narrative of transition into English, previously discussed as a paradigmatic model of immigrant life writing. Both of them have been influenced by poststructuralist views of language and translation that privilege a free flow of textuality and intertextual borrowings as well as attention to the play of difference within and outside the subject. If texts and subjects can be seen as "always already" translated since they carry the mark of otherness within, translation becomes obsolete. Although Hoffman and Kamboureli engage in practices that can clearly be recognized as translational, both exhibit similar distrust of translation and use translation as a negative concept. However, they conceptualize its shortcomings from different perspectives: Hoffman grapples with linguistic and cultural displacement, hoping to discover some "essence" underneath the postmodern fragmentation, while Kamboureli locates failures of translation precisely in a danger of fixity and finality of the product. In a sense, then, they exemplify two different approaches to "loss" in translation that have been sketched above in the context of Ricoeur's theory of mourning and Derrida's *pharmakon*.

A common thread in their narratives is an obsession with accent as a sign of irreducible difference and excess of the untranslatable. An auditory equivalent of a "visible" marker of otherness, accent, according to Derrida, "indicates a hand-to-hand combat with language in general; it says more than accentuation. Its symptomatology invades writing" (*Monolingualism* 46). It functions as a shibboleth, a feature of pronunciation that identifies one as a member of a particular group, and therefore constitutes an obstacle to or a protective guard against the possibility of full translation or full assimilation. For both Hoffman and Kamboureli, a migration into English as a second language has entailed a loss of kinship through severing their ties to a mother tongue and a loosening of the ethnocultural bonds to their communities of origin. It might be helpful here to recall

Gustavo Pérez Firmat's study of Spanish bilingual writers, where he introduces a distinction between tongue, idiom, and language, which complicates the dichotomous source-target dynamics of loyalties and betrayals that we have been tracing so far in translation, making the issue of losses and gains much more nuanced and complex. A tongue (*lengua*) is corporal, verbal, and intimate, based on familial ties; an idiom (*idioma*) is locative, regional, place-bound, a native tongue rather than a mother tongue; finally, language (*lenguaje*) is an abstract structure detached from both person and place: "If a speaker's relation to a tongue is affective, and that to an *idioma* is cultural, his or her relation to *lenguaje* is cognitive" (Firmat 18). The ties binding a bilingual subject to these languages can be quite knotty, compounding the difficulties, if not the impossibility, of self-translation. Accent always reveals the subject's belonging to some elsewhere, to another idiom. Aligning the politics of accent with the phantasm of "a purity of language," Derrida reminisces that "One entered French literature only by losing one's accent" (*Monolingualism* 41). Interestingly, for Hoffman and Kamboureli the relationship to the English language supersedes the family and ethnic ties connoted by mother tongues and native idioms. They both share a high investment in writing and the written and have chosen the professions of writer and literary critic as routes of self-translation through which to enter literature in English. However, a self-reflexive focus on language does not resolve the textual and social problems of erasure of difference and untranslatability. As immigrants who have not lost their accents, they have become sensitized to linguistic ethnocentrism and conservatism of the host culture, where the policing of accent may serve symbolically as another form of social construction of otherness, supplanting or supplementing the marking of the body through ethnicity and race.

In Hoffman's and Kamboureli's life narratives, ethnicity becomes a problem of language and translatability. Consequently, there is a movement from éthnos to éthos, reflecting the need for "ethical writing" of otherness, which also manifests itself through the problematics of translation. I would like to add that "ethics" here is used in Kristeva's sense of challenging the monological subject or in Cixous's sense of gesturing toward the other. Through this insistence on ethics, Hoffman and Kamboureli also repoliticize life writing, providing contrapuntal readings of ethnicity to the Anglo-dominant ones which are confined to the context of national culture rather than diasporic negotiations of identity. Extrapolating from Ien Ang's discussion of the possibilities of mobilizing the productive tensions between "here" and "there" in the constructions of diasporic identities and cultures, one can say that diaspora can be conceptualized from the position of nostalgia, as exile from some lost or imaginary homeland; from the perspective of multiculturalism, as self-ethnicization prescribed by the dominant culture; or from the third space of translation, as hybridity and creative syncretism. It is usually the first two types of diasporic imagination, identified respectively with lost origins and hyphenated biculturality, that tend to decry the losses of translation and "construct the space of that ambivalent in-between-ness as an empty space, the space that gets crushed in the cultural translation from one side to the other in the bipolar dichotomy of 'where you're from' and 'where you're at'" (Ang 558). Hoffman and Kamboureli explore these tense power dynamics—in ways that can be both complicitous and contestatory—involved in the production of diasporic subjects as "ethnic" in the postmodern sense that Ang gives to ethnicity as a provisional and partial site of identification for the subject caught up in the ambivalent space of the hyphen.

Eva Hoffman's *Lost in Translation: A Life in a New Language*

> Something enormous is always lost in translation. Something insidious seeps into the gaps, especially when amateur linguists continue to compare, one-for- one, language differences and then put forth notions wide open to misinterpretation. (Amy Tan, "The Language of Discretion")

Unlike Mary Antin, who practically had to invent a form of immigrant autobiography by adapting traditional American models, Eva Hoffman's entry on the scene of life writing is accompanied by a combined sense of historical contingency and postmodern revisionism. Although self-reflexive moments can be found even in conventional personal narratives, *Lost in Translation* is innovative in its thematic focus on language and translation not so much as tools of immigrant survival but as semiotic fields of self-construction and self-exploration. As the title suggests, her life writing is subsumed by the project of translation operating within the economy of loss, in contrast to Antin's optimistic philosophy of a remainder. To account for Hoffman's pessimistic view of translation, I want to read her narrative symptomatically, taking my point of departure from trauma theorists who have documented the continuity of trauma in the lives of children of Holocaust survivors. Following Freud, Cathy Caruth writes that the structure of trauma consists "not in the forgetting of a reality that can hence never be fully known, but in an inherent latency within the experience itself [which means that] the traumatic event is not experienced as it occurs, [but] it is fully evident only in connection with another place, and in another time" (8). I argue that Hoffman's parents' memories of the Holocaust have had a great impact on her life writing and that she can be seen as speaking "out of the crisis of [her] own survival" (Caruth 10).[1] However, the economy of loss evident in her narrative is not simply attributable to the "postmemory" of the Holocaust, but is amplified by other losses related to her displacement through immigration and her experience of intellectual anxiety and dis-ease of postmodernity, all of which cause "a hole in the symbolic network that cries out to be mended, rehearsed, revised," to use Peggy Phelan's definition of trauma (105). Writing, articulation, and theorizing, as part of Hoffman's translation therapy, to which she brings intellectual control and detachment, offer some sense of mastery yet cannot quite eradicate the loss. Despite her post-Holocaust and postmodern skepticism about the possibility of order and continuity, there is a residue of nostalgia for wholeness and unity, along with the need to cling to a tradition of Jewish secular humanism, manifest in her text.

Lost in Translation records three phases in the process of self-translation, parallel to her movement across three different diasporas: from Poland ("Paradise" of Part One), through Canada ("Exile" of Part Two), to the United States ("The New World" of Part Three). This overriding chronological structure is continually challenged from within as Hoffman mixes time layers and speaks in a discontinuous voice, from the intersections of multiple cultural codes, contradictory discourses, and competing ideologies.

In Part One, covering her Polish childhood, translation from Polish into English appears on many different levels, from specific lexical items, to fictionalized dialogues with her Polish friends and relatives, and intercultural translation from the Polish- into the English-speaking context. Polish vocabulary is used sparingly, usually as single words highlighting the specificity of forms of address (for example, *Pan, Pani, ciocia,* and *dama* as "Mr.," "Mrs.," "auntie," and "lady," respectively) and of place names (the *Planty, Sukiennice*). Several lexical items receive periphrastic explanations, signalling the absence of any direct equivalent in English. For example, *kogelmogel* is described as "a creamy, thick, sweet mixture of egg yolk and sugar, butter, and cocoa," while the word *banieczki*—cuppings—conjures a description of the entire procedure (LT 50). There are, however, a few words—concepts that are crucial to Hoffman's construction of cultural difference. These include *tęsknota* ("a word that adds to nostalgia the tonalities of sadness and longing" [LT 4]), to which she returns several times in an untranslated form, as well as *polot* ("a word that combines the meanings of dash, inspiration, and flying," which she associates with "the true Polish values" ([LT 71]). Whenever Polish seeps into the narrative, it is to convey a sense of local colour, to authenticate the speaker's linguistic competence, and to draw attention to the untranslatable. Even though Hoffman's young persona, Ewa, never questions the symbolic preponderance of the Polish language and culture in that stage of her life, her environment is by no means monolingual. She registers class inflections of speech around her and remembers her parents speaking in Yiddish—"the language of money and secrets" (LT 14). Occasionally, she even uses the Jewish idiom when talking about *sabbath, hallah, schlemiels,* and *chutzpa.* She recollects summer holidays in the Tatra mountains, where *górale*, a mountain folk, "speak a somewhat different dialect of Polish from us" (LT 18). The linguistic universe of Polish is also ruptured by the presence of the unspeakable, by the silences made conspicuous by her parents' elisions of war references. They refer to the Holocaust simply as the Thing (LT 25). Finally, in an ironic reversal, English encroaches upon young Ewa's world as the language of the totally other when she hears the unpronounceable name of Vancouver, a foreign destination the family is bound for, which sounds to them like "Vantzo-ouver" (LT 84).

The entire Part One is an attempt to translate Hoffman's young self into English by retelling her childhood experiences in a new language, using translation as a prosthesis of "origins" that have been missing in the second language. In this sense, the book's subtitle, "Life in a New Language," not only is future-oriented, but also refers to the past retold. The term "metastory" (LT 25) is her label for such autobiographical anamnesis of an adult returning to the past through the medium of another language in order to reintegrate that past into the fabric of her new life. Eventually, she will be able to declare that she can "trust" English to speak her childhood and thus to keep what has been lost. It is important to understand the split in her narrative focalization so as to prevent hasty generalizations about the account of Hoffman's life in Poland as "idealized."[2] In fact, her grown-up persona, Eva, often qualifies and relativizes young Ewa's emotional enthusiasm. The "Edenic" glow of her childhood memories has the power of myth on her imagination, but Hoffman is well aware that "the myths run deep, and we believe them ourselves, for years and decades to come" (LT 42). If she dresses her departure from Poland in the imagery of expulsion from paradise, she simultaneously leaves no doubt that this paradise is already contaminated by the spectres of war, the trials of survival under the communist regime, and the menace of anti-Semitism.[3] The irony of the labels applied to the three parts of her journey can be lost if we take her imagery at face value.

Part Two describes her arrival in Canada in 1958 as a transitional period in her North American makeover. An interval between the past and the future, Canada is a literal scene of translation, the in-between space that she never really wants to inhabit. Using psychoanalytic imagery, she describes her "birth into the New World," at the age of thirteen, through "the primal scream" of a nightmare associated with uprooting and being thrown into the "incomprehensible space" of a new continent (LT 104). In contrast to Antin and Salverson, Hoffman's young persona initially exhibits no eagerness to learn English, which she finds "harsh-sounding." According to Gustavo Pérez Firmat, this defensive reaction is common among many second-language migrants who try to disparage or silence "the intrusive language" when it "threatens to take over areas of experience occupied by [the] mother tongue" (19). Ewa's entry into the school system is a traumatic moment of "careless baptism," appending new "identification tags" to her and her sister Alina, who henceforth become "Eva" and "Elaine," the names neither can even pronounce yet (LT 105). She perceives this forceful translation of their names as violation and objectification. During the process of second-language acquisition that follows, the young persona experiences what the grown-up narrator explains in terms of structuralist severance of any natural relation between the signifier and the signified. Ewa discovers that "the translation doesn't work" (LT 107), and words such as "envious," "happy," or "disappointed" do not communicate the same content to her in English as the Polish words do. A failure of translation is manifest in the "loss of a living connection" between words and things (LT 107). Obviously, for Hoffman, translation is not just the question of verbal equivalence, but also that of finding cultural connotations and complex emotional shadowing of particular words that are intensely personal. It proceeds not just from language to language, but "from the word back to its source, to the feeling from which it springs" (LT 107). Alienated from Canadian culture, Ewa encounters the problem of semantic segmentation as her limited knowledge of the macro-context restricts her ability to interpret the range of meanings of different lexical items. Hence she has difficulty trying to classify people as "nice," "kind," or "silly," as these words carry different connotations in her mother tongue. A sense of linguistic disorientation is exacerbated by her atrophying Polish, leading to a loss of her "interior language" that cannot yet be compensated for by her inadequate English (LT 107). The world around her is covered with "the verbal blur," and she fears that she is losing her identity. The grown-up narrator theorizes this condition of "wordlessness" that affects many dispossessed people as a "speech dis-ease" that can cause neurosis and eventually lead to rage and violence. Indeed, Ewa's linguistic displacement at this stage of her life accounts largely for her experience of "immigrant rage."

Diary writing becomes Ewa's way of moulding a new English-speaking persona. She chooses to write in English since Polish has become "a dead language, the language of the untranslatable past" (LT 120). Her intimate use of writing, from the position of immigrant or ethnic exclusion which Derrida links to interdiction or jealousy of the dominant language around itself, can be seen as motivated by "a certain mode of loving and desperate appropriation of language and through it of a forbidding as well as forbidden speech" (*Monolingualism* 33). However, her "written self" constructed in English is split in translation into a private persona whom she would have been had she grown up in Poland and another, impersonal self "refracted through the double distance of English and writing," giving her a sense of self-voyeurism, of watching herself perform (LT 121).[4] In her discussion of mirroring in bicultural texts, Judith Oster views the moment of splitting that occurs when immigrant narrators face their mirrors as "the reverse of the Lacanian 'mirror stage,' when the baby acquires a sense of unified 'self' through the mirror image, an illusion of wholeness" (77). As the young immigrant Ewa conducts an imaginary dialogue with her would-have-been, the Cracow Ewa is her mirror returning to her an image of her artificial splitting in translation.[5] Watching her English self emerge from writing, she observes:

> When I write, I have a real existence that is proper to the activity of writing—an existence that takes place midway between me and the sphere of artifice, art, pure language. This language is beginning to invent another me. However, I discover something odd. It seems that when I write (or, for that matter, think) in English, I am unable to use the word "I." I do not go as far as the schizophrenic "she"—but I am driven, as by a compulsion, to the double, the Siamese-twin "you."
> (LT 121)

This seems to support Derrida's point that the autobiographical "I" is the most difficult to translate because it is not independent of language but articulated differently through different languages (*Monolingualism* 29). Unable to use "I" in English, Ewa resorts to the second-person "you," the dialogic pronoun which transports her back to the immediate presence of her Polish persona. Interestingly, while the English "I" is a linguistic construct, this Polish persona seems to have a "natural" connection to herself. When the signifier is severed from the signified, denaturalization of language applies only to English while Polish still remains "the most unmediated language" (LT 120), a mimetic instrument, preserving a "natural" connection between words and things, as in Hoffman's elaborate comparison of the Polish *rzeka* with the English *river* (LT 106).[6]

During her Canadian phase, Hoffman also finds out that learning the semiotics of culture is part of learning the language, and that the body signifies differently in Polish and in English. She begins to develop a "semiotic" way of looking at the world around her as text, of reading its signs and staying alert to their deeper meaning. Ewa's attempts to assimilate require her to translate gender scripts according to the local notions of femininity and masculinity, as well as mastering complex symbolic codes such as the rituals of dating (LT 149) or "the rules and constraints of sexual behavior" (LT 150). Her troubled attempts at translation as acculturation in Part Two are grounded in nostalgia for the lost "original" language and the "authentic" self lodged in her fading mother tongue. For a certain time, her young persona exists in the negative space of translation, "in the stasis of a perpetual present," highlighting the differences between the source and the target culture and finding it impossible "to throw a bridge between the present and the past" (LT 117). This stage marks the formation of her "provisional" nascent new self (Eva's ghost). At the same time, this part of the narrative most resembles earlier immigrant success stories. However, like other "writers of memory," such as Nabokov, Milosz, and Kundera, Hoffman endorses "the regressive dangers of both forgetfulness and clinging to the past" (LT 116). Consequently, she treats language as "a crucial instrument" in overcoming "the stigma of [her] marginality" (LT 123) and even struggles with her accent, perceived as a class marker. Since her musical "ear" cannot bear hearing English distorted, she embarks on a rigorous program of self-improvement that will open the doors of American universities to her. In the end, she not only masters the language, but also manages to graft it successfully onto her body, transforming her body image and revising her aesthetic criteria of beauty in the process. She reports gradually becoming less demonstrative, less emotional, more restrained, and more reserved. With her revamped self-image, she simultaneously adopts a new, more pragmatic value system, rejecting her Polish dream to be a pianist as no longer a priority.

Part Three describes a major stage of Eva's linguistic education after she begins her university studies in Texas. A sense of loss is now more acutely felt in relation to a new American reality surrounding her in the present rather than her Polish past and what-might-have-been. Interestingly, she comes to inhabit English as her second language from the top down, in a reverse order from a native speaker's progression of literacy. Thus before she accumulates layers of colloquial and domestic vocabulary, she learns to express abstract, intellectual ideas in academic language: "For me, this is an elementary rather than an advanced language, a language I learn while I'm still in my English childhood. It does not have to make its way through layers of other vocabulary, and I can juggle it with resistless ease" (LT 181). Since she has a relatively limited grasp of the particulars and feels "lost in the wash and surf of inexactly understood words" (LT 180), dealing with abstractions is easier for her than dealing with particulars. Paradoxically, she can excel in New Critical literary close readings precisely because of her "verbally deprived condition" (LT 181). As a result, she acquires expertise in locating symbolic patterns: "repeated symbols, patterns of words, recurring motifs, and motifs that pull against each other" (LT 182). However, what she bemoans not being able to access is the music of the language, the pleasure and beauty of its surface texture that are lost in "the translation from the sounds to their definition" (LT 180). The interval it takes her to move from wrestling with Yeats's poem in her undergraduate years to being fully attuned to Eliot's words after she finishes graduate school is filled with hard work on improving her English.

"Obsessed with words," she is working on her vocabulary, hoping to "incorporate the language, make it part of my psyche and my body" (LT 216). A sort of linguistic absolutist, she not only believes that articulation is everything and nothing fully exists until it is articulated, but she also wants articulation "that says the whole world at once ... as if the totality of the world and mind were coeval with the totality of language" (LT 217). Hoffman's perfectionism is reminiscent of Derrida's "hyperbolism," an excessiveness which he, too, as a Franco-Maghrebian Jew experienced as the absolute need "to speak in good French, in pure French" (*Monolingualism* 49), which is perhaps a protective mechanism on the part of the subject who perceives himself or herself as threatened by expropriation from the language that jealously guards its boundaries. Still, her inner voice echoes in Polish when she ponders decisions about marriage, divorce, or choice of a profession. But she never loses her distrust of translation, even when she successfully crosses over into English and eventually can dream in English, feel the beauty of poetry in English, or be comfortable making love in English. In a Sapir-Whorfian manner, she seems to believe that language determines one's perception of reality and that there is "cultural memory" encoded in it (LT 211). Regarding the hypothesis of linguistic relativity, Pérez Firmat confirms that for many bilinguals it has a subjective affective truth-value, even if its scientific verification is impossible, and that "there is a 'special' or 'restricted' linguistic relativity rooted in the historical tongue ties of individuals or communities" (13). Hoffman's bilingualism possibly explains why her attitude to language is characterized by the coexistence of dual and contradictory romantic and postmodern tendencies, influenced by "the wholeness of childhood truths" and "the divisiveness of adult doubt" (LT 273). On the one hand, language is like an organic substance. She envisions English words as "bits of chromosomal substance trying to rearrange itself ... in her bloodstream" (LT 243). On the other hand, as she desperately tries to repossess her voice in a new language, she compares herself to "a silent ventriloquist" inhabited by fragmented voices (LT 220). She replaces organic metaphors with references to postmodern images of quilting or a mosaic of fragments, which are thematically linked to the imperfect patchwork of memory and translation.

In this part of the narrative, translation takes one more turn in a brief moment of self-retranslation when she returns twice to visit Poland. She now finds that she is linguistically alienated from some aspects of Polish life and has to ask for help in translating from English into Polish.[7] As she admits, "If I tried talking to myself in my native tongue, it would be a stumbling conversation indeed, interlaced with English expressions" (LT 272). Nevertheless, she still deliberately uses occasional linguistic calques from Polish in such sentences as "It's only psychological" (LT 221); "It's capital" (LT 236); or her father's "Don't let them spit in your kasha" (LT 237). These expressions foreground the uniqueness of her linguistic situation and show how her two languages affect each other: "When I speak Polish now, it is infiltrated, permeated, and inflected by the English in my head. Each language modifies the other, crossbreeds with it, fertilizes it. Each language makes the other relative" (LT 273). Hoffman's two-way translation is thus both inwardly and outwardly oriented; projecting herself into the future and retrieving her past are part of the same project of overcoming her arrest in the middle (the present), which she views as a predicament typical of the condition of emigration. Struggling against self-defeating nostalgia and alienation, she attempts to strike a balance between what Werner Sollors calls "descent" and "consent" models of ethnicity, which he uses to foreground the differences between "contractual and hereditary, self-made and ancestral, definitions of American identity" (*Beyond* 6).[8] She moves between the culture of descent and the culture of consent, "without becoming assimilated—that is, absorbed—by [her] new world" (LT 211). However, even though she gains an understanding of translation as an ongoing process, she ends her narrative with an Edenic scene in her friend's garden, suggesting her "arrival" in a new language, when she can finally enjoy being "here" and "now." In a way, then, her model of acculturation remains integrationist as she relies on two mechanisms of coping: assimilation ("passing") and finding a "fixed centre" in her past.

Hoffman's self-translation provides fascinating insights into the dynamics of cross-cultural identity formation. She moves from the initial condition of "being split by the difference" to seeing herself as the sum of her languages, including "the language of my family and childhood, and education and friendship, and love, and the larger, changing world" (LT 273–74). However, there are still conspicuous polarities and contradictions in her constructions of identity. Her grown-up self is a truly postmodern "hybrid" (LT 221): split, fractured, multiple, invented, and reinvented, just as the real-life authorial persona straddles multiple identities: Jewish, Polish, Canadian, American, and currently expatriate American in London. In the American phase of her translation therapy, she is trying on different identities: a pianist, an academic, a New York intellectual, and finally a writer. Yet, despite all the effort she puts into carving out for herself a "professional, self-confident, American identity" (LT 248), she admits that there is always insecurity underneath, an awareness of a "lack of 'typological fitness,'" synonymous with a fear of being exposed as not "one of their own" (LT 244). Moreover, she never quite abandons a desire to hang onto some sort of unity and continuity of the self. It can be argued that her perception of a loss of wholeness, or what Danuta Zadworna Fjellestad calls "exile from selfhood into subjectivity" (141), is not necessarily the result of Hoffman's experience of immigration. Living in a diaspora and being an immigrant can be conducive to a loose sense of identity; therefore, even Hoffman's pre-immigration self can be seen as already divided. The usurper complex and bitter references to "atavistic anxieties" (LT 249) have deeper roots, recalling her parents' ordeal of being Jewish in a hostile, anti-Semitic environment.

The memory of the Holocaust has a profound effect not only on her parents but also on Hoffman, who carries the scars of the past, struggling to assert her "essential humanity" against the historical legacy of trauma.[9] Listening to the stories of suffering, she grows up with the "ever-present tug" of death (LT 7), a legacy of "excess darkness" (LT 253) that does not leave her even in her mature life. Her parents have adopted two opposite attitudes to the Holocaust experience: while her father prefers to suppress his memories, her mother insists on the importance of remembering. Both survivors have developed a life-centred philosophy focused on the present moment and on the possibility of happiness for their children. At the same time, war has left them with a certain sense of absurdity and anarchic irrelevance of any official authority. Hoffman inherits this sense of unpredictability and irrationality of life as well as a propensity to take risks. However, she can never shake off the burden of the past and the guilt associated with her inability to go as near her parents' pain as she thinks she should (LT 25). In early childhood, this anxiety takes the form of a refusal to eat. Later she adopts denial—also one of her parents' coping mechanisms—telling herself that "there are no useful lessons I can derive from my parents' experience; it does not apply to my life" (LT 25). Still, there are several passages in the narrative that suggest Hoffman's awareness of the impact and the burden of the legacy of being a child of Holocaust survivors. "I come from the war" is how she explains her predicament: "I have only struggled with specters—[my parents'] specters among others—while they have battered themselves against hard realities" (LT 129). That part of her historical bequest explains why at the age of thirteen she already does not know what "peace of mind" feels like (LT 129). As a successful New York intellectual, she meets other people of her generation, survivors' children like her, who are afflicted with similar problems. She reflects on the inexplicable suicide of her first love Marek and on her friend Zofia's depression:

> I think, sometimes, that we were children too overshadowed by our parents' stories, and without enough sympathy for ourselves, for the serious dilemmas of our own lives, and who thereby couldn't live up to our parents' desire—amazing in its strength—to create new life and to bestow on us a new world. And who found it hard to learn that in this new world too one must learn all over again, each time from the beginning, the trick of going on. (LT 230)

The continuing impact of the Holocaust trauma has shaped Eva's responses to the world around her. Its effects can be recognized in her filial obligation and guilt, a desire to protect her parents, a sense of impermanence and non-belonging, and a subterranean craving for stability and essence.

There are also other aspects of her Polish Jewish identity that may have been formative for her. Being a Jew in postwar Poland meant being an outsider, a stranger. It was "one of those whispered, half-secret subjects" (LT 57). But Hoffman's mother instills in her that despite the threat of anti-Semitism, asserting her Jewishness is a matter of honour. Although her family is assimilated, which has been a survival strategy chosen by many Polish Jews, it nevertheless maintains certain Jewish traditions and keeps a safe distance of disaffiliation learned from the lessons of history. Her parents perform a precarious balancing act, poised between passing and being ready to leave any time the political climate becomes dangerous. In a truly paradoxical manner, their exodus, like that of many other Polish Jews, was one of those "departures that are neither entirely chosen nor entirely forced, and that are chosen and forced at the same time" (LT 83). Perhaps these aspects of her childhood experience can serve as an explanatory background for Hoffman's adoption of ironic distance, intellectual nonconformity, and suspicion of dogma. It also puts in perspective her criticism of the Polish Jewish community in Vancouver, which she finds pretentious in its pursuit of the comforts of middle-class life; it explains as well her questioning attitude toward what she calls "a choice of different ways to be Jewish" (LT 145). When her younger sister enrols in a Hebrew school, Eva voices her objections to Alinka's "embrace of ethnic exclusivity" that "rubs against the equation ... between Jewishness and a kind of secular humanism" which makes sense for Eva (LT 144). Finally, during Hoffman's return visit to Cracow, she quietly reaffirms her Jewish identity even though this subject causes embarrassment or compensatory responses in her interlocutors. On this and other occasions, she refuses, however, to turn her Jewishness into some essentialized identity that would define her position of moral superiority.

Life in Poland prepares her to cope with the sense of discontinuity, contingency, and cognitive disjunction that later become the staple of her immigrant experience. She learns survival strategies in her childhood: from her parents' Holocaust memories; from the knowledge of their own marginality as a Jewish family in largely Catholic Poland; from the absurdities of life under the communist system polarized between the two mega-symbols of Soviet Russia and America. Living in the culture of duplicity, she is exposed to the doubletalk, to different "histories" taught at school, to the coexistence of official discourse and counter-discourse. These are the sources of her political savvy, her fledgling consciousness of social hierarchies, and her ability to read "the nuances of class" (LT 13). And yet, in her personal mythology, this Polish childhood is coded as the space of the familiar, of the lost unity and wholeness, whereas her American adulthood connotes fragmentation and divisiveness, splintering and insecurity. She is nostalgically committed to the myth of complete "selfhood" while living a life of diasporic dispersion that actually deconstructs that myth. The country of her childhood becomes a symbol of that lost holistic paradise, providing her with the centre that holds (LT 74). Significantly, its two most important gifts are language and music. While for Antin and Salverson a discovery of the library belongs to the New World experience, Hoffman's initiation into "the riches of Araby" (LT 26) happens in her native tongue. The young Ewa is a voracious reader, fascinated with the power of words to awaken her fantasies and desires. In reading she can experience for the first time how fluid the boundaries of the self are. Similarly, music speaks to her as books do, letting her "know how anyone in the world feels ... Music is a wholly adequate language of the self—my self, everyone's self" (LT 72). Her lifelong fascination with music is in tune with her romantic belief in the "honesty" of tone (LT 70). Later, as a writer, she will attempt to treat language like a musical instrument to get the right "melody" from it. At the same time, the discipline and practice required for a career in music instill in her an ethic of hard work and self-realization that will be great assets for a future immigrant.

Canada, her new country, becomes a place of exile primarily because it is associated with linguistic uprooting, but also because the young Ewa has to watch helplessly her family's economic destitution as they start out their new life with nothing. Initially at the mercy of rich benefactors, her parents find it difficult to fit in. With her father "peddling junk" and her mother cleaning other people's houses, they are in her eyes "relegated to aspiration and failure" (LT 111). Like Antin and Salverson, Ewa is particularly worried about her father, whose spirits are dampened by a constant struggle against poverty. Polite, constrained, bland, uneventful, boring, and dull are the adjectives that keep coming back in her Canadian memories. Echoing Salverson's sentiments, Hoffman analyzes the sociopolitical and propagandistic deceptions of the Canadian government that attracts immigrants without putting in place "support systems to ease the 'newcomers' first steps" (LT 125). Later she similarly deconstructs the meaning of the American Dream, juxtaposing her apparent success with different expectations of her parents or even more marginalized people like her Brazilian house cleaner. Even so, it is the United States that is the "real" New World to her, Canada being discarded as too peripheral for her American self. It figures as a transitional zone, a place inhabited by her young immigrant self and her working-class, "ethnic" parents. As an antidote to the initial absence of status in North American society, she develops two strategies: cultivating her "essential humanity which [she] learned to believe in as a Jewish girl in Poland" (LT 139) and embracing her immigrant displacement as a form of epistemic privilege. The relative position of immigration allows her to "triangulate," that is, project herself into different cultural spaces until all versions of reality appear arbitrary (LT 170). These are her coping mechanisms in the situation of unbearable marginality and anonymity.

Most of Part Three chronicles the process of Hoffman's Americanization, her transition from the role of "an exotic stranger" to the status of an ordinary person. Tired of the state of "attractive otherness," she tries "to break out of [her] difference and reclaim a state of ordinariness in which, after all, we want to live" (LT 179). The imagery she uses occasionally plays on the traditional frontier motif: the new land to which an immigrant arrives is "an uncharted landscape"(LT 173) to be tamed and made one's own. While her rhetoric reveals her strong investment in the power of dominant cultural ideologies, it inadvertently exposes the ethnocentric norms of American culture, implying that immigrant realities are peripheral and somehow less real, existing perhaps beyond "a state of ordinary reality" (LT 202).[10] Still, in this context, the "exoticism" of her Polish memories has an important function. To forestall a potential risk of turning her project of translation into a simple story of assimilation, she clings to her past, trying to salvage some sense of the self that would give her "distinctive shape and flavor" (LT 205). The contradictory task she sets for herself involves finding "a way to lose [her] alienation without losing [her] self ... bend[ing] toward another culture without falling over" (LT 209). At the same time, she is aware of the impossibility of her project: "In a splintered society, what does one assimilate to? Perhaps the very splintering itself ... I share with my American generation an acute sense of dislocation and the equally acute challenge of having to invent a place and an identity for myself without the traditional supports" (LT 197). If she identifies postmodern splintering as a specifically American condition, she remains not fully assimilated precisely because of her residual longing for stability, anchoring, and home, which are the concepts grounded in her romantic metaphysics of childhood.

Hoffman philosophically accepts dislocation as "the norm rather than the aberration in our time" and uncritically embraces the gain of immigrant mobility as part of the exhilarating changes of postmodernity: "New York, Warsaw, Teheran, Tokyo, Kabul—they all make claims on our imagination, all remind us that in a decentered world we are always simultaneously in the center and on the periphery, that every competing center makes us marginal" (LT 275). Leaving aside an offhand levelling of life in the world's metropolis with that in impoverished and politically troubled places, based on her cultural self-definition, I cannot but suspect that she has travelled from centre to centre, substituting the centrality of New York for that of Cracow in her childhood. She describes herself as

> a professional New York woman, and a member of a postwar international class; somebody who feels at ease in the world, and is getting on with her career relatively well, and who is as fey and brave and capable and unsettled as many of the women here—one of a new breed, born of the jet age and the counterculture, and middle-class ambitions and American grit. (LT 170)

This passage reveals a New Yorker's perception of the world, the confidence stemming from living in "an imperial center whose currency is the international standard and whose language is the Esperanto of the modern world" (LT 251). Clearly, she already speaks here from a position of power, as someone who has gained access to education and class privilege, which legitimizes her narration of an immigrant success story.

Ultimately, Hoffman's translation is about negotiating power through language, from the desire for absolute mastery of the English language to the achievement of a coveted editorial position in one of America's most prestigious papers. Apart from intuitive associations of language with empowerment and control, which can partly explain her celebration of words and the cult of articulation, her adoption of English as the language of writing and self-expression already presupposes the necessary disarticulation of her mother tongue and loss of her ethnic self. As Magdalena Zaborowska notes, Hoffman even "marries an extraordinarily talented conversationalist and ... is thus mediated into America by others: as the nonnative speaker of English she marries *into* the new language, and as the foreign sexual body she is legitimized as the wife of an American male" (232). But more than a union with "a native-born," it is writing in English that is truly her means of symbolic entry into the dominant culture. Her Polish becomes the language of "the other," the memory of the preverbal state of "wholeness" associated with childhood that "had no word" (LT 217). In contrast to this "muteness" or "voicelessness" in Polish, her English represents the fullness of articulation. Thus, the story of her transition from East to West re-enacts a literacy narrative about finding a voice in English. By chronicling the process of crossing over to the mainstream, dramatized as a struggle for agency and control of the metropolitan language, she foregrounds the asymmetry between the two cultures, reinforcing the symbolic domination of her American identity. Such complicity with the dominant culture ensures that immigrant autobiographies can gain access to the printed world, which, according to Paul Eakin, can only happen "through an intermediary belonging to the dominant class that controls the production and consumption of such texts" (88).

Like any other text, Hoffman's narrative is implicated both by the material conditions of its production and by different kinds of discourses she draws on in the performative reiteration of cultural scripts of identity. The combination of what she incorporates from the available repertoire, what she discards, and what she underplays produces the possibility of conflicted readings. Sidonie Smith offers the following description of such performative acts:

> It is as if the autobiographical subject finds him/herself on multiple stages simultaneously, called to heterogeneous recitations of identity. These multiple calls never align perfectly. Rather they create spaces or gaps, ruptures, unstable boundaries, incursions, excursions, limits and their transgressions. ("Performativity" 20)

A vision of immigrant subjectivity that emerges from Hoffman's performance is a paradoxical site of conservatism and subversion: of clinging to the past so as to provide oneself with the fixed centre, the stable core, the source of continuity and identity, while at the same time embracing variety, difference, heterogeneity that may challenge the very notion of the continuous or unitary self. Several traditions and influences, often incompatible, seem to be woven into the fabric of her self-presentation. Most notable among them are a tradition of Polish romanticism, with its individualistic cult of the difficult, artistic personality, and American pragmatism, with its Horatio Algerian reverence for the self-made hero. In her case, both are filtered through the contemporary ambience of postmodern skepticism and Jewish "secular humanism," as well as the admixture of

American transcendentalism with its ideals of individualism, nonconformity, and civil disobedience.

When Carole Boyce Davies speaks of "migratory subjectivity" replacing nationhood, I think of Hoffman as a nostalgic version of such a migrant traversing geographical and discursive spaces. In the history of the Jewish diaspora, we find a prototype of Davies's migratory subject in the figure of the wandering Jew. It seems that Hoffman endorses this identity via Antin, whose biography she summarizes and whom she quotes at length: "I felt the pang, the fear, the wonder, and the joy of [emigration]. I can never forget, for I bear the scars. But I want to forget—sometimes I long to forget … It is painful to be consciously of two worlds. The Wandering Jew in me seeks forgetfulness" (LT 163). In Hoffman's words, her own perspective is always slightly "askew" in relation to generally accepted opinions. Confronted with the demands of a Jewish diasporic community to reject her Polish past, she refuses to follow the prevalent sentiments. Her intellectual honesty propels her to take the risk of going against the grain and showing her nonconformity, as she did in her historical interpretation of the Polish-Jewish relations in *Shtetl: The Life and Death of a Small Town and the World of Polish Jews*, published in 1997, where she managed to hold the middle ground of translation without going for easy equivalences. Still, in *Lost in Translation*, despite eloquent acknowledgements of her "hybridity," she fails to embrace the condition of in-between-ness as a performative space from which to challenge rather than internalize the dominant norms of her bicultural conditioning. Opting for a more self-consolidating position, she thus forgoes the opportunity to turn her complex location into the source of radical cultural questioning and redefinition. Her fear of in-between-ness, earlier recognized as distrust of translation, stems from its associations with oppression, with "an amphibian" position of marginality (LT 13). When she expresses her dread of "getting lost in the middle" (LT 118), she might well mean her fear of getting lost in the space of translation.

Compared with her major predecessor Mary Antin, Hoffman significantly shifts emphasis in her narrative to loss and distrust of translation, a strategy enhanced by her relentless brooding on untranslatablity. Antin ostensibly celebrates the gains of translation, occasionally "tainted" by evidence of the untranslatable which breaks through the surface exhortation of the possibility of translating the immigrant self into the American self. Extremely revealing are Hoffman's observations on the similarities and differences between Antin's narrative and her own story. She sees their lives as following similar trajectories, so closely that it seems almost uncanny to her. But unlike her "ancestress," she can focus more intensely on her interiority and use her grown-up voice, exploring topics of sexuality and the body that were off limits earlier in the century. She also stresses the fundamental split in perception that separates their parallel accounts. According to Hoffman, Antin's story is firmly anchored in such traditional certainties as "a belief in self-improvement, in perfectability of the species, in moral uplift" (LT 164). By contrast, the zeitgeist of postmodernity denies her such comforts:

> A hundred years ago, I might have felt the benefits of a steady, self-assured ego, the sturdy energy of forward movement, and the excitement of being swept up into a greater national purpose. But I have come to a different America, and instead of a central ethos, I have been given the blessings and the terrors of multiplicity. (LT 164)

The above passage, in clichéd terms, signals Hoffman's alertness to the decentralizing processes affecting not only contemporary individual life stories, but also collective cultural self-definition. However, despite her consciousness of a different, postmodern episteme separating her from Antin, upon closer examination she may as well be playing a more traditional chord.

There is certainly some intertextual borrowing in the fashioning of Hoffman's younger persona that reflects her fascination with Antin's narrative voice. However, beside Antin, there is another great autobiographer whose influence on Hoffman—rarely examined fully by her critics—cannot be underestimated. The similarities between *The Education of Henry Adams* and Hoffman's text go well beyond her borrowing of his method of geodetic triangulation, openly acknowledged in her narrative (LT 160). Henry Adams's autobiography is a giant project in which he develops a complex interpretive system that actually resembles intersemiotic translation moving back and forth between narratives of history, science, and personal experience. In his preface Adams declares that he wanted to reverse the autobiographical method of Augustine's *Confessions* by working from unity to multiplicity. This multiplicity affects not only the concept of the self—for Adams and Hoffman caught in the challenging moments of transition to modernity and postmodernity, respectively—but also the form that deliberately incorporates diverse and heterogeneous discourses. Similar to *The Education of Henry Adams*, Hoffman's text is a blend of autobiographical narrative, history, political commentary, ethnography, philosophy, and cultural criticism. She even shares Adams's association of the romantic vision of unity with childhood.[11] As in Adams's autobiography, the overriding structure of Hoffman's narrative remains chronological and linear. However, Adams dismisses as artificial this basic structure of the historical narrative, based on sequence and a relation of cause and effect (382). He finds that the process of history, including also autobiographical history of the subject, operates in ways that can be described as chaotic, "convertible, reversible, interchangeable attractions of thought" (386). In response to the distortions of linear time, Adams—and Hoffman after him—adopts the method of triangulation, which allows a historian and an autobiographer to "keep his alignment with past and future" (395). Hoffman's narrative similarly repeats the movement from unity to multiplicity. Like Adams, who found in the Middle Ages "the point in history when man held the highest idea of himself as a unit in a unified universe" (435), Hoffman uses her childhood as such a point from which to fix a position for herself and to project herself into the future.[12] Triangulation as a narrative method describes the consciousness of Adams's "new man" and Hoffman's immigrant subjectivity as "born of contact between the new and the old energies" (H. Adams 500).

Subversion of the dominant culture, potentially inscribed in the project of translation, cannot be fully realized in Hoffman's project, largely because she adopts the traditional, androcentric model of autobiography. Despite her appropriation of poststructuralist rhetoric, she is still drawn to the concept of essential selfhood whose experience can be of universal value. In its celebration of power and control, of individual triumph over the language, the narrative shows complicity with the tradition of bourgeois autobiography as "a progressive narrative of individual destiny, from origin through environment and education to achievement" (Smith, *Subjectivity* 19). In contrast to the functionalist uses of life writing in the ethnographic narratives discussed previously, Hoffman continues the earlier traditions examined in Antin's and Salverson's autobiographies, writing for introspective and aesthetic purposes. She embraces the ethos of detached individualism that Regenia Gagnier associates with bourgeois subjectivity: "a meditative and self-reflective sensibility; a faith in writing as a tool of self-exploration; an attempt to make sense of life as a narrative progressing in time ... and a belief in personal creativity, autonomy, and freedom for the future" (265). At all stages of her self-translation, Hoffman leans toward the hegemonic values of a culture she passes through, identifying with middle-class models of acculturation that differ mostly in their belonging to different geographies and different histories.

Smaro Kamboureli's *in the second person*

> I was no longer a foreigner with no ground to stand on. I had landed in the English language. (Julia Alvarez, "My English")

Smaro Kamboureli came to Canada from Greece in 1978, after a brief stay in the US as a graduate student, and has since enjoyed a successful academic career as critic and editor of Canadian literature. The publication of *in the second person* in 1985 slightly precedes the academic "mainstreaming" of Canadian multicultural writing and the concurrent surge of interest in feminist autobiography studies; as a result, the book has not received the critical attention it deserves and, regrettably, still remains out of print. It is a borderline text in relation to both Canadian ethnic/immigrant and mainstream autobiography, and as such it is uniquely positioned to unsettle the construction of margin-centre, the goal which Kamboureli consistently pursues also through her scholarly, critical work. In contrast to Hoffman, Kamboureli does not reveal any immediate "ethnic" or "immigrant" literary predecessors. Rather, she speaks to a "national" tradition of such Canadian genres as literature of exploration and the long poem.

Since linguistic displacement appears to be of immediate concern in her text, translation—viewed literally and metaphorically—can be a suitable means of analyzing a complex web of relationships between language, memory, immigrant self, desire, and the body. She extends the range of autobiographical strategies through linguistic and formal experimentation, so that the experimental form itself becomes a metaphor of border identity. Cutting across different genres, she employs a mixture of narrative, poetry, anecdotes, quotations, aphorisms, jokes, dreams, memories, and journal entries to piece together a non-unitary, fragmented self. The relation between autobiographical structures and territorial metaphors is crucial to her project of subverting the dominant codes of subjectivity, language, and place. She foregrounds the asymmetry between her "old" Greek (pre-emigration) self and her "new" English-mediated subjectivity, at the same time showing that the "I/you" is a place occupied by many selves. Consequently, she moves toward multiplicity and polyphony even though her voice is set up as dialogical and open to the second person.[13] The historical subject Kamboureli embodies a paradox of simultaneous membership in the elite circles of academe and in the overdetermined category "immigrant woman" or an "ethnic." Her critical and creative interventions have given a new meaning to the category of "immigrant woman writer," running counter to liberal mainstream constructions of ethnicity and racialized difference. Discourses of ethnicity developed in her oppositional and contestatory writing necessitate a search for new formal and thematic possibilities of immigrant life writing—rejecting traditional constructions of the other that produce a monolithic "ethnic" subject. In her text, the ethnic split is a heightened symptom of other divisions and fractures defining a discursive condition of the postmodern subject.

At the beginning of *in the second person*, the author's persona, Smaro, prepares to leave for the States and recalls burning her diary and other juvenilia written in Greek. This gesture of *auto-da-fé*—which finds its doubling in the text through references to Elias Canetti (isp 22) and a bonfire made out of the "greek alphabet" (isp 59)—is intended as "a way of erasing personal traces, traces of language, whose absence could set [her] free and open" to adopt a second language (isp 7). In a serendipitous coincidence, Robert Kroetsch, an eminent Canadian poet and Kamboureli's real-life husband, discusses the ethnic paradigm in terms of its concealed story of "the necessary death—the death, that is, out of one culture, with the hope that it will lead to rebirth in another" (90). A similar rhetoric permeates Hoffman's opening scene of departure from the Polish shores that makes her feel like her "life is ending" (LT 3). However, while Hoffman views death by emigration as the originary trauma, which for Hélène Cixous marks "an inaugural scene, from which writing sprouted" (*Three Steps* 8), Kamboureli's Smaro deliberately stages her own symbolic death—also the death (or murder?) of the mother tongue. She starts with "lack" as a necessary condition of desire, with a blank page to be filled with words, for as Cixous says, "to begin (writing, living) we must have death" (*Three Steps* 7). From the ashes of Smaro's Greek diaries and her old self, a phoenix emerges: a woman flying across the sky (isp 22). In her parting ritual we can already recognize the moment of linguistic rupture, a refusal to envision continuity or coexistence of her Greek and English linguistic selves, the agonistic view of bilingualism that is consistent with her repudiation of the possibility of translation, or even the need for translation. In fact, the book starts with a disclaimer: "Writing in broken english does not mean translating from one language to another" (isp 9), and it ends with a warning: "The only danger lurks in the act of translation" (isp 87).

From the Greek dedication, to other Greek phrases and words scattered throughout the text, Kamboureli employs the Greek language in the manner that she herself describes as "playing hide-and-seek with one's mother tongue" (isp 7). Except for occasional single words, most of the Greek expressions remain untranslated, although, with a few exceptions, they have been transcribed in the Latin alphabet and can be read out loud by any reader to reproduce the sound of the Greek language. Moreover, the vocabulary includes a vast array of theoretical terms, most of them of Greek origin (anamorphosis, metaphor, metonymy, polis, mnemic, dionysiac, hieroglyphics, metamorphosis, agonistic, hymen, exegesis, etc.) but also quite a few French concepts (*différance, langue, jouissance*). The authorial persona reads and paraphrases Lacan, Foucault, Bataille, Leiris, and Kristeva, and introduces a whole plethora of intertextual allusions or direct quotations from such writers as Nicole Brossard, Phyllis Webb, Daphne Marlatt, Mary Meigs, Anais Nin, George Seferis, and Virginia Woolf, as well as references to film (Pasolini), music, and photographs. The text harks back to such mythological structures as the myth of metamorphosis or "an Orphic journey" (isp 9)—Smaro's form of underworld descent to meet the shadows of her past selves (Rao 252). Similarly, she encodes the thematics of dream, memory, and forgetting through the Greek figurations of Tantalus, Mnéme, and Léthe. The resulting heteroglossia makes the body of the text comparable to "a collage of foreign fingertips pulsating" (isp 73).

The foregrounding of heterogeneity and difference that do not yield to translation is both disjunctive and performative. In addition to Greek, French, and Latin intrusions, other disjunctive strategies in the text comprise the use of the very form of the journal rather than a seamless narrative; a facsimile of Smaro's handwriting in journal headings; and the dramatic splitting of pronouns into multiple personas visualizing "untranslatable differences" (isp 29). Since the polyglossia is also polyphonic, *in the second person* experiments with graphic and semantic devices that convey the sound of speech as opposed to the silence of writing. The tension between speech and writing, the interiority of the body and the exterior of the body, can be approximated through a process of intersemiotic or synesthetic translation, from ear to eye, or from speech to writing:

> is it speech that betrays
> our otherness the other cannot sign
> the signature lies in the phoné speaks
> the distance/s (isp 35)

Only breathing and music offer "a story without words," a "language" that does not betray (isp 40). The tortured relation between speech and body is captured in a crude phonological joke quoted from a newspaper, mimicking the accented speech of a Carlos Faria, obviously an ethnic subject, "age toidy-nine, fwawm Bwooklyn" (isp 20). In Smaro's case, "My language"—described as locked within the body (isp 19)—refers to both her "rusty" Greek and her "bastard" English, one buried within the body while the other yet unborn. Doubly "exiled by virtue of sound" (isp 20), the English-speaking part of herself has "a greek accent" while her Greek self discovers that she speaks "greek with an english accent" (isp 35). The violence of the splitting can sometimes be expressed only through scream, which Kamboureli describes as "the language of the inarticulate" (35) that can articulate her linguistic condition of "being on the edge of two languages," with its connotations of marginality.

There are striking similarities in the ways both Hoffman and Kamboureli are preoccupied with accent as a marker of otherness. Sociolinguist Rosina Lippi-Green reminds us that standardization is related to power as an instrument of social control and exclusion. It sanctions the need to notice other people's accent and to be aware of one's own:

> The myth of standard language persists because it is carefully tended and propagated. Individuals acting for a larger social group take it upon themselves to control and limit spoken language variation, the most basic and fundamental of human socialization tools. The term *standard* itself does much to promote this idea: we speak of one standard and in opposition, non-standard, or substandard. This is the core of an *ideology* of standardization which empowers certain individuals and institutions. (Lippi-Green 59)

According to Lippi-Green, a standard language ideology, tied to the myth of a homogeneous nation-state, shapes the lives of immigrants in that it justifies "restriction of individuality and rejection of the *other*" (73). People who cannot or at least do not try to lose their foreign accent often risk being stigmatized or cut off from rights and privileges of citizenship. Not surprisingly, both authorial personas, Eva and Smaro, are tempted by a dream of passing; both, however, realize the loss involved in shedding their individually marked voices. Accent as a shibboleth reveals the body marked by excess, leading to the recognition of the impossibility of passing but also its undesirability. Smaro refuses complicity with the imaginary standard by accepting her "otherness" as inescapable in any language: "My accent is the sonorous indicator of the scission that gives my self its shape. I want to get rid of my accent but I also want to keep it. In either case I will be a loser" (isp 11). What she risks is that her claim to linguistic competence will be questioned by self-appointed gatekeepers. Quite tellingly, she dreams about speaking French—the language of poststructuralism and the academy—with no trace of an accent.

While Kamboureli's use of language is palimpsestic, the same process occurs on the level of textuality and of subjectivity, which are thus treated as isomorphic structures. Other "texts" are visible beyond the layers of writing much the same as several subject positions are available to the "I." Structurally, *in the second person* is a text that might be described in Derridean terms as "invaginated," folding into itself, with its two parts, "An open parenthesis" and the journal, overlapping in time and mirroring each other.[14] "An open parenthesis" contains five pages of reflective writing, a meditation on personal, linguistic, and geographical displacement attendant to the immigrant condition—already aptly named by the book's title as living and writing "in the second person." "Parenthesis"—etymologically, an act of inserting, a fragment that is set off or departs from the main text—encodes a central idea of her text, her "parent thesis." *Open* parenthesis also suggests a refusal of closure. Prefaces are supposed to be of supplementary nature, but an open parenthesis is associated with a parallel activity that never ends (perhaps also gesturing to Kamboureli's literary and cultural criticism). The journal that follows is a poetic and dramatic enactment of the themes signalled in "An open parenthesis"—a polyphonic orchestration of different voices refracted through the self. According to Kamboureli, the self "keeps changing. It's like that Greek monster: you kill it, but it grows another head" (Williamson 34). The use of Greek introduces another voice, that of the untranslatable other. In this intimate, dialogic exchange, "the other is her and it and him and him and me" (isp 70). Eleonora Rao observes that the splintering of the self into different pronouns sometimes occurs within a single entry. For example, in the section "January 18, 1981," the authorial persona moves between the first, second, and the third person, "literally and figuratively 'suspended' between these identities" (Rao 248). While a "person" may equally well be a mask, a dramatic role performed and acted out, or the new persona who has grown a "second skin," the other sometimes takes on the identity of the loved ones: "relatives, lovers, husband, friends and countries" (Tostevin, "The Muses" 224). "i. me. you. the other. one word emotionally multiplied" (isp 79)—the pronoun "you" has the power to interpellate the reader as well. But the anaphoric "you" not only suggests speaking in the voices of others; the second person also points to a "secondary" (not primary)—and thus inferior—position occupied by the other, the abject part of the immigrant self. The possibility of such reading is sustained by a rather volatile nature of the relationship between the "I" and "i," ranging from accusations and threats to confusion, rivalry, and "nostalgia for togetherness" (isp 48).

Subjectivity for Kamboureli is troped as a linguistic condition. Elsewhere, she jokingly refers to her "past Greek/post-Greek condition" (S. Roy 269), which can be taken as a pun on postmodern provisionality and tentativeness of any post-humanist constructions of subjectivity. In *in the second person*, as the authorial persona admits, "The doubleness of my language becomes the precursor of my personality" (isp 11). However, unlike Hoffman's narrative, there is no need for Kamboureli to arrive at a resolution of this "doubleness" or at least to reconcile different parts of the self by means of translation. The process of translation is never completed and never materializes into a finished "product." This lack of finality, presupposing identification rather than identity, is what, according to Derrida, characterizes autobiographical discourse, where "identity is never given, received, or attained; only the interminable and indefinitely phantasmagoric process of identification endures" (*Monolingualism* 280). Kamboureli's subject captures this ongoing performative process of trying on different identities by means of parody of the mechanical learning of conjugation: i play, you play, s/he plays, it plays, we play, etc. (isp 75), reminding us that immigrant narratives are also accounts of second-language acquisition. However, where Hoffman's experience of "radical disjoining between word and thing" (LT 107) is associated with her transition from Polish into English, Kamboureli's persona has an insight into "that realm of language where words as signs are not yet divided into signifiers and signifieds. The borderline that marks the conflict between the first and second language marks as well the stage of language where words are beings in themselves prior to becoming the proper names of things" (isp 10). While in *Lost in Translation* the divisions within the subject are staged as a split between the mother tongue and the "foreign" tongue, here it is the return of what must be sacrificed in the name of patriarchal logos prior to the emergence of a "natural" language: the foreignness within, or *différance*. Greek and English as any other "natural" languages belong to the order of monological rationality that suppresses this "other" side of language. In contrast to Hoffman's groping toward some hidden "essence" or genuine "emotion" embodied by language, it seems that Kamboureli is less obsessed with articulation as a form of mastery over language and is willing to turn her experience of linguistic displacement in both languages into a symbol of the postmodern subject's condition.

The text offers abundant evidence of its reliance on postmodern theories and poststructuralist tools in constructing a model of discontinuous, heterogeneous, and fragmented subjectivity. Derrida's concept of *différance* as both difference and deferral of meaning is given a prominent place in Smaro's discourse about the impossibility of stabilizing the subject's identity and pinning down the exact difference between her Greek self ("the being that was nourished by the mother tongue") and her Canadian self (the one "bathed in a language other than my mother tongue"): "The distance in the eye of the beholder is not one of difference, but of differ*a*nce" (isp 10). Rejecting fixity, wholeness, and completeness in her vision of the subject, she approximates what Kristeva calls *sujet-en-proces* (subject-in-the-making or subject-in-process/on trial).[15] Kamboureli's subject "is constantly becoming its other, what it is not, what it can be, ultimately, what it is being" (isp 10). The use of the progressive tense in the last phrase underscores a processual, mobile, and unfixed nature of subjectivity. The same applies to memory, which is understood as "the act of remembering" rather than a product of remembering (isp 43). On several occasions, she has expressed her concern with "the dynamics of an existence [rather] than a fixed ethnic identity" (S. Roy 267). She defines "the ethnic subject" as always in a transitional state ("The Technology" 205). Similarly, in the portrait of the ethnic subject of the journal Kamboureli adopts a model of writing that emphasizes the dynamics of production over the actual product. However, notwithstanding the fact that the subject is produced in language, or rather as we said earlier, on the edge of two languages, this subject is not viewed as cut off from the realm of the social. It is not a solipsistic self, a mere discursive product, or a trace in language. Instead, as this subject is constantly reaching towards the other within and without, a dialogical staging of its encounters with otherness becomes a symbolic manifestation of the subject's ethics of sociality.

The question of ethics in her narrative relates intertextually to the influence of Kristeva's Bakhtin-inspired critique of monologism that has been noted in Kamboureli's text by one her readers, Dawne McCance. Referring to Kristeva's view of monologism as coercive reinforcement of "an unethical moral code," operating according to the "either/or *law of the excluded middle*," McCance considers *in the second person* as enacting Kristeva's model of a dialogical subject-in-process in answer to the contemporary ethical imperative to challenge and transform the autonomous humanist subject of ethics (26–27). This traditional model has been predicated upon the notion of responsibility to the self rather than relationality to the other.

The dialogical stance adopted by Kamboureli's persona is a direct attempt to escape the violence of monologism and to restore the transgressive and forbidden pleasure of being (for/with) the other in the erotic merging of discourse and desire: "living on the edge of two languages, on the edge of two selves named and constructed by language, liberates the self from a monologic existence. The self becomes a being of multiple meanings and *jouissance* and many little deaths" (isp 11). According to Barbara Godard, translation in *in the second person* is treated with suspicion because it "would lead to the substitution of one language for the other, a suppression that would reinstate a monologic discourse. It is crucial to remain attentive to the 'double scene' of representation, of enunciation" ("The Discourse" 181). Writing in another context about the relation between translation and the ethnic subject, Kamboureli quotes Derrida's view of translation from *Writing and Difference* that seems pertinent to this perception of a threat of monologism and its inner contradictions. Translation destroys the evidence of one's visibility while

> at the same time [ensuring] that [one] remains visible. This infraction of strategies, this breach of logic sums up ... the process of translation to which the ethnic has to surrender. Like the materiality of words which cannot be translated or carried over to another language (Derrida 210), the materiality of the ethnic self, the materiality of what resides in the margins, must be relinquished in order to survive. ("Of Black Angels" 20)

In another essay, similarly linking ethnicity to the reading and translation of difference, Kamboureli puts forth a distinction between the terms "immigrant" and "ethnic," saying that the former "is an outsider whose difference is defined by her or his origins, whereas the ethnic subject's difference (however visible or pronounced its traces of difference might be) is defined by the surrounding culture" ("The Technology" 208). In the same essay she analyzes translation in the Canadian Multiculturalism Act, a bilingual document in which English and French both claim the status of a source text rather than a translation of the other. There, again, translation is interpreted as posing a threat to the irreducible difference of the other.

Since the ethical implications of Kamboureli's case against translation are associated with the danger of monologism, translation—which to her seems to be equivalent to erasure of heterogeneity and heteroglossia, or what we have earlier associated with the figure of *pharmakon*—does not seem to be a viable option for the ethnic subject. As she explains to an interviewer, "I didn't want to define my so-called 'ethnic' identity; I wanted instead to explore the plurality of my immigrant experience ... there is no precise figure in the mirror, on the page, to gaze at" (Williamson 34). Her self-consciousness about her accent is turned into a parable of ethnicity as a linguistic condition of "exiled speech." Pondering the historical transmutations of the word "barbarian" as a source of improper speech, she turns to the condition of contemporary migrants:

> There is also another kind of foreigner, another kind of barbarian, who moves away so far from her origin that she has no home to go back to: she, then, becomes a stranger to her mother (country). This foreigner does not travel with a camera hung around her neck. She doesn't have to revise herself. Instead, she must re-invent herself. I'm talking about those foreigners we have come by a twist of syntax to call ethnics. All it takes is changing the position of the word *ethnic* from that of an adjective to that of a noun. We all have ethnic origins, but only she is an ethnic. Sometimes called members of minority groups, or immigrants, or migrants, ethnics are condemned, or blessed depending on your point of view, to never lose their barbarity. ("Of Black Angels" 16)

A modern-day counterpart of ancient "barbarians," immigrants are forced into the space of abjection. In marked contrast to Hoffman's persona, Smaro introduces herself as an immigrant "without a family ... who left [her] country not out of deprivation or disillusion" (isp 9). She foregrounds ethnicity as a position—both chosen and imposed—to speak from. However, instead of being recognized by others in her personal complexity, she is seen reductively as a specimen "of the Greek stereotype [she] is supposed to represent" (isp 8). Since the word "immigrant" excludes and essentializes, Smaro constantly has to deal with imposed or presumed homogeneity: "I am what Canadians have made of me, those anonymous faces that turn toward me when they hear my accent (not my voice)" (isp 9). Where boundaries of language and identity are asserted through normative monolingualism, accent is associated "with difference viewed as lack and maneuvered into a position of marginalization" ("The Technology" 216).

However, as soon as the subject enters the "double scene" of enunciation, the text opens itself to the possibility of subversion and resistance to the hegemonic versions of ethnicity. When Smaro pronounces her past and her Greek language as "what I cannot leave" (isp 8), powerlessness ("cannot" in the sense of "am unable to") gives way to affirmed obligation ("cannot" in the sense of "shouldn't"). The stigma of otherness is accepted as a position of epistemic privilege of a "double view" (isp 8) from which to conduct a critique of essentialist constructions of ethnic and national identities within both mainstream and immigrant communities. With emphasis on *différance* rather than sameness, ethnicity can be turned into a vantage point if one can abandon nostalgia for unity and embrace the myth of metamorphosis. The construction of a multiply localized self is, paradoxically, a position of enunciation that frees her from a sense of inferiority. Immigration displaces a habitual perception of the self and, through defamiliarization, allows her to see herself as an artifice, or a work in progress: "apoikos, a woman away from home" (isp 15). Choosing the politics of multiple locations of the subject allows her to confront the staleness of ethnic essentialism.[16] Smaro's comments on Greek émigrés "returning home every few years loaded with … German marks and American dollars" (isp 14), the oppressiveness of Greek nationalism "soiled by national blood" (isp 15), Greek Americans who "hadn't given up any of their old habits" (isp 31), as well as her hostility toward the Greek peasant woman with baskets at the airport—all these reveal an ambivalent relation to the Greek diaspora. Read side by side with Kamboureli's theoretical statements, *in the second person* insists on the importance of difference within éthnos: "By bracketing my ethnicity, while still speaking in an accented voice, I wish to articulate the hybrid position of an ethnic who, without seeking to abscond from her origins, seeks to blend together the foreign within and the foreign outside" ("Of Black Angels" 16).[17] Smaro's "Greek self" subverts dominant notions of ethnicity as ethnography, with its connotations of the exotic, strange, separate. After all, even her pre-emigration self is not homogeneous, but already cosmopolitan, already Americanized, already "translating"—listening to jazz, Herbie Hancock, or Chuck Berry. Consequently, she refuses to "frame" herself from within such categories as gender, race, class, and diaspora because they are not "stable and coherent, internally invaried" (*Scandalous* 4).[18]

Smaro's "foreign" name and her accented speech refer to an elsewhere and thus point to the intersection of language and place as a site where identities are constructed: "Not place and language. But place of language"—the self as "the place of language" (isp 11). Place names begin to appear in the journal after her return to Greece, constituting a kind of chronographic and cartographic mapping of her life, the writing of the "where" of the subject inserted into geography (geo-auto-graphy).

Together with journal chronology, the use of place names belongs among "the technologies whereby a text constructs the historical individual" (Smith, *Subjectivity* 106). However, since for a diasporic subject the question of identity—of "Who am I?"—can no longer be answered positively, it seems to be replaced by the question of place: "Where am I?" The importance of "Where?" becomes even more nagging in the autobiographical text which enacts a crisis of mimetic representation, frustrating conventional expectations to be like a mirror or a metaphorical "photograph" of a person. As Timothy Dow Adams notes in his study of the connections between life writing and photography, both have the power "simultaneously to display and conceal" (241). In other words, a photograph is like writing in that it also dissimulates the image of the subject—exactly like the black-and-white photograph showing the author's dark profile on the back cover of the book, accompanied by bpNichol's blurb calling it an "adjournal—a record of delay and departure." In the journal, Smaro's reaction to her own photograph is similar to looking at a picture of a stranger as she recalls her multiple faces from the past and the roles she used to play. The meaning of "home"—as well as that of the self—is drifting as the fractured subject disappears into textual folds. At different points, Thessaloniki, Winnipeg, Canada, language, even "self" are accepted and/or rejected as "home." While for Hoffman to be at home means to be centred, for Kamboureli there is no fixed ground for home as home is constructed not around a place but in relation to people, those "others" (including one's own split selves) who only pass through the "where" of geography or a written page (isp 27).

Staged as a psychomachia of the internal splitting of the subject, the agonistic narrative plays itself as a repeated pattern of escape and return from/to ethnicity and locality, imposing the structure of *Bildungsroman* in the form of literacy narrative or quest narrative, combined with a travel journal. The geographic trajectory of Smaro's travels parallels a constant movement back and forth between several languages, including Greek and English, poetic language and theory, silence and breathing. Such combination of formal and stylistic conventions corresponds with the descriptions of the genre of the long poem.[19] In her typology of the Canadian long poem Ann Munton recognizes the presence of "the autobiographical, the keeping of a diary, the personal as well as work-related discoveries, the documentation of a quest, the search for understanding" as features of contemporary long poems (Munton 93). Kamboureli's journal shares all these features, adding to them a list of other common traits such as discontinuity, self-reflexivity, linguistic experimentation, and concern with travel and map-making, albeit in her case it is inner rather than outer exploration, substituting consciousness for wilderness. Whatever continuity exists in the poem, it is the continuum of the writing process itself as well as the reading process. Ironically, Kamboureli's insertions into this generic tradition produce the effect of "invagination": a Greek-Canadian invigorating a specifically Canadian or national tradition that has its literary roots in ancient Greece. Consequently, she claims the genre not as an immigrant or a stranger, but as someone whose "entitlement" to this form predates its current use and is historically legitimized by her "hereditary" proximity to the archetypal long poem, the Greek *Odyssey*.[20] The choice of the generic convention, then, can also be seen as consistent with her overall project of subverting ethnic or national essentialism that seeps into constructions of identities, languages, and even genres.[21] It is quite opportune that the historical subject, Kamboureli the critic, is an expert on the long poem, having published *On the Edge of the Genre: The Canadian Long Poem* (1991), where she lists textual plurality and "betweenness" as major characteristics of the genre.

The use of the second person, lack of teleology, silences and omissions are strategies that undermine the unitary subject of traditional autobiography and its unified structure that aims to achieve narrative coherence. The serial form of the journal diary itself unsettles generic boundaries in that it does not conform to the normative expectations of linearity and closure. Traditionally associated with women's writing, the journal diary creates an illusion of immediacy and unpredictability of experience while also flaunting its artifice. Its fragmentariness and heterogeneity are considered congenial to writing that cannot be sustained over extended periods of time. As a gendered form, encoding the intimate and the personal, it provides a private, potentially transgressive space away from public prohibitions and constraints. But the experimental journal is more than just a genre; it also functions as a physical object, the white pages on which writing takes place. A shape-shifting, hybrid form, the journal is never a finished product but is always in process. It is treated as an analogue of the self in that both deal with cumulative experience and memory: "It writes itself. Leaf by leaf it grows. It begets its own shape" (isp 13). A silhouette, a contour to be filled out, the journal is a metonymy of the performative "I." The relationship between the two is reversible: the self writes the journal, but the journal also writes the self, "recreates me with difference, with writing" (isp 18). Kamboureli finds images and metaphors that approximate her situation, such as playing hopscotch or being only an amanuensis. She relies on the agonistic structure of conflicting desires, inscribing her warning against the naturalizing effects of translation and assumptions of transparency in the life writing text. Not surprisingly, similar to her distrust of translation, she has qualms about the limits of the journal form: "After the publication of *in the second person*, I became too conscious of keeping a journal and so I quit after a while. Not that all the journal entries there are 'real,' as some people seem to think, but situating a private discourse within a public realm changed my relationship with the form. In fact, it put an end to it" (Tostevin, "Women" 96). Provisionality and tentativeness must extend beyond the text, leaving space for the historical subject who has the right to remain beyond the text's grasp. These are the issues the textual persona openly voices upon reading Anais Nin's *Diaries*, finding them "inauthentic" despite Nin's efforts to achieve the effect of authenticity, which manage only to evoke "realism rather than reality" (isp 17).

The dynamics of Kamboureli's constructions of subjectivity as well as her engagement with ethnicity suggest that she posits herself in the space of the hyphen, or the space of in-between. Signalling "the desire (and the ability) to be both 'here' and 'there,'" the hyphen, according to Kamala Visweswaran, "enacts a violent shuttling between two or more worlds" (116). She further quotes Trinh Minh-ha, arguing that "the challenge of the hyphenated reality lies in the hyphen itself: the *becoming* [in Minh-ha's case] Asian-American; the realm in-between, where predetermined rules cannot apply" (Visweswaran 119). Smaro's performance of diasporic subjectivity through her writing documents both the impossibilty of assimilation and a rejection of ethnocentrism. Her quest is not completed and no resolution is offered; only writing remains (isp 66). In comparison with the model seen in Hoffman, considered in terms of Werner Sollor's "conjunctive" and "disjunctive" immigrant acculturation, Kamboureli refuses both to move toward the centre and to embrace ethnicity as otherness, choosing instead the space in-between, the space of becoming, or the space of the hyphen. Smaro seems to be fascinated with the aesthetics of international travel, of being in transit, hopping planes, and waiting in airports. Similar to Hoffman's older persona's, her easy mobility inevitably brings us back to the question of the "Where?" of the subject, to the ethics of being in transit, or to different nomadic modalities of transnationalism. Referring to Radhakrishnan's discussion of transnationalism, specifically to his insistence on the importance of asking the question "Where are you from?" Kamala Visweswaran also links the question of identity and geography to the sites of privilege and loss, but sounds a cautionary note: "The question 'Where are you from?' is never an innocent one. Yet not all subjects have equal difficulty in replying. To pose a question of origin to particular subjects is to subtly pose a question of return, to challenge not only temporally, but geographically, one's place in the present" (115). For Smaro, who is not an autoethnographer, the privileges of transnationality are associated with the danger of narcissistic looking in rather than voyeuristic looking out. Eleonora Rao reads the ending of the book as Smaro waiting at the airport for her flight, reading Lacan, and "not engaging with other human beings" (258). More recently, in *Scandalous Bodies*, Kamboureli the critic distances herself from such solipsism and commits to a different ethical position of responsibility, the one that is self-reflexive of its own aporias and that attends to the production of knowledge and to "power relations usually concealed behind the force of knowledge" (26).

While the hyphen in "Greek-Canadian" that frames the subject can function as a slash, signalling a distance, separation, or exclusion, the hyphen as a sign of in-between-ness can be translated into a hymen. The visual slash in Smaro's declaration: "to absolve to set or pronounce free by writing a journal i pronounce my/self free" is reinterpreted as "hyménas" (isp 64). Yet another meaning of the hymen gradually crystallizes in the text, that of marriage between a Greek and a Canadian. As a concluding image of *in the second person*, it gives a new dimension to "hyphenated identity," at the same time as it foregrounds a new philosophical framework from which to interpret this kind of writing. The entire journal can be reinterpreted as enacting Derrida's "logic of the hymen," developed mostly in his essay on Mallarmé, "The First Session," and subsequently applied to his thoughts on translation in "Des Tours de Babel." According to this logic, the "event" mimed in life writing is not "mimetic"—there is no "imitated," that is, a signifier has no fixed and stable signified. The act of writing—the movement of revelation and concealment, difference and deferral—is the "content." The inscription of a life "is no longer comprehended within the process of truth but on the contrary comprehends *it*" (Derrida, "The First Session" 159). The operation of the hymen produces "the effect of content" that is "nothing other than the space of writing"—as "a hymen (a closeness and a veil)" does not unveil any presence, does not "represent" ("The First Session" 160). It only sets up a stage—"a yet unwritten page"—for the possible construction of selves and identities that are not a priori givens but effects of writing and interpretation.

Kamboureli's concept of life writing at work in the text seems to gesture toward Derrida's reading of the hymen: "the visibility (which remains outside) of the visible that is being effectuated" ("The First Session" 160). The hymen, like autobiography, involves revealing and concealing, re-membrance and a membrane, a material trace. Etymologically connected to membrane, envelope, or textile—all of which stand in between the inside and the outside—the hymen opens up the space of the "yet unwritten page." As Derrida comments on Mallarmé: "What is produced is an absolute extension of the concept of writing and reading, of text, of hymen, to the point where nothing of what *is* can lie beyond them" ("The First Session" 177). As a sign of "in-between-ness," the hymen is related to such signs as marriage, identity, and difference. Associated with "hymn" and "marriage," the hymen "is first of all a sign of fusion, the consummation of a marriage, the identification of two beings, the confusion between the two" ("The First Session" 161). This rhetoric of marriage and hyphen is put to productive use also in the context of translation. In his comments on Benjamin's metaphor comparing the relationship between original and translation to that of the broken fragments of the amphora that have been reconstituted lovingly into the whole, which is not identical but in which the same amphora can be recognized, Derrida works his way toward an extended description of this relationship: "The urn [the amphora] is one with itself though opening itself to the outside—and this openness opens the unity, renders it possible, and forbids its totality. Its openness allows receiving and giving" ("Des Tours" 190). As he points out, this image deconstructs the mimetic model of translation, or for that matter of any other representation, as passive imitation, reproduction, or copy of something that is original, real, or true. On the contrary, translation is not "subjected to the law of reproduction" but rather to the promise of marriage and growth, produced through the non-hierarchical coupling and reconciliation between two languages:

> A translation espouses the original when the two adjoining fragments, as different as they can be, complete each other so as to form a larger tongue in the course of sur-vival that challenges them both. For the native tongue of the translator, as we have noted, is altered as well ... It is what I have called the translation contract: hymen or marriage contract. ("Des Tours" 191)

The hymen, then, can join a sequence of other similar figurations of translation that we have already encountered in earlier readings of life writing, such as *pharmakon*, crypt, hyphen, or invagination, all of which can be used to explain the necessary mutuality of the translation contract, its in-between-ness, and the impossibility of demarcating any inside/outside distinctions. It also stands as a vivid reminder that it is only in translation that any alliance, agreement, or obligation, any coming together of self and other, can take place, and that is only if it can be heard in two languages at once.

The operation of the hymen applies to Smaro's relationship with the "other"—whether the dialogic "you" interpellates her Greek self, the reader, or Robert, her Canadian fiancé. The journal is punctuated with calls to and from Robert and brief glimpses of their life together. The effect of simultaneous presence and absence produced by the enunciative silences of this figure of authority and desire verges on a Freudian parody: the ego—the "I," struggling with the "other"—her id (the "presence whose scent" follows her [isp 13]), supervised by the super-ego, Robert, who comes to represent the symbolic order of the target language and culture in the excess of signification produced by writing. "Robert's" presence exceeds the intentionality of the text. It complicates Kamboureli's relationship to English—after all, it is "her husband's tongue" (Godard, "The Discourse" 181)—and her situation as a writer, premised on both the difficulty (challenge) and the privilege of being married to a "great Canadian writer." The book's dedication to him and the signifying forces at work in the text, through the presence of "Robert's" persona, evoke a larger literary context: the Robert Kroetsch phenomenon.

Kroetsch's writing constitutes the silent intertext that encircles Smaro Kamboureli's writing. Her 1985 essay "Locality as Writing" addresses a similar question of absence and centrality (or displacement) of the other in Eli Mandel's long poem. She focuses on Mandel's wife's Preface described as "the seam that connects the empirical historicity of *Out of Place* with its presence as a text. This junction ... reveals, too, the presences that Eli Mandel erased in the poem, without, however, denying their centrality" (Kamboureli, "Locality" 268). Not only is Robert Kroetsch such a presence in *in the second person*, but several of his essays can be seen as intertexts of Kamboureli's book. In particular, echoes of "The Fear of Women in Prairie Fiction: An Erotics of Space" and "For Play and Entrance: The Contemporary Canadian Long Poem" reverberate in *in the second person* although the writers' shared passion for the long poem and preoccupation with ethnicity, desire, and language exceed these two instances of intertextual encounter. In an interview with Sukhmani Roy, Kamboureli actually mentions that her text is in a way a rewrite of "An Erotics of Space" (269), her oblique answer to the question "How do you make love in a new country?" on which Kroetsch's essay is suspended. The entry of February 10, 1981, bounces off this question:

> How do I make love in a new country?
> How does my body draw foreign figures of desire
>   on another body?
> How do I love in a new language?
> Every time I embrace the body of love I also embrace all these
> questions. My difference is his rival. (isp 23)

The book contains the answer. The erotics of space becomes, in her case, the erotics of language, played out in the dynamics of desire and distance, or difference and deferral, that characterize the Derridean conception of language as a play of *différance*. Similarly, Robert Kroetsch in "For Play and Entrance" discusses the "grammar of delay" that dictates the rules in both lovemaking and in writing the long poem (117). Elaborating on the long poem as travel and its "complex relationship to the idea of love," he names "separation and delay and fulfillment" as their basic elements in common (Kroetsch 130). The importance of this particular intertext for *in the second person* is signalled by direct paraphrases; for example, Kroetsch's heading for section 15, "the erotic and erratic erotic" (126), reappears—ironically—as "the erratic become erotic" (isp 70).

The marital metaphor and the trope of lovemaking are central to Kamboureli's writing. They reoccur in her essays on the use of myth and on Nin's *Diaries* (the latter piece actually bearing the title "Discourse as Intercourse"); they also appear in her creative meditation on the relationship between fiction and theory, called "It Was Not a Dark and Stormy Night," where fiction and theory are holding each other in the erotic embrace. The erotic is also a hidden subtext of *in the second person* viewed as an epithalamion, that is, a poem celebrating a marriage. The erotics of in-betweenness is generated constantly in the text that situates itself on the edges. As Kamboureli says of the condition of "living on the edges of two languages," it means living in the space of "jouissance and many little deaths" (which is a French expression for orgasms) (isp 11). The space of in-between is also chosen through her positioning of herself as a diasporic writer, with a constant displacement and deferral of desire it entails. Living in-between two languages is like living in a state of continuous lovemaking. Much the same as the space of hymen/marriage, it is also the space of translation as a process. Perhaps such metaphors can illuminate her distrust of translation as a product associated with the danger of "being translated" —which of course resembles a fear of fulfillment as putting an end to the generativity of desire.

Kamboureli's early essay "Dialogue with the Other: The Use of Myth in Canadian Women's Poetry" (1983) is important for her refusal of "the dialectics ... of *logos* versus *eros*," opting instead for the marriage of eros and logos and for the dialogic space in-between: "Their dialogic discourse operates according to the principle of difference rather than the principle of opposition" (108). *in the second person* inscribes itself in a tradition of women's writing that uses myth to "recover the voice that was spirited away from them." The following statement from the essay applies to her own use of dialogic discourse:

> Myth for the woman poet becomes the space where the different faces of the self encounter each other. It becomes the locus of a constant undoing, the place of a dialogue between the mirror image and the real face of reality. Myth, then, in Canadian women's poetry, is at once a discourse of love and a figure of difference. ("Dialogue" 108)

Like many Canadian long poems, *in the second person* is a love poem with a difference, mapping an itinerary of desire bound to a particular time and place. According to Derrida, the inscription of a date always entails a kind of signature. Dates assign singularity to the event, pointing to the here-and-now of the act of writing. They also point to a dialogical character of the poetic journal as a space where a potential meeting with the other can occur in time. In Derrida's words, "poetic writing offers itself up in its entirety, to dating ... a poem is en route from a place toward 'something open' ('an approachable you'), and it makes its way 'across' time, it is never 'timeless'" (*Acts* 371). Like a love letter—a proxy for a lover—Kamboureli's poetic writing of desire opens itself to "dating" and at the same time presents itself for a rendezvous or an encounter with the other.

Concluding Remarks

The distrust of translation expressed in *Lost in Translation* and *in the second person* seems to be derived from different conceptualizations of translation by Eva Hoffman and Smaro Kamboureli. While both writers are inclined to privilege translation as a noun rather than a process, as a final product in a series of linguistic and semiotic transfers, their negative assessment of the potential effects of translation stems from divergent motives and ideologies. For Hoffman, who remains a humanist at heart and never quite abandons her essentialist longing for "truth," translation is impossible. A translated self or even the subject's past experiences translated into a new language are marked by irrecuperable loss of "authenticity." Writing from within a cultural diagnosis of dislocation of the self as a stable locus of organizing consciousness, she is haunted by the history of trauma, which leads to a desire to re-member herself as the subject of autobiographical anamnesis. Her refusal to give up a dream of essence creates a performative illusion of the autonomous self of translation, shrinking the distance between the person who writes and the narrating "I" and contributing to the effect of transparent representation, despite all poststructuralist caveats in the text. On the other hand, for Kamboureli, versed in poststructuralist theories of language as always translative and foreign to itself, translation is redundant or obsolete. She devalues translation as a fixed product precisely because of a theoretical threat it poses to the idea of unarrested movement of *différance*. The symbolic closure of a "translated" self or life invalidates a desire for the possibility of endless semiosis and cancels the erotics of in-between-ness that grants the subject a degree of freedom from totalization. In other words, where Hoffman bemoans the loss of the non-translatable, Kamboureli embraces non-translatability as a "value" lost in translation. Yet, paradoxically, even though neither of them consciously explores in her project the epistemological usefulness of the trope of translation reconceived as a process, they both engage performatively in translation as part of their ongoing negotiations of language and subjectivity.

More than any other narratives discussed so far in this book, with the exception of Kikumura's *Through Harsh Winters*, *Lost in Translation* and *in the second person* rationalize their constructions of subjectivity in a self-reflexive manner by recourse to theory. Perhaps a partial explanation of their common predilection for combining the theoretical with the experiential in their life writing is the fact that both Hoffman and Kamboureli chose to establish academic careers as a point of entrance into a new country. They both inhabit what Hoffman jokingly calls the "college country"—a position which is already slightly off-centre but which nevertheless grants certain tangible privileges. Seconding Mary Antin, Hoffman tends to idealize this "democratic educational system" and "a democratic ideology of reading," which never make her feel like "an outsider poaching on others' property." She feels that "in this country of learning, [she is] welcomed on equal terms" (LT 183–84). Still, even if academic life is sometimes less unproblematic than it appears to Hoffman, each writer records working on her doctoral dissertation as an important phase of her acculturation. However, the role played by theory differs significantly in each text. In *Lost in Translation*, Hoffman uses sociolinguistic insights and generalizations about postmodernity as a context in which her life writing is embedded. Kamboureli's text, on the other hand, enacts deconstructive concepts performatively, opening yet another space of in-between at the interface of life writing and theory. As she suggests elsewhere, alluding to the debates about "fictionalysis" conducted on the pages of the feminist journal *Tessera*, she wants to demystify "the split between theory and writing (fiction/poetry)" as "each other's doubles" rather than binaries (Kamboureli, "It Was Not" 63–64). Referring to the etymological roots of theory in "Behold. Be. Hold" ("It Was Not" 63), she views the relationship between theory and writing as the loving embrace. According to Kamboureli, theory can "re/tell what the writer has left untold" ("It Was Not" 64). It is what she calls "'the third term' ... positing another version of experience through the foregrounding of language" (Tostevin, "Women" 87). The importance of theory lies in its "enabling us to read the world, its offering alternate methods of thinking, showing how images and genders are constructed" (Tostevin, "Women" 95).

Another common motif linking the two diasporic narratives discussed in this chapter is nostalgia, thematically related to the economy of loss endorsed by both writers. The nostalgia experienced by Kamboureli's persona is split at the root, combining the Greek *nostos* (return home) with *aleos* (pain) and thus signalling a dis-ease connected with this homecoming. For Hoffman, whose entire family was uprooted, there is no "home" to return to, no return to plenitude and wholeness, only "the return to a contingent, historically grounded present" (Burgess 93). Still, the politics of nostalgia in both texts suggests a certain gendering of home as a place of stasis, with the travel/home opposition corresponding to the dynamic/static and active/passive paradigms traditionally associated with the maternal and the feminine space. In a sense, both Eva and Smaro must leave home and make it in the male-dominated world of the academy and exile. Their failure to recognize that there is also movement in the home, together with their chosen alignment with theory and intellect, suggests that in order to succeed they have made choices culturally valorized as "masculine." However, it is precisely through their choices that both writers challenge the dominant gender codes.

Both narratives inscribe the immigrant gendered body as the body speaking with an accent. According to Magdalena Zaborowska, "a perfect linguistic crossing" is impossible "for those who come to a new country too late to lose their foreign accents and word sensibilities" (240). Why are people like Kamboureli and Hoffman aware of their accents? Such manifestation of what might be perceived as "linguistic insecurity"[22] seems to confirm the pervasive ideology of the myth of standardization related to power as an instrument of social control and exclusion of non-native speakers. It sanctions the need to notice other people's accent and to be aware of one's own (Lippi-Green 59). However, accented speech is capable of betrayal only when the "white" body speaks. An important thing to remember when considering the experience of the body in translation is that it is always there, but also differentiated by the possibility of passing and assimilation, or being locked up in "difference" through racialization, not just through language. Eva's revamping of her body image (of which learning English is a part) is possible because of her unacknowledged whiteness.[23] Privileges of whiteness, education, and attained social position, with a relatively easy access to publishing, differentiate Hoffman and Kamboureli from many other immigrant women, women of colour like Kikumura's mother, or others whose life writing has been invoked through many epigraphs in this book. Like the Amy Tan quotation cited earlier in this chapter, their stories make us aware of a different kind of loss, a different meaning of the phrase "lost in translation," referring to what is lost in the cracks and crevices of language when translation gives rise to racial and ethnic stereotypes. Perhaps, then, in the case of Hoffman and Kamboureli it is pointless to talk about writing in "borrowed tongues" as these two writers "master" English, making it intimately and passionately their own by taking it into their logo-erotic embrace.

Chapter 4

Translation as Allegorical Metafiction
Marlene Nourbese Philip and Jamaica Kincaid

>Child   all i have to give
>is English which hates/fears your
>black skin
>
>make it dance   sing
>to sunlight on the Caribbean
>(Claire Harris, *Drawing Down a Daughter*)

Postcolonial Tropologies

We have examined different possibilities of diasporic writing of migrancy as translation performed from the position of self-ethnicization and/or postmodern nostalgia. The writers analyzed in the previous chapters focus mostly on the genealogical functions of translation and its mediating role in the processes of cross-generational transmission of languages and cultures and the possibility of sur-vival through their symbolic marriage or memorializing inscriptions. With Marlene Nourbese Philip's *Looking for Livingstone: An Odyssey of Silence* (1991) and Jamaica Kincaid's *The Autobiography of My Mother* (1996), we come to the situation where there is only the target language and where the need for sur-vival demands creative invigoration, bending and blending, reshaping and transforming of the monolanguage, so as to escape its abusive power and to graft onto it what it has repressed as its own negativity. It becomes not so much the way of using English as "a borrowed tongue" as using it with "borrowed claws" (Derrida, *Monolingualism* 66). What makes Philip and Kincaid different from other immigrant women writers discussed before is the fact that they inflect migrancy and postmodernity with postcoloniality, a condition whose political, socio-economic, cultural, and philosophical consequences still shape our global reality.[1] Born in Tobago and Antigua, respectively, Philip and Kincaid embody the discontinuities of Caribbean history and carry this history with them when they migrate to North America, one to Toronto and the other to New York. It is a history marked by colonial conquest, slavery, imperialism, and foreign domination, as well as cultural resistance and struggle for independence. The Caribbean bears the memory of brutal ruptures and displacements: the genocide of indigenous peoples, the Middle Passage of Africans, and the enforcement of slavery, indentured labour, poverty, and exploitation of the region, followed by the indignities of forced economic migration to the West, which in turn brings with it exposure to systemic racism and discrimination. For African Caribbean diasporic subjects, the experience of migrancy cannot be detached from the background of this colonial legacy. Speaking from a male perspective, Edouard Glissant describes the enslaved African as the "stripped migrant" who

> could not bring his tools, the images of his gods, his daily implements, nor could he send news to his neighbours, or hope to bring his family over, or reconstitute his former family in the place of deportation. Naturally, the ancestral spirit had not left him; he had not lost the meaning of a former experience. But he will have to fight for centuries in order to recognize its legitimacy. The other migrant, also stripped to essentials, retained all of that. (50)

Echoes of this "nonhistory" (Glissant 62), of the programmatic extinction of languages, cultures, and kinship ties through the slave trade and plantation economy, together with the damages inflicted on individual and collective identities by colonial education, reverberate in the cultural memory of the descendants of enslaved Africans, who "have had to invent mythologies of their own, stories and allegories of 'self' and 'other' that can translate this complex heritage" (Lionnet, "Of Mangoes" 322).[2]

Growing from a crisis of colonial encounter, history, and geography, Philip's and Kincaid's texts function in the framework of postcolonial autobiography, a type of writing which cannot free itself from the hauntedness of the past and can be seen as caught up in the reactive structure of *ressentiment*—resentment against imperialism, colonialism, racism, Eurocentrism, and white supremacy, a long list of what Frantz Fanon calls "travelling companions" of the postcolonial subject (65). At the same time, this type of writing exhibits its creative strength in deconstructing established modes of thinking and representation while seeking possible transformation of received forms of cultures, identities, and languages in order to accommodate a diversity and richness of Caribbean diasporic experiences. Philip and Kincaid belong to the tradition of Caribbean intellectuals who decentre English and French as imperial languages and decolonize structures of representation that duplicate in language the material practices of colonial domination and subordination. In contrast to the autobiographies by European or Asian immigrants, who confront English from the position of bilingual alterity, the African Caribbean writers are faced with a different dilemma of alienation from English and the devaluation of a Creole language, or Caribbean demotic, as a language that evolved from English in the contact zones of plantation culture. This situation poses a challenge different from the politics of language analyzed earlier in other narratives, where translation has been a matter of vertical flows, albeit often two-directional, between two languages and cultures that may have been encoded as "weaker" or "stronger" but have nevertheless been seen as "foreign" to each other. In the case of writers who use both Creole and English, it is more accurate to talk about a linguistic continuum, which in turn makes their relation to English different from monolingual English speakers.

In the Caribbean, a linguistic choice depends on the context of communication, allowing the speaker to switch language registers to underscore class and race differences, or levels of familiarity and intimacy. The use of Creole, or patois (Kincaid's preferred term)[3] can have several affective functions, expressing group allegiance, values, and modalities different from those of the dominant language, or serving to establish a restricted context. The choice to speak the language of lower social prestige, a vernacular tongue that "exists in the shadow, as it were, of an official language" (Bell 51), can also be a political decision when Creole becomes a signifier of resistance, providing a link to history and "to speakers of other New World creoles and even to Africa in ways that standard English cannot" (Bell 53). Edward Kamau Brathwaite's concept of the "nation language" has been embraced precisely to challenge the primacy of standard or "proper" English which is perceived as capable of articulating only Eurocentric experience, alien to the Caribbean. Exposing the devaluation of creolized languages as linked to linguistic imperialism, Caribbean writers point to regimes of linguistic standardization as a form of "mastery" over, and control of, "substandard" dialects.[4] An ongoing critique of such hegemonic practices is integral to the project of challenging hierarchies of languages and cultures that have been created by colonialism.

This kind of hierarchy of "superior" and "inferior" Englishes that mark their historical bearers must be distinguished from the verticality of the relationship between English and immigrant mother tongues studied before, where a "mother tongue" changes between the generations of mothers and daughters, giving rise to the need for intergenerational translation. What sets apart these narratives of immigration from the narratives of post-slavery is the fact that in the latter there is no passing of the mother tongue between mother and daughter. Rather, what is exchanged is a loss of a story to pass on, so what is transmitted carries no promise of equivalence to be found through translation as it already comes "with the mark of untranslatability on it" (Spivak, "The Politics" 195). The types of translation we have been dealing with in narratives of immigration are driven by what Barbara Godard describes as "a logic of identity and equivalence," engaged in pursuit of some form of "con/version" of the immigrant self into its translated version that would be compatible and intelligible from within the target language and culture. For Philip and Kincaid, the catastrophic events of the past, with their subsequent erasure and loss of the mother tongue, have created a challenge of non-translation rather than translation proper, forcing their writing into "a logic of non-identity or contradiction" (Godard, "Writing between Cultures" 93). As much as it can be politically expedient in their case to refuse to translate their difference, contesting any possibility of "con/version" in a white supremacist culture, they engage in producing "re/versions," to use Godard's term again, that is, resistant, revisionist, recuperative horizontal translations (or trans-versions) that tell the story "across" while reinvigorating their linguistic and cultural identities.

With the enduring effects of the wounds of colonialism and racism on African Caribbean subjectivity, it is not surprising that the narratives written by Philip and Kincaid exemplify "return migrations," revisiting the sites of trauma in the literal, geographic sense, but also metaphorically, in the sense of wounding representations and the scars they have left on languages and bodies. While *Looking for Livingstone* stages an imaginary journey through Africa, *The Autobiography of My Mother* returns to Dominica to explore the indigenous Carib connection in Kincaid's genealogy, with both texts providing counter-discourses to Western constructions of Africa and indigenous peoples that have been inextricably bound up with negativity through the images of "savages" and Africa as a "dark continent." In response to such negative discourse, from the mid-twentieth century, Africans in francophone and anglophone Africa, the Caribbean, North America, and Britain have "constructed and reconstructed collective political 'memories' of African culture to form a cohesive structure to shield them from racist ideology and oppression" (White 118). The concepts of a return migration to Mother Africa and, in the Caribbean context, a return to the pre-Columbian paradise signal a tendency toward essentialist constructions of mythic origins and identity, and reveal that too often "diasporas conceive of themselves ... within the cognitive grid of a Western paradigm of identity reconceived from a marginal position" (Roberts 188). This is the foundation of the critiques of the movement of Négritude, defined as "the sum of the cultural values of the black world" (Senghor 28) that allows people of African descent all over the world to affirm their shared identity. Although Aimé Césaire, who coined the term in 1947, and Léopold Senghor, generally considered as one of the main philosophers of Négritude, have defended the concept against reductive interpretations, the proponents of Négritude have been viewed—by Fanon among others—as defining themselves oppositionally against white racism and prejudice and theorizing from within the binary space framed by white culture.[5] Engaging intertextually with this body of thought, both Philip's and Kincaid's texts effectively complicate any monolithic accounts and demonstrate that notions of purity or authenticity cannot be recouped in a postcolonial world.

Caribbean cultures have been historically capable of absorbing world influences and transfiguring them into "a new syncretic culture, as elements from Africa, Europe, Asia and the Caribbean became absorbed, worked and reworked into a new and distinctively 'Creole' culture" (Chamberlain 154). Glissant, the most influential theorist of *Créolité*, embraces creolization as an idea of "the unceasing process of transformation," linked to diasporsim, hybridity, or *métissage*, and the creation of contact zones, or liminal, transnational spaces.[6] "The poetics of creolization is the same as a cross-cultural poetics," associated with openness, blurring the boundary between inside and outside, deconstructing the myth of "unique" origins (Glissant 142). It must be noted, however, that among anglophone Afro-Caribbeans creolization is primarily associated with contact languages, and that Creole "as language is always open to multilingual influence and blending without subservience to a dominant culture" (Collier 297).[7] Creolization, then, can be related to the non-hegemonic practices of transculturation and translation, which preserve traces of heterogeneity and heteroglossia rather than insisting on the erasure of difference. But writing is translative even when the chosen language is English or French, instead of Creole. It can also generate creative processes of creolization, becoming "a means of translating into the colonizer's language a different sensibility, a different vision of the world, a means therefore of transforming the dominant conceptions circulated in the more standard idiom ... [English] is appropriated, made into a vehicle for expressing a hybrid, heteroglot universe" (Lionnet, *Postcolonial* 13). Language performances enacted in Philip's and Kincaid's narratives allow us to contextualize their attitudes to English in the above terms as translation that takes a form of creolization, focusing on language and the structures of thought and representation that can be produced through it.

Consequently, I view *Looking for Livingstone* and *The Autobiography of My Mother* as examples of allegorical metafiction, both engaged in a "creolized" approach to translation, in the sense of producing new meanings at the interfaces of several different languages (Creole and English, colonial and postcolonial, literal and figurative, masculine and feminine discourses, among others). As postcolonial allegories, they embody a mode of narration organized around a rhetorical structure that allows for indirection and multiple substitutions, making it a favoured form of expression for the oppressed. Both texts then can be described as tropological narratives: centred on rhetorical figures and their subversion, performing rhetoric while simultaneously attempting its deconstruction as a tool of domination. Used in this way, translation becomes a strategy of deconstructive mimicry,[8] a performance that stands authority on its head while also displaying the double consciousness of the gendered postcolonial subject. Double consciousness is one of the most important tropes of postcolonial subjectivity, derived from W.E.B. Du Bois's metaphor of the veil that splits the African American subject in two, creating "this sense of always looking at one's self through the eyes of others" (45), a sense of inner conflict and alienation resulting from the imposition of racism and stereotyping (including internalized attitudes) by the dominant culture. This kind of experience forces the subject into double discourse and double-voicedness, leading to the adoption and performance of masking strategies such as the practice of mimicry. In Philip's and Kincaid's texts, the echoing voice of mimicry is multidirectional and resonates on several levels: from the general predicament of a postcolonial writer, like Echo, "doomed" to repetition, to the echoes of dominant and suppressed traditions playing against each other, the noisy chunks of negativity persistently echoing in the head, and, finally, the maternal "echo" in the subject. But rather than falling into passive echolalia, this voice assumes a resistant stance of signifying, an African American rhetorical strategy which relies on repetition in order to inscribe difference.[9] Both *Looking for Livingstone* and *The Autobiography of My Mother* are signifying texts whose rhetoric simultaneously reveals and obscures, employing indeterminacy and indirection in order to subvert ethnocentric Western designations of African people, their languages, and their cultures.

Marlene Nourbese Philip's *Looking for Livingstone: An Odyssey of Silence*

> But to the Door of No Return which is illuminated in the consciousness of Blacks in the Diaspora there are no maps. This door is not mere physicality. It is a spiritual location. It is also perhaps a psychic destination. Since leaving was never voluntary, return was, and still may be, an intention, however deeply buried. There is as it says no way in; no return. (Dionne Brand, *A Map to the Door of No Return: Notes to Belonging*)

Marlene Nourbese Philip's *Looking for Livingstone: An Odyssey of Silence* is a short, experimental text which is, however, extremely sophisticated and rich in interpretive possibilities. Even its placement under the rubric of life writing begs the question as the narrative persistently obfuscates any reference to "life," instead miming the autobiographical function through incorporated conventions of travel diary, parody of autoethnographic writing, and trauma testimony. Nevertheless, I argue that Philip develops an elaborate allegory as a metafictional mask, behind which she conducts her deconstructive and re-constructive philosophy of language, from her position as a writer of African Caribbean descent, burdened with the legacy of enslavement, colonization, and racism. As a consequence of brutal dispossession of the African in the New World, language—standard English—comes to her as a colonizer's "gift," in a double sense of inheritance and poison.[10] Through birthright, she also inherits another language, Creole or Caribbean demotic, the speech of the marginalized that has evolved from English through processes of creolization.

Philip's strategies of creolization can be discerned on the level of textual practices that might be qualified as translative. How is *Looking for Livingstone* a project in translation? In terms of patterns of translation discussed in other chapters, Philip's text combines different kinds of translation, from translation as language transfer to cultural translation, adding to them translation as parsing of discourse and retranslation in Godard's sense of "re/version." The narrative symbolically enacts a linguistic passage of the author/Traveller caught between a dominant and a marginalized language (English and Caribbean demotic) to a new synthesis, where the perspective and sensibility of a marginalized language-user blends with the existing medium of English, forging a new kind of self-conscious language—a "living stone" cleansed of "the pollute/ the profane in word," that is, a residue left by English as the language of oppression (LFL 39). This alchemical process is constantly supported by the work of cultural translation performed by the "Caucasianist" ethnographer's gaze trying to interpret "white man's" cultural discourses. At the same time, another translative strategy, parsing, is adopted as a way of unravelling meanings encoded in words. It is identified in a crucial moment in the text, in the last poem before the narrator's encounter with Livingstone: "How parse the punish/ in Silence/ Noun/ Verb/ absent a Grammar" (LFL 59). Parsing serves the analytical and deconstructive function of unmaking language, offering an insight into its "hostile" grammar, where, for example, the noun "silence" can be turned into a more threatening verb "to silence." Finally, there is a task of retranslation as "re/version," an attempt to reinscribe the African's silence without turning it into words, without converting the truth of the oppressed into the oppressor's language. If the subject is seen as forced into translation, literally and metaphorically, through the Middle Passage and erasure of reference, retranslation can bring her back to language in a resistant way, refusing familiarization with the target culture while also bearing witness to the lost origin(al).

Alternately defined through exile or immigration, Philip has been categorized as an African Caribbean writer living in Canada or an Afro-Caribbean Canadian writer. But she has a much more complex diasporic sense of identity, and in her 1997 essay "A Genealogy of Resistance" she describes herself as "a post-colonial, postmodern, hybridized, Afro-Saxoned, anglicized, African 'West Indian' woman" (24). This inventory alone testifies to her openness to heterogeneity and syncretism. In an earlier piece of life writing, "Echoes in a Stranger Land," included as an introduction to *Frontiers*, she acknowledges being a product of two predominant traditions central to her work: the white colonial tradition, tied to her British education, and the Afrocentric tradition, tied to the collective race memory of Afro-Caribbeans. She has honoured the latter tradition through self-naming, choosing the West African name "Nourbese" (which she now spells NourbeSe), meaning "marvellous child" in Benin, as "an invocation of ancestry, passage and journey" (Sanders 82). Situating herself at the crossroads of European and African traditions, she echoes a familiar trope of double consciousness, which for a multiply displaced African Caribbean diasporic subject is more than double and may comprise the braiding of several traditions. But this double or multiple consciousness can be turned into a form of epistemic privilege, allowing her to question and deconstruct hegemonic meanings from her position as a "translator" skilled in multiple "languages," the dominant and the marginalized ones, while at the same time experiencing a disjuncture between a sense of self and the world view that can be articulated through them.

Philip extends Edouard Glissant's reflection on a "forced poetics" and the anguish caused by the colonized subject's experience of incompatibility between desire and expression (Glissant 120). In the essay called "Absence of Writing or How I Almost Became a Spy," included at the beginning of *She Tries Her Tongue, Her Silence Softly Breaks*, Philip formulates the concept of "i-mage" which echoes Glissant's meditation on the problems of self-expression negated or stifled by "the opposition between a language that one uses and a form of expression that one needs" (Glissant 121). The concept of "i-mage" is drawn from "the Rastafarian practice of privileging the 'I' in many words," which Philip adopts to bring African subjectivity into discourse (*She Tries* 12), striving to inscribe the autobiographical where it has been banned or excluded from dominant representations. According to her, Africans removed from Africa lost "their power to create, control, and even understand their own i-mages ... [as they] lacked that needed matrix in which the autonomous i-mage-maker could flourish" (*She Tries* 13). Moreover, English in the Caribbean was the language of oppression and brutalization, "etymologically hostile and expressive of the non-being of the African" (*She Tries* 15). However, with the obliteration of African languages in the New World, she has no other tool "to create and express i-mages about herself, and her life experiences" (*She Tries* 16). The poem "Discourse on the Logic of Language" graphically expresses the condition of the stuttering African subject whose father tongue is also the language of "m/othering" (Doray and Samuel 37):

> my father tongue is a foreign lan lan lang
> language/
> l/anguish
> anguish
> a foreign anguish
> is english (*She Tries* 56)

For the African Caribbean writer using English as her medium, this "anguish of English" is a major paradox and challenge: how to reclaim its i-mage-making power while at the same time exposing English as tainted by imperialism and colonial domination. However, Philip refuses to limit the experience of the African artist either to working in standard English or to working in the Caribbean demotic: "It is *in the continuum of expression* from standard to Caribbean English that the veracity of the experience lies" (*She Tries* 15). She thus avoids identification with either of the extreme positions exemplified by Braithwaite, who heightens the use of Creole, and Derek Walcott, who remains invested in the power of the master tongue. Carole Boyce Davies offers a feminist critique of this phenomenon of "the anxiety of the tongue" (156) affecting African and Caribbean postcolonial writers and suggests that this anguish should be read in gendered terms as "male."[11] Such male colonial angst is part of a cultural mythology of the Caribbean, but it finds a different expression in Caribbean women's writing, which emphasizes female creativity and resilience not only to cultural imperialism but also to sexist oppression. Women's writing reveals that both languages can be used to marginalize women through patriarchal discourses of Caribbean nationalism and white colonial supremacy.

In the poem "Discourse on the Logic of Language" (*She Tries*)[12] Philip uses a bricolage of texts, including fragments of slaveholders' edicts as ethnographic exhibits "from the archive of imperialism" (Godard, "Rape" 420). The edicts reveal a deliberate policy to separate and break any familial or ethno-linguistic bonds that the slaves might have preserved as well as stating an explicit prohibition of the use of vernacular languages, punishable by removal of the tongue. These quotations are juxtaposed with two other texts. One is a poem lamenting the loss of the mother tongue while the other is a narrative of birth telling of the mother licking her newborn of "the creamy white substance covering its body"—a literalized metaphor of cleansing the body from a white layer of imposed language. The absence of the mother tongue is translated here into the mother's tongue. But the image paradoxically also reminds us that the white substance is necessary for birth, and for articulation as bringing meaning into the world. Through such images, Philip can engage in "questioning the tongue as organ and concept" ("Managing" 297) and begin to deconstruct the father tongue/ mother tongue binary which tends to naturalize motherhood. By claiming that she has "no mother/ tongue/no mother to tongue/no tongue to mother," she refuses to embrace Creole as the idealized "mother tongue" while at the same time asserting her entitlement to English as her expressive medium. Similar to deconstructing motherhood in Black feminist theory, by such critics as Patricia Hill Collins, the concept of "mother tongue" must be deconstructed in the Caribbean and migrant contexts. The name "mother tongue" is derived from the association of the child's acquisition of language through contact with the mother in the early years. However, a connection with children is broken and denied to slave mothers, indigenous mothers, working-class mothers, or migrant mothers working away from their families, as part of the transnational circuit of cheap labour. Consequently, the concept of "mother tongue" must be seen as gendered, classed, and racialized through the white middle-class ideology of motherhood, which romanticizes and essentializes the mother's role in the process of reproduction of exclusionary national identities.

For Philip, Caribbean demotic is an "oral link to a different historical past" (Lionnet, *Autobiographical* 1–2). Her linguistic continuum between standard English and marginalized "englishes" becomes a site of resistance and creative cross-breeding in a struggle to forge a medium capable of accommodating the past, present, and future experiences of the African Caribbean diasporic subject whose links to her own and her peoples' histories have been destroyed by the violence of geographic and linguistic displacement. Symbolic imperialism, privileging the dominant group's values and perspectives, inflicts damage and renders invisible the experiences of a colonized people. The continuing effects of this violent history haunt Philip's narrative, which must therefore do the work of mourning and remembering while also *re*-membering the loss by means of cultural and linguistic processes of creolization whose operations inform the metafictional allegory in *Looking for Livingstone*. Traces of this horrific past and its consequences in the present in the collective African postmemory of trauma can be found in the narrative in the form of creative negotiations of counter-memory. However, in order to create counter-memory, those who have survived need "to break through the dead tissue [of] colonial ideology" (Glissant 62) or, in Philip's terms, to "lick off" the white substance of language. In Philip's narrative this deconstruction of the imposed and inherited forms of self-expression and representation, as well as construction of counter-memory, is performed from the gendered perspective of a female migrant, the itinerant narrator called The Traveller.

Looking for Livingstone follows and in a way expands Philip's meditations on language, racism, and colonialism, included in *She Tries Her Tongue, Her Silence Softly Breaks*. A sense of double dislocation from Africa and the Caribbean that informs her text creates multiple tensions in relation to the two traditions embodied by David Livingstone, a missionary, doctor, and explorer, representative of England, and by imaginary Africa, a vast continent where the anonymous Traveller retraces Livingstone's steps. While The Traveller's "odyssey" turns into a symbolic return migration to the scene of originary rupture and displacement of the African body that deprived it of the mother tongue, Philip's metafictional goals include the aesthetic, philosophical, and political exploration of the interrelatedness of African Caribbean diasporic subjectivity, language, and place. The Traveller's relationship to Africa as a mindscape, as a space of the interior, parallels her physical, psychic, and spiritual disconnection. In the process, Philip through The Traveller effectively defamiliarizes presumptions and conventions of Eurocentric discourses used by the colonizers to enslave the African and to mask the erasure of African history, language, and culture. The text parodically mimics ethnographic utopias of explorers who, at different times, searched for Eldorado, the Promised Land, or the Ultima Thule, thus implicitly suggesting links between imperialism and utopia, between colonial utopian projects and the historical plundering of Africa, of its people and resources. Returning to Africa, The Traveller "is combating the colonizers' geographic violence, their right to explore, chart, and finally bring the world under control" (Karamcheti 183). This continuing subjugation has been supported in European philosophical thought by discursive constructions of Africa as a continent without history and without civilization, culminating in Hegel's classic formulations in his *Philosophy of History*: "What we actually understand by 'Africa' is that which is without history and resolution, which is still fully caught up in the natural spirit" (in Snead 63). For the European, the African is placed in relation of absolute alterity, occupying the negative space outside all European conceptions of the subject.[13] Philip's critique of Eurocentrism and imperialism is translated into an allegorical battle between WORD and SILENCE, the battle which plays itself out on the level of psychoanalytic, historiographic, ethnographic, and literary subversions of the dialectic of the colonizer's WORD versus the African's SILENCE.

The psychoanalytic subtext is evident in "the theme of recuperation and recovery implicit in The Traveller's journey" (J. Harris 10), and in the ironic encoding of her identity quest in terms of the maternal and the paternal imagery. Referring to English as an abusive parent, she stages a metaphorical return to the womb of Africa and re-enacts its primal rape, showing herself as a hybrid child born of this violation. She thus invokes classic goals of psychoanalytic theory: to discover the site of trauma unknown to the subject and articulate it, thereby banishing its ongoing psychological impact. Accordingly, the key to this aspect of her narrative allegory is provided by The Traveller's dreams. In the first dream, Livingstone's phallic word penetrates the silence of her vagina before contemplating his impotence (LFL 25) whereas in the second she is "blown up like a sow" trying to give birth to "the monstrous product" of his word and her silence, conceived in her womb (LFL 26). These two dreams exemplify Philip's practice of signifying as a form of indirect critical engagement with received racist stereotypes. Her hyperbolically animalistic metaphors poke fun at Western sexual fantasies associating blackness with wildness and bestiality; at the same time, the conflation of language and sexuality can be seen as a way of talking back to European fears of miscegenation and obsession with language purity, embedded in the colonial power dynamics of control and ownership of "white" language and "white" body.[14] Philip confounds psychoanalytic expectations by replacing the act of articulation, privileged in Freudian and Eurocentric thought, with the act of silence, often devalued by Western cultures as "passive." Additionally, *Looking for Livingstone* reveals the site of trauma as located not in an easily isolated moment, but rather in an ongoing impact of cultural rupture which, moreover, has not been repressed in the Freudian sense but has been suppressed in the colonial sense. The imagery of pregnancy and birth foregrounds the convergence of language, power, and the body's racialized and gendered identity, where The Traveller's body becomes the ravished body of Africa—both "territories" claimed and possessed by Livingstone's word. Needless to say, on the metafictional plane, this image also reflects Philip's dilemma as a writer. The Traveller's quest for Livingstone can be read as an allegorical life narrative of the author obsessed with English (Livingstone, her father tongue), "trying to engender by some alchemical practice a metamorphosis within the language from father tongue to mother tongue" ("Absence" 24). The alchemy of her writing in *Looking for Livingstone* turns Livingstone-English into a living stone, her own metamorphosed matrilineal language, or into a living tone, a live speech. In a similar vein, Dawn Thompson interprets the transformation of the proper name "Livingstone" (tongue turned to stone) into a common noun, as "tongue turned to stone" is transformed into "livingstone" (64).

When the text opens, The Traveller has already initiated her quest, for which she has borrowed a motto from Livingstone: "I will open a way to the interior or perish"—a signal that her journey is also a journey of self-discovery and that "this text functions in autobiographical space" (Thompson 76). The parallel, and yet simultaneously opposed, nature of Livingstone's and The Traveller's individual quests is immediately established, with Livingstone cast in the role of her double. While he ostensibly seeks to map the external, The Traveller is involved in mapping her "interior." Where Livingstone attempts to impose language and meaning—his word—onto the silence of Africa, The Traveller moves toward an understanding of the richness and variety of what has been perceived as silence. Philip's metaphor of the interior is reminiscent of other constructions of collective memory of the African diasporic subject, such as Dionne Brand's "door of no return," which casts a similar "haunting spell on personal and collective consciousness in the Diaspora" (Brand 25). Within that spectral psychological space, The Traveller and Livingstone are "both heirs to a common language, albeit to different linguistic experiences ... [and] remain forever sensitive to each other" (*She Tries* 21). Philip writes that England is, for better or worse, part of the African experience "as much as the experience of the African in the Caribbean and the New World is part of the English collective experience" (*She Tries* 20). Consequently, The Traveller's obsession with Livingstone echoes Philip's own anguish about English and England. Elsewhere she speaks of her ambivalent attitude to this side of her genealogy: "In what part of my body is this thing lodged? That they have planted within me. What is it? ... this desire to have england. inside. within me! so that to rid myself of it i needs must turn myself inside out. Expose the darkest, softest parts to the light" (*Genealogy* 25). The way she describes her education resembles the process of turning the colonial subject into "a mimic man," envisioned in Macaulay's writing and described by Bhabha as "the effect of a flawed colonial mimesis, in which to be Anglicized is *emphatically* not to be English ("Of Mimicry" 87). Philip's Traveller also mimics Livingstone, in her own faltering way retracing the erratic patterns of his itinerary.

The Traveller's inevitable confrontation with Livingstone is central to Philip's project of disrupting the official hegemonic narrative of colonialism and its legacy of historiographic misrepresentation. The subversion of colonialist versions of history proceeds through deconstruction of linear historical time, intended to place the counter-narrative outside of the Western discursive framework. The fact that the search for Livingstone takes The Traveller "eighteen billion years—the age of the universe" (LFL 60) provides an important clue to the calendar system adopted to mark different stages of her allegorical journey. While she progresses by moving backwards to reach Livingstone, she also, hyperbolically, traverses billions of years and re-visions inherited histories and myths, including the traditions of Christianity and slavery, in the process symbolically undoing the Middle Passage through a ritual of rebirth. Marking each year "the year of our word" is an ironic acknowledgement of the creative power of language—"our word" substituted for the Christian God, "the Lord"—to construct "realities" and "facts." At the same time, it also suggests the competing linguistic and epistemic universes of Livingstone and The Traveller, who questions the nature of historical knowledge by showing that what counts as "fact" is constructed and authorized by power. As she observes: "A fact is what anyone, having the power to enforce it, says is a fact. Power—that is the distinguishing mark of a fact" (LFL 67). Stanley and Livingstone, ironically presented as "white fathers of the continent" (LFL 7), have perpetrated the myth of Africa as a utopian no-place, uncharted territories associated with timelessness and undated origins, a place awaiting to be "discovered" and renamed. Their maps are defined as "crude pictures" projected by the mind, a topographic imposition of patterns infused with dominant subjectivity rather than objective "facts." One way of subverting such colonialist representations, which strip the continent of its identity and history and treat it like a blank and barren wilderness, is to invoke indigenous presence—the native guides who led Livingstone to the places he claimed to have "discovered," or the original names that had been erased through his renaming of Africa's geography. Since relatively little knowledge has been preserved of ancestral history, Philip chooses a powerful trope to remind us of those forgotten origins: Africa's stolen past, cultural myths, images, and languages are represented metonymically as Silence, where Silence means not so much absence as a different form of presence juxtaposed to the colonizers' phallic Word.

However, in discourses of Afrocentricity, the recourse to Africa as a locus of origin, pan-African identity, and common destiny often constructs images of ancient tribal cultures of mythic and compensatory rather than historical character. The Traveller's Africa is no less imaginary. In Stuart Hall's words, "Africa is the name of the missing term, the great aporia, which lies at the centre of [Black] cultural identity and gives it meaning which, until recently, it lacked" (394). For an African Caribbean diasporic subject, one troubling aspect in the connection between Africa and the Caribbean is the issue of African complicity in the transatlantic slave trade, or the originary betrayal of Mother Africa selling her children. According to Rhonda Cobham, "African collusion in the trade was the rule rather than the exception" (883fn). Yet another meaning of silence as cultural taboo can be derived from the fact that "modern African writing, like modern African society, tends to acknowledge the slave trade, and African participation in it, only indirectly" (Cobham 873). The descendants of the enslaved have an ambivalent relationship to this part of African history, which further complicates any unproblematic reclamation of the African past in the Afro-Caribbean diaspora, where Africa "is also the place that forgot to protect her own; that devoured her children in the pursuit of the promise of wealth" (Cobham 875). While identification with African traditions remains a vital tool of cultural resistance in Caribbean consciousness, it should not be idealized or used to reinforce reductive binary constructions of good-and-evil or black-and-white, a kind of thinking which Frantz Fanon calls "manicheism delirium" (183).

The Traveller's journey is a journey through the Silence of Africa, a metaphor literalized through the names of different imaginary African societies that she visits, all being anagrammatic versions of the same word: SILENCE. To challenge the colonizing gaze, she parodies the imagery of sexual domination and submission, which animates traditional male narratives of exploration and conquest. Conquest, exploration, travel are shown as gendered, definitely coded as patriarchal exploits of the arrogant men like Stanley, declaring to Livingstone that "a continent awaits us—like a whore" (LFL 25). Philip's "feminized" Africa, populated by tribal communities of women, serves as a powerful symbol of the violence inflicted on women and indigenous peoples by the paternalistic assumptions that men and Europeans have made about our/their silence (Currie 124). Women's bodies, black and white—since Livingstone's wife is also seen as "sentenced" to silence—are used as wombs, or denied through repressive, idealized models such as Queen Victoria or the Virgin Mary. The narrative contains a fictional letter from Mary Livingstone to her husband, revealing the "howling silence" of her solitude and abandonment (LFL 29). The fact that The Traveller gains wisdom from African women and that she can extend compassion to the white British woman is a reminder for women of the need to find solidarity among themselves rather than being seduced by the male rhetoric and colluding with imperialist projects. Interestingly, there are also reports of gendered differences in the accounts of African complicity with the slave trade. Cobham notes that African male and female writers adopt differing perspectives: the former often present African collaborators as a monstrous aberration while the latter "present the slave trade as a social institution that involved a range of ordinary people [including] upstanding members of their communities" (883f). Once again, in different cultural contexts, women's writing probes beyond officially sanctioned patriarchal metanarratives.

Ethnographic violence finds its most striking critique in the difference between the "multicoloured quilt of Silence," woven by The Traveller, and The Museum of Silence that she visits. The ritual of making the quilt that she learns from one of the tribes, a process through which she can use both word and silence, allows her to find a transformative power of her own Silence. The art of weaving, of braiding together multiple yarns or threads, is a metaphor for women's creativity, gesturing toward the concept of *métissage* and the poetics of creolization, as opposed to the imperial rule of the monolanguage.[15] The Traveller's dialogic learning of how to weave disparate elements is contrasted with The Museum's ethnographic appropriation of "the many and varied silences of different peoples," which are commodified as museum objects, "labelled, annotated, dated, catalogued" (LFL 57), and put on display as artifacts severed from their context in ritual and culture, rendered meaningless or distorted.[16] The curators who laugh at her demands that these objects be returned to their rightful owners make her realize the value of protective silence: the oppressed should not disclose all their secrets to the oppressor to avoid appropriation. In the course of her quest, the signifier "silence" acquires different meanings, finally crystallizing into the small-"s" silence and the capital-"S" Silence, the former inflicted on the African by colonizers and the latter representing the totality of African heritage. In the climactic encounter with Livingstone, The Traveller rejects the temptation to replace her silence with words: "if I had words, he said, i could be a witness to all that had gone wrong. I could speak out, condemn—i could even blame them." However, she prefers to remain faithful to her Silence, "the only thing … that is not contaminated" (LFL 65). The Traveller thus refuses to accept the imposition of the word, signalling a stance contrary to Eurocentric hegemonic practices. By seeking not to fill the silences in the historical record but to testify to their presences, she undermines the record, as well as the way of reading other people's histories and cultures presumed to be represented. Silence that foregrounds such perceived "absences" becomes a way of seeing (as there is a "lence"—lens—in silence), a form of counter-discourse of resistance allowing her to reverse the agency, shifting the gaze from the colonizer to the colonized. A twofold purpose of her quest becomes apparent: she breaks her silence ("the sentence of her silence" imposed by his word) while at the same time discovering and surrendering to the Silence of the African.

The fact that The Traveller's journey through Africa is meant to be a parody of ethnographic discourse is also evidenced by her self-reflexive use of the form of travel diary, complete with dated entries on her "discovery" and sojourn in different civilizations. Her text performatively presents itself as equipped with maps and photographs, including her photographs with Livingstone—an ironic reversal of the genre of ethnographic pictures with the natives. Elsewhere, Philip actually refers to herself as a "Caucasianist," that is, "an ethnological observer of the institutional practices of white society" (Godard, "Rape" 416). Moreover, the text goes one step further in problematizing representation, including its own, by attaching a spurious editorial apparatus at the end of The Traveller's account. The "Author's Note" appended to the text converts the book itself into a museum artifact, suggesting a challenge to the notion of an "original" document. As Kristie McAlpine writes, "In a piece of work that so comprehensively challenges the ideologies of discovery ... there are no originals, clean pages or pure states to discover, only representations and facsimiles" (139). As a result, Philip's own narrative risks being caught in a conundrum that often characterizes ironic double-discourse: to parody ethnographic representations, the text must rewrite them with a difference, thus risking their reinforcement. Moreover, the structure of allegory opens the text to the danger noticed by Myriam Chancy, namely, to neocolonization by means of universalizing interpretations (102), thus raising a series of questions: How does Philip's text resist collapsing Africa into another utopia or reinscribing the code of the exotic? Can her own relationship to Africa be unmediated by one form of ethnography or another? Can layers of "white man's discourse" be peeled off her representation? However, it must be admitted that any universalizing reading can only be performed at the cost of ignoring the signifying aspect of the text and the ethical thrust of her allegory.

The use of parodic repetition and re-enactment underlines Philip's critical outsider's position both within and without these discourses. She escapes the danger of duplicating the colonizer's stance in her constructions of "Africa" through the self-reflexive practice of mimicry rather than mimesis. As already mentioned, the figure of mimicry, premised on the ambivalence of "almost the same, but not quite" (Bhabha, "Of Mimicry" 86), is a sign of double articulation, at once resembling and subverting dominant representations, disrupting the authority of what it approximates. Philip's mimicry of ethnographic discourse inscribes "the colonial text erratically, eccentrically across a body politic that refuses to be representative, in a narrative that refuses to be representational" (Bhabha, "Of Mimicry" 88). Once again, such mimicry establishes that what is at stake is not the nostalgia for Africa as "originary territory," but rather the investment in language as a site of political struggle. Philip "remains caught in a border dialogue between mimicry, alerity, silence" (Godard, "Rape" 408), refusing to replace colonial ethnographic utopias with some "contrapuntal" versions of utopian pan-Africanism. The link between word and Africa, between text and place, is forged by one of the poems interspersed with the narrative, in which Africa is viewed as a page to be filled with words:

>   Beyond the beckon in
>   beyond
>   the last sea
>   the ultima Thule
>   where space is
>   the page
>   blank
>   ignorance made monstrous (LFL 17)

The blank page of Africa is a metafictional metaphor which conflates the identities of The Traveller and the writer-poet and makes isomorphic their respective quests for Livingstone and for the "living stone" of language with which to build the "edifice" of Philip's text. The end of the poem suggests the direction of this double quest:

>   to find the bang that was
>   beginning
>   big
>   beyond
>   the wait in horizon
>   the straight line margin
>   in circles
>   widening
>   into ever
>   from the silence of
>   stone
>   dropped (LFL 18)

Such self-reflexive moments and emphasis on historical discontinuities make it possible to place *Looking for Livingstone* in the category of postmodern historiographic metafiction as a mode of narrating the past in a self-conscious manner so as to problematize history by opening it up to the present. Linda Hutcheon, who coined the term, suggests that by engaging in the process of rewriting history, historiographic metafiction subscribes to the view that "there are only *truths* in the plural, and never one Truth" (109). However, Philip's text never falls into celebration of historical indeterminacy. On the contrary, it repeatedly stresses the need to decolonize our knowledge of history, becoming an allegory of the diasporic writer's journey of unsaying Western ethnographic representations without condescending to fill the silences left by them.

When Arwhal, the weaver woman who becomes her lover, tells The Traveller, "The word does not belong to you—it was owned and whored by others long, long before you set out on your travels ... But to use your silence, you have to use the word" (LFL 52–53), she also expresses a predicament faced by Philip and other writers from oppressed or marginalized groups and who are alienated from hegemonic discourses. As bell hooks observes, "it is difficult not to hear in standard English always the sound of slaughter and conquest" (296). Repeating Adrienne Rich's words—"This is the oppressor's language/ yet I need it to talk to you."— hooks is compelled to think of the oppressive monolanguage

> of standard English, of learning to speak against black vernacular, against the ruptured and broken speech of a dispossessed and displaced people. Standard English is not the speech of exile. It is the language of conquest and domination. In the United States it is the mask which hides the loss of so many tongues, all those sounds of diverse native communities we will never hear, the speech of the Gullah, Yiddish, and so many other unremembered tongues. (296)

hooks, however, recognizes the importance of repossessing the language and claiming it "as a space of resistance" (297). Such "reinvented and remade" language would become a counter-language for a Black community (hooks 297). Similarly, Philip admits that working with the oppressor's language—which she describes as "the only one [she has]"—means for her a challenge to use that language so as "to subvert the inner and hidden discourse—the discourse of [her] non-being" ("Managing" 296). What she manages to achieve in *Looking for Livingstone* is, through the creative alchemy of creolization, to produce a series of i-mages that symbolically re-constitute African diasporic subjectivity in language. She claims her right to be housed in English, rather than being "hostage" to it—a creative and ethical transformation envisioned also in Derrida's reflection on his relationship with French in colonial Algeria, which through a semantic chain passing from hostage to hostile, host, and hospitable, arrives at the idea of hospitality in language that also coincides with Ricoeur's ideal of translation (*Monolingualism* 14).

Philip's Traveller, a woman descended from enslaved Africans, is an allegorical figure of multiple, syncretic subjectivity, symbolically braiding the realities of migrancy, of double consciousness, of cultural fragmentation. Her appellation as "Traveller" reinforces the idea of a subject who is in transition, a subject-in-process, through whom the collective experience, past and present, is articulated, reassessed, and transformed. Moreover, Philip's dedication "To the ancestors," as well as The Traveller's reconstruction of ancestral kinship communities from which she learns different meanings of silence, reveals the importance and vitality of lineage in the construction of diasporic subjectivity, consistent with the importance of the spirit of ancestral kin in Caribbean culture, where it "acts as a powerful binding force and dynamic in families" (Chamberlain 160). Symbolically, mothers, grandmothers, and "othermothers"[17] represent the multiplicity of voices and subject positions braided and woven into the diasporic subject's consciousness, including also the interlocutory relation to the voices of the other(s) within the self. This consciousness is constantly shaped and reshaped by memory, which, through its relation to imagination and imaginative structures, destabilizes any notion of a fixed and bounded identity. Mae Gwendolyn Henderson's trope of "speaking in tongues," used for black women's writing, is relevant here as it suggests speaking "in a plurality of voices as well as in a multiplicity of discourses" (262), which characterizes Philip's language.

The subjectivity emerging from Philip's narrative is also an integrative feminist subjectivity. In the context of her critique of white supremacist colonial patriarchy, the gender and race of The Traveller signify in multiple ways in relation to male explorers like Livingstone, with whom she partly identifies, but also in relation to British Victorian "lady" travellers like Mary Kingsley, or women like Mary Livingstone, a daughter of an English missionary and her husband's companion on several of his expeditions, who died of malaria on the lower Zambezi. Having an African woman occupy the position historically associated with popular narratives written by Victorian women travellers in Africa not only serves as an ironic reminder of white women's stake in the project of empire building, but also destabilizes gender as a category inflected through racialization. At the same time, through empathy for Livingstone's abandoned wife, colonizers' women are present as victims of white sexism. Philip reminds her readers of the negative binary representations of black and white women: "Victoria/Queen or Jemimah" next to "whore-wife" or "virgin-slut" (Wolf 109). By foregrounding the anti-racist feminist consciousness of the complex interlocking of racism, sexism, and colonialism, Philip's text moves beyond a simplistic binary schema of male/female, black/white, or European/non-European, into the interstitial spaces of translation, which opens up the possibility of making connections among multiple cultural codes and ideologies and relating them to one another.

The poetics of creolization in the text leaves its mark also in relation to generic conventions, cross-breeding the strategies familiar from a long-established tradition of African American life writing and the more recent aesthetics of Négritude. Discussing African American autobiography as a dynamic, eclectic genre, Alison Easton describes its process of adaptation and evolution from slave narratives, which "started by taking discourses of the dominant white culture, in particular those of individualism and political independence, the picaresque, the spiritual autobiography and abolitionist fiction and polemic" (177). Philip's text performs similar adaptations, combining Western traditions of travel writing, poetry, allegory, and the philosophical tale with the aesthetic paradigms of Négritude, which, according to Léopold Senghor, include de-emphasizing individual self; dialogic set-up; anti-realism; the symbiosis of the arts through poetry, song, and rituals; and movement and rhythm:

> Africa teaches that art is not photography; if there are images they are rhythmical ... For it is rhythm—the main virtue, in fact, of negritude—that gives the work its art and beauty. Rhythm is simply the movement of attraction or repulsion that expresses the life of the cosmic forces; symmetry and asymmetry, repetition and or opposition: in short, the lines of force that link the meaningful signs. (34)

Philip's prose and poetry privilege orality with its rhythms of repetition and stuttering, melodic naming, riffing, and the switching of language registers (Godard, "Rape" 432). Even the inscription of silence can be seen as an oral element (DeFehr 49). The textual abdication of the realist narrative is symptomatic of the rejection of Eurocentric structures. Similar to Senghor's anti-mimetic aesthetics, Edouard Glissant associates mimesis—the obsession with imitation—with violence: "The mimetic impulse is a kind of insidious violence" (18). Instead, in *Caribbean Discourse*, he discusses the African and the Creole folktale as a model of "a stylized reading of the real" (83). The tale can "combat the sometimes paralyzing ... yearning for history" and can "react to a gap in history by simply acknowledging it." Unlike myth, which "consecrates the word," the folktale attacks "the sacred status of the written word" (84). However, the tale can sometimes be a vehicle for myth. Philip's narrative combines the tale and the mythic mode. It has the fragmented nature of the Creole folktale and exhibits what Glissant calls "the emphatic emptiness of the landscape." Glissant's comment on the landscape in the Creole folktale is a fit description of the setting in *Looking for Livingstone*: "landscape is reduced to symbolic space and becomes a pattern of succeeding spaces through which one journeys" (129). Similarly, Philip's treatment of time corresponds to Glissant's perception of the Caribbean poetics of time in which the dimension of time is neither harmonious nor linear. According to him, the advance of time is "marked by a polyphony of dramatic shocks, at the level of the conscious as well as unconscious, between incongruous phenomena or 'episodes' so disparate that no link can be discerned" (106–7).

As a decolonizing text,[18] engaged with subversion of dominant discourses, Philip's *Looking for Livingstone* is translative by virtue of its creative transformation of the received referential codes:

> Like translation, subversion is always a twice-written discourse, transforming an original text by supplementation. Like translation, subversion is always referential to another text, conceding priority, even if only chronological, to that other text, and negotiating some kind of dominant/submissive relationship with it. But unlike linguistic translation, subversion seeks to displace, replace, or deface the original text rather than seeking primarily to supplement it. (Karamcheti 185)

But Philip's text becomes more than subversion when it strategically reverts to silence. As a "re/version" that stages an impossible dialogic encounter between "your word *against* my silence," it dodges the expectation to assume a supplementary role in relation to the European "original." Its paradoxical performance of this silence testifies to a crisis of representation that cannot be explained through conventional literary historical narratives of anxiety of influence, cultural continuity, or indebtedness to tradition. Her resistant translation reveals the aporias of the concept of gift giving that has animated our discussion of translation's genealogical and invigorating functions. What the idealized rhetoric of giving masks is the fact of unequal economic exchanges that sustain capitalist rationality, which appropriates the "gifts" from its others—women or colonized peoples—by stealing their bodies, resources, and labour, or alternately, imposes as "gifts" (of language, writing, "civilization," modernity, economic development—the list can go on) what it considers a debt to be repaid. Philip's creative intervention exposes such Eurocentric economies of the counterfeit gift as a site of ideological oppression linked to the systemic inequalities and exploitive power relations of late capitalist postmodernity.

It seems that in *Looking for Livingstone* translation reaches its limit, becoming a liberatory practice of creolization, deconstructing those theories and practices of translation that insist on boundaries. Most important, however, it deconstructs ways of thinking about language as "property" and language as "proper," in other words, language as the arena of domination and standardization. When The Traveller teaches Livingstone the pronunciation of the *proper* name (in a double sense of "correctness" and "property") of the Victoria Falls, an English substitute for the original native name Mosioatyuna, meaning "the smoke that thunders" (LFL 7), she shows that a claim to control correctness and property rights in languages is always an arbitrary imposition. bell hooks views the normative use of standard English by white supremacist society as "a weapon to silence and censor" and to suppress non-English voices (299). Against this policing of imperial boundaries, she calls for "the acknowledgement and/or celebration of diverse voices and consequently diverse languages and speech [that disrupt] the primacy of standard English" (hooks 300). From this perspective, perhaps the sense of Philip's words might one day be changed: "The word does not belong to you"—it belongs to everyone.

Jamaica Kincaid's *The Autobiography of My Mother*

> This tongue that I have mastered
> has mastered me;
> has taught me curses
> in the language of the master
> has taught me bondage
> in the language of the master
> I speak this dispossession
> In the language of the master (Abena Busia, "Caliban")

Like *Looking for Livingstone*, *The Autobiography of My Mother* is the allegorical staging of translation of colonialism into life writing. Set in colonial Dominica, before the independence in 1967, it spans the life of Xuela Claudette Richardson, from her birth, which coincides with her mother's death, to the age of seventy, when she tells her story, preparing to die. The theme of abandonment functions as a unifying element of Kincaid's allegory, its meanings emerging palimpsestically through the layering of Xuela's grief: as a motherless child betrayed by her father; a girl and woman devalued by patriarchy; a national subject brutalized by her country; a racialized colonial "other" defined through the Eurocentric gaze; and a speaker excluded from language because of her gender, poverty, and race. On the metafictional level, parallel motifs converge in the challenges faced by Jamaica Kincaid, a writer bequeathed with a postcolonial legacy of *ressentiment* and negativity not dissimilar from her protagonist's. Consequently, a multi-level thematic allegory linking abandonment with the history of colonialism expands into an antithetical literary allegory signifying on the received notions of subjectivity, agency, and autobiographical genre. The colonial violence that engenders the subject remains deeply entrenched in the project of self-representation, and it is easy to misunderstand this text through a(n)esthetic readings removed from the painful historical and sociopolitical contexts.[19]

As a signifying structure, Kincaid's text dialogically invokes and responds to an extensive network of intertextual references, ranging from particular works, to styles, traditions, genres, and theoretical discourses. From a black female postcolonial perspective, it tells a story reminiscent of Charlotte Bronte's *Jane Eyre* and Jean Rhys's *Wide Sargasso Sea*, whereas through its title it conjures Rosellen Brown's *The Autobiography of My Mother*, published in 1976, and Gertrude Stein's *The Autobiography of Alice B. Toklas*. In addition to allegory and biblical allusions, it engages with classical myth and African and Caribbean folklore as it endows the narrator with the characteristics of Echo, Narcissus, and Persephone, as well as Mammywata, the West African river goddess and trickster figure.[20] Apart from its obvious affinities with Caribbean and African American philosophy, reinforced by the book's dedication to Derek Walcott, Kincaid's narrative is a site of intersection of many theoretical intertexts derived from psychoanalysis, trauma theories, postcolonial theories, feminist theories, or queer theories of fetishism and sadomasochism. Some of the theoretical concepts that can be (or have been) applied to the text include Freud's pre-Oedipal phase and narcissism, Lacan's mirror stage, Kristeva's abjection,

Melanie Klein's theory of artistic creation, Nancy Chodorov's and Luce Irigaray's maternal ethics, or Anne Cheng's melancholy of race. This quick overview does not yet exhaust the possibilities of contextualizing Kincaid's writing, but I want to argue that the most relevant intertext for *The Autobiography of My Mother* is Frantz Fanon's *Black Skin, White Masks* (1952). In relation to Fanon's text, Kincaid's narrative performs what Henry Louis Gates Jr. in his discussion of Ralph Ellison calls "formal signifying," understood as a complex and inherently polemical relationship based on repetition and inversion that, to use Ellison's words, takes the form of "*a technical assault against the styles* which have gone before" (in Gates 294), which results in inscribing continuity with a difference.

In fact, Kincaid's book might be seen as a translation into fiction of Fanon's philosophical essay, offering a female gendered response to his quest for disalienation of the black colonial subject. Both texts experiment with new ways of writing postcolonial (in the sense of "post-contact") subjectivities and attempt to carve out new heterogeneous spaces for life writing that moves between theory and experience, experience and fictionalization.[21] Both projects are "haunted by the problems of love and understanding" (Fanon 8), foregrounding their common affective, political, and epistemological dimensions. Both grow from an understanding that no "purity" of identity is possible for the colonized and the colonizers alike, deconstructing the rigid binarism of black and white. Fanon's "black skin" and "white masks" are both surface screens onto which a culture obsessed with "epidermalization" projects meaning and value. He pursues the consequences of Du Bois's double-consciousness, interpreted as the black subject's "double alienation" from "his own race" and from the Europeans "who shaped him into their own image" (64). For him, as for Kincaid, the psychic and the social texts are intertwined, and the problem of racism and stereotyping is "the product of a psychological-economic system" (35), grounded in the material conditions and ideology of colonialism.[22] Hence, they both offer an indictment of whiteness and European culture with its "myths of progress, civilization, liberalism, education, enlightenment, refinement" (Fanon 194).

Xuela, Kincaid's black schoolgirl in Dominica, can be viewed as a counter-response to Fanon's "black schoolboy in the Antilles, who in his lessons is forever talking about 'our ancestors, the Gauls,' identifies himself with the explorer, the bringer of civilization, the white man who carries truth to savages—an all-white truth" (147). Kincaid seems to supply an answer to the aporia of black femininity in Fanon, redirecting onto Xuela, a black colonial woman, Fanon's stated purpose of helping "the black man to free himself of the arsenal of complexes that has been developed by the colonial environment" (30). Through her portraits of typical colonial characters, she also reproduces similar divisions and hierarchies in Dominica as those described by Fanon in Martinique: the inferiority of blacks, the superiority of white-identified Dominicans like Xuela's father, and the privileged position of whites. Her Dominica is "the small world" of people ravaged by terror, brutality, greed, and self-hate, whose subjectivity has been destroyed by colonialism, leaving them with no empathy, no pity, no "instinct to protect the weak" (AMM 20). It is a reality without love and solidarity, where fear and distrust create further separations and divisions. However, the most important commonality between Fanon and Kincaid is the spirit of defiance and the rejection of crippling "amputations" imposed by colonial constructions of Black subjectivity that Fanon summarizes in the following passage:

> I was responsible at the same time for my body, for my race, for my ancestors. I subjected myself to an objective examination, I discovered my blackness, my ethnic characteristics; and I was battered down by tom-toms, cannibalism, intellectual deficiency, fetishism [*sic*], racial defects, slave-ships, and above all else, above all: 'Sho' good eatin.'" (112)

Xuela's negations echo Fanon's: "My Negro consciousness does not hold itself out as a lack. It *is*. It is its own follower" (135). Through her interrogations of what it means to be human, Kincaid also shares Fanon's concern with humanism, different from the Eurocentric tradition of humanist ethics, with its universalistic sources in self (Kant), god (Christianity), or the other (Levinas). For Fanon, the existence of racism poses an ethical dilemma that hits him head-on: "I am enraged, I am bled white by an appalling battle, I am deprived of the possibility of being a man. I cannot dissociate myself from the future that is proposed for my brother. Every one of my acts commits me as a man. Every one of my silences, every one of my cowardices reveals me as a man" (88–89). For this kind of anti-racist humanism, the problem of restoring humanity to a human being involves an ethical obligation to recognize, name, and oppose any form of racism and exploitation.

A closer look at the first paragraph of *The Autobiography of My Mother*—beginning with the sentence, "My mother died at the moment I was born, and so for my whole life there was nothing standing between myself and eternity; at my back was always a bleak, black wind" (AMM 3)—reveals similarities to Fanon's figurative statement of his intention to descend "into a real hell" and to explore Black subjectivity as "the zone of nonbeing" (8). At the same time, Kincaid's passage epitomizes her characteristic writing strategies that I will discuss under the rubric of allegorization, rhetoricity, indeterminacy, or negativity, as well as the theme of abandonment. The entire opening stages a mini-allegory of the birth of an African Caribbean diasporic subject. A palimpsestic effect of the superimposition of the Middle Passage ("a bleak, black wind" at her back) and the genocide of the Caribs (her mother's death) captures the complex histories caught up in the economy of loss and gain. Introducing the allegorizing impulse, the paragraph also introduces a poetics of indeterminacy as well as the rhetoric of negativity that animates the entire text. The narrator's "backward and forward" look might be said to enfold her heterogeneous braided traditions (African and indigenous Carib—the past—and Caribbean and European—the future of the newborn orphan). With her life framed by death, she is thrown into this negative space of nothingness ("the black room of the world"). Based on the substitution of mother/mother tongue and the images of blackness bracketing her life as "standing on the precipice" and crossing into "nothing" ("at my end was nothing"), it is possible to read these images in terms of the condition of the postcolonial subject whose life recapitulates the rupture of the Middle Passage, between the loss of the mother tongue (and the maternal narrative) and the space of non-being marked by the father tongue and his symbolic order, from which she is excluded. The passage signals the themes of dispossession, loss, and lack ("more of some of the things I had scarcely had at all") as well as the motif of the melancholy of race ("overwhelmed with sadness and shame and pity for myself"), while setting the tone for the narrative through the affective function of the narrator's self-description as "vulnerable, hard, and helpless" (AMM 4). Even the elements of Kincaid's literary signifying are already identifiable in these opening lines, which gesture to Dante's *Divine Comedy*, another multi-level allegory, with its epic beginning *in medias res* and descent into hell and purgatory—a journey to the underground to meet the dead. Using a black female narrator who "in the middle of [her] life" gains self-understanding, Kincaid's text is recoding the meaning of the spiritual quest and rewriting a famous topos of Western literature: writing as dealing with the spirits.

The Autobiography of My Mother is a hyper-rhetorical text punctuated with "metaphorical asterisks" (223) to signal its continually productive rhetoricity. The build-up of allegorical meanings in the text occurs through the performative and symbolic structure of unveiling, which is both a rhetorical figure and a strategy of double discourse, alluding to Du Bois's image of the veil that splits the consciousness of the African American subject, but also to Fanon's "white mask" that represents colonial mimicry and alienation. Unveiling as an "allegorogene" (Bal 61) generates multiple meanings, for example through the proliferation of the imagery of clothing. Xuela's mother appears to her in dreams, descending a ladder, with only a foot and a hem of her dress visible, suggesting the elusiveness of her Carib heritage. Even the visual "bookmarks" inserted between the chapters perform the movement of unveiling, gradually revealing what might be Xuela's or her mother's likeness, a *trompe l'oeil* of the (auto)biographical truth uncovered.[23] However, the text also signals that there are limits to any unveiling of truth, particularly in a postcolonial and poststructuralist frame. Clothing or masking may be adopted to protect the subject from a threat or terror. Xuela's withdrawal from self-disclosure with her white husband Philip Bailey, a refusal "to allow him an entry into [her] deepest thoughts" (226), doubles as a warning for the reader to keep a respectful distance. Similarly, the "allegorogenic" function of clothing contributes to the possibility of metafictional reading of such images as Ma Eunice's dress: "Dirt had made it old, but dirt had made it new again by giving it shadings it did not have before, and dirt would finally cause it to disintegrate altogether" (10). Ma Eunice, a figure of the laundress who returns in Kincaid (and also in Fanon), is a charged representation of gendered colonial poverty, ironically suggesting the ubiquity of dirt in colonialism. At the same time, the old colonial garb of her dress rewoven by dirt refracts Kincaid's method of retelling negated stories through denegation. Finally, clothing is also related to the abstract, moral level of her allegory, reminiscent of medieval morality plays such as "Everyman," where unclothed and naked, oppressors and oppressed must reckon with life, faced with death as "the only reality ... the only certainty, inevitable to all things" (228).

As a form of resistant, polemical discourse, Kincaid's narrative is also involved in what might be called genealogical revisionism, conducted, on the one hand, through the practice of (un)naming and, on the other hand, through reclaiming her maternal inheritance, both acts partaking of the dynamic of unveiling of what is not apparent to the eye or to consciousness. The topos of (un)naming has a long-standing tradition in African diasporic writing, where it functions as a symbolic gesture of self-possession performed by the formerly enslaved subjects. Kimberly Benston discusses unnaming as an act "that sees all labels formulated by the master society ('they') as enslaving fictions" (151). Kincaid's narrator remains anonymous for one-third of the narrative and reveals her name for the first time through identification with her mother:

> "Xuela Claudette Desvarieux." This was my mother's name, but I cannot say it was her real name, for in a life like hers, as in mine, what is a real name? My own name is her name, Xuela Claudette, and in the place of the Desvarieux is Richardson, which is my father's name; but who are these people Claudette, Desvarieux, and Richardson? To look into it, to look at it, could only fill you with despair; the humiliation could only make you intoxicated with self-hatred. For the name of any one person is at once her history recapitulated and abbreviated. (AMM 79)

Her mother, an abandoned Carib child with the name "Xuela" written on a piece of cloth found on her, was discovered by a Catholic nun who renamed her after herself. The name "Xuela" survived this ethnocentric attempt to imprint the baby with "an inaugural mark of enslavement" (Benston 158) and was passed on to the daughter, becoming her badge of resilience. By contrast, her stepbrother was named after her father, Alfred, who in turn was named after Alfred the Great, the English king. The foreign name not only proved fatal for the boy, who died young, but it brought sterility and lack of fulfillment for her father, a colonial functionary, who failed to produce a "dynasty." Xuela does not blame her father for his own name but holds him responsible for perpetuating a (deadly) colonial legacy through his son's naming. Her own name functions oppositionally through multiple possible encodings of indigeneity, Caribbeanness, Africanness, or even the tradition of anti-racist resistance and poststructuralist indeterminacy. "Xuela" is reminiscent of the title of Edward Kamau Brathwaite's 1987 book *X/Self*, but also of "Zulu" and of the "X" in the name of Malcolm X as "a symbol not of something unnamable but of something unknowable—the inaugural African identity that was usurped during Middle Passage" (Benston 153), or her unknown Carib ancestry. The "X" in Xuela's name evokes both the anonymity of the allegorical subject and the self that is crossed out, "under-erasure" and/or "in-process," through its constant rapprochement with death. Moreover, the name Xuela Claudette Richardson is an extradeigetic pointer directing us to Kincaid's real name, Elaine Potter Richardson, and to her habit of recycling familial names so as to draw her protagonists into an autobiographical space that defies the conventional boundaries between fiction and autobiography as well as the inside/outside demarcations of her texts.²⁴

There is an important connection between the urge to unname and the need to reject the authority of colonial discursive constructs, thematized through a juxtaposition of the observing self and the colonial gaze. In a lengthy meditation Xuela ponders the wonder of human existence and a beholding, loving look that follows this wonder from infancy to old age, implicitly contrasting this nurturing look with the situation of the subject abandoned to the lovelessness of the colonial gaze:

> All this is something so wonderful to observe, so wonderful to behold; the pleasure for the observer, the beholder, is an invisible current between the two, observed and observer, beheld and beholder, and I believe that no life is complete, no life is really whole, without this invisible current, which is in many ways a definition of love. No one observed and beheld me, I observed and beheld myself; the invisible current went out and it came back to me. I came to love myself in defiance, out of despair, because there was nothing else. (AMM 56–57)

The allegorical possibilities of reading this passage are numerous: on the literal level, it is the story of her coping with maternal abandonment; on the moral level, it is a parable of the ethics of human relationships founded upon love and the imperative of "witnessing" to the presence of other human beings, which has been perverted under colonialism; on the metafictional level, it is an apology for autobiography as an act of (self)love, a substitute for witnessing. Xuela observes and beholds not only herself; she refracts her colonial environment, all the while refusing to be absorbed into the dominant ways of seeing. As a result, she becomes an unnaming voice for everything she observes, assuming historical and individual agency and autonomy and passing to a different order of representation.

Xuela's complex genealogy allows her to become the voice of the repressed history of the Caribbean, braiding together the four strands of her Carib, African, Dominican, and European heritage. It demonstrates how creolization of these diverse and conflicted influences and traditions complicates any simplistic reading of diasporic identities. While each part of her legacy is wrought up with pain, it is her maternal inheritance that is the most potent source of identification for her, an identification which reveals a gaping absence at the core of her self through its grounding in the originary act of matricide, allegorically echoing the historical genocide of indigenous people that has pre-empted any possibility of "wholeness" for the Caribbean diasporic subject. Xuela's dreams, expressive of her longing to see the face of her absent mother, introduce the figure of anacoluthon, an elliptical device that points to the haunting presence of an absent companion, as "at once the motor, the motivation, and the dramatic emotion" of her narrative (Derrida, "Le Parjure" 222). As a figure of accompaniment, defined as "letting stand alone a word that calls out for another as companion," the anacoluthon "speaks of lack, solitude, aloneness, mourning in the language" (Derrida, "Le Parjure" 215) and implicates Xuela's narrative as "a wanting narrative" both in the sense of desire and lack. At the same time, the image of being trapped under the heel of the dead mother holds the ambivalence of having to deal with the oppressive bearing of the past.

The unveiling of Xuela's Carib legacy is counterpointed with her reflection on the condition of the African descendants on the island, who are described as humiliated and suffering from self-loathing. From both ancestral groups, she takes her strength to resist oppression and survive. Using indigenous knowledge, she teaches herself about medicinal and poisonous herbs and plants. Although Africa to her is a distant place on the map, and she rejects the defeated, vanquished aspect of being African, she indirectly establishes continuity with Africa by embracing Creole African folklore and obeah. She aligns herself with this outlaw knowledge, deconstructing colonialism's distortion and devaluation of native lives and beliefs. A cultural and epistemic "murder" of non-European traditions from a position of Eurocentric superiority leaves the colonized in shame and denial of their own beliefs. She refuses to be silenced and defiantly accepts the truth considered to be "the belief of the illegitimate, the poor, and the low" (38). At the same time, through her father's ancestry, she also embodies the entwined histories of slavery and white slaveholders. Caught in between divided loyalties to the "victor" and to the "vanquished," her father chooses to identify with dominant values and embraces the legacy of his white "Scots-man" father, accumulating wealth unusual for a man of African descent. Xuela interprets her father's colonial mimicry as a sign of defeat, in which the conquered worship the conquerors' gods: religion and capitalism (symbolized by money). However, even while exposing the damages in colonial society she never ceases to signify against those truly responsible for these damages, hinting at the colonizers' cruelty and greed as the "original" model translated into colonial "mimics" like her father.

Kincaid's text delivers a scathing critique of white supremacy, which not only passes off its privilege as invisible, but also obscures its economic motives. The profit made from colonialism, from stealing commodities from far-away places, is used to hide "the forced labor, the crippling, the early death of the unnamed many" (135). Focusing on language as an ideological filter, she exposes its false "translations" between the empirical and the cognitive categories when the spoils of colonialism are renamed as "English tea," "English cocoa," or "English silk." In a brilliant example of signifying, Xuela deconstructs the words of a religious hymn whose author asks Jesus to be his "Master and [his] friend." With different connotations of "master" to the slaves, she dismisses "this Master and friend business" as impossible because white man as master "cannot be a friend" (134). Asking his god to be his master and friend, the white man "asks for himself the very thing he cannot give" (138). Yet, in her depiction of the two portraits of English colonial types in Philip Bailey, a doctor and naturalist who embodies white dominant rationality, and Moira, his first wife who embodies white superiority and dominance, Xuela pierces beyond the appearances of power. She discovers that they, too, are damaged by colonialism, which causes spiritual death and dehumanization on both sides. However, "the despair of the victor and the despair of the vanquished" are incommensurate because of "the bottomless well of pain and misery that the conquered experiences" (192). Raising the question of justice and responsibility, the narrator's voice spans a complex register of ridicule, judgement, and compassion, all of which still reinforce the indictment of whiteness as locked up in denial of its own transgressions, and hence forfeiting even the possibility of self-forgiveness premised on the ability to confess. As she claims, "to forgive yourself for your transgressions against others is not a right that anybody can claim" (220).

The allegorizing of the island's history finds a powerful correlative in the descriptions of the landscape and the sea. Xuela attaches great importance to the formative influence of "the meeting of people and place," believing that consciousness is shaped by physical surroundings. Dominica is described as "a false paradise ... at once beautiful, ugly, humble, and proud; full of life, full of death" (32), surrounded by the mass grave of the ocean in which the slave traders' ships and their cargo lay buried. For Xuela, the experience of natural beauty is the source of comfort because, in contrast to people, nature "was itself; nothing could be added to it; nothing could be taken away from it" (26), even though people can contaminate it with death. While she dreams of repossessing the land that used to belong to the Caribs, her denied maternal inheritance, she rejects her father's inheritance, a piece of land he bought for her as an investment. Xuela's father represents the capitalist venture economy which has encroached upon the land to exploit its resources. We learn that as a young boy he received a gift of an egg and turned it into enormous profit, which he then gave to his father, who left for Scotland and never came back. This tale of the profit derived from a gift, followed by a betrayal by the European father, illustrates a "*père*-version" (Kristeva's term) of the economy of the gift that replaces traditional sharing and reciprocity with modern self-interest. The indigenous economy of the gift extends also to the gift of the land and the sea, to the entire island whose beauty is lost on those who have erected on it a system that breeds cruelty, greed, and misery. In terms of moral allegory constructed by Kincaid's text, the meeting of people and place under colonialism leads to an inevitable disjunction between beauty and ethics. This unveiling of beauty in the middle of despair, which Xuela describes as occurring "in parts, not all at once" and as giving her a "feeling of gladness at the sight of the new and strange, the unfamiliar" (62), can serve as a metafictional metaphor that approximates the effect of Kincaid's own writing, which deals with the translation of pain into an aesthetic form.

Kincaid's narrative offers a dark vision of the colonial diaspora, haunted by dispossession, non-belonging, and absence. Such negativity weighs heavily on the possibility of self-representation of the African Caribbean female subject, who must speak from within and against "a ruling episteme" that privileges the white masculine norm, forcing her to inhabit "the reality of that always-insisted-on difference" (Cheng 7). Xuela's voice manages to create a counter-ideology to the totalizing discourses of racism and patriarchy by strategically placing her in the space of negativity and saturating her language with rhetorical and syntactic negations. She situates herself outside of the social order, as "a person who doesn't understand money or love" (184), and refuses to accept belonging to a race or a nation, which she perceives as "the crime of ... identities" (226). Kincaid's signifying on the notion of unreliable narrator, through Xuela's repeated denials of the accuracy and truthfulness of her comments, works against the Western will to clarity and the oppressive binary logic of rationalism, complicating any unequivocal recuperation of the "truth" of the subject. Moreover, the choice of negativity is also evident in the textual constructions of resistant, subversive subjectivity that defiantly literalizes the Eurocentric and patriarchal definitions of the subject through "blackness" and "femininity" conceived of as "lack." By flaunting Xuela's status as a disinherited daughter, emphatically "not a son," the text genders the tradition of the hidden polemic with the received ideas of blackness and femininity as negative essences, as "others" defined "negatively vis-à-vis a master who is the only 'proper' person and full subject of history" (Lionnet, "Of Mangoes" 330). In this sense, Kincaid's narrator literally embraces the externally imposed negativity, turning it into her own contestatory space: "the respectable, the predictable—such was not to be my own destiny" (73). When the content of the "self" is disfigured by the patriarchal, racist gaze, refusal and negation become forms of negotiation of agency from a position of exclusion, of twisting power out of oppression. Xuela's stance of "negative affirmation" (Benston 157) forces us to rethink agency, showing that internalization of oppression is a reductive notion and that dominant, normative meanings can be disrupted through signifying.

The use of antiphrastic language, which relies on negation, refutation, and indeterminacy, is associated with the acquisition of subjectivity and the emergence of anti-hegemonic discourse. Analyzing the role of negation in the course of language acquisition, Julia Kristeva notes that not only does the beginning of the use of negation coincide with the mirror stage, with the subject's separation and splitting from the mother, but also that negativity is a crossroads that allows us to capture the "production of this subject as a [heterogeneous] process, an intersection—an impossible unity" (*Revolution* 118). Such "subject in process/on trial" uses the language abundant in negative statements and rejection, thereby disrupting accepted linguistic structures and established ideologies of the dominant social order (of the family, state, or the body proper) while conducting the struggle against the signifier. For Kristeva, this negativity of the text, when it becomes a driving force of the signifying process, "produces new cultural and social formations which are innovative and—under specific conditions ... subversive" (*Revolution* 162). Kincaid's narrative seems to be governed by heterogeneous rejection and therefore is representative of what Kristeva calls "a revolutionary social practice" (*Revolution* 191), or what Deleuze and Guattari subsume under the category of "minor literature" (where "minor" stands for "revolutionary").[25] Xuela adopts the position of a heterogeneous subject within the dominant symbolic order, speaking from within the system, but through the logic of negativity and rejection. It is a position in which she cannot be "othered" (like foreignized translation), assimilated (like domesticated translation), or pushed out and confined into a pluralized "third space" of translation. Rather, her "re/version" allows her a radical reworking and transforming of meaning from within the system itself, looking for new ways of translating between thought and world.[26] From the hegemonic perspective, such "re/version" is "perverse" and must be expelled outside of the system into the sphere of abjection. As a heterogeneous border-subject, the abject constantly threatens the wholeness, solidity, and identity of a social order from which it is expelled but for which it remains present as an ambiguous marker and reminder of the fluidity of limits, rules, and confines. The subject of abjection is the one who "neither gives up nor assumes a prohibition, a rule, or a law; but it turns them aside, misleads, corrupts; uses them, takes advantage of them, the better to deny them" (Kristeva, *Powers* 8), Likewise, Xuela refuses to internalize the "law" but ingests it in order to spew it back, to assume it with a difference, exposing its errors by means of rhetorical manipulation and signifying. Kristeva recognizes the courage of the subject in incorporating and unveiling abjection in order to challenge homogeneity as "eminently productive of culture" (45), capable, like Kincaid, of devising languages and literary works in which "the abject collapses in a burst of beauty that overwhelms us" (*Powers* 210).

It may be tempting to see Xuela as Kincaid's response to a personality type that Fanon calls "a black abandonment-neurotic" (79). Quoting Germaine Guex's psychoanalytic work on this type of pre-Oedipal neurosis, Fanon describes such a person as egocentric, aggressive, vengeful, deprived of affective security, and possessed by "an overwhelming feeling of impotence in relation to life and people" (73). The abandonment-neurotic has an acute sense of being "the Other" and therefore is always on guard, always in a shaky position: "Imprisoned in himself, locked into his artificial reserve, the negative-aggressive feeds his feeling of irreparable loss with everything that he continues to lose" (Fanon 78). Like this neurotic type discussed by Fanon, Xuela has experienced an abusive childhood and adolescence, marked by lack of love and understanding, which explains her "inner melancholy" (Fanon 74). Likewise, she has been early "apprenticed to loneliness" (Fanon 75). However, while Fanon contends that the neurotic structure of an individual is simply a reaction to conflicts "arising in part out of the environment and in part out of the purely personal way in which that individual reacts to these influences" (81), Kincaid's narrator actively resists the possibility of pathologizing her condition and shifts a diagnosis onto a culture that produces symbolic abandonment and exclusion. "Neurosis" then can be used more accurately as a metaphor for the violations of human rights perpetrated under colonialism and in its aftermath rather than a description of Xuela's psychic structure. In fact, far from accepting the "affective devaluation of self" that characterizes Fanon's neurotic (76), she negotiates her agency by means of strategies that allow her not only to cope with the status of the object thrust upon her, but also to put colonialism and racism on trial. In this, she is akin to Kristeva's subject of abjection, constituted as the excluded, the outside-of-meaning, and situated "at the boundary of what is assimilable, thinkable" (*Powers* 18).

Xuela has a gift of tongue, and, consequently, her greatest triumph is as an artist, in the execution of her narrative. Letter writing, which she begins at the age of seven, is established as another metafictional "allegorogene." It teaches her about the power of writing to effect change in her situation as, indeed, her father comes to rescue her from the school ordeal. While it makes her realize the value of writing as interpersonal exchange that grows from the need for communication and requires the presence of the other, letter writing at the same time allows her to become practised in the use of double discourse and to navigate the risks of self-exposure and the possibility of misreading. Her narrative is a disguised letter meant for her absent mother. A story of the defeated translated into a linguistic tour de force, it embodies a kind of performative paradox of agency: a painful acquisition of language is turned into a useful tool for self-expression and a substitute for connection. Significantly, her entry into writing is immediately recognized as running against gender and class norms prescribed in her world: "It was well known that a person in the position that I was expected to occupy—the position of a woman and a poor one—would have no need whatsoever to write a letter" (AMM 18). It is but one in a series of acts defying a gender identity scripted according to patriarchal, colonial expectations. Stepping outside all conventions, she would not wear the uniform of femininity and would reject sexual modesty and motherhood. But she also avoids the trappings of the binary logic of victim–victimizer, or male–female, recognizing that in her world no simple assignment of moral judgement or blame is possible. Observing and recording the reality of suffering, her own and that of women and men around her, Xuela adopts a stance of non-indifference to pain. Her acts of renunciation constitute a symbolic refusal of reproduction of the pain of colonialism, of the whole legacy of "origins" into which one is born. The self-knowledge she gains after the abortion, looking at her reflection in the river, reveals her as anti-Narcissus, to whom Eurocentric psychoanalytic theories cannot apply literally. She begins to embrace herself in order to find comfort in a willed act of self-love as a precondition of survival: "No matter how swept away I would become by anyone or anything, in the end I allowed nothing to replace my own being in my own mind" (100).

Fanon describes the black body as "overdetermined from without" (116), associating blackness with the burden of "corporeal malediction" produced by negative and devaluing representations of black bodies in white discourse (11). Xuela's calm resolve to resist the colonial gaze which imposes meaning onto her body echoes his decision to reject fiery polemic and self-defensive refutation for the sake of a more detached and methodical "digging into his own flesh to find a meaning" (Fanon 9). However, in contrast to Fanon's anxious black man who "cannot escape his body" (65), Kincaid's narrator chooses the consolation of her black female body and claims the full right to re-signify its value to her while also signifying through it. Transgressing the standards of "civilization," she mockingly literalizes racist associations of the African body with nature by flaunting her sensual pleasure in touching herself and enjoying her intimate smells. She withdraws into the immediate, sensory territory of her embodiment, into celebration of her corporeality, loving what she has been told to hate (32). Examining herself in a broken piece of mirror, she voices total acceptance of her body against Eurocentric beauty norms (58). The centrality of the body in Kincaid's narrative, as well as her focus on rendering the phenomenological experience of embodiment, contributes to her de-emphasizing the Western metaphysics of subjectivity. The metaphor of Xuela touching herself poses a challenge to the predominance of vision in Western epistemology as a masculinist way of organizing, subordinating, and controlling reality. Her immersion in the sensory world of sight, touch, hearing, and smell, registering her perception of texture, pain, and pleasure, might be seen as related to her critical stance against the privileged status of the gaze, its reductiveness and objectification. As a contact sense, touch is metonymic; "the surface of the toucher and the touched must partially coincide," providing "contiguous access to an abiding object" (Grosz 98). Touch foregrounds the dual status of the body as a threshold between being the subject and being the object, which is one of the main paradoxes of autobiographical representation. In tactile perception "the gulf between subject and object is never so distant as in vision" (Grosz 101). There is a fundamental reversibility "between touching and being touched, between seeing and being seen" (Grosz 100), which is lost to the gaze of the imperial "I." If this reversibility helps us to undo the power of dualistic thinking (subject/object), then autobiography as touching oneself, which embodies this reversibility, has a potential to change our habitual patterns of thought and to develop new epistemologies of the subject.

Xuela's signifying through the body finds a strong expression in her treatment of sexuality, bringing to mind again Fanon's preoccupation with the theme of racialized sexuality and sexualized race, specifically his reference to biology and genitality as racist marks attached to the black body. While in the "othering" discourses used by Europeans the racialized body connotes animalistic physicality, racialized sexuality has been associated with deviance and excessive carnal appetites. Kincaid's text refracts this arrogant, fetishizing gaze and hyperbolizes the European libidinal fantasies through Xuela's unabashed sexuality, which has been linked to narcissism and sadomasochism.[27] However, her attitude to sex must be understood in the context of her struggle for agency as yet another example of ironic mimicry, where the oppressed subject embraces her sexual abjection in a gesture of mock-compliance, transforming it effectively into powerful transgression. Such is the case of her sexual initiation at the age of fifteen, where she manipulates her limited agency, from being watched by Monsieur LaBatte while she is masturbating, to holding his gaze and directing the scene, until she is ordered to remove her clothes. Although the entire episode apparently plays on the ambivalence of rape/seduction, it leaves no doubt as to the affective impact of this act on Xuela, who comments: "The inevitable is no less a shock just because it is inevitable" (AMM 69).

Similarly, one of the longest sexual scenes in the novel, the enactment of sadomasochistic, or S/M, sexuality between Xuela and Philip Bailey, challenges the dynamics of dominance and submission fundamental to the patriarchal and colonial contract. The image of "an Afro-Carib woman bound by her European lover, then following the steps typical of S/M psychodrama" (Holomb and Holomb 969) is loaded with painful associations. Echoing Xuela's first punishment by Ma Eunice, it triggers a similar allegorizing impulse and becomes "redolent of the relationship between captor and captive, master and slave, with its motif of the big and the small, the powerful and the powerless, the strong and the weak" (10). But unlike that early cameo of the girl kneeling on stones, the scene of mature Xuela's self-bondage allows her to repossess her objectified body by shifting the gendered and racialized notions of control and vulnerability, power and passivity, agency and bondage. Consistent with the textual irony of repetition with a difference, Xuela's image is an uneasy recollection of the scenes of whipping preserved in the cultural memory of slavery. The performance of S/M sexuality, with a palimpsestic historical trace of "slave and master," is also a reversal of colonialism, where "fantasies" were turned into a horrifying reality. S/M then can be taken as a productive analogue for the economy of Kincaid's narrative that situates itself in the space of the slash, suggesting cutting or being cut off rather than connection. In the context of our earlier remarks on the interstitial spaces occupied by translation, the slash represents a different mode of "in-between-ness" compared to the hyphen operating in other, mostly white, immigrant figurations of translation, which are more or less assimilatory in kind. The slash in Kincaid's racialized text is also the slash of "re/version," underscoring exclusion and distance, that is, a more tense dynamic in the positioning of the translating and the translated subject.[28]

At the same time, the enactment of the colonial/sexual fantasies of bondage implicates the reader as voyeur in the scene. There is a slippage in the narrative voice from "I" to "you," which momentarily unsettles the diegetic boundary, drawing the reader into Xuela's room, which is filled with "hisses, gasps, moans, sighs, tears, bursts of laughter" that "would make you cover your ears unless they came from inside you, until you realized that they came from inside you; all these sounds came from me" (AMM 155). This "you" refers to Xuela as participant as well as to the reader as voyeur, perhaps also to Xuela as reader. Her elaborate description of Philip Bailey's skin, "thin and pink and transparent, as if it were on its way to being skin but not yet reached the state that real skin is" (152), constructs whiteness—Philip's and potentially the reader's—as a ghostly presence in this scene of colonial encounter. We can see here a conflation of metaphor and metonymy, identification and contiguity. What begins with S/M as a metaphor for colonial relations gets transformed into a metonymy of the reader's complicity or implication in the history of colonialism and slavery, throwing the reader into this whirl either through the inheritance of white privilege or a legacy of oppression. The metaphor of S/M does not exhaust the possible interpretations of Xuela's suffering, which can also be viewed in terms of trauma and its latency and the need to put pain to a creative use. Paradoxically, a performance of what is considered out of bounds, or "dehumanizing" sexuality, restores Xuela back to her "humanity," lifting her out of the role of passive victim or the defeated. Interestingly, the text "doubles" these themes in its own effect on the reader, who is provoked to devise interpretive and affective strategies in order to cope with the "pain" of reading Xuela's story. As a result, Kincaid's narrative stands as a vivid reminder of the importance of pain in the experience of reading in practising literary criticism, but also in pedagogy and education, as an aspect of witnessing trauma and confronting difficult histories from which we cannot extricate ourselves.

As mentioned before, crucial to unveiling this painful history is the way language is made to function as a vehicle for the narrative of colonialism, language which is simultaneously an instrument of oppression and empowerment. As a tool of cultural imperialism, it is used to justify exclusion and stereotyping, leading to delegitimizing, devaluing, or silencing of the speech of "others." It can literally be turned into hate speech and curses accompanying acts of abuse or punishment that Xuela is subjected to in childhood. However, any attempt to assign intrinsic meaning and value to English and Creole, based on simplistic binary constructions of "bad" and "good," or "father tongue" and "mother tongue," is constantly subverted by Xuela's (and Kincaid's) demonstration that it is the history and the uses language is put to, rather than its essential qualities, that define its status and effectiveness in any particular context. The politics of language in Dominica translates colonial relations into a hierarchically ordered system, including standard English, a vernacular, creolized form of English, and French Creole, or patois. English for Xuela is encoded with power linked to colonial and patriarchal oppression, and used by her father as part of his colonial mimicry. She resorts to English when she needs to project her strength: "I was not physically robust, my voice was weak, I was female, I spoke to [my father] only in English, proper English" (AMM 195). Similarly, at school the students speak proper English, but among themselves they use French patois, which is devalued and disrespected as "the language of the captive, the illegitimate" (74), used by the poor, by the defeated, and by women. When her stepmother, who is of African background, speaks to her in French Creole, Xuela perceives it as an attempt to make her illegitimate, to associate her "with the made-up language of people regarded as not real—the shadow people, the forever humiliated, the forever low" (30–31). As much as patois is devalued, it is also the informal and intimate language. Xuela's father speaks patois only within the family circle, or with those who had known him since childhood. The fact that he speaks to her in English rather than French Creole or creolized English can be seen as a mark of his class aspirations, but also an indicator of a distance between him and Xuela. Her late entry into speech at the age of four occurs when she asks about her father: "Where is my father?" She poses the question in English, though she has never heard anyone speak it in Ma Eunice's house. Similar to Marlene Nourbese Philip's anguish of English, she associates English with the pain of separation. Her first utterance in English might be interpreted allegorically as setting up her inquiry into history and colonialism (Morris 954).

On the other hand, Xuela links Creole, the language of the "vanquished," with an African Caribbean identity. A trajectory of her changing attitudes to Creole, from her refusal to speak it as a child, to embracing it in her old age, is related to the development of her anti-colonial attitudes, her postcolonial subjectivity, and woman-centred identity. She ends up using patois in communicating with her white husband, who in turn uses English, "speaking to each other in the language of our thoughts," neither submitting to the language of the other (219). She literally becomes a translator for him: "He now lived in a world in which he could not speak the language. I mediated for him, I translated for him. I did not always tell him the truth, I did not always tell him everything. I blocked his entrance to the world in which he lived" (224). The arrangement she describes mirrors the narrator's positioning vis-à-vis the reader and introduces translation as a metafictional trope for the text written in English but "originating" in the subject who admittedly thinks in Creole. This "mark" of translation attached to the text functions as a sign of its resistance to transparent reading and identification; it insists on preserving a residue of difference, keeping the reader at further remove from Xuela's narrative. It models the obverse of her experience of disconnect between language and reality in colonial education, where signifiers come before signifieds and refer to "somewhere else, somewhere far away" (12), like "The British Empire"—the first words she learned to read, as she named the invisible power that controlled her world.

Articulating from within the crisis of colonial languages, the text is replete with the presence of other, non-verbal languages, including body language, gesture and touch, the language of sensory perceptions, or communication through silences. This preference for the physical and the concrete over the abstract, for staying close to the body and avoiding concepts that define and contain, affects to a large extent the narrative choice of style, a choice which, according to some linguists, is always political (Talib 132). Consequently, not only Kincaid's relationship to English and Creole, but also her stylistic grounding in the phenomenological and the corporeal, should be recognized as facets of her politics of language. However, notwithstanding her critique of cultural imperialism and white supremacy that have bestowed English on her through the colonial system of education, Kincaid—like Fanon—insists on her right to dismiss or tap that legacy for her own purpose. For Fanon, speaking Creole (or dialect) "closes off the black man [and] perpetuates a state of conflict in which the white man injects the black with extremely dangerous foreign bodies. Nothing is more astonishing than to hear a black man express himself properly, for then in truth he is putting on the white world ... [saying] *no* to those who attempt to build a definition of him" (36). Fanon's argument can be used to support Kincaid's logic in her choice of standard English and her mimicry of European literary models. What Victoria Burrows calls "Kincaid's strategy of literary *backchat* and postcolonial reversal" (74) is another way of saying "no" to those who try to impose their definitions on her. Kincaid refuses to give up Milton despite the fact that she studied him under the British rule; she refuses to "forget John Milton because it involves a painful thing. I find John Milton very beautiful ... I am sorry that the circumstances of how I got to know it were horrid ... but since I know it, I know it and I claim every right to use it" (in Burrows, 74).

The attitude to language and literary tradition in *The Autobiography of My Mother* encompasses both borrowing and rupturing the conventions of autobiographical writing. Kincaid's repeated claim that her texts are autobiographical rubs against such performances of the genre that put into question the classic tenets of the autobiographical contract premised upon truth telling and identity of the text's narrator and its signatory. Adopting the metafictional form of the novel as a vehicle for her serial project of self-representation, including *At the Bottom of the River* (1983), *Annie John* (1986), *Lucy* (1991), *Autobiography of My Mother*, and *My Brother* (1997), she literalizes a fictionalizing impulse behind any construction of the autobiographical subject. Xuela as the autobiographer's figure deconstructs the unreliability of the scene of self-representation as a site of active re-membering and forgetting. Similarly, seriality, related to repetition with a difference, reveals the autobiographical subject as a function spread over several segments, a force that does not refer to a transcendental subject but rather is a vector, a movement of translation. A disruption of the convention of autobiographical authorship occurs already in the title, *The Autobiography of My Mother*, which challenges the concept of Western autobiography as "the psycho-phenomenology of the self, the egology" (Derrida, "Le Parjure" 208). The title signals a certain generic displacement or dislocation from traditional boundaries between autobiography and biography, foregrounding the interdependence of self and others and creating a confusion over authorship and ownership of selves and stories—a strategy which resonates with larger themes pertaining to questions of property rights over language and forcing us to inquire "why these questions matter so much and what they reveal about our intellectual and cultural imperatives" (Donnell 127). Such playing with the generic conventions of autobiography continues Kincaid's dialogue with Eurocentric constructions of truth, origin, and identity, exemplified earlier by her deconstruction of the relationship between metaphor and metonymy. The title is both a metonymy, substituting "my mother" for "myself," and a metaphor, using the word "autobiography" as a figure for the self.

The auto/biographical conflation in the title takes us back to the motif of borrowing that is central to life writing, where the story of the self cannot be told apart from stories of others and where anamnesis is bound up with the ethics of intersubjectivity. A visual allegory of the tensions created by the title is offered by the book's front and back covers, which function as a parergon, both a supplement and a part of the text. They show two pictures of women: one assumably a portrait of the fictional protagonist, the other a photograph of the actual author. They both frame and are framed by the title, insinuating themselves as images of the "mother" and the "daughter." They reveal Kincaid's book as a two-sided text hinged on the concept of autobiography working both inward and outward: as an autobiography of a subaltern woman re-membering the absent Carib mother and as Kincaid's autobiographical inscription of her ancestry.[29] Toward the end, Xuela's voice saying "I was new, the pages of my life had no writing on them, they were unsmudged, so clean, so smooth, so new" (AMM 214–15), becomes a metafictional metaphor of the book as an anthropomorphized "incarnation" of the author. Since photographs appended to a publication "open possibilities for grounding a viewer's experience in a life before and beyond the text" (Egan 9), the cover also visualizes the book as a veil, splitting the subject "Kincaid" along her African Caribbean roots and her American persona looking at us from a conventional author photograph on the back cover. This invaginated framing structure blurs the boundary between the inside and the outside, establishing a visual link between the text and the world. At the same time, it directs us toward a view of autobiography as an allegorical inscription of genealogy: Who am I? What am I born of? The daughter as Persephone, "per-se-phoning," that is, voicing herself through her mother's story, embodies the condition of the autobiographical subject. As noted by Susan Suleiman, psychoanalytic theory—one of Kincaid's intertexts—"places the artist, man or woman, in the position of the child" (357). If we accept this idea, Kincaid can be seen as literalizing Roland Barthes's suggestive metaphor for a writer as "someone who plays with the body of [her] mother" (in Suleiman 357).

I have previously referred to the figure of anacoluthon as one of the productive tropes in Kincaid's narrative. The way her text constructs the relationship between the autobiographical self and other selves suggests the possibility of reading autobiography as a form of anacoluthic discourse, which is illustrated by the following passage:

> This account of my life has been an account of my mother's life as much as it has been an account of mine, and even so, again it is an account of the life of the children I did not have, as it is their account of me. In me is the voice I never heard, the face I never saw, the being I came from ... This account is an account of the person who was never allowed to be and an account of the person I did not allow myself to become. (AMM 227–28)

Xuela's words conjure a multiplicity of voices, producing a dispersion of identity that threatens "the word and the concept 'I'" (Derrida, "Le Parjure" 200). The anacoluthon is a rhetorical figure capable of evoking these multiple presences and capturing the interplay of autobiography and biography. The anacoluthic substitution is realized through the use of the denegative form: "I am not." Xuela as the narrator is destined to denegation, in relation to her mother as well as the dominant gaze, opening up the text to the possibility of multiple substitutions of the subject. According to Derrida, "basically, the anacoluthon interrupts forever the relation of self, the possibility of a relation to self, or even an absolute and absolutely absolved confession of self, a report-confession. We are not present to the truth of this *us* and when we are present, the truth is not there" ("Le Parjure" 229). Viewed as anacoluthic discourse, this type of autobiography by the disenfranchised subject, haunted by negativity, potentially leads to a critique, subversion, resistance, and deconstruction of dominant concepts or fictions of "self" and conventions of self-representation.

Finally, the book's title can also be read to suggest that the text, writing self through other, can be seen as symbolically incorporating and devouring the mother. On the one hand, such an interpretation is consistent with reading Xuela as a Freudian melancholic subject who "recuperates and 'takes in' the lost object by 'identifying' with it" (Cheng 177). On the other hand, a cannibalistic "ingestion" of the mother's body by the daughter who is telling her story invokes an extended metaphor harking back to the associations of Caribs with cannibalism in colonial discourse. As Kathryn Morris notes, "a performance of incorporating the spirit of a fallen body into one's own" is "paradigmatically similar to Kincaid's exculpation of the Carib woman's history" (958). Similar to Marlene Nourbese Philip's polemic with imperial ethnographic and travel narratives, Kincaid's text indirectly speaks to a tradition of European constructions of indigenous peoples of the Caribbean as primitive, cannibalistic, wild, and hyper-sexualized. Ironically, in addition to the initial error of misnaming, mistranslation lies at the root of such constructions as "Columbus's translations of his Arawak guides' descriptions of the Carib Indians merged 'Carib' and 'cannibal' and brought the image of the flesh-eating West Indian savage to Europe" (Anatol 940).[30] Critics such as Eugenio Matibag recognize cannibalism as a trope that haunts the imagination of modern Caribbean writers whose narratives undertake "a search for identity in the traces left by Antillean 'forerunners,' while at the same time ironizing the implicit search for origins" (in Morris 956). In Kincaid's text, we discover a semantic layering of cannibal, Caliban, Carib, and Caribbean that not only creates a palimpsestic effect, but together with her reliance on word/image, metaphor, and allegory, leads to a rhetorical intensity that throws every semantic unit into a self-conscious play of signification. In addition, the chain of cannibal, Caliban, Carib, and Caribbean captures a vast thematic scope of the narrative that spans colonial representation, language, maternal legacy, history, and identity.

Anthropophagy, then, might be used as a metaphorical figuration of the working of both autobiography and translation in Kincaid's narrative, in particular when applied to her use of language and literary tradition. The metaphor of cannibalism has an established place in non-Eurocentric theories of translation coming from Latin America, especially from Brazil, where it is used to rethink the relationship between the Old World and the New World.[31] Brazilian theorists claim that by "devouring Europe," the formerly colonized can "break away from what was imposed upon them. And at the same time, the devouring could be perceived as both a violation of European codes and an act of homage" (Bassnet and Trivedi 4–5). Rather than denying European influences, the digestive metaphor emphasizes the possibility of absorbing the other's strength and transforming it by going back to indigenous elements. As a result, what has been experienced as foreign and oppressive can be turned into a source of health and nourishment for the translator. In a telling gesture, close to the end of the narrative, Xuela dresses her white husband in white and herself in black, paradoxically repeating the racial marking while also reversing its significance and inscribing a new meaning of history and social justice. With Philip Bailey leaving only a white-on-white trace, the Old World's domination fades away from history. What persists is Xuela's voice as black marks written on white pages.

Concluding Remarks

In the signifying texts discussed in this chapter, both The Traveller and Xuela can be interpreted as variations of the trickster figure, "ever punning, ever troping, ever embodying the ambiguities of language ... repeating and simultaneously reversing in one deft, discursive act" (Gates 285). This kind of double discourse not merely exposes language and rhetorical conventions that serve to legitimize social differences, but also creatively mobilizes its own textual rhetoric to produce difference differently. Xuela's language displaces her within well-established modes of enunciation, but defamiliarization is not produced through the use of Creole, but through the use of English, whose signifying rhetoric precludes transparency and closure. This effect is reminiscent of the one found in Marlene Nourbese Philip's poetry, where parsing also destabilizes meaning and never allows for transparency. The use of tropes serves the purpose of undermining the colonial language and representation and transforming our constructions of reality. Similar to Philip, Kincaid's style of repetition and negation is strongly anti-mimetic, and hence it participates in challenging the certainties of dominant conventions of Western literary realism. Writing about the importance of repetition in black culture, James Snead observes that "all representational conventions such as literary realism suppress repetition and verbal rhythm in the telling in favor of the illusion of narrative verisimilitude." Since it is based on the assumption that outside reality is knowable and "exhaustible in its manifestations" (73), realism is thus suitable for maintaining the status quo, and as such it is often a target of oppositional or subversive representations.

A different discussion of the problem of autobiography's representation of the real has been offered by Leigh Gilmore in the context of the relationship between metaphor and metonymy. She describes traditional Western privileging of metaphor as a figure of identity that mirrors the self in both real life and autobiography (*Limits* 101). Notably, Philip's and Kincaid's practice of allegory deconstructs the relationship between metaphor and metonymy, challenging the regimes of truth in autobiography from a position of the subject who has been denied the right to self-representation. If allegory is an act of displacement and reframing, The Traveller's as well as Xuela's life (a vehicle of the metaphor) is constantly reframed by a larger narrative of colonialism (its tenor), one that borrows its meaning from the other and turns allegory into an extended metaphor. But the relationship between the subject's life and (post)colonial history is also metonymical, as one is part of the other. If Xuela's life is a story of pain, it is because colonialism represents infliction of pain. In a parallel vein, if The Traveller enacts a journey through Africa, it is because of the historical rupture of the Middle Passage. Such deconstruction through a chiasmus, or a cross-over, allows to activate both sides, metaphor and metonymy, preventing the stifling imposition of "truth," "sameness," and "identity," as, for example, in such interpretations of these texts that fail to read metonymically and pathologize Xuela as "a repellent heroine" or impose the universalizing lens on The Traveller's journey.

Situating themselves as outsiders within their own language, both Marlene Nourbese Philip and Jamaica Kincaid perform the work of translation as creative transformation and resistance to being fixed in the position of the "other." They both use allegorical life writing in order to inscribe their own names as subjects of the history of oppression and epistemic violence that has persistently misnamed them and misrepresented their stories. Divided by the slash and alienated from the inherited language, they nevertheless commit to dialogue from within this divide, translating from the space of the slash of "re/version," propelled by the impulse to testify and re-vision individual and collective narratives of the past that shape their subjectivity in the present. While both texts explore how language and subjectivity function in the frame of postcoloniality, Philip's narrative concentrates on the ideological working of discourse whereas Kincaid's examines how subjectivity is mediated through colonial representations and whether it can be intelligible outside of that frame. Taken together, their texts address questions of grievance and grief, applying the perspective of justice on the one hand, naming a violation of human rights and demanding its recognition, while on the other hand processing the psychic effects of this colonial violence from the ethical perspective of mourning.

While Philip casts herself as an ethnographic traveller and Kincaid as an heir to a lost maternal narrative, each writer symbolically enacts her version of autobiographical anamnesis whose primary goal is, according to Derrida, "to remind *myself*. Myself. To remind myself, to myself as myself" (*Monolingualism* 9). Constructing a poetics and politics of relation to history and genealogy, Philip and Kincaid rely on metafiction to foreground a political contestation around language and representation that defines their predicament as postcolonial writers. However, they manage to escape being trapped in denial or reversal of the dominant system as they refuse to engage with power on its own terms, either by leaving the silences unanswered, like Philip, or, like Kincaid, rejecting the binary hierarchy of languages and cultures altogether. Instead, they both embrace textuality as a translative practice of creolization, claiming their right to borrow, transform, and use any language as their own and freeing themselves from any externally imposed restriction or obligation.

Conclusion

Sometimes, yes, I do feel like a kind of cultural Frankenstein, when those who speak only English regard my fluency in 'their' language as freakish, an interesting but somewhat grotesque mimicry of a language which belongs to them but was only lent to me. (Minfong Ho, "The Winter Hibiscus" 162)

The question as to when one should "mark" oneself (in terms of ethnicity, age, class, gender, or sexuality, for example), and when one should adamantly refuse such markings, continues to be a challenge. For answers to this query remain bound to the specific location, context, circumstance, and history of the subject at a given moment. (Trinh Minh-ha, "An Acoustic Journey" 8)

A massive uprooting of dualistic thinking in the individual and collective consciousness is the beginning of a long struggle, but one that could, in our best hopes, bring us to the end of rape, of violence, of war. (Gloria Anzaldua, *Borderlands/La Frontera: The New Mestiza* 8)

Marlene Nourbese Philip's and Jamaica Kincaid's situation vis-à-vis the English language illustrates what Jacques Derrida calls "a logical contradiction," the impossibility he expresses in one sentence: "I only have one language, yet it is not mine" (*Monolingualism* 2). Although this paradoxical "monolingualism" is most traumatically embodied by postcolonial subjects like Philip and Kincaid, Derrida posits the truth of this condition for any subject of language, including diasporic subjects like himself, a Franco-Maghrebian Jew, or bilingual subjects like the other immigrant women discussed in this study, or even "native" speakers of dominant languages adopted by these immigrants. Following Derrida, I have made a distinction between universal and empirical conditions of displacement in language that always clash with the law of the "proper," whether it invokes property rights to language or the rules of correctness. By exposing the fallacy of equivalence and transparency, the philosophies of translation examined in the preceding chapters challenge the "proper" and confirm the truth of "an essential alienation in language—which is always of the other" (*Monolingualism* 58). What immigrant women's life writing as idiomatic testimony—that is, narrative accounts grounded in concrete singular and historical circumstances—contributes to our understanding of the relationship of the subject to language is that this relationship always has a political dimension and material consequences. Such narratives "phenomenalize" the laws of language and translation and allow us to repoliticize what is at stake in translation as both a linguistic and cultural transfer, namely, the power of monolanguage and the suppression of the effects of plurality.

The politics of monolanguage still remains undeconstructed in contemporary thought despite a relative undoing of such categories as gender, race, ethnicity, and identity as monolithic or essential "properties" of the subject. Monolingual hegemony is derived from the nineteenth-century ideal of linguistic nationalism and the importance of the nation-state as a territorial unity where one language is spoken. However, the linguistically and culturally homogeneous national space has been and continues to be contested by today's transnational diasporas, which resemble "an older archetype: the multilingual trading city" (Shell 685). Yet, people still view themselves as attached to a "mother tongue" and situate as "foreigners" second-language users of such an international language as English. In designating primary or secondary rights to a language, we are still caught in the metaphysics of origin and reaffirm the "legal fiction" of the mother tongue as "the originary and irreplaceable place of meaning" (*Monolingualism* 91). For Derrida, this monolingualism characterizes an essential *coloniality* of every culture,

> which tends, repressively and irrepressibly, to reduce language to the One, that is, to the hegemony of the homogeneous. This can be verified everywhere, everywhere this homo-hegemony remains at work in the culture, effacing the folds and flattening the text. To achieve that, colonial power does not need, in its heart of hearts, to organize any spectacular initiatives: religious missions, philanthropic or humanitarian good works, conquest of markets, military expeditions, or genocides. (*Monolingualism* 40)

Any subject who claims exclusive possession of language or feels the unease of speaking a language that is "not my own" might be seen as having internalized this colonizing drive of culture and exhibiting complicity with the order of property and identity. No one can claim "natural possession" or "ownership" of language because such claims—whether by the colonizer or the dominant culture—are based on "politico-phantasmatic constructions" imposed "through rhetoric, the school, or the army" (*Monolingualism* 23). Consequently, following Levinas, for whom "the essence of language is friendship and hospitality," Derrida proposes to view language as "expression" rather than "generation or foundation," substituting affiliation for the familial and national ties (*Monolingualism* 91). As we have seen, translation delivers a promise of relational possibilities on many levels, from theoretical formulations to personal explorations of subjectivity and attitudes to alterity.

Working from a thesis that immigrant women's life writing can be viewed as performances in translation has helped us to visualize that the "I" of autobiographical discourse never precedes the language(s) in which it is produced and articulated, and that—as Derrida says—"it is not independent of language in general" (*Monolingualism* 29). However, the power to say "I" and to be heard is not something everyone can take for granted. Although most of the authors discussed here have been motivated in their choice of English as the language of expression by a desire to write from a paradigm of multiplicity and heterogeneity, that is, a desire to tap a liberatory potential of English, at the same time they reveal its liability to be used as a tool of oppression. Examined through their attitudes to translation, these narratives make us understand that language plays a major role in social classification and stratification and that we need to question linguistic categories that serve to exclude. Immigrants may reveal complicity with or resistance to an ideology of symbolic and cultural imperialism and language standardization. But more often, they rely on the dynamics of translation as a figure of possible transformation of exclusionary power discourses that impose monolingual regimes and discipline the "foreign" others. Reading their life writing through the conceptual framework of translation provides evidence of the need to attend carefully to language as a primary site where boundaries are constituted, boundaries to our thinking that reinforce material separations in social life for many subjects whose human rights remain unrecognized or violated. For several writers discussed here a vexing question is not what is lost and found in translation but rather how to deal with finding loss and keeping what is lost.

It seems that in today's criticism of autobiography and life writing still not enough attention is given to the importance of language as translation practice. My approach to immigrant women's life writing from the perspective of contemporary theories of translation reveals complications of language, identity, and identification that confound such census-imposed categories as first language and second language, traditionally applied to immigrants in a new country. The concepts of "mother tongue," or first language, and "borrowed tongue," or second language, are inadequate. The texts I have analyzed unsettle any claims of the law of the "proper" in more than one sense, engaging the questions of "propriety" and "property" in politicized ways, by foregrounding issues of competence in a language that is supposedly "not one's own" and by interrogating the languages of oppression and colonization. On the one hand, the writers expose and challenge regimes of standardization that limit language diversity and variety of expression and operate on many axes, from assigning a "first-" or "second-language" status to policing accent. On the other hand, they try to perform deconstruction of dominant discourses and re-construction of counter-discourses. These narratives force us to acknowledge that both the myth of literacy and the myth of a standard language must be examined as part of the processes of disciplining through discourse. Language and accent often become points of gatekeeping, as Rosina Lippi-Green reminds us, "because we are forbidden, by law and social custom, and perhaps by a prevailing sense of what is morally and ethically right, from using race, ethnicity, homeland or economics more directly ... to turn away, to refuse to recognize the other" (64).

The analyses of immigrant women's life writing demonstrate that translation must be acknowledged not only as a linguistic but also as a social process, tied to every attempt to bring meaning to the "I." Disclosing complex histories and processes of identification, effected through multi-practices of translation on many levels of discourse, the narratives of immigrant women's experiences illustrate the movement from bicultural and bilingual models of immigration and translation to plural modes of belonging and identity that come closest to the examples of diasporic consciousness and creolization. Openly or surreptitiously, migrant texts legitimize alternative forms of subjectivity, knowledge, literacy, and offer counter-discourses to the dominant ones. Searching for "third space" in-between categories, such narratives open up the interstitial or liminal space of change and transformation, of mixing and blurring. Through their use of language, they question and destabilize monolithic categories of identity described by Derrida as "this concept of which the transparent identity to itself is always dogmatically presupposed by so many debates on monoculturalism or multiculturalism, nationality, citizenship, and, in general, belonging" (*Monolingualism* 28). Consequently, migrant texts invite us to rethink models of identity as not necessarily determined by place of birth and nationality and to view them in terms of provisional, shifting, and contingent identifications and mobile alliances. My reading of these texts reaffirms that the oppositional dualist models of translation and cultural self-definition are no longer useful as a paradigm by which to understand migrant identities and that the end of this model means the beginning of a new epistemic era characterized by the emergence of different ways of thinking about language and identity in new transnational contact zones, premised upon a recognition of heterogeneity.

If academic institutions can be viewed as a microcosm of such transnational contact zones, I am convinced that we can benefit from the findings of research on life writing and translation in trying to learn to read each other's stories, listen to multiple voices, and find the possibility of plurivocal exchanges in cross-cultural, multilingual, globalized, and indigenized contexts. Seeing connectedness and communication at the root of translation, Paul Ricoeur injects hope into his vision of interlinguistic hospitality that would bind us in an exchange of our different narratives. Theories of translation as a mode of ethical relationship to the other could help scholars to test the usefulness of translation in thinking across our differences as well as finding the language of the "in-between" through which to interrogate together race politics, ethnic exclusions, and (hetero)sexism of dominant social, literary, and cultural institutions. There is also the possibility of linking this research on how translation and women's life writing pose a challenge to binary thinking and teach respect for the work of difference, to discussions about interdisciplinarity and the possibility of building feminist and other progressive communities. Finally, relating the concept of translation as "equivalence without identity" not only to ethics but also to epistemology, we can learn humility in accepting limits to our ability to "know" everything and renounce the need for totalization, fullness, wholeness, unity, perfection, and control.

Using Derrida's reflections on "monolingualism of the other" as a way of concluding this book allows me to reiterate what immigrant women's life writing has richly demonstrated, namely, that language belongs exclusively to no master, no dominant culture. Ultimately, these women challenge the concept of speaking and writing in "borrowed tongues" since no property rights can be asserted over any language. Life writing as translation has taken many forms in the nearly eight decades spanned by the texts in this study. Together they provide a radical basis for a political project: to destroy the perception and power claims that language (English) is "owned" and can be used as a legitimate instrument of exclusion; to write to a future free from the terrors of monolanguage.

Notes

Notes to Introduction: Migrations of Theories

1 The theoretical possibilities of bridging autobiography and translation studies began to be explored only recently. In fact, the 2008 International Auto/Biography Association (IABA) conference had translation as its theme. I have found three book-length studies, beginning with Mary Besemeres's pioneering *Translating One's Self: Language and Selfhood in Cross-Cultural Autobiography*, Martha Cutter's *Lost and Found in Translation: Contemporary Ethnic American Writing and the Politics of Language Diversity*, and most recently, Bella Brodzki's *Can These Bones Live? Translation, Survival, and Cultural Memory*. Besemeres's title is, however, a little misleading since in addition to autobiography, she also examines modernist fiction and poetry written by "language migrants." She is overly suspicious of poststructuralist approaches to language and self, which inform my own perspective, and her overall concern is "how a particular self at any time depends for its expression on a particular natural language" (10). Cutter's book applies translation to American ethnic writing and Native American writing, including a few autobiographical texts. Her approach, however, differs from mine in that she focuses less on questions of translation and subjectivity than on the politics of multilingualism in the context of US multiculturalism. Finally, Brodzki grounds her argument in the poststructuralist theories of translation elaborated by Walter Benjamin and Jacques Derrida, focusing on translation's links to cultural survival and memorialization, trauma and memory, whereas I focus more on issues of power and subjectivity. Moreover, in the European context, the interest in globalization and its effects has spurred several attempts to rethink the connection between translation and identity, most notably in Michael Cronin's *Translation and Identity*, which links translation to migration and new forms of cosmopolitanism. Similarly, *Translating Identity and the Identity of Translation*, edited by Madelena Gonzalez and Francine Tolron, uses the problematic of translation to examine the changing politics of identity in its local and global manifestations in postcolonial societies, in search of "a new postnational form of literary studies better equipped to take into account the interculturalism of contemporary life and its altered identities" (viii).

2 My choice of the term "life writing" over "autobiography" is consistent with a long-established tradition in autobiography studies where "life writing" has been used to encompass non-canonical or hybrid forms of autobiographical practices. See, for example, Donald Winslow's dictionary (1980); Evelyn Hinz's "Speculative Introduction: Life-Writing as Drama," in a special issue of *Mosaic* (1987); K.P. Stich's 1988 definition of "life-writing" as "a hybrid form [which] blurs the distinction between autobiography, autobiographical novel, and fictional autobiography" (*Reflections* 16); Shirley Neuman's entry on "Life-Writing" in *Literary History of Canada: Canadian Literature in English* (1990); and Helen Buss's "Writing and Reading Autobiographically," Introduction to *Prairie Fire*'s 1995 "Life Writing" Issue. More recently, Margareta Jolly explains that she chose life writing for the title of her encyclopedia "because of its openness and inclusiveness across genre, and because it encompasses the writing of one's own or another's life" (ix). Also Cynthia Franklin and Laura E. Lyons assert that from the 1980s onwards, "autobiography studies was redefined as 'life writing,' in order to accommodate ... the emergence of new testimonial forms" (ix).

3 Note the ambivalent construction of "host" that places the immigrant as a parasite or, in a more benign way, a recipient of hospitality.

4 Derrida's earlier engagement with Jakobson can be found in "Des Tours de Babel," where he critiques the presupposition of "the unity and identity of language" in Jakobson's theory of translation (173).

5 As part of decentring translation studies, Maria Tymoczko advocates "broadening the definition of translation and breaking the hold of Eurocentric stereotypes of translation" by including "forms and modes of cultural interface that are related to translation but distinct from it" such as postcolonial literature ("Reconceptualizing" 27). Immigrant life writing can obviously be included in this interface. She critiques Eurocentric assumptions of monolingualism built into translation studies, premised on the equation of nation with language; privileging of written literacy over orality; individualistic rather than collective models of meaning production; and the ahistorical assumption that cultural mixing and hybridity are contemporary phenomena resulting from globalization.

6 I use close reading following the example of feminist narratology, that is, as a more contextual than formalist approach. See Warhol.

7 Lefevere prefers to talk of a "conceptual grid" and a "textual grid." For example, cultural differences and specificities belong to the former while genre is part of the latter (76). His theory of rewritings posits translation as one among many forms of reprocessing and representing source texts. Regarding the broadening of translation, Maria Tymoczko cites Gideon Tury's definition of translation as "any target language text which is presented or regarded as such within the target system itself, on whatever grounds" ("Reconceptualizing" 21).

8 Here is an expanded definition of a bilingual: "A bilingual may be defined as a person who has two linguistic systems which s/he uses for communication in appropriate situations. In a bilingual or multilingual situation 'transfer' or 'interference' is inevitable. This transfer will work both ways, each language influencing the other. One system may be more dominant than the other" (Prasad 46–47). On the other hand, a translingual is a person who writes "in more than one language or in a language other than [his or her] primary one" (Kellman ix).

9 Roy Pascal's modernist *Design and Truth in Autobiography* (1960) dismisses the majority of autobiographical productions as lacking literary quality and considers

only a few autobiographies as worthy of consideration. See also the special issue of *Life Writing* (April 2007), especially Geok-lin Lim and Kyungah Hong's introduction.

10 See also Bella Brodzki's claim that autobiographical narratives (fictionalized or not) are predicated "on a principle of the 'I' as a repeatable singularity across time and space." Women's narratives also seek "to diffuse and displace this singularity by remaking it as heterogeneous and performative" [as each 'I' indeed is] (*Can These* 75).

11 Derrida critiques Benjamin's genealogical model because it maintains the dualism of the original and translation even though it reverses the relationship between them, seeing the original as indebted to translation ("Des Tours" 180).

12 See Sathya Rao's critique of universalism and indeterminacy of Derrida's deconstruction, or Bryan Reynolds's comments on "infinite supplementation of meaning" (278). However, contrary to claims of "unlimited" play of signification, Derrida insists that reading is always "bounded" by its contexts.

13 I share resistance that many critics show towards the term "minority" as "useful" for defining "majority." For example, Zamora speaks of the need "to complicate the notion of 'minority' as it has been used historically in the United States, with its implication of marginalization and isolation from some vaguely defined 'mainstream'" (2).

14 These three areas of life writing as different projects in translation resemble three interlinked types of movement between different systems of signs (where each system is already pluralized): intersemiotic (between genres), intralingual (within the same language), and interlingual (between two or more languages).

15 Critical writing on autobiography viewed as a predominantly male-defined genre dates back at least to the1960s, which saw the publication of Roy Pascal's book. For a historical review of theories of autobiography, see Charles Berryman, who looks mostly at male models of the genre. Sidonie Smith and Julia Watson in their Introduction to *Women, Autobiography, Theory: A Reader* offer the most comprehensive review of the field of autobiography studies from a feminist perspective. A useful survey of the Canadian scene of autobiographical criticism is provided in Julie Rak's "Introduction."

16 In her Introduction, Jelinek juxtaposes the male and female traditions of autobiographical writing, based on characteristic differences between essentialized "male" and "female" experiences; she postulates that "different criteria are needed to evaluate women's autobiographies, which may constitute, if not a subgenre, then an autobiographical tradition different from the male tradition" (6). A general tendency to "totalize" and treat as separate the two strands of "male" and "female" autobiography has been usefully criticized by Jeanne Costello, who argues that we need "not only to revise our criteria for assigning women's texts to an autobiographical tradition, but also to reassess our sense of the field of men's autobiographies" (132).

17 It was the only essay on women's autobiography published in James Olney's *Autobiography: Essays Theoretical and Critical* (1980), a collection which introduced poststructuralist perspectives into the study of autobiography.

18 For some examples of these genres, see Smith and Watson's collection of essays (*De/Colonizing*), as well as the studies by Caroline Steedman, Anne Goldman, Susanna Egan, Suzette Henke, Miriam Fuchs, and Leigh Gilmore's analysis of trauma and testimony (*The Limits*). The study of autobiography has been extended to embrace such "everyday" uses of autobiographical practices as application forms, interviews, and family photography. See Smith and Watson's *Getting a Life*, a collection devoted to "backyard ethnography." In Canada, two recent collections have significantly

widened the scope of autobiographical criticism, moving it toward interdisciplinarity (see Rak, and Kadar et al., *Tracing*).

19 Whitlock and Poletti also use the term "autography" in their introduction to the special issue of *Life Writing* on graphic life writing. There has been an attempt to launch yet another concept, that of "biotext." As Fred Wah explains, "biotext" or "biofiction" is "a happier term, compositionally, [than autobiography and life writing] since it indicates the possible brush with certain narrative tropes" (97).

20 The term is Michele Causse's. It refers to "the language of man or Andros (in other words, the expression of a consciousness-experience sexed/gendered in the masculine)" (Mezei 9).

21 See Paolo Bartoloni's discussion of Benjamin's conception of memory as the spatialization of time (27).

22 Julia Kristeva in "Women's Time" defines gender as a function of the translation between various discourses and the body, enacted within the parameters of the subject's positioning in relation to the sociosymbolic contract (21).

23 To clarify the distinction, in the US context Karen Christian describes "immigrant literature" as works by foreign-born writers who have settled permanently in the United States. This type of writing in English focuses on making the US the immigrant's new home, emphasizing rebirth and conversion. By contrast, "ethnic literature" reflects bilingual and bicultural interaction. She notes that "immigrant writing frequently articulates an *ethnic* consciousness. For this reason, I do not consider the categories 'immigrant literature' and 'ethnic literature' to be mutually exclusive" (Christian 169).

24 The material conditions of translation can be used as a crucial factor of differentiation between different types of migrants. "Travellers" such as pioneers, settlers, or tourists, remain in possession of the master's tongue, whereas for "ethnics" or "immigrants" translation moves in the opposite direction, from the mother tongue, into the master's language (Bartkowski 86).

25 What Moya does not explain is how these social categories and/or subjective identities are constituted, how they are formed, maintained, and become available. In this respect, poststructuralist theories of the relationship between subjectivity and discourse, of how the subject is constituted through agency and subjection, are more helpful.

26 Not surprisingly, traditional approaches to immigrant autobiography are also coded in dualistic terms as theories of split identity caused by the caesura of immigration, predicated on the notion of bounded nation-states and hyphenated identities, which also fit the model of translation as a transfer of meaning from the source to the target language. For example, William Boelhower's definition of the genre of immigrant autobiography as an organization of a "double self" and "two cultural systems" is steeped in the dualisms of the Old World and the New World (*Immigrant* 29).

27 An interesting observation made by Kathleen Shields confirms that despite the existence of many varieties of French- and English-influenced Creole languages, in educational settings "normative, centralizing conceptions still prevail" (229).

28 A different criticism is offered by Rey Chow, who views Bhabha's concept of hybridity as reviving in the guise of "deconstruction, anti-imperialism, and 'difficult' theory ... an old functionalist notion of what a dominant culture permits in the interest of maintaining its own equilibrium" ("Where Have" 131). Recent attempts in postcolonial studies to move beyond the hybridity paradigm interpret it as still premised on the binary structure of colonialism and show preference for "transnationality" which does not depend on any originary space (Ghosh-Schellhorn 23).

29 Chow quotes Jean Laplanche, whose reading of Benjamin corresponds with my interpretation of Derrida reading Benjamin: "Benjamin participates in ... the 'anti-auto- or self-centered' movement of translation ... a movement that doesn't want translation to be self-enclosed and reduce the other to the terms of that self, but rather a movement out toward the other" (Chow, *Primitive* 189).

30 A useful description is offered by Betty Bergland: "to avoid implications that we know a coherent self contained in pronoun references, I will distinguish (minimally) between the historical subject, referring to the biological life; the autobiographical narrator, the "I" who writes the narrative; and the autobiographical subject the speaking "I" in the narrative" ("Postmodernism" 137). The distinction is further elaborated by Sidonie Smith and Julia Watson into a theory of the autobiographical "I" that comprises the historical "I," the narrating "I," the narrated "I," and the ideological "I" (*Reading Autobiography* 72–8).

Notes to Chapter 1: Literacy Narratives

1 Antin's career must be qualified as "meteoric," to use her own words from a letter to the publisher, written in 1926, which she stylized as an obituary (Salz 108). She suffered a nervous breakdown after separating from her husband, Amadeus Grabau, who showed pro-German sympathies during the First World War. Similarly, in the 1920s, she experienced stark political disillusionment with the government's restrictionist policies.

2 The most influential racialized classification of immigrant groups, provided by American sociologist William Z. Ripley's *The Races of Europe* (1899), contrasts the desirable "Teutons or Baltics from Northern Europe" with populations of central and southern Europe, the former stereotyped as "stolid, reserved, and independent" and the latter depicted as feminized—fickle, passionate, and impulsive (Irving 20).

3 The genre of spiritual autobiography, defined as "a narrative of selected experiences" including the motif of a journey, religious conversion, and the hunger for education, was previously used by Phillis Wheatley, Benjamin Franklin, Booker T. Washington, and Frederick Douglas (Salz xvi). The tradition of Jewish-American autobiography, with Antin as one of its pioneers, includes Abraham Cahan, Rose Cohen, Ludwig Lewisohn, M.E. Ravage, Elizabeth Stern, Anzia Yezierska, and Isaac Bashevis Singer, as well as Jacob Riis, whose autobiography *The Making of an American* (1901) Antin mentions in her letter to Ellery Sedgwick (Salz 52).

4 The Irish and the Chinese, who came in the mid-nineteenth century, were the only groups in the first wave treated with overt prejudice (Payant xvii).

5 Betty Bergland mentions thirty-four printings, two re-editions, and frequent anthologizing ("Ideology" 102). The 1997 Penguin edition includes a new necessity of reading Antin's text against the grain of its surface rhetoric of Americanization. Most notably, Sidonie Smith, Aranzazu Usandizaga, Kirsten Wasson, and Magdalena J. Zaborowska offer counter-interpretations, looking for disruptions, subversions, double-coding, and oppositional discourses working from the margins of the text.

6 How deeply ingrained were expectations of immigrant gratitude on the part of American readers can be seen in the historical Antin's confrontation with Ruth Woodsmall, the author of a scathing letter accusing Antin of ingratitude to her adopted homeland, following the publication of *Those Who Knock on Our Gates*. Antin makes her stand clear: "After having made my cordial acknowledgments [in *The Promised Land*], I proceed, like any other American, to study and think and criticize [the many sins of omission]" (Salz 79).

7   In fact, Antin's narrative yields itself to the kind of exegesis that has been part of the Ashkenazic tradition, which Eva Hoffman in *Shtetl* describes as the method of "pilpul" or pepper: "looking for those grains of pepper that disturbed the harmony of the text and that might therefore be a clue, an opening, to further truths" (100). It is an apt description of what might be viewed as a prototype of Derrida's deconstruction.

8   Wendy Zierler quotes the voices of several Jewish critics who condemned Antin's book as a "religio-cultural striptease" for the benefit of her American Gentile friends (4). Countering this tendency, Evelyn Salz, editor of Antin's letters, reclaims and reinterprets her legacy as "the first documenter of Russian Jewish history in English" (xxii). She also chronicles Antin's support of Zionism.

9   In a reading that might be congenial to my project, Janet Burstein attempts to apply the metaphor of translation to Antin's text. Unfortunately, she preserves the linearity of "the Russian original" and "the American translation" and views translation simply as channelling feelings into words (18). As Antin's text demonstrates, the "original" may resist translation and/or is itself selectively constructed, available as already "translated."

10 She was actually thirteen not eleven when she wrote the pamphlet. According to Werner Sollors, Antin's father falsified her age on the school certificate to secure two more years of schooling for her ("Introduction" xxvii–xxviii). Besides, the title contains an error of naming, which she accepted, substituting the Polish "Plotzk" for Antin's "Polotzk," a Russian town on the Dvina, near Vitebsk. Zangwill in his Foreword consistently refers to Antin as "the gifted Polish girl" (9).

11 In her letter to Israel Zangwill, written when she was eighteen and a half, she complains that one of her rich patrons, Mrs. Hecht, is trying to impose social taboos on her: "Mrs. Hecht said I was getting too big to be a girl, I must be a young lady. I mustn't go out alone with Mr. Grabau ... I must be properly chaperoned on all occasions. I must and I mustn't a hundred horrid things. Are you going to be one of those who think a girl *must* be a lady when she gets to be sixteen and a half [*sic*], whether she is anxious for the honor or shudders at the thought of it? Then you will laugh at me when I tell you that it nearly broke my heart to become 'grown up,' and it made me positively ill, so that I couldn't go to school for a few days. It worries me still. Wouldn't *you* let me be a girl till I was tired of it?' (Salz 22).

12 In addition, young Antin is left without any support during her adolescence and, baffled by the changes in her body, turns for advice to her teacher, Miss Dillingham. Note the unintentionally comic effect in her use of the generic "man" in reference to herself, when she learns that her mood swings are just symptoms of growing up, "as anybody will know who was present at the slow birth of his manhood" (PL 216).

13 Salz mentions that another Jewish immigrant from Russia, Emma Goldman, despite her radical anarchist views, did not participate in the suffrage movement either. I suspect that as immigrant women, both Antin and Goldman may have felt alienated from the women's movement dominated by white middle-class leadership that exhibited "maternalistic" condescension toward immigrants.

14 However, she still considers her schoolmates "democratic" and blames herself for the fact that "our intimacy ended on the steps of the school-house" (PL 231). One wonders why she refuses deeper analysis, of which she shows herself perfectly capable, of the hypocrisy and inequitable relations in American society. Indeed, her words often suggest blindness or self-delusion: "So my companions and I parted on the steps of the school-house, in mutual respect; they guiltless of snobbishness, I innocent of envy. It was a graciously American relation, and I am happy to this day to recall it" (PL 231–32).

15 Antin seems to combine the Whitmanesque "I" with the humanistic pride in the "immortal" self, reflected also in her endorsement of the idea that ontogeny recapitulates phylogeny: "I am a wonderful thing, being human ... I am the image of the universe, being myself ... I am the repository of all the wisdom of the world" (PL 197). She is both ageless/ancient and young ("the endless ages have indeed throbbed through my blood" [PL 285])—the rhetoric partly inspired by natural science, partly by transcendentalism.

16 In her letter to Ellery Sedgwick (July 19, 1911), she ponders using a different name ("Esther Altmann") in the text "to take the edge off the boldness of my confessions" and to protect the privacy of her "heroes and heroines" (Salz 53).

17 Betty Bergland identifies the "enormous contradictions" between Antin as "the Autobiographical Subject" and "the Historical Antin" ("Ideology" 109); she speaks, however, of the text's failure to articulate the position of the immigrant subject as a grown-up, sexual, and ethnic being. Evelyn Salz refutes such claims as absurd.

18 This passage has been vastly commented upon by such critics as Kirsten Wasson (177) and Sidonie Smith. Smith invokes the memory of the cheesecake as "a recipe of sensuality, of taste, smell, touch, of pleasure" interrupting "the narrative of Americanization with the whiff of the repressed, the return to the mother of childhood, the imaginative return to the motherland (even if not a national motherland)" ("Cheesecake" 127).

19 To this day, there is no definitive biography or a critical monograph assessing her entire output.

20 For example, Craig criticizes her ethnocentrism in the superlative portrayal of Icelandic culture, which he sees ironically as a mirror-like reflection of English-Canadian ethnocentrism and racism (86).

21 See Kristjana Gunnars's interpretation of *Confessions* in the context of the genre (1986), Barbara Powell's article discussed later (1992), Helen Buss's inclusion of Salverson in the tradition of Canadian women's autobiography (1993), or Wendy Roy's reading of the book as an example of working-class autobiographical writing (2005).

22 It is not my intention to "essentialize" this type of autobiography. As Françoise Lionnet has convincingly argued in her reading of Augustine, this model of masculine autobiography can also be read for the presence of the feminine. Besides, in Rousseau we can discern strategies of evasion and dissimulation, in addition to self-consciousness in the use of artifice, that already undermine the concept of a unified subject.

23 For example, Gunnars builds her interpretation of Salverson's text on a contrast between the traditions of confession and autobiography, which parallels her split self. The divided self is seen as "doubled: once between the 'ethnic' and the 'non-ethnic', again between 'female' and 'male' worlds" (152).

24 Unlike Antin, who did not inherit any tradition of organized women's movement from her ethnic group, Icelandic women have a documented history of feminist activism prior to their immigration history in Canada. Upon arrival in Manitoba, they founded women's organizations and edited their own feminist journal *Freyja* (woman). This history is only marginally acknowledged by Canadian mainstream feminist historians (see Kinnear). One might speculate that this background history of competing feminisms colours Salverson's attitude to the figure of Nellie McClung, whom she recalls respectfully but bitterly in connection with the publication of *The Viking Heart*. In fact, at the suggestion of McClung, Salverson added the opening chapter for which she was later attacked by her community.

25 J.S. Woodsworth's *Strangers within Our Gates* (1909) was written partly in response to intolerance and prejudice against immigrants. He was supportive particularly of non-English-speaking Europeans, pleading for their acceptance on the basis of their assimilability. This kind of discourse of assimilation is marked by racist exclusion of racialized minorities, not considered assimilable. In Winnipeg, at the beginning of the century, foreigners were segregated in the North End ghetto. Scandinavians and Germans were the quickest to climb the social ladder, probably because of their "cultural closeness to Anglo-Canadians" (Stich, "Introduction" xii).

26 Similar attitudes are reflected in *The Viking Heart*, most notably in the story involving the "Noble Savage" character Old Joe.

27 See also *The Viking Heart*, where English is celebrated as "this new tongue which was a key to all manner of excellent things" (47). It is instructive to recall here Israel Zangwill's comment on Mary Antin's choice of English, from his Preface to *From Plotzk to Boston*: "Her capacity to handle English—after so short a residence in America—shows that she possesses also the instrument of expression. More fortunate than the poet of the ghetto, Morris Rosenfeld, she will have at her command the most popular language in the world" (8).

28 Talal Asad offers a critique of modernism as a cultural movement that consciously employed multilingual, intertextual references and quotations as part of its challenge to bourgeois values. The result of having these "foreign" elements incorporated was an enrichment rather than subversion of "modern world culture," which, according to Asad, "has no difficulty accommodating unstable signs and domesticated exotica, so long as neither conflicts radically with systems of profit" ("A Comment" 331).

Notes to Chapter 2: Immigrant Crypto(auto)graphy

1 Anthropology and ethnography are understood respectively as theorizing and gathering information about cultural and/or racial others.

2 Caroline B. Brettell makes a distinction between "life history" and "life story," seeing the latter as more suitable to emphasize the constructedness of a narrative of one person's life (224), which also accounts for my preference for the term "life story." According to Mary Jean Corbett, the term "memoir" is used "to denote not an autobiographical text that tells a story about a centered self, but one in which the writing subject recounts stories of others and events or movements in which she and/or her other subjects have taken part" (262f).

3 The crypt resembles another structure in Derrida's topology of textuality, namely, the structure of invagination, the term he sometimes uses to describe the folds of the text where the inside becomes the outside and vice versa.

4 Incidentally, Bella Brodzki observes that the Derridean premise in *The Ear of the Other*, regarding "the scene of translation" as inscribed "'within the scene of inheritance,'" is reflected also in the debt binding Derrida to Walter Benjamin's "The Task of the Translator" ("History" 207).

5 Although for Cosslett et al. subjectivity is "an effect produced by autobiography" (10), her definition of intersubjectivity moves beyond the textual so as to encompass all kinds of "relationships in which the narrator is embedded" (3), including other selves, cultural, social, and historical metanarratives, as well as interactions with the audience.

6 Autoethnography has been defined by Mary Louise Pratt as one of the arts of the contact zone, used by the colonized to reclaim the right to look at themselves rather than be looked at by the colonizer. To Deborah Reed-Danahay, autoethnography

is defined as "a form of self-narrative that places the self within a social context" (9). Marlene Kadar ("The Discourse") uses "bioethnography" to distinguish it from "autoethnography" in one of its specific meanings as self-reflexive ethnography.

7   The tradition of Japanese American autobiography preceding and/or surrounding Kikumura's book includes Mine Okubo's *Citizen 13660* (1946), Monica Sone's *Nisei Daughter* (1953), Jeanne Houston's *Farewell to Manzanar* (1973), Charles Kikuchi's *The Kikuchi Diary* (1973), and Yashiko Uchida's *Desert Exile* (1982).

8   This strategy can be contrasted with that of such practitioners of feminist oral history as Tomoko Makabe, the author of *Picture Brides: Japanese Women in Canada*, which is also a translation from Japanese into English. The author, herself an immigrant from Japan, gathers the stories of five Issei women who all grew up in Japan during the Meiji period (1868–1912), a period associated with male privilege. Like Kikumura, Makabe deals with the issues of the "ordinariness" of their experience, poverty, and suffering, and the problem of exclusion and discrimination. She emphasizes the frequently overlooked fact that in addition to their domestic duties, Issei women worked equally with their husbands in the production process, including farming and the fishing industry. Part of her analysis concerns the differences between women's and men's approaches to such issues as anti-Asian racism, and especially her perception that Japanese women generally tend to downplay discrimination.

9   Surprisingly, Rayson considers Kikumura and her mother to be incompetent witnesses to the relocation. Her review dismisses Kikumura as almost third generation rather than Nissei and questions the mother's reliability as a simple farmer preoccupied with domestic hardships rather than the meaning of political events around her.

10   In Communist Poland, the topic of Soviet deportations was a taboo. Until 1989, any published work appeared only in exile. The best-known example of such memoirs written in English is *The Dark Side of the Moon* (1947), with T.S. Eliot's preface. As Bogusia Temple notes in her interviews with British "Sybiraki" (Polish survivors of Siberia), people's accounts of their experiences in Siberia were "more than background information, since they formed a part of the sense of identity of those relating them, as well as of a sense of community generally" (23).

11   The book *Marynia, Don't Cry*, published by the Multicultural History Society of Ontario (MHSO), contains two memoirs, of which the other, a much shorter narrative, called "Three Generations (The Deputat Family)," represents a different genre of oral history, transcribed by Barbara Glogowska and translated from the Polish by Irma Zaleski. Glogowska, who describes herself as a family friend, focuses on the narrative of immigration as progress from rags to riches and celebrates the self-made man, Mike Deputat, who is at the centre of this family history.

12   Norman Davies reports that interwar Poland was "a society in which two-thirds of the population was engaged in subsistence agriculture and where one-third consisted of national minorities" (412–13). Peasant masses lived in poverty, following a brief revival of the rural economy in 1928–29, after which it never recovered from decline. Official unemployment figures, estimated at 10 percent in 1936, concealed the far more serious unemployment in rural areas, estimated at about 45 percent. The territories where the Kojders came from constituted Poland's most backward region, the so-called "Polska-B" (Second-Class Poland).

13   The memories recorded by Kojder as representative of peasant classes stand in sharp contrast with "upper-class" accounts by affiliates of the bourgeois Polish government in exile such as Wanda Stachiewicz's *Journey through History: Memoirs* (1985).

Bogusia Temple, a British scholar of Polish descent, ponders the instability of terms such as "Polish" or "working class," reminding us that such terms are provisional and contested; therefore, the content of the pronoun "we" can be indeterminate. As she contends, "I do not abandon terms such as 'Polish,' or 'woman' or 'working class,' since they are used by people as ways of describing their connection to the social world. These ascriptions are, however, occasioned and purposeful and can be challenged" (22).

14 In the translation reproduced by Kojder the first line of Adam Mickiewicz's romantic manifesto of youthful rebellion and individualism is replaced by a bathetic rhyme which substitutes a singular metaphor ("man is but a skeleton") for the poet's catastrophic vision of dead nations as masses of skeletons populating the earth ("szkieletow ludy").

15 "Ethnocultural Voices" is one of MHSO's serial publications which additionally include "Studies in Ethnic and Immigration History," "Conference Proceedings," and the journal *Polyphony*. Kojder's book is the only one in the series dealing with the Polish immigrant culture; however, there were other books on Poles in Canada published earlier by the MHSO. Its editorial board is composed of scholars and community researchers who often have their own ties to immigrant cultures and are committed to multiculturalism. Manuscripts submitted for publication in any of the MHSO's publishing programs are written in English, but it does not seem that the Society subscribes to any philosophy or specific policy around translation. However, despite the MHSO's monolingualism exhibited through its published materials, the Society has collected over 7,000 hours of oral history interviews, some of which have been recorded in languages other than English. In the current fiscal climate, with the Society relying solely on volunteers, the MHSO cannot afford to pay for transcription and translation of these tapes.

Notes to Chapter 3: Experimental Self-Translations

1 According to Caruth, "for those who undergo trauma, it is not only the moment of the event, but of the passing out of it that is traumatic ... *survival itself*, in other words, *can be a crisis*" (9). *Lost in Translation* has generally been read as an immigrant narrative of acculturation rather than a second-generation Holocaust-survivor narrative. This perception may have changed since the 2004 publication of Hoffman's volume of reflection on the meaning of the Holocaust, *After Such Knowledge: Memory, History, and the Legacy of the Holocaust*, where she coins the term "hinge generation" to refer to the situation of children of survivors who are the link between history and memory. Marianne Hirsch refers to this generation as "the generation of postmemory," which has been haunted by their parents' trauma and called to secondary witnessing.

2 For example, Hirsch is annoyed by Hoffman's "nostalgically Edenic representation of Poland" and her displacement of "her parents' suffering with her own happiness" ("Pictures" 77). However, approaching Hoffman's text through trauma as well as paying attention to the ironic distance in perspective can mitigate such criticism.

3 Hearing another immigrant woman's confession, Hoffman does not find the woman's nostalgia for the paradise of her childhood unusual, but she comments: "The wonder is what you can make a paradise out of. I told her that I grew up in a lumpen apartment in Cracow, squeezed into three rudimentary rooms with four other people, surrounded by squabbles, dark political rumblings, memories of wartime

suffering, and daily struggle for existence. And yet, when it came time to leave, I, too, felt I was being pushed out of the happy, safe enclosures of Eden" (LT 5).

4 A similar splitting is also dramatized in Smaro Kamboureli's *in the second person*, the other narrative I will be discussing in this chapter, although I suspect that the mirror metaphor would be rejected by Kamboureli as too mimetic.

5 Although I am not pursuing psychoanalytic interpretation of Hoffman's narrative, it is worth noting that in the text she applies translation as a tool of dream analysis, reading bilingual puns that appear in her dream "about the fear of time, in which the word *chronos* and the Polish *chronić*, which means to protect, are elaborately interwoven" (LT 243). The conflation of "time" and "protect" suggests that memory if crucial to her project of self-translation.

6 Similarly, Danuta Zadworna Fjellestad talks about Hoffman's tendency to "naturalize" Polish phenomena while seeing their American counterparts as "constructed." For example, Polish dating conventions seem "natural" (LT 142), whereas American courtship rules are seen as artifice. The same applies to Hoffman's valorization of her mother as aligned with "nature"—through her intuitive understanding of people—as opposed to herself as "culture." While Fjellestad notices that Hoffman is "exiled from what she experiences as 'nature' into the American culture" (136), she forgets to add that at this point she is also cut off from Polish-Jewish culture.

7 Curiously, this part shows that Hoffman reserves for the American part of her story the privilege of resisting totalization, refusing narrative closure, and dismissing "any confidently thrusting story line" as "a sentimentality, an excess, an exaggeration, an untruth" (LT 164). However, in relating the lives of her Polish childhood peers, she more readily exhibits a predilection for closure and confinement, reducing their fate in her brilliant verbal cameos to the chilling finality of failure.

8 E. San Juan, Jr. criticizes Sollors's binary model for "its stress on normative assimilation or integration" and for its repression of the legacy of racism and colonialism, consistent with the liberal idea of cultural pluralism (22–23).

9 Several critics downplay her Jewishness as a primary source of her "difference," since it gets continually displaced in her attempts at "passing" first in Poland, then in the United States. Zaborowska claims that Hoffman's Jewishness "does not have as profound effect on her identity as it did on the daughters of orthodox rabbis like Yezierska or Stern half a century earlier" (229).

10 William Boelhower, discussing Mary Antin and the xenophobic pressure of the dominant culture, notices that "most immigrant/ethnic autobiographers sought to pass themselves off as Americans by didactically copying and promoting officially acceptable behavioral codes" (*The Future* 127).

11 According to Henry Adams, the notion of the ego as whole and unitary finds its fullest expression in a child's vision: "The older the mind, the older its complexities, and the further it looks, the more it sees, until even the stars resolve themselves into multiples; yet the child will always see but one" (398–99).

12 Adams projects himself from unity into "Twentieth-Century Multiplicity … With the help of these two points of relation, he hoped to project his lines forward and backward indefinitely" (435).

13 Kamboureli's friend Lola Lemire Tostevin comments on the title in a letter to the author: "I find myself wondering if it doesn't suggest a duality of a subject split only in two, when, in fact, so many of your 'journal' entries assert the 'naming of plurals'" ("Women" 75).

14 In an interview, Kamboureli "narrated how she happened to unearth her own diaries in a drawer and felt that she was not the person who wrote them. The diary-journal

written in *in the second person* is a 'play' on those two diaries; one in Greek the other in English. The poem 'June 8, 1982' talks about these three diaries" (S. Roy 266).
15. See the first chapter of *Revolution in Poetic Language* and McCance's article in *Tessera*, to which I refer later in my discussion.
16. As a necessary caveat to the endorsement of "locality," it is important to remember that, elsewhere, Kamboureli cautions against potentially "detrimental effects of self-location" and "intellectual swindling" that the pressure to assume a fixed location may lead to. Progressively identifying with the position of a diasporic critic, she reminds us of the presence of "elements that are unassimilable, that extend beyond the binary structure within which the diasporic critic has traditionally situated herself" (*Scandalous* 22).
17. See Kamboureli's comment: "The pressure I felt to position myself, instead of resolving my tensions, kept pointing to various layers of my subjectivity, revealing my identity to be unsettled, continuously disrupted, determined by different alliances on different occasions" (*Scandalous* 5).
18. In *Scandalous Bodies* Kamboureli elucidates her views on ethnicity and other markers used to situate a person and admits that her questioning of identity categories derives from the reflection initiated by *in the second person*: "I began to see the material signs of my body—including my whiteness (the whiteness of a southern European) and my accent—as stress signs symptomatic of the condition of the social body I was trying to understand. I had become a medium of representation" (4).
19. Barbara Godard is among the first readers to place *in the second person* within the genre of Canadian long poem ("The Discourse").
20. See Robert Kroetsch's essay "For Play and Entrance: The Contemporary Long Poem," where he places the contemporary Canadian long poem in the line of continuity with Homer's *The Odyssey* (*The Lovely Treachery* 120).
21. Smaro refuses the role of "native informant" (nota bene, the role that Eva Hoffman cherishes while translating both ways: Eastern Europe to her American friends and, subsequently, America to her Polish friends): "Although I am Macedonian like Aristotle, I am not a mimetic being, a signified brand. I am expected to be homogeneous at the expense of my personal heterogeneity. I've said 'No' to those who invited me to recite Homer by heart" (isp 8).
22. Rosina Lippi-Green uses this term coined by Labov "to describe how speakers of peripheralized languages subordinate and devalue their own language in line with stigmatization which originates outside their communities" (174).
23. Jennifer Browdy de Hernandez, in her comparative essay on Hoffman and Audre Lorde, draws attention to a relative privilege of white immigrants: "For all her sense of herself as an outsider, Hoffman meets with much less systemic resistance in her struggles to find a place for herself than does Lorde, [who is black and lesbian]" (31).

Notes to Chapter 4: Translation as Allegorical Metafiction

1. There has been a lot of debate in critical literature about the accuracy of the term "postcolonial," suggesting not only that it is a Eurocentric term, privileging the European moment in history, but also that it downplays the reality of colonialism for indigenous peoples and neocolonialism in the era of globalization. I concur with Françoise Lionnet's understanding of "postcolonial" less in terms of periodization or a new economic reality than in terms of "'postcontact': that is, as a condition that [already] exists within, and thus contests and resists, the colonial moment itself

with its ideology of domination" (*Postcolonial* 4). Consequently, she views such phenomena as Négritude and Frantz Fanon's writing, which was produced during the colonial period, as already "postcolonial."
2   Similarly, Frantz Fanon contrasts the dominant culture's attitudes to white and Black migrants, showing how racialization and Eurocentrism work in the context of speaking with an accent. Using an example of a German or a French person, he says: "I can hardly forget that he has a language of his own, a country, and that perhaps he is a lawyer or an engineer there ... [But a Black person] has no culture, no civilization, no 'long historical past'" (34). I might add that the specificity of African Caribbean immigrants' experience sets them apart not only from their European counterparts but also from African Americans native to the United States, for whom the topos of the Middle Passage functions mostly in the context of exclusion from citizenship and represents, according to Heike Paul, "the reverse/repressed side of immigration and the immigrant experience" (18). Philip's and Kincaid's work, stemming from a history of multiple displacements, confounds a tendency to cast immigrant experience and African American experience in oppositional terms based on race and necessitates careful attention to different histories of immigration and racialization.
3   Patois is described simply as colloquial language, and Creole as a contact language which is more stable and can be a person's native language (Talib 124).
4   Lippi-Green reminds us that there are no linguistic criteria but only social criteria for identifying dialects, and "a dialect is perhaps nothing more than a language that gets no respect" (43).
5   Fanon's strong critique of Négritude as "an anti-racist racism" (132) is derived from his opposition to any counter-constructions of Black subjectivity based on essentialist associations with rhythm, sensuality, etc.
6   Glissant prefers to use the concept of creolization to that of *métissage*, which he perceives as tainted by its association with racist discourses of hybridity. As already mentioned in the Introduction, Françoise Lionnet has salvaged the concept of *métissage* for the feminist study of postcolonial autobiography in her *Autobiographical Voices*.
7   According to Derrida, creolization is the inner structure of each language suppressed by monolingual regimes; it is how each language grows, by being "open to the most radical grafting, open to deformations, transformations, expropriation, to a certain a-nomie and de-regulation" (*Monolingualism* 65).
8   I discuss Philip's use of mimicry in more detail later in this chapter. Suffice it to say here that this concept has special currency in postcolonial theory, especially since it has been re-theorized by Homi Bhabha. Originally associated with a degrading condition of a colonial "mimic man," doomed to imperfect translation as imitation of the "superior" (English) original, it has been taken up and resignified through the possibility of becoming adopted self-consciously as a defiant, resistant strategy. Like parody, mimicry is a form of repetition with a difference, relying on intertextual and cultural flows. However, while parody often operates within the same cultural context, mimicry might be described as cross-cultural parody, based on the assumption of rigid cultural and racial boundaries.
9   Henry Louis Gates Jr. traces signifying back to African mythology and African American folktales of the Signifying Monkey, a popular trickster figure. Referring to signifying as "the slave's trope," a metaleptic, trope-reversing trope, he adds that it is "a trope that subsumes other rhetorical tropes, including metaphor, metonymy, synecdoche and irony (the 'master' tropes)," as well as a chain of related rhetorical

tropes which include figures of negation, repetition, substitution, and reversal (286). He views signifying as akin to Mikhail Bakhtin's "double-voiced" or dialogical discourse of parodic imitation and a hidden or internal polemic, and sees its manifestations everywhere in Black culture, from African American literature and literary history, to the rhetorical patterns of the Black vernacular, to hip hop music.

10 One can say that "gift" is always contaminated by its association with "poison" through the German word *das Gift*, the duplicity or undecidability that recalls my earlier comments on Derrida's use of *pharmakon*.

11 Carol Boyce Davies mockingly sums up this colonized male anxiety as "Oh God! This tongue is not mine. It gives me hell and angers me but I cannot part with it" (158).

12 The title "Discourse on the Logic of Language" also signals intertextual borrowings from Glissant, who in *Caribbean Discourse* speaks of the difficulty to attain expression that is "not part of the internal logic of [the dominant] language" (121).

13 Henry Louis Gates Jr. adds that a pernicious tendency in Western discourse to associate the trope of blackness with absence goes back at least to Plato's *Phaedrus* (315).

14 It is possible to make a link here between a threat of "monstrosity" as a result of "improper" sexual and linguistic mixing and the problem of standardization. In fact, standardization has a colonial legacy: "the rise of the notion of what standard English should be developed ... hand in hand with the rise of British colonialism" and the notion of "King's English" "might have arisen as a reaction to the threat of foreign corruption of the language. Thus 'King's English' is defined negatively by fears of what English should not be rather than what it is or should be" (Talib 15).

15 Coincidentally, the etymological meaning of *métis* or *méstizo*, the roots of the word *métissage*, "derives from the Latin *mixtus*, 'mixed,' and its primary meaning refers to cloth made of two different fibers" (Lionnet, *Autobiographical* 14).

16 Krishna Sarbadhikary observes that for the African the museum is a symbol of appropriation and silencing: "In this site of 'racial oppression' a double erasure takes place: erasure of the ritualistic context within which African cultural objects existed, and erasure of the circumstances of their severance from the places of belonging" (112).

17 Patricia Hill Collins defines "othermothers" as "women who assist bloodmothers by sharing mothering responsibilities" in African American communities (178).

18 Susan Rudy Dorscht describes decolonizing writing as "writing into the English language experience and syntax, and thus ways of thinking, seeing, and being, that are not only foreign to it but also rendered unthinkable, invisible, unspeakable, and certainly unlivable within it" (134).

19 For example, Lizabeth Paravisini-Gebert offers a dark, non-redemptive reading of the text, judging Xuela as "damaged beyond repair" (163), "a repellent heroine" (149) unable to engage with "her fellow human beings" (150). Another Eurocentric reading is offered by Elizabeth West, who downplays the trauma of colonialism, focusing on Xuela's "spiritual desolation," which makes her unable "to construct a meaningful identity" (3).

20 Rhonda Cobham discusses Xuela as an incarnation of Mammywata, whom she links to both Africa and the Caribbean: "Combining the characteristics of males and females, colonizer and colonized, the Mammywata [is] related to those creolized cultural spaces where Pidgin English is spoken in Nigeria, and where European influence existed" (871).

21 In its rich heterogeneity, Fanon's text might even be regarded as offering models of autobiographical criticism, through a series of symptomatic readings of life writing

such as Mayotte Capécia's memoir *Je suis Martiniquaise* (1948) and René Maran's autobiographical novel *Un homme pareil aux autres* (1947). Incidentally, interesting relays of meaning occur if one looks at Derrida's testimony in *Monolingualism of the Other* as a repetition with a difference of Fanon's, whose self-analysis of colonial alienation is, in turn, refracted and gendered in Kincaid's text.
22 The presence of Fanon as an intertext also justifies frequent readings of Kincaid in terms of psychoanalysis. However, I argue that for Fanon and Kincaid alike, psychoanalysis can be viewed as an extended poetic system, with its own stock of favourite images and metaphors. Fanon offers a great critique of psychoanalysis, or rather of its limitations and its false, useless universalism that tends to ignore the material context of the experience, its historical, economic, social circumstances: "The discoveries of Freud are of no use to us here. What must be done is to restore this dream *to its proper time* ... and *to its proper place*" (104).
23 But the illustrations can also represent re-membering of the absent Carib mother, a process that reaches its conclusion with the book's ending, when there's only the mother as the book. The images can also be read as her "cut up" body. This is an example of indeterminacy that prevents totalization and signals a refusal to be mastered.
24 One cannot overlook the fact that the historical Kincaid participates in the same tradition of signifying/significant name changes in "an effort to forge a more adequate representation of a 'post'-colonial subject" (Gilmore, *Limits* 103). Although not in fact from Jamaica, she uses 'Jamaica,' as opposed to Antigua, where she is from, or Dominica, where her maternal roots are, "to signify her Caribbean roots as well as mark her status as a 'rootless' cosmopolitan migrant" (Bernard 119).
25 Deleuze and Guattari mention three characteristics of "minor literature," all of which apply to Kincaid's narrative. First, minor literature is not written in the language of a minority, but rather comes from a deterritorialized major language, like English in the Caribbean. Second, minor literatures exhibit a political consciousness. Third, minor literatures are "*collective assemblages of enunciation*" (Deleuze and Guattari 18). This aspect relates to Kincaid's experiment with the autobiographical subject as a necessary function for the collective experience to be told.
26 I want to add that this position differs from a simple reversal and revaluation, as in celebratory approaches to difference such as, for example, the movement of Négritude. Nor is it an "add-on" approach characteristic of demands for recognition in identity-based movements. For me, this radical reworking from within describes Kincaid's critical insider/outsider place in contemporary American literature: both mainstream and oppositional, staking a high claim to "the literary" and deterritorializing it.
27 The centrality of pain in Kincaid's narrative may account for the possibility of reading it in relation to theories of sadomasochism or S/M, justified, for example, by Fanon's psychoanalytic approach to colonialism. Holomb and Holomb try to "theorize possible intersections of S/M and colonialism" as it applies to Kincaid (969), similar to Fanon's theorization of possible intersections of psychoanalysis and colonialism.
28 Regarding the hyphen, here is a different example of its use in Xuela's narrative: "And it was from that life that those people [the enslaved Africans] were taken away by the Scots-man or some other hyphenated man who cannot exist as just a man but only with a hyphen" (AMM 187). In this passage, the narrator dismantles the European myths of cultural superiority and uses the Middle Passage to rewrite the meaning of the hyphen. A hyphen here means denial of humanity through "the crime

of identity"; "the Scots-man" is also half-human because he commits the crime of slavery.

29 Kincaid's photograph and the cover image as two sides of the book can also be related to a different way of thinking about translation that decolonizes the concept from its Eurocentric presuppositions. To illustrate, let me quote here Maria Tymoczko's explanation of a Chinese concept of translation as "turning a page": "In China text and translation are related as the front and back of the object, or perhaps as the positive and negative of the same picture" ("Reconceptualizing" 22).

30 The pervasiveness of such representations is evident from the early accounts of Columbus's journeys and Pere Labat's 1693–1705 memoirs, to William S. Birge's 1900 description of his trip to the Carib reserve in Dominica, *In Old Roseau*. Hinged upon the binaries of European/"other," Christian/pagan, or civilized/barbaric, these discourses of alterity served to reinforce the idea of white superiority and justify the brutal conquest of the Caribs. As Morris observes, the Caribs had to be marked with brutality and violence "so that the barbarity that would be enacted upon them would appear to be justifiable" (958).

31 This complex metaphor first emerged in Oswald de Andrade's *Manifesto Antropofago* (1928) as "an irreverent verbal weapon and a form of resistance" to mental colonialism of Brazilian culture, and was taken up again by Haroldo de Campos in the 1960s to the 1990s "as both a metaphor and a philosophy of culture" (Vieira 96). As a "reversible" metaphor, it can be turned back onto Europe, which has brought savage capitalism and imperialism "devouring" the rest of the world.

Works Cited

Adams, Henry. *The Education of Henry Adams: An Autobiography*. 1918. Boston: Houghton Mifflin, 1961.
Adams, Timothy Dow. *Light Writing and Life Writing: Photography in Autobiography*. Chapel Hill: U of North Carolina P, 2000.
Alarcon, Norma. "Chicana's Feminist Literature: A Re-vision through Malintzin/or Malintzin: Putting Flesh Back on the Object." In Moraga and Anzaldua, eds., *This Bridge* 182–90.
Alvarez, Julia. "My English." In *Something to Declare: Essays*. New York: Plume, 1998. 21–29.
Alvarez, Roman, and Carmen-Africa Vidal, eds. *Translation, Power, Subversion*. Clevedon, England: Multilingual Matters, 1996.
Anatol, Gizelle Liz. "Speaking in (M)other Tongues: The Role of Language in Jamaica Kincaid's *The Autobiography of My Mother*." *Callaloo* 25.3 (2002): 938–53.
Ang, Ien. "On Not Speaking Chinese: Postmodern Ethnicity and the Politics of Diaspora." In Morag Shiach, ed., *Feminism and Cultural Studies*. Oxford and New York: Oxford UP, 1999. 540–64.
Antin, Mary. *From Polotzk to Boston*. Boston, MA: W.B. Clarke, 1899.
———. *The Promised Land*. 1912. New York: Penguin Books, 1997.
Anzaldua, Gloria. *Borderlands/La Frontera: The New Mestiza*. San Francisco: Spinsters/Aunt Lute, 1987.
———. "Speaking in Tongues: A Letter to Third World Women Writers." In Moraga and Anzaldua, eds., *This Bridge* 165–74.
Asad, Talal. "A Comment on Translation, Critique, and Subversion." In Dingwaney and Maier, eds., *Between Languages* 325–32.
———. "The Concept of Cultural Translation in British Social Anthropology." In James Clifford and George Marcus, eds., *Writing Culture: The Poetics and Politics of Ethnography*. Berkeley: U of California P, 1986. 141–64.

Ashcroft, Bill, Gareth Griffiths, and Helen Tiffin. *The Empire Writes Back: Theory and Practice in Post-colonial Literatures*. New York: Routledge, 1989.

Ashley, Kathleen, Leigh Gilmore, and Gerald Peters, eds. *Autobiography and Postmodernism*. Amherst: U of Massachusetts P, 1994.

Bal, Mieke. *A Mieke Bal Reader*. Chicago: U of Chicago P, 2006.

Bammer, Angelika, ed. *Displacements: Cultural Identities in Question*. Bloomington: Indiana UP, 1994.

Banting, Pamela. *Body Inc. A Theory of Translation Poetics*. Winnipeg: Turnstone P, 1995.

Bartkowski, Frances. *Travelers, Immigrants, Inmates: Essays in Estrangement*. Minneapolis: U of Minnesota P, 1995.

Bartoloni, Paolo. *On the Cultures of Exile, Translation, and Writing*. West Lafayette, IN: Purdue UP, 2008.

Bassnett, Susan, and Harish Trivedi, eds. *Post-colonial Translation: Theory and Practice*. New York and London: Routledge, 1999.

Bell, Sharon Masingale. "In the Shadow of the Father Tongue: On Translating the Masks in J.S. Alexis." In Dingwaney and Maier, eds., *Between Languages* 51–74.

Benjamin, Walter. "The Task of the Translator." Trans. Harry Zohn. *Illuminations*. New York: Schocken Books, 1969.

Bennington, Geoffrey. "Deconstruction and Ethics." In Nicholas Royle, ed., *Deconstructions: A User's Guide*. New York: Palgrave, 2000. 64–82.

Benstock, Shari, ed. *The Private Self: Theory and Practice of Women's Autobiographical Writings*. Chapel Hill: U of North Carolina P, 1988.

Benston, Kimberly W. "I yam what I am: The Topos of (Un)naming in Afro-American Literature." In Henry Louis Gates Jr., ed., *Black Literature* 151–72.

Benveniste, Emil. *Problems in General Linguistics*. Coral Gables, FL: U of Miami P, 1971.

Bergland. Betty. "Ideology, Ethnicity, and the Gendered Subject: Reading Immigrant Women's Autobiographies." In Donna Gabaccia, ed., *Seeking Common Ground: Multidisciplinary Studies of Immigrant Women in the United States*. Westport, CT: Praeger, 1992. 101–21.

———. "Postmodernism and the Autobiographical Subject: Reconstructing the 'Other.'" In Ashley et al., eds., *Autobiography* 130–66.

Berman, Antoine. *The Experience of the Foreign: Culture and Translation in Romantic Germany*. Trans. S. Heyvaert. Albany: SUNY P, 1992.

Bernard, Louise. "Countermemory and Return: Reclamation of the (Postmodern) Self in Jamaica Kincaid's *The Autobiography of My Mother* and *My Brother*." *Modern Fiction Studies* 48.1 (Spring 2002): 113–38.

Berryman, Charles. "Critical Mirrors: Theories of Autobiography." *Mosaic* 32.1 (1999): 71–84.

Besemeres, Mary. *Translating One's Self: Language and Selfhood in Cross-Cultural Autobiography*. Bern: Peter Lang, 2002.

Bhabha, Homi K. "Frontlines/Borderposts." In Bammer, ed., *Displacements* 269–72.

———. "How Newness Enters the World: Postmodern Space, Postcolonial Times and the Trials of Cultural Translation." *The Location of Culture*. New York and London: Routledge, 1994. 212–35.

———. "Of Mimicry and Man: The Ambivalence of Colonial Discourse." *The Location of Culture* 85–92.

Boelhower, William, ed. *The Future of American Modernism: Ethnic Writing between the Wars*. Amsterdam: VU UP, 1990.

———. *Immigrant Autobiographies in the United States*. Verona: Essedue Edizioni, 1982.

Bourdieu, Pierre. *The Field of Cultural Production: Essays on Art and Literature*. Ed. Randal Johnson. New York: Columbia UP, 1993.

Brand, Dionne. *A Map to the Door of No Return: Notes to Belonging*. Toronto: Doubleday Canada, 2001.

Brettell, Caroline B. "Blurred Genres and Blended Voices: Life History, Biography, Autobiography, and the Auto/Ethnography of Women's Lives. In Reed-Danahay, ed., *Auto/Ethnography* 224–46.

Brodzki, Bella. *Can These Bones Live? Translation, Survival, and Cultural Memory*. Stanford, CA: Stanford UP, 2007.

———. "History, Cultural Memory, and the Task of Translation in T. Obinkaram Eschewa's *I Saw the Sky Catch Fire*." *PMLA* 114.2 (1999): 206–19.

Brodzki, Bella, and Celeste Schenck, eds. *Life/Lines: Theorizing Women's Autobiography*. Ithaca and London: Cornell UP, 1988.

Brooke-Rose, Christine. *Remake*. Manchester: Carcanet, 1996.

Brossard, Nicole. *These Our Mothers, Or: The Disintegrating Chapter*. Trans. Barbara Godard. Toronto: Coach House, 1983.

Burgess, Marilyn. "'Imperfect Homecomings': Exile, Feminist Video and the Lure of the Maternal." *Topia* 2 (1998): 91–103.

Burrows, Victoria. *Whiteness and Trauma: The Mother–Daughter Knot in the Fiction of Jean Rhys, Jamaica Kincaid, and Toni Morrison*. New York: Palgrave Macmillan, 2004.

Burstein, Janet. "Translating Immigrant Women: Surfacing the Manifold Self." In Joyce Antler, ed., *Talking Back: Images of Jewish Women in American Popular Culture*. Hanover and London: Brandeis UP and UP of New England, 1998. 15–29.

Busia, Abena P.A. *Testimonies of Exile*. Trenton, NJ: Africa World Press, 1990.

Buss, Helen M. *Mapping Our Selves: Canadian Women's Autobiography*. Montreal and Kingston: McGill-Queen's UP, 1993.

———. *Repossessing the World: Reading Memoirs by Contemporary Women*. Waterloo, ON: Wilfrid Laurier UP, 2002.

———. "Writing and Reading Autobiographically." *Prairie Fire* 16.3 (Autumn 1995): 5–15.

Butler, Judith. *Gender Trouble: Feminism and the Subversion of Identity*. New York: Routledge, 1999.

Carbonell, Ovidio. "The Exotic Space of Cultural Translation." In Alvarez and Vidal, eds., *Translation* 79–98.

Caruth, Cathy. *Trauma: Explorations in Memory*. Baltimore and London: Johns Hopkins UP, 1995.

Chamberlain, Mary. "The Global Self: Narratives of Caribbean Migrant Women." In Cosslett et al., eds., *Feminism* 154–66.

Chancy, Myriam J.A. *Searching for Safe Spaces: Afro-Caribbean Women Writers in Exile*. Philadelphia: Temple UP, 1997.

Chanfrault-Duchet, Marie-Françoise. "Textualization of the Self and Gender Identity in the Life-Story." In Cosslett et al., eds., *Feminism* 61–75.

Cheng, Anne Anlin. *The Melancholy of Race*. New York: Oxford UP, 2001.

Cheyfitz, Eric. *The Poetics of Imperialism: Translation and Colonization from The Tempest to Tarzan*. Philadelphia: U of Pennsylvania P, 1997.

Chow, Rey. *Primitive Passions: Visuality, Sexuality, Ethnography, and Contemporary Chinese Cinema*. New York: Columbia UP, 1995.

———. "Where Have All the Natives Gone?" In Bammer, ed., *Displacements* 125–51.

Christian, Karen. *Show and Tell: Performing Identity in U.S. Latina/o Fiction*. Albuquerque: U of New Mexico P, 1997.

Cixous, Hélène. "The Laugh of the Medusa." Trans. Keith Cohen and Paula Cohen. In Elaine Marks and Isabelle de Courtivron, eds., *New French Feminisms: An Anthology*. New York: Schocken, 1981. 244–64.

———. *Three Steps on the Ladder of Writing*. Trans. Sarah Cornell and Susan Sellers. New York: Columbia UP, 1993.

Cobham, Rhonda. "'Mwen na rien, msieu': Jamaica Kincaid and the Problem of Creole Gnosis." *Callaloo* 25.3 (2002): 868–84.

Collier, Gordon. "A Disunified Field Theory of Creolization." In Bénédicte Ledent, ed., *Bridges across Chasms: Towards a Transcultural Future in Caribbean Literature*. Liège: Language and Literature, 2004. 293–301.

Collins, Patricia Hill. *Black Feminist Thought: Knowledges, Consciousness, and the Politics of Empowerment*. 2nd ed. New York: Routledge, 2000.

Corbett, Mary Jean. "Literary Domesticity and Women Writers' Subjectivities." In Smith and Watson, eds., *Women* 255–63.

Cosslett, Tess, Celia Lury, and Penny Summerfield, eds. *Feminism and Autobiography: Texts, Theories, Methods*. London and New York: Routledge, 2000.

Costello, Jeanne. "Taking the 'Woman' Out of Women's Autobiography: The Perils and Potentials of Theorizing Female Subjectivities." *Diacritics* 21 (1991): 123–34.

Couser, G. Thomas. *Altered Egos: Authority in American Autobiography*. New York: Oxford UP, 1989.

Craig, Terrence L. "The Confessional Revisited: Laura Salverson's Canadian Work." *Studies in Canadian Literature* 10.1–2 (1985): 81–93.
Cronin, Michael. *Translation and Identity*. New York: Routledge, 2006.
Culley, Margo. *American Women's Autobiography: Fea(s)ts of Memory*. Madison: U of Wisconsin P, 1992.
Currie, Noel Elizabeth. Review of Marlene Nourbese Philip's *Looking for Livingstone*. *Canadian Literature* 145 (Summer 1994): 122–25.
Cutter, Martha J. *Lost and Found in Translation: Contemporary Ethnic American Writing and the Politics of Language Diversity*. Chapel Hill: U of North Carolina P, 2005.
Davies, Carole Boyce. *Black Women, Writing and Identity: Migrations of the Subject*. New York: Routledge, 1994.
Davies, Norman. *God's Playground: A History of Poland*, vol. 2: *1795 to the Present*. Oxford: Oxford UP, 1981.
Davis, Kathleen. *Deconstruction and Translation*. Manchester, UK: St. Jerome Publishing, 2001.
Dawson, Mark. "In Place of Another Here the First Word Is ..." *Parallax* 15.1 (2009): 1–4.
DeFehr, Wayne. "Some Places to Take a Dull Ear: The 'Silent' Agent in Nourbese Philip's *Looking for Livingstone*. *Open Letter* 9.2 (1995): 45–52.
Deleuze, Gilles, and Félix Guattari. *Kafka: Toward a Minor Literature*. Trans. Dana Polan. Minneapolis: U of Minnesota P, 1986.
de Lotbiniere-Harwood, Susanne. *The Body Bilingual: Translation as a Rewriting in the Feminine*. Toronto: Women's Press, 1991.
de Man, Paul. "Autobiography as De-Facement." In *The Rhetoric of Romanticism*. New York: Columbia UP, 1984.
Derrida, Jacques. *The Ear of the Other: Otobiography, Transference, Translation*. Lincoln: U of Nebraska P, 1988.
———. "The First Session." Trans. Barbara Johnson. In Derek Attridge, ed., *Acts of Literature*. New York: Routledge, 1992. 127–80.
———. "*Fors*: The Anglish Words of Nicolas Abraham and Maria Torok." Trans. Barbara Johnson. In Nicolas Abraham and Maria Torok, *The Wolf Man's Magic Word: A Cryptonymy*. Minneapolis: University of Minnesota Press, 1986.
———. "The Law of Genre." Trans. Avital Ronell. In Derek Attridge, ed., *Acts of Literature*. New York: Routledge, 1992. 221–52.
———. *Monolingualism of the Other; or, The Prosthesis of Origin*. Trans. Patrick Mensah. Stanford: Stanford UP, 1998.
———. "'Le Parjure,' *Perhaps*: Storytelling and Lying ('abrupt breaches of syntax')." Trans. Peggy Kamuf. In Carol Jacobs and Henry Sussman, eds., *Acts of Narrative*. Stanford, CA: Stanford UP, 2003. 195–234.
———. "Des Tours de Babel." Trans. Joseph F. Graham. In Joseph F. Graham, ed., *Difference in Translation*. Ithaca, NY: Cornell UP, 1985. 165–207.

Devy, Ganesh. "Translation and Literary History: An Indian View." In Bassnett and Trivedi, *Post-colonial* 182–88.

Dingwaney, Anuradha, and Carol Maier, eds. *Between Languages and Cultures: Translation and Cross-Cultural Texts*. Pittsburgh: U of Pittsburgh P, 1995.

Donnell, Alison. "When Writing the Other Is Being True to the Self: Jamaica Kincaid's *The Autobiography of My Mother*." In Polkey, ed., *Women's Lives* 123–36.

Doray, Jocelyne, and Julian Samuel, eds. *The Raft of Medusa: Five Voices on Colonies, Nations and Histories*. Montreal: Black Rose Books, 1993.

Dorscht, Susan Rudy. "Decolonizing Canadian Writing: Why Gender? Whose English? When Canada?" *Essays on Canadian Writing* 54 (1994): 124–52.

Du Bois, W.E.B. *The Souls of Black Folk*. New York: Signet Classics, 1969.

Eakin, Paul. *Touching the World: Reference in Autobiography*. Princeton: Princeton UP, 1992.

Easton, Alison. "Subjects-in-Time: Slavery and African-American Women's Autobiographies." In Coslett et al., *Feminism* 169–182.

Egan, Susanna. *Mirror Talk: Genres of Crisis in Contemporary Autobiography*. Chapel Hill: U of North Carolina P, 1999.

Eldred, Janet, and Peter Mortensen. "Reading Literacy Narratives." *College English* 54.5 (1992): 512–39.

Fanon, Frantz. *Black Skin, White Masks*. Trans. Charles Lam Markmann. New York: Grove Press, 1967.

Firmat, Gustavo Pérez. *Tongue Ties: Logo-Erotocism in Anglo-Hispanic Literature*. New York: Palgrave Macmillan, 2003.

Fjellestad, Danuta Zadworna, "'The Insertion of Self into the Space of Borderless Possibility': Eva Hoffman's Exiled Body." *MELUS* 20.2 (1995): 133–47.

Flotow, Luise von. *Translation and Gender: Translating in the 'Era of Feminism.'* Manchester: St. Jerome Publishing; Ottawa: U of Ottawa P, 1997.

Franklin, Cynthia, and Laura E. Lyons. "Editor's Introduction: Bodies of Evidence and the Intricate Machines of Untruth." *Biography* 27.1 (Winter 2004): v–xxii.

Friedman, Susan Stanford. "Women's Autobiographical Selves: Theory and Practice." In Benstock, ed., *The Private Self* 34–62.

Fuchs, Miriam. *The Text Is Myself: Women's Life Writing and Catastrophe*. Madison: U of Wisconsin P, 2004.

Gagnier, Regenia. "The Literary Standard, Working-Class Autobiography, and Gender." In Smith and Watson, eds., *Women* 264–75.

Gagnon, Madeleine. "Mother Tongue and Women's Language." In Godard, ed., *Collaboration* 88–95.

Gates, Henry Louis, ed. *Black Literature and Literary Theory*. New York: Routledge, 1984.

George, Rosemary Marangoly. "Traveling Light: Of Immigration, Invisible Suitcases, and Gunny Sacks." *differences* 4.2 (1992): 72–99.

Ghosh-Schellhorn, Martina. *Steep Stairs to Myself: Transitional Autobiography*. Trier: Wissenschaftlicher Verlag, 2008.

Gilmore, Leigh. *Autobiographics: A Feminist Theory of Women's Self-Representation*. Ithaca, NY: Cornell UP, 1994.

———. *The Limits of Autobiography: Trauma and Testimony*. Ithaca, NY: Cornell UP, 2001.

———. "The Mark of Autobiography: Postmodernism, Autobiography, and Genre." In Ashley et al., eds., *Autobiography* 3–18.

Gilroy, Paul. "Diaspora and the Detours of Identity." In Kathryn Woodward, ed., *Identity and Difference*. London: Sage Publications, 1997. 299–346.

Glissant, Edouard. *Caribbean Discourse: Selected Essays*. Trans. J. Michael Dash. Charlottesville: UP of Virginia, 1989.

Gluck, Sherna Berger, and Daphne Patai, eds. *Women's Words: The Feminist Practice of Oral History*. New York: Routledge, 1991.

Godard, Barbara, ed. *Collaboration in the Feminine: Writing on Women and Culture from Tessera*. Toronto: Second Story Press, 1994.

———. "The Discourse of the Other: Canadian Literature and the Question of Ethnicity." *The Massachussetts Review* 31.1–2 (1990): 153–85.

———. "Introduction: The Moving Intimacy of Language." In Nicole Brossard, *Intimate Journal*. Toronto: Mercury Press, 2004. 5–24.

———. "Rape by Grammar: Marlene Nourbese Philip's Hyphenated Tongue or Writing the Caribbean Demotic between Africa and the Arctic." In Georgiana M.M. Colvile, ed., *Contemporary Women Writing in the Other Americas: Contemporary Women Writing in Canada and Quebec*. Vol. 3. Lewiston/Queenston/Lampeter: Edwin Mellen P, 1996. 407–42.

———. "Theorizing Feminist Discourse/Translation." *Tessera* 6 (1989): 42–53.

———. "Writing between Cultures." *TTR* 10.1 (1997): 53–99.

———. "Writing Resistance: Black Women's Writing in Canada." In Vevaina and Godard, eds., *Intersexions* 106–15.

Godard, Barbara, and Coomi S. Vevaina. "Crossings." In Vevaina and Godard, eds., *Intersexions* 1–54.

Goldman, Anne E. *Take My Word: Autobiographical Innovations of Ethnic American Working Women*. Berkeley: U of California P, 1996.

Gonzalez, Jennifer A. "Autotopographies." In Gabriel Brahm and Mark Driscoll, eds., *Prosthetic Territories: Politics and Hypertechnologies*. Boulder, CO: Westview Press, 1995. 133–50.

Gonzalez, Madelena, and Francine Tolron, eds. *Translating Identity and the Identity of Translation*. Newcastle, UK: Cambridge Scholars P, 2006.

Grossman, Ibolya (Szalai). *An Ordinary Woman in Extraordinary Times*. Toronto: Multicultural History Society of Ontario, 1990.

Grosz, Elizabeth. *Volatile Bodies: Toward a Corporeal Feminism*. Bloomington and Indianapolis: Indiana UP, 1994.

Gunew, Sneja. "Feminism and the Policy of Irreducible Differences: Multiculturalism/Ethnicity/Race." In Sneja Gunew and Anna Yeatman, eds., *Feminism and the Politics of Difference*. Halifax: Fernwood, 1993. 1–19.

Gunnars, Kristjana. "Laura Goodman Salverson's Confessions of a Divided Self." In Shirley Neuman and Smaro Kamboureli, eds., *A Mazing Space: Writing Canadian Women's Writing*. Edmonton, AB: Longspoon/NeWest, 1986. 148–53.

Hall, Stuart. "Cultural Identity and Diaspora." In Williams and Chrisman, eds., *Colonial Discourse* 392–403.

Harris, Claire. *Drawing Down a Daughter*. Fredericton, NB: Goose Lane Editions, 1992.

Harris, Jennifer. "*Looking for Livingstone: An Odyssey of Silence*, or an Odyssey of Marlene Nourbese Philip: Life-Writing the Unwrite-able." Unpublished manuscript. 1997. 1–16.

Hellerstein, Kathryn. "In Exile in the Mother Tongue: Yiddish and the Woman Poet." In Mae G. Henderson, ed., *Borders, Boundaries, and Frames: Essays in Cultural Criticism and Cultural Studies*. New York: Routledge, 1995. 64–106.

Henderson, Mae Gwendolyn. "Speaking in Tongues: Dialogics, Dialectics and the Black Woman Writer's Literary Tradition." In Williams and Chrisman, eds., *Colonial Discourse* 257–67.

Henke, Suzette A. *Shattered Subjects: Trauma and Testimony in Women's Life Writing*. New York: St. Martin's P, 2000.

Hermans, Theo. "Norms and the Determination of Translation. A Theoretical Framework." In Alvarez and Vidal, eds., *Translation* 25–51.

Hernandez, Jennifer Browdy de. "On Home Ground: Politics, Location, and the Construction of Identity in Four American Women's Autobiographies." *MELUS* 22.4 (1997): 21–38.

Hinz, Evelyn. "A Speculative Introduction: Life-Writing as Drama." *Mosaic* 20.4 (1987): v–xii.

Hirsch, Marianne. "The Generation of Postmemory." *Poetics Today* 29.1 (2008): 103–28.

———. "Pictures of a Displaced Girlhood." In Bammer, ed., *Displacements* 71–89.

Ho, Mingfong. "The Winter Hibiscus." In Josip Novakovich and Robert Shapard, eds., *Stories in the Stepmother Tongue*. Buffalo, NY: White Pine P, 2000. 161–78.

Hoffman, Eva. *After Such Knowledge: Memory, History, and the Legacy of the Holocaust*. New York: Public Affairs, 2004.

———. *Lost in Translation: A Life in a New Language*. New York: Penguin Books, 1989.

———. *Shtetl: The Life and Death of a Small Town and the World of Polish Jews*. Boston: Houghton Mifflin, 1997.

Holomb, Gary E., and Kimberly S. Holomb. "'I made him': Sadomasochism in Kincaid's *The Autobiography of My Mother*." *Callaloo* 25.3 (2002): 969–76.

Holte, James Craig. *The Ethnic "I": A Sourcebook for Ethnic-American Autobiography*. Westport, CT: Greenwood P, 1988.

hooks, bell. "'this is the oppressor's language/ yet I need it to talk to you': Language, a Place of Struggle." In Dingwanwy and Maier, eds., *Between Languages* 295–301.
Huff, Cynthia, ed. *Women's Life Writing and Imagined Communities*. New York: Routledge, 2005.
Hutcheon, Linda. *A Poetics of Postmodernism: History, Theory, Fiction*. New York: Routledge, 1988.
Irigaray, Luce. *This Sex Which Is Not One*. Trans. C. Porter and C. Burke. Ithaca, NY: Cornell UP, 1985.
Irving, Katrina. *Immigrant Mothers: Narratives of Race and Maternity, 1890–1925*. Urbana: U of Illinois P, 2000.
Jakobson, Roman, "On Linguistic Aspects of Translation." In Lawrence Venuti, ed., *The Translation Studies Reader*. New York: Routledge, 2000. 113–18.
Jelinek, Estelle C. *Women's Autobiography: Essays in Criticism*. Bloomington: Indiana UP, 1980.
Jolly, Margareta, ed. *Encyclopedia of Life Writing: Autobiographical and Biographical Forms*. Chicago: Fitzroy Dearborn, 2001.
Joseph, May, and Jennifer Natalya Fink, eds. *Performing Hybridity*. Minneapolis: U of Minnesota P, 1999.
Kadar, Marlene. "Coming to Terms: Life Writing—From Genre to Critical Practice." In Marlene Kadar, ed., *Essays on Life Writing: From Genre to Critical Practice*. Toronto: U of Toronto P, 1992. 3–16.
———. "The Discourse of Ordinariness and 'Multicultural History.'" *Essays on Canadian Writing* 60 (1996): 119–38.
———. "Introduction: What Is Life Writing?" In *Reading Life Writing*, ed. Marlene Kadar. Toronto: Oxford UP, 1993. ix–xv.
———. "Whose Life Is It Anyway? Out of the Bathtub and into the Narrative." In Kadar, ed., *Essays* 152–61.
Kadar, Marlene, Linda Warley, Jeanne Perreault, and Susanna Egan, eds. *Tracing the Autobiographical*. Waterloo, ON: Wilfrid Laurier UP, 2005.
Kamboureli, Smaro. "Dialogue with the Other: The Use of Myth in Canadian Women's Poetry." In Ann Dybikowski, Victoria Freeman, Daphne Marlatt, Barbara Pulling, and Betsy Warland, eds., *In the Feminine: Women and Words/Les femmes et les mots*. Conference Proceedings 1983. Edmonton: Longspoon Press, 1985. 105–9.
———. *in the second person*. Edmonton, AB: Longspoon, 1985.
———. "It Was Not a Dark and Stormy Night." In Godard, ed., *Collaboration* 63–67.
———. "Locality as Writing: A Preface to the 'Preface' of *Out of Place*." *Open Letter* 6.2–3 (1985), 267–77.
———. "Of Black Angels and Melancholy Lovers: Ethnicity and Writing in Canada." The Caroline Heath Lecture. *Freelance* 21.5 (1993): 15–20.

———. *Scandalous Bodies: Diasporic Literature in English Canada*. New York: Oxford UP, 2000.

———. "The Technology of Ethnicity: Law and Discourse." *Open Letter* 8.5–6 (1993): 201–17.

Kaplan, Caren. "Resisting Autobiography: Out-Law Genres and Transnational Feminist Subjects." In Smith and Watson, eds., *De/Colonizing* 115–38.

Karamcheti, Indira. "Aimé Césaire's Subjective Geographies: Translating Place and the Difference It Marks." In Dingwaney and Maier, eds., *Between Languages* 181–97.

Kellman, Steven G., ed. *Switching Languages: Translingual Writers Reflect on Their Craft*. Lincoln: U of Nebraska P, 2003.

Kikumura, Akemi. *Through Harsh Winters: The Life of a Japanese Immigrant Woman*. Novato, CA: Chandler and Sharp, 1981.

Kim, Myung Mi. "Into Such Assembly." In Soyini D. Madison, ed., *The Woman That I Am: The Literature and Culture of Contemporary Women of Color*. New York: St. Martin's P, 1994. 93–94.

Kincaid, Jamaica. *The Autobiography of My Mother*. New York: Farrar Straus Giroux, 1996.

Kinnear, Mary. "The Icelandic Connection: Freyja and the Manitoba Woman Suffrage Movement." In Nuzhat Amin et al., eds., *Canadian Woman Studies: An Introductory Reader*. Toronto: Inanna, 2000. 79–85.

Kojder, Apolonja Maria, and Barbara Glogowska. *'Marynia Don't Cry': Memoirs of Two Polish-Canadian Families*. Toronto: Multicultural History Society of Ontario, 1995.

Kristeva, Julia. *Desire in Language: A Semiotic Approach to Literature and Art*. Trans. Thomas Gora, Alice Jardine, and Leon Roudiez. New York: Columbia UP, 1980.

———. *Powers of Horror: An Essay on Abjection*. Trans. Leon Roudiez. New York: Columbia UP, 1982.

———. *Revolution in Poetic Language*. Trans. Margaret Waller. New York: Columbia UP, 1984.

———. "Women's Time." Trans. Alice Jardine and Harry Blake. *Signs*, 7.1 (1981): 13–35.

Kroetsch, Robert. *The Lovely Treachery of Words: Essays Selected and New*. Toronto: Oxford UP, 1989.

Layoun, Mary N. "Translation, Cultural Transgression and Tribute, and Leaden Feet." In Dingwaney and Maier, eds., *Between Languages* 267–91.

Lefevere, André. "Composing the Other." In Bassnett and Trivedi, eds., *Post-colonial* 75–94.

Lejeune, Philippe. *On Autobiography*. Trans. Katherine Leary. Minneapolis: U of Minnesota P, 1989.

Levinas, Emmanuel. *Outside the Subject*. Trans. Michael B. Smith. Stanford: Stanford UP, 1994.

Lim, Shirley Geok-lin. *Among the White Moon Faces: An Asian-American Memoir of Homelands*. New York: Feminist Press, 1996.

———. "Immigration and Diaspora." In King-kok Cheung, ed., *An Interethnic Companion to Asian American Literature*. New York: Cambridge UP, 1997. 289–311.

Lim, Shirley Geok-lin, and Caroline Kyungah Hong. "Introduction: The Postmodern Dilemma for Life Writing: Hybridizing Hyphens." *Life Writing* 4.1 (April 2007): 3–9.

Lionnet, Françoise. *Autobiographical Voices: Race, Gender, Self-Portraiture*. Ithaca, NY: Cornell UP, 1989.

———. "Of Mangoes and Maroons: Language, History, and the Multicultural Subject of Michelle Cliff's *Abeng*." In Smith and Watson, eds., *De/Colonizing* 321–45.

———. *Postcolonial Representations: Women, Literature, Identity*. Ithaca and London: Cornell UP, 1995.

Lippi-Green, Rosina. *English with an Accent: Language, Ideology, and Discrimination in the United States*. New York: Routledge, 1997.

Lorde, Audre. The Master's Tools Will Never Dismantle the Master's House." *Sister Outsider: Essays and Speeches*. Freedom, CA: Crossing P, 1984. 110–13.

———. *Zami: A New Spelling of My Name*. Freedom, CA: Crossing P, 1982.

Ma, Sheng–mei. *Immigrant Subjectivities in Asian American and Asian Diaspora Literatures*. Albany, NY: SUNY P 1998.

Makabe, Tomoko. *Picture Brides: Japanese Women in Canada*. Trans. Kathleen Chisato Merken. Toronto: Multicultural History Society of Ontario, 1995.

Marlatt, Daphne. "Musing with Mothertongue." *Readings from the Labyrinth*. Edmonton: NeWest, 1998. 9–14.

———. "Self-Representation and Fictionalysis." In Godard, ed., *Collaboration* 202–6.

Mason, Mary G. "The Other Voice: Autobiographies by Women Writers." In Olney, ed., *Autobiography* 207–35.

McAlpine, Kristie. "Narratives of Silence: Marlene Nourbese Philip and Joy Kogawa." In Serge Jaumain, Marc Maufort, and Lucette Nobell, eds., *The Guises of Canadian Diversity: New European Perspectives*. Amsterdam: Rodopi, 1995. 133–42.

McCance, Dawne. "Julia Kristeva and the Ethics of Exile." *Tessera* 8 (Spring 1990): 23–39.

Mezei, Kathy. "Traverse." *Tessera* 6 (1989): 9–10.

Miller, Nancy K. *Getting Personal: Feminist Occasions and Autobiographical Acts*. New York: Routledge, 1991.

———. *Subject to Change: Reading Feminist Writing*. New York: Columbia UP, 1988.

Minh-ha, Trinh T. "An Acoustic Journey." In John C. Welchman, ed., *Rethinking Borders*. Minneapolis: U of Minnesota P, 1996. 1–17.

———. *Framer Framed*. New York: Routledge, 1991.

Mintz, Susannah B. *Unruly Bodies: Life Writing by Women with Disabilities*. Chapel Hill: U of North Carolina P, 2007.

Molloy, Sylvia. "The Unquiet Self: Spanish American Autobiography and the Question of National Identity." In Hortense J. Spillers, ed., *Comparative American Identities: Race, Sex, and Nationality in the Modern Text*. New York: Routledge, 1991. 26–39.

Moraga, Cherríe. *Loving in the War Years*. 1983. Expanded Second Edition. Cambridge, MA: South End P, 2000.

Moraga, Cherríe, and Gloria Anzaldua, eds. *This Bridge Called My Back: Writings by Radical Women of Color*. New York: Kitchen Table: Women of Color P, 1981.

Morris, Kathryn E. "Jamaica Kincaid's Voracious Bodies: Engendering a Carib(bean) Woman." *Callaloo* 25.3 (2002): 954–68.

Moya, Paula M.L. "What's Identity Got to Do with It? Mobilizing Identities in the Multicultural Classroom." In Linda Martin Alcoff, Michael Hames-Garcia, Satya P. Mohanty, and Paula M.L. Moya, eds., *Identity Politics Reconsidered: Future of Minority Studies*. New York: Palgrave Macmillan, 2006. 96–117.

Mukherjee, Arun. "Introduction." *Sharing Our Experience*. Ottawa: Canadian Advisory Council on the Status of Women, 1993. 1–35.

Munton, Ann. "The Long Poem as Poetic Diary." *Open Letter* 6. 2–3 (1985): 93–106.

Neijmann, Daisy L. "Laura Goodman Salverson, Guttormur J. Guttormsson, and the Dual World of Second-Generation Canadian Authors." *Scandinavian-Canadian Studies* 8 (1995): 19–36.

Neuman, Shirley. "Life-Writing." In W.H. New, ed., *Literary History of Canada: Canadian Literature in English*. Second Edition, Volume Four. Toronto: U of Toronto P, 1990. 333–70.

———, ed. *Reading Canadian Autobiography. Essays on Canadian Writing* 60 (Winter 1996).

Niranjana, Tejaswini. *Siting Translation: History, Post-structuralism, and the Colonial Context*. Berkeley: U of California P, 1992.

Olney, James, ed. *Autobiography: Essays Theoretical and Critical*. Princeton: Princeton UP, 1980.

Oster, Judith. "See(k)ing the Self: Mirrors and Mirroring in Bicultural Texts." *MELUS* 23.4 (1998): 59–83.

Palumbo-Liu, David. *Asian/American: Historical Crossings of a Racial Frontier*. Stanford, CA: Stanford UP, 1999.

Paravisini-Gebert, Lizabeth. *Jamaica Kincaid: A Critical Companion*. Westport, CT: Greenwood P, 1999.

Pascal, Roy. *Design and Truth in Autobiography*. Cambridge, MA: Harvard UP, 1960.

Paul, Heike. *Mapping Migration: Women's Writing and the American Immigrant Experience from the 1950s to the 1990s*. Heidelberg: U.C. Winter, 1999.

Payant, Katherine B. "Introduction: Stories of the Uprooted." In Katherine B. Payant and Toby Rose, eds., *The Immigrant Experience in North American Literature: Carving Out a Niche*. Westport, CT: Greenwood Press, 1999.

Perreault, Jeanne. *Writing Selves: Contemporary Autography*. Minneapolis: U of Minnesota P, 1996.

Phelan, Peggy. *Mourning Sex: Performing Public Memories*. New York: Routledge, 1997.

Philip, Marlene Nourbese. *Frontiers: Essays and Writings on Racism and Culture*. Stratford, ON: Mercury Press, 1992.

———. *Genealogy of Resistance and Other Essays*. Toronto: Mercury P, 1997.

———. *Looking for Livingston: An Odyssey of Silence*. Toronto: Mercury Press, 1991.

———. "Managing the Unmanageable." In Selwyn R. Cudjoe, ed., *Caribbean Women Writers: Essays from the First International Conference*. Wellesley, MA: Calaloux Publications, 1990. 295–300.

———. *She Tries Her Tongue, Her Silence Softly Breaks*. Charlottetown, PE: Ragweed P, 1989.

Polkey, Pauline, ed. *Women's Lives into Print: The Theory, Practice and Writing of Feminist Auto/Biography*. London: Macmillan Press, 1999.

Powell, Barbara. "Laura Goodman Salverson: Her Father's 'Own True Son.'" *Canadian Literature* 133 (1992): 78–89.

Prasad, G.J.V. "Writing Translation: The Strange Case of the Indian English Novel." In Bassnett and Trivedi, eds., *Post-colonial Translation* 41–57.

Pratt, Mary Louise. *Imperial Eyes: Travel Writing and Transculturation*. New York: Routledge, 1992.

Proefriedt, William A. "The Immigrant or 'Outsider' Experience as Metaphor for Becoming an Educated Person in the Modern World; Mary Antin, Richard Wright and Eva Hoffman." *MELUS* 16.2 (1989–90): 77–89.

Radhakrishnan, R. "Ethnic Identity and Post-Structuralist Difference." *Cultural Critique* 6 (1987): 199–221.

Rak, Julie. "Introduction." In Julie Rak, ed., *Auto/biography in Canada: Critical Directions*. Waterloo, ON: Wilfrid Laurier UP, 2005. 1–29.

Rao, Eleonora. "Customs and Immigration: Smaro Kamboureli *in the second person* and the Airport of Language." *Textus: English Studies in Italy* 6 (1993): 241–58.

Rao, Sathya. "From a Postcolonial to a Non-Colonial Theory of Translation." In Naoki Sakai and Jon Solomon, eds., *Translation, Biopolitics, Colonial Difference*. Hong Kong: Hong Kong UP, 2006. 73–94.

Rayson, Ann. "Beneath the Mask: Autobiographies of Japanese-American Women." In Martine Watson Brownley and Allison B. Kimmich, eds., *Women and Autobiography*. Wilmington, DE: Scholarly Resources Books, 1999, 131–47.

Reed-Danahay, Deborah E., ed. *Auto/Ethnography: Rewriting the Self and the Social*. Oxford, UK: Berg Publishers, 1997.

Reynolds, Bryan. *Transversal Subjects: From Montaigne to Deleuze after Derrida*. New York: Palgrave Macmillan, 2009.

Rich, Adrienne. *Blood, Bread, and Poetry: Selected Prose*. New York: Norton, 1986.

Ricoeur, Paul. *On Translation*. Trans. Eileen Brennan. New York: Routledge, 2006.

Roberts, Richard. "The Construction of Cultures in Diaspora: African and African New World Experiences." *The South Atlantic Quarterly* 98.1–2 (1999): 177–90.

Roy, Sukhmani. "In the Third Person: An Interview with Smaro Kamboureli." In Vevaina and Godard, eds., *Intersexions* 265–69.

Roy, Wendy. "'The Ensign of the Mop and the Dustbin': The Maternal and the Material in Autobiographical Writings by Laura Goodman Salverson and Nellie McClung." In Rak, ed., *Auto/biography* 247–62.

Russell, Catherine. *Experimenthal Ethnography: The Work of Film in the Age of Video*. Durham, NC: Duke UP, 1999.

Salverson, Laura Goodman. *Confessions of an Immigrant's Daughter*. 1939. Toronto: U of Toronto P, 1981.

———. *The Viking Heart*. 1947. Toronto: McClelland and Stewart, 1975.

Salz, Evelyn, ed. *Selected Letters of Mary Antin*. Syracuse, NY: Syracuse UP, 2000.

Sanders, Leslie. "Marlene Nourbese Philip's 'Bad Words.'" *Tessera* 12 (Summer 1992): 81–89.

San Juan, E., Jr. "The Cult of Ethnicity and the Fetish of Pluralism: A Counterhegemonic Critique." *Cultural Critique* 18 (1991): 215–29.

Sarbadhikary, Krishna. "Weaving a 'Multicoloured Quilt': Marlene Nourbese Philip's Vision of Change." *International Journal of Canadian Studies* 10 (1994): 103–18.

Senghor, Léopold Sédar. "Negritude: A Humanism of the Twentieth Century." Williams and Chrisman *Colonial Discourse* 27–35.

Sengupta, Mahasweta. "Translation as Manipulation: The Power of Images and Images of Power." In Dingwaney and Maier, eds., *Between Languages* 159–79.

Shell, Marc. "Afterword." In Marc Shell and Werner Sollors, eds., *The Multilingual Anthology of American Literature: A Reader of Original Texts with English Translations*. New York: New York UP, 2000. 684–92.

Shields, Kathleen. "The Centre That Dare Not Speak Its Name: Translatability and Non-translation in Contemporary France." In Stephen Kelly and David Johnston, eds., *Betwixt and Between Place and Cultural Translation*. Newcastle, UK: Cambridge Scholars Publishing, 2007. 229–39.

Simon, Sherry. *Gender in Translation: Cultural Identity and the Politics of Translation*. New York: Routledge, 1996.

———. "Translating and Interlingual Creation in the Contact Zone: Border Writing in Quebec." In Bassnett and Trivedi, eds., *Post-colonial Translation* 58–74.

Smith, Sidonie. "Cheesecake, Nymphs, and 'We the People': Un/National Subjects about 1900." *Prose Studies* 17.1 (1994): 120–40.

———. "Identity's Body." In Ashley et al., eds., *Autobiography* 266–92.

———."Performativity, Autobiographical Practice, Resistance." *a/b:Auto/Biography Studies* 10 (Spring 1995): 17–33.

———.*Subjectivity, Identity, and the Body: Women's Autobiographical Practices in the Twentieth Century*. Bloomington: Indiana UP, 1993.

Smith, Sidonie, and Julia Watson, eds. *De/Colonizing the Subject: The Politics of Gender in Women's Autobiography*. Minneapolis: U of Minnesota P, 1992.

———. *Getting a Life: Everyday Uses of Autobiography*. Minneapolis: U of Minnesota P, 1996.

———. *Reading Autobiography: A Guide for Interpreting Life Narratives*. 2nd ed. Minneapolis and London: U of Minnesota P, 2010.

———. *Women, Autobiography, Theory: A Reader*. Madison: U of Wisconsin P, 1998.

Snead, James A. "Repetition as a Figure of Black Culture." In Gates, ed., *Black Literature* 59–79.

Soliday, Mary. "Translating Self and Difference through Literacy Narratives." *College English* 56.5 (1994): 511–26.

Sollors, Werner. *Beyond Ethnicity: Consent and Descent in American Culture*. New York: Oxford UP, 1986.

———. "Introduction" to Mary Antin's *The Promised Land*. New York: Penguin Books, 1997. xi–lx.

Spivak, Gayatri Chakravorty. *A Critique of Postcolonial Reason: Toward a History of the Vanishing Present*. Cambridge, MA: Harvard UP, 1999.

———. "The Politics of Translation." *Outside in the Teaching Machine*. New York: Routledge, 1993. 179–200.

———. "Translation as Culture." *Parallax* 6.1 (2000): 13–24.

Stachiewicz, Wanda. *Journey through History: A Memoir*. Toronto: Canadian Polish Research Institute, 1985.

Stanton, Domna S., ed. *The Female Autograph: Theory and Practice of Autobiography from the Tenth to the Twentieth Century*. Chicago and London: U of Chicago P, 1984. Piscataway, NJ: Rutgers UP, 1986.

Steedman, Carolyn. *Landscape for a Good Woman: A Story of Two Lives*. New Brunswick, NJ: Rutgers UP, 1986.

Stich, K.P. "Introduction." In Salverson, *Confessions* v–xvi.

———. *Reflections: Autobiography and Canadian Literature*. Ottawa: U of Ottawa P, 1988.

Sturken, Marita. *Tangled Memories: The Vietnam War, The AIDS Epidemic, and the Politics of Remembering*. Berkeley: U of California P, 1997.

Suleiman, Susan Rubin. "Writing and Motherhood." In Shirley Nelson Garner, Claire Kahane, and Madelon Sprengnether, eds., *The (M)other Tongue: Essays in Feminist Psychoanalytic Interpretation*. Ithaca and London: Cornell UP, 1985. 352–77.

Talib, Ismail S. *The Language of Postcolonial Literatures: An Introduction*. New York: Routledge, 2002.

Tan, Amy. "The Language of Discretion." In Paul Escholz, Alfred Rosa, and Virginia Clark, eds., *Language Awareness*. New York: St. Martin's P, 1994. 352–59.

Temple, Bogusia. "Terrible Times: Experience, Ethnicity and Auto/Biography." In Polkey, ed., *Women's Lives* 22–33.

Tessera: La Traduction au féminin/Translating Women 6 (1989).

Thompson, Dawn. *Writing a Politics of Perception: Memory, Holography, and Women Writers*. Toronto: U of Toronto P, 2000.

Tostevin, Lola Lemire. "The Muses Have Learned to Write: The Journal Diary Crosses Borders and Boundaries in Canadian Women's Writing." In Geoffrey Davis, ed., *Crisis and Creativity in New Literatures in English Canada*. Amsterdam: Rodopi, 1990. 215–26.

———. "Women of Letters: Correspondence with Smaro Kamboureli." *Subject to Criticism: Essays*. Stratford, ON: Mercury P, 1995. 73–104.

Tymoczko, Maria. "Post-colonial Writing and Literary Translation." In Bassnett and Trivedi, eds., *Post-colonial Translation* 19–40.

———. "Reconceptualizing Western Translation Theory: Integrating Non-Western Thought about Translation." In Theo Hermans, ed., *Translating Others*. Manchester, UK: Jerome Publishing, 2006: 13–32.

Usandizaga, Aranzazu. "Two Versions of the American Dream: Mary Antin's *The Promised Land* and Agnes Smedley's *Daughters of Earth*." In Gert Buelens and Ernst Rudin, eds., *Deferring a Dream: Literary Sub-Versions of the American Columbiad*. Basel: Birkhauser Verlag, 1994. 37–47.

Van Herk, Aritha. "The Ethnic Gasp." In Christie Verduyn, ed., *Literary Pluralities*. Peterborough, ON: Broadview Press, 1998. 75–80.

———. "Writing the Immigrant Self: Disguise and Damnation." *In visible Ink*. Edmonton, AB: NeWest Publishers, 1991. 173–89.

Venuti, Lawrence, ed. "Genealogies of Translation Theory: Schleiermacher." *TTR* 4.2 (1991): 125–50.

———. *Rethinking Translation: Discourse, Subjectivity, Ideology*. New York: Routledge, 1992.

———. "Translation, Community, Utopia." In Lawrence Venuti, ed., *The Translation Studies Reader*. New York: Routledge, 2000. 468–88.

Vevaina, Coomi S., and Barbara Godard, eds. *Intersexions: Issues of Race and Gender in Canadian Women's Writing*. New Dehli: Creative Books, 1996.

Vieira, Else Ribeiro Pires. "Liberating Calibans: Readings of Atropofagia and Haroldo de Campos' Poetics of Transcreation." In Bassnett and Trivedi, eds., *Post-colonial* 95–113.

Visweswaran, Kamala. *Fictions of Feminist Ethnography*. Minneapolis: U of Minnesota P, 1994.

Wah, Fred. *Faking It: Poetics and Hybridity, Critical Writings 1984–1999*. Edmonton, AB: NeWest Press, 2000.
Warhol, Robyn R. "Guilty Cravings: What Feminist Narratology Can Do for Cultural Studies." In David Herman, ed., *Narratologies*. Columbus: Ohio State UP, 1999.
Warren, Catherine Elizabeth. *Vignettes of Life: Experiences and Self-Perceptions of New Canadian Women*. Calgary, AB: Detselig, 1986.
Wasson, Kirsten. "A Geography of Conversion: Dialogical Boundaries of Self in Antin's *Promised Land*." In Ashley et al., eds., *Autobiography* 167–87.
Wegierski, Mark. "A Review of *Marynia Don't Cry*." *The Samaritan Review* (January 1998): 519–20.
Weisser, Susan Ostrov. "'What Kind of Life Have I Got?' Gender in the Life Story of an 'Ordinary' Woman." In Smith and Watson, eds., *Getting* 249–70.
West, Elizabeth J. "In the Beginning There Was Death: Spiritual Desolation and the Search for Self in Jamaica Kincaid's Autobiography of My Mother." *South Central Review* 20.2–4 (2003): 2–23.
White, Frances E. *Dark Continent of Our Bodies: Black Feminism and the Politics of Respectability*. Philadelphia: Temple UP, 2001.
Whitlock, Gillian. *Soft Weapons: Autobiography in Transit*. Chicago and London: U of Chicago P, 2007.
Whitlock, Gillian, and Anna Poletti. "Editor's Introduction: Self-Regarding Art." *Biography* 31.1 (Winter 2008): v–xxiii.
Wildeman, Marlene. "Daring Deeds: Translation as Lesbian Feminist Language Act." *Tessera* 6 (1989): 31–40.
Williams, Patrick, and Laura Chrisman, eds. *Colonial Discourse and Postcolonial Theory: A Reader*. New York: Columbia UP, 1994.
Williamson, Janice. "Sounding the Difference: An Interview with Smaro Kamboureli and Lola Tostevin." *Canadian Forum* 66 (1987): 33–38.
Winslow, Donald J. *Life-Writing: A Glossary of Terms in Biography, Autobiography, and Related Forms*. 2nd ed. Honolulu: U of Hawaii P, 1980.
Wolf, Doris. "Moving Out of 'the or of either': Reading Black Liberatory Subjectivity in Philip's *Looking for Livingstone*." *Open Letter* 9.2 (1995): 45–52.
Wong, Nellie. "In Search of the Self as Hero: Confetti of Voices on New Year's Night: A Letter to Myself." In Moraga and Anzaldua, eds., *This Bridge* 177–81.
Wong, Sau-Ling Cynthia. "Immigrant Autobiography: Some Questions of Definition and Approach." In Paul Eakin, ed., *American Autobiography: Retrospect and Prospect*. Madison: U of Wisconsin P, 1991. 142–70.
Yamamoto, Traise. *Making Selves, Making Subjects: Japanese American Women, Identity, and the Body*. Berkeley: U of California P, 1999.
Zaborowska, Magdalena J. *How We Found America: Reading Gender through East European Immigrant Narratives*. Chapel Hill: U of North Carolina P, 1995.
Zamora, Lois Parkinson, ed. *Contemporary American Women Writers: Gender, Class, Ethnicity*. Harlow, UK: Longman, 1998.

Zierler, Wendy. "In(ter)dependent Selves: Mary Antin, Elizabeth Stern, and Jewish Immigrant Women's Autobiography." In Katherine B. Payant and Toby Rose, eds., *The Immigrant Experience in North American Literature: Carving Out a Niche*. Westport, CT: Greenwood P, 1999, 1–16.

Index

A
abjection, 155, 159, 197, 208–209, 211
Abraham, Nicolas, and Maria Torok, 95
accent, 5, 49, 56, 66, 90, 131–32, 138, 153–55, 159–60, 171, 226, 241n2; as shibboleth, 131, 154
Adams, Henry, 149–50, 239n11, 12
Adams, Timothy Dow, 161
Alarcon, Norma, 20
Alger, Horatio, 55, 66, 112, 147
allegory, 39, 50, 52, 173, 178–79, 183–97, 200–201, 203–206, 211, 216, 218–19
alterity, 3, 29, 32, 34, 36, 91, 184, 191, 225
Alvarez, Julia, 151
Anatol, Gizelle Liz, 218
Andrade, Oswald de, 244n31
Ang, Ien, 23, 31, 132–33
Antin, Mary, 38, 41–68, 73, 77, 79, 80, 82, 83, 84–85, 86, 88–91, 93, 96, 97, 108, 119, 123, 126, 133, 136, 144, 148–49, 150, 169, 233–35nn1–24, 239n10
Anzaldua, Gloria, 15, 18, 20, 25, 223
Aristotle, 4
Asad, Talal, 93–94, 121, 236n28
Ashcroft et al., 24
assimilation, 5, 22, 28, 31–32, 38, 41–44, 48, 51–53, 55–57, 61, 63, 69–70, 78–79, 82, 84, 86, 88–89, 91, 93, 95, 99, 113, 120, 123–24, 128, 131, 138, 141, 145, 163, 171, 212
Augustine, 69, 90, 149, 235n22
autobiography, as anacoluthic discourse: 204, 216–17; autobiographical subject, 7–8, 14–15, 28, 38, 64, 66, 72, 77, 122, 137, 162, 169, 210, 215–16; confession and, 38, 44, 64, 66, 69–70, 90–91, 93, 128, 217; crypto(auto)graphy, 39, 94–95; ethnic a.: 7, 20–21, 25, 38, 93, 99, 124, 151; feminist criticism of, 10–11, 13–16, 21, 73–74, 105, 126, 150, 151; genre of, 2, 5, 13–16, 38, 66, 91, 105, 150, 197, 215, 231n15, 16, 232n26; Jewish American a., 46, 233n3; spiritual a. and conversion narrative, 31, 37, 46, 47, 84, 194, 233n3; supplementarity of, 6–7; as thanatography, 96; truth in, 10, 13, 64, 66, 70, 90, 97–98, 101, 164, 201, 206, 215, 217, 219; witnessing in, 65, 80, 114, 203, 212
autoethnography, 15, 16, 37, 48, 98, 101, 126, 131, 164, 179, 236–37n6

B
Bakhtin, Mikhail, 157, 242n9
Bal, Mieke, 201
Banting, Pamela, 17
Barthes, Roland, 216
Bartkowski, Frances, 232n24
Bartoloni, Paolo, 232n21

Index

Bassnett, Susan, and Harish Trivedi, 129, 218
Bataille, Georges, 153
Bell, Sharom Masingale, 175
Benjamin, Walter, 8, 10, 33, 34, 35, 96, 121, 165, 229n1, 232n21, 233n29. *See also* Derrida: on "The Task of the Translator"
Bennington, Geoffrey, 36–37
Benstock, Shari, 14, 16
Benston, Kimberly, 201–202, 207
Benveniste, Emil, 26
Bergland, Betty, 233n30, 5, 235n17
Berman, Antoine, 42–43, 69, 76, 99
Bernard, Louise, 243n24
Berry, Chuck, 160
Berryman, Charles, 231n15
Besemeres, Mary, 229n1
Bhabha, Homi, 12, 29–31, 33, 186, 190–91, 232n28, 241n8
bilingualism, 6, 19, 25, 38, 119, 132, 140, 152, 158, 175, 223, 230n8
body, 17–18, 27, 44, 53, 54, 59–60, 67–68, 71, 74–75, 84–85, 90, 111, 132, 138, 149, 151, 153–54, 171, 176, 185, 186, 196, 210, 214
Boelhower, William, 232n26, 239n10
Bourdieu, Pierre, 24
bpNichol, 161
Brand, Dionne, 179, 186
Brathwaite, Edward Kamu, 175, 182, 202
Brettell, Caroline, 130–31, 236n2
Brodzki, Bella, 10, 97, 121, 229n1, 231n10, 236n4; and Celeste Schenck, 14
Bronte, Charlotte, 197
Brooke-Rose, Christine, 16
Brossard, Nicole, 16, 153
Brown, Rosellen, 197
Burgess, Marilyn, 170
Burstein, Janet, 234n9
Busia, Abena, 196
Buss, Helen, 15, 73–74, 94, 230n2, 235n21
Butler, Judith, 8, 53

C

Cahan, Abraham, 233n3
Canetti, Elias, 152
Capécia, Mayotte, 243n21
capitalism, 23, 25, 60, 80, 82, 197, 204, 206, 244n31
Carbonell, Ovidio, 41
Caruth, Cathy, 111, 133–34, 238n1
Causse, Michele, 232n20
Césaire, Aimé, 177
Chamberlain, Mary, 177, 193
Chancy, Myriam, 190
Chanfrault-Duchet, Marie-Françoise, 100
Cheng, Anne, 198, 206, 217
Cheyfitz, Eric, 6
Chodorow, Nancy, 105, 198
Chow, Rey, 29, 32, 232n28, 233n29
Christian, Karen, 232n23
citizenship, 2, 5, 23, 46, 48, 60–63, 78, 79, 91, 100, 112–14, 154
Cixous, Hélène, 17, 18, 26, 35, 96, 129, 132, 152
Cobham, Rhonda, 187–89, 242n20
Cohen, Rose, 233n3
Collier, Gordon, 177
Collins, Patricia Hill, 183, 242n17
colonialism, 2, 11, 12, 24, 25, 31, 33, 80–81, 129, 174, 176, 181–83, 184, 186, 194, 197–98, 201, 203–205, 208–209, 211, 213, 219–20, 243n27
Corbett, Mary Jean, 236n2
Cosslett et al., 97, 126, 236n5
Costello, Jeanne, 231n16
Couser, Thomas, 46
Craig, Terrence, 78, 235n20
creolization, 39, 175, 177–79, 183, 189, 192–94, 197, 203, 213, 221, 226, 241nn6–7
Cronin, Michael, 229n1
Culley, Margo, 16
Currie, Noel Elizabeth, 188
Cutter, Martha, 229n1

D

Dante, 200
Davies, Carole Boyce, 20, 29–30, 148, 182, 242n11

Davies, Norman, 115, 237n12
Davis, Kathleen, 7, 37
Dawson, Mark, 121
de Campos, Haroldo, 244n31
deconstruction, 6–7, 10, 15, 53, 165, 175, 178, 182–83, 186, 198, 215–17, 220, 234n7
DeFehr, Wayne, 194
Deleuze, Gilles, and Félix Guattari, 3, 23, 68, 207, 243n25
de Lotbinière-Harwood, Susanne, 19
de Man, Paul, 96
Deputat, Mike, 237n11
Derrida, Jacques: critique of Jakobson, 4, 230n3; critique of liberal humanism, 33; critiques of, 231n12; crypt, 38, 76, 94–96, 117, 120, 126, 166, 236n3; debt and gift, 10, 38, 40, 68, 96–97, 107–109, 195–96; "Des Tours de Babel," 8, 10, 21, 32–33, 37, 51, 164, 165, 188, 230n4; *différance*, 7, 125, 153, 156–57, 160, 167, 169; *The Ear of the Other*, 4, 64, 68, 93, 95, 97, 120, 122–25, 130, 236n4; "The First Session," 164–65; "Fors," 95, 117; hymen, 164–66, 168; invagination, 155, 162, 166, 216; law of genre, 15; "Le Parjure," 204, 215, 217; *Monolingualism*, 29, 37, 43, 124–25, 130–32, 137–39, 156, 173, 193, 220, 223–27, 241n7, 243n21; otobiography, 64, 127; pharmakon, 21, 35, 130, 131, 158, 166, 242n10; on "The Task of the Translator" (Benjamin), 8–10, 33–35, 37, 76, 96, 118, 165, 229n1, 231n11, 233n29, 236n4; *Writing and Difference*, 158
Devi, Mahasweta, 33
Devy, Ganesh, 129
diary, 137, 152, 162–63, 167, 179, 190, 240–41n14
diaspora, 2, 5, 21, 23, 27, 31, 47–48, 52, 58, 129, 132–33, 134, 141, 144, 148, 160, 167, 173–74, 177, 179–80, 183, 185–86, 188, 193, 206, 224
Dingwaney, Anuradha, and Carol Maier, 27
Donnell, Alison, 215

Doray, Jocelyne, and Julian Samuel, 181
Dorscht, Susan Rudy, 242n18
Douglas, Frederick, 233n3
Du Bois, W.E.B., 24, 178, 198, 201

E
Eakin, Paul, 98, 147
Easton, Alison, 194
Egan, Susanna, 216, 231n18
Eldred, Janet, and Peter Mortensen, 44, 59
Elliot, T.S., 139, 237n10
Ellison, Ralph, 198
epistemology, 12, 44, 149, 160, 181, 187, 198, 204, 210, 220, 227; binary thinking, 11, 16, 17, 23, 28–29, 41, 71, 72, 74–75, 82, 170, 188, 194, 206, 209, 210, 213, 223; insider/outsider perspective, 104, 190; knowledge production, 26, 30, 31, 58–59, 67, 125, 128, 164; mind–body dualism, 84–85, 59–60
ethics, 3, 5, 9, 12, 18, 29, 31, 33–37, 39, 43, 97, 101, 107, 126, 132, 157–58, 163–64, 190, 199, 203, 206, 216, 220
ethnicity, 2, 5, 21–23, 46, 64, 69, 71, 75, 77, 81–82, 90, 100, 118, 122, 127, 132–33, 141, 151–52, 158–61, 163, 166, 224
ethnocentrism, 32, 35, 37, 43, 56, 70–71, 81, 83, 91, 93, 103, 129, 132, 145, 163, 179, 184, 202
exile, 21–23, 45, 47, 49–50, 52, 99, 116, 129, 133, 141, 144, 154, 159, 170, 180

F
Fanon, Frantz, 174–75, 177, 188, 198–201, 208, 210–11, 214–15, 241nn1–2, 241n5, 242n21, 243n22, 27
femininity, 19, 53–54, 74, 87, 90, 138, 198, 206–207, 209
feminism, 15, 17, 18, 20, 27–28, 30, 34, 39, 55, 61, 73, 75, 80, 82, 98, 114, 115, 122, 170, 193–94, 227, 234n13
fictionalization, 45, 76–77, 117, 134, 198, 215
fictionalysis, 16–17, 170
Firmat, Gustavo Pérez, 132, 136, 140

Fjellestad, Danuta Zadworna, 141, 239n6
Flotow, Louise von, 117, 118
Foucault, Michel, 153
Franklin, Benjamin, 233n3
Franklin, Cynthia, and Laura E. Lyons, 230n2
Freud, Sigmund, 74, 95, 133, 166, 185, 197, 217, 243n22
Frey, James, 10
Friedman, Susan Stanford, 14, 105
Fuchs, Miriam, 231n18

G
Gagnier, Regenia, 116, 150
Gagnon, Madeleine, 16, 19
Gates, Henry Louis, Jr., 198, 219, 241n9, 242n13
gender, 2, 5, 8, 11, 13–14, 17, 19–20, 34, 44, 49, 52–55, 69–70, 71–75, 82, 83, 87, 90, 100, 106–108, 112, 114–16, 122, 125, 138, 160, 162, 170–71, 178, 182–83, 185, 188, 193–94, 197–98, 201, 206, 209, 211, 224, 232n22
George, Rosemary Marangoly, 48, 102–103
Ghosh-Shellhorn, Martina, 232n28
Gilmore, Leigh, 13–14, 16, 219, 231n18, 243n24
Gilroy, Paul, 23
Glissant, Edouard, 174, 177, 181, 183, 194–95, 241n6, 242n12
globalization, 1, 12, 21, 24, 39, 229n1
Glogowska, Barbara, 237n11
Gluck, Sherna Berger, and Daphne Patai, 94
Godard, Barbara, 9, 10, 11, 12, 19, 70, 84–85, 158, 166, 176, 180, 182, 190, 191, 194, 240n19
Goldman, Ann, 231n18
Goldman, Emma, 234n13
Gonzalez, Jennifer, 16
Gonzalez, Madelena, and Francine Tolron, 229n1
Grossman, Ibolya, 41, 124
Grosz, Elizabeth, 210
Grove, Frederick Philip, 46
Guex, Germaine, 208

Gunew, Sneja, 22, 86
Gunnars, Kristjana, 235n21, 23

H
Hall, Stuart, 187
Hancock, Herbie, 160
Harris, Claire, 173
Harris, Jennifer, 184
Hegel, Georg Wilhelm Friedrich, 184
Hellerstein, Kathryn, 52
Henderson, Mae Gwendolyn, 193
Henke, Suzette, 231n18
Hermans, Theo, 5
hermeneutics, 4, 6, 20, 36
Hernandes, Jennifer Browdy de, 240n23
Hillis Miller, J., 129
Hinz, Evelyn, 230n2
Hirsch, Marianne, 19, 238n1, 2
Ho, Mingfong, 223
Hoffman, Eva, 38, 129–51, 152, 154, 156, 159, 161, 162, 163, 168–71, 184, 234n7, 238–239n, 240n21, 23
Holomb, Gary E., and Kimberly S. Holomb, 211, 243n27
Holte, James Craig, 48
Homer, 240n20, 21
hooks, bell, 15, 192, 196
Houston, Jeanne, 237n7
Huff, Cynthia, 15
Hutcheon, Linda, 192
hybridity, 1, 4, 12, 25, 27, 30–33, 90, 91, 127, 133, 141, 148, 160, 162, 177–78, 180, 184, 232n28

I
identity, 3, 7, 12, 22–23, 25, 29, 31, 33, 35–36, 38–39, 73, 79, 84, 89, 119, 124, 127, 130, 133, 137, 141, 147, 152, 155–57, 159, 160–61, 164, 176, 177, 183, 185, 187, 193, 203, 206, 224
ideology, 2,3, 11, 26, 27, 70, 71, 78, 114, 126, 134, 145, 169, 183, 190, 198, 226
immigration, 23–24, 42, 45, 46–47, 49, 78–79, 100, 103, 114, 116, 126, 141, 143, 159–60, 174, 176, 180
imperialism, 2, 6, 20, 24–25, 32–33, 80, 91, 174–75, 182, 183, 184

indigeneity, 2, 12, 20, 24, 80–81, 174, 176, 187, 188, 200, 202–204, 206, 217–18
individualism, 14, 49, 55, 97, 104, 105, 114, 115, 147–48, 150, 194
intersubjectivity, 96, 97, 105, 107, 216, 236n5
Irigaray, Luce, 18–19, 198
Irving, Katrina, 233n2

J
Jakobson, Roman, 3–5
Jelinek, Estelle C., 13–14, 231n16
Jolly, Margareta, 230n2
Joseph, May, and Jennifer N. Fink, 31

K
Kadar, Marlene, 16–17, 124, 237n6; Kadar et al., 232n22
Kamboureli, Smaro, 38, 127, 129–33, 151–71, 239–240n4n–21
Kant, Immanuel, 34
Kaplan, Caren, 15
Karamcheti, Indira, 184, 195
Kellman, Steven, 230n8
Kikuchi, Charles, 237n7
Kikumura, Akemi, 38, 93–94, 97, 99–114, 122, 124–28, 131, 169, 171
Kim, Myung Mi, 46
Kincaid, Jamaica, 39, 173–79, 196–221, 223, 242nn19–20, 243n22–28, 244n29
Kinnear, Mary, 235n24
Kipling, Rudyard, 78
Klein, Melanie, 198
Kojder, Apolonja Maria, 38, 93–94, 97, 100, 114–28, 131, 237–38nn12–15
Kristeva, Julia, 36, 86, 132, 153, 157, 197, 206–208, 209, 232n22, 240n15
Kroetsch, Robert, 152, 166–67, 240n20
Kundera, Milan, 138

L
Labov, William, 240n22
Lacan, Jacques, 137, 153, 164, 197
La Malinche, 20, 88
language: acquisition of, 44, 55–56, 83, 119, 136, 156, 183, 207, 209; and agency, 12, 18–20, 25, 39, 48, 87, 106, 147, 189, 207–209, 211; as androcentric, 2, 17–20; commodification of 5, 21, 26, 31, 100, 103; and communication, 8, 36, 67, 70, 72, 97, 104, 175, 209; and domination, 2, 6, 20, 24–25, 30, 31, 39, 87, 94, 175, 180–82, 193, 196, 212–14; linguistic displacement, 3, 21–22, 45, 77, 131, 137, 151, 155–56, 183, 224; monolanguage and monolingualism, 4, 20, 24, 33–34, 36, 37, 42, 50, 99, 129, 135, 159, 173, 175, 189, 192, 223–24, 228; mother tongue, 13, 21, 25, 35, 37, 132, 136, 146, 152, 156–57, 176, 182–83, 184, 185, 200, 213, 224, 226, 232n24; and otherness, 7, 22, 29, 156, 224; plurality of, 3–4, 8, 19, 33, 34, 51, 117, 193, 224; standardization, 24, 50, 99, 154, 171, 175–76, 183, 192, 196–97, 213, 225–26, 242n14; translingualism, 6, 21, 230n8
Laplanche, Jean, 233n29
Layoun, Mary N., 88
Lefevere, André, 5, 230n7
Leiris, Michel, 153
Lejeune, Philippe, 10
Levinas, Emmanuel, 36, 199, 225
Lewisohn, Ludwig, 233n3
life writing, 2, 13, 15–18, 25–26, 29–33, 36–37, 87, 91, 96, 105, 115, 124, 152, 161, 164–66, 169, 170, 171, 179, 194, 197–98, 220, 224, 230n2
Lim, Shirley Geok-lin, 21, 23; Lim and Kyungah Hing, 231n9
Lionnet, Françoise, 2, 14–15, 174, 178, 183, 207, 235n22, 240n1, 242n15, 241n6
Lippi-Green, Rosina, 24, 154, 171, 226, 240n22, 241n4
literacy, 20, 38, 41, 44, 53, 55, 56–58, 82, 85, 89, 119, 131, 139, 147, 161
Longfellow, Henry Wadsworth, 56
long poem, 38, 151, 161–62, 167, 168, 240n19
Lorde, Audre, 2, 15, 99, 240n23

M

Ma, Sheng-mei, 100
Macaulay, Thomas Babington, 186
Makabe, Tomoko, 98, 237n8
Malcolm X, 202
Mallarmé, Stéphane, 33, 164, 165
Mandel, Eli, 166
Maran, René, 243n21
Marlatt, Daphne, 16–18, 85, 153
Mason, Mary G., 14
Matibag, Eugenio, 218
McAlpine, Kristie, 190
McCance, Dawne, 157, 240n15
McClung, Nellie, 235n24
Meigs, Mary, 153
memoir, 10, 90, 94, 100, 115, 119, 121, 128, 236n2
memory, 17, 38, 67–68, 85, 96–97, 98, 111, 118, 120–21, 134, 140, 142, 151, 153, 157, 162, 174, 177, 180, 183, 186, 193, 211, 232n21
metaphor, 6, 10–11, 75, 153, 178, 182, 185, 188, 191, 212, 216, 218, 219–20
métissage, 16, 177, 189, 241n6, 242n15
metonymy, 9, 68, 153, 162, 187, 210, 212, 216, 219–20
Mezei, Kathy, 4, 232n20
Mickiewicz, Adam, 122, 238n14
Miller, Nancy K., 14, 15
Milosz, Czeslaw, 138
Milton, John, 215
mimicry, 53, 178, 184, 186, 190–91, 201, 204, 211, 213, 215, 241n8
Minh-ha, Trinh T., 21, 125, 163, 223
Mintz, Susannah B., 16
Molloy, Sylvia, 90
monologism, 17, 19, 36, 37, 76, 132, 156–58
Moodie, Susanna, 46
Moraga, Cherîe, 20
Morris, Kathryn E., 213, 217, 218, 244n30
Moya Paula, 22, 232n25
Mukherjee, Arun, 22
multiculturalism, 21–22, 28, 42, 44, 83, 94, 98–99, 123–24, 127, 133, 151, 158, 229n1
Munton, Ann, 161

N

Nabokov, Vladimir, 138
nationalism, 5, 20, 23, 37, 46, 48, 49, 64, 75, 79–80, 84, 87–89, 116, 121, 160, 162, 182, 183
nation-state, 21, 23, 31, 79, 100, 111–12, 114, 123, 124, 132, 148, 151, 154, 197, 206, 224, 232n26
negativity, 173, 177, 179, 184, 197, 200, 206–207, 217
Neijmann, Daisy, 69
neoliberalism, 2, 39
Neuman, Shirley, 127, 230n2
Nin, Anais, 153, 163, 167
Niranjana, Tejaswini, 25, 29, 31–32

O

Okubo, Mine, 237n7
Olney, James, 231n17
oral history, 15, 38, 94, 96, 97–99, 105, 115, 120, 122, 127, 128
Ostenso, Martha, 46
Oster, Judith, 137

P

Palumbo-Liu, David, 113–14
Paravisini-Gebert, Lizabeth, 242n19
Pascal, Roy, 230n9, 231n15
Pasolini, Pier Paolo, 153
Paul, Heike, 241n2
Payant, Katherine B., 233n4
performance, 7–9, 11, 15, 19, 27–28, 31, 53–54, 64, 84, 90, 121, 127, 147, 148, 153, 155–56, 162–63, 169, 170, 178, 190, 195, 201, 212, 225
Perreault, Jeanne, 16
Phelan, Peggy, 134
phenomenology, 6, 27, 37, 74, 75, 210, 214, 215
Philip, Marlene Nourbese, 39, 173–97, 213, 217, 219–21, 223, 242n12
photography, 127, 153, 161, 190, 194, 216
Plato, 4, 242n13
postcolonial theories, 2, 6, 11, 12, 24, 30–34, 39, 93, 129, 173–75, 177–78, 180, 197–98, 200–201, 214, 220, 232n28, 240n1

postmodernism, 7, 12, 14, 31, 39, 129, 131, 133, 140, 141, 145–47, 152, 156–57
postmodernity, 23, 134, 149, 170, 174, 196
poststructuralism, 3, 5, 7, 31, 33, 131, 150, 155, 157, 169, 201, 202, 229n1, 231n17
poverty, 2, 23, 49, 58, 60–62, 69, 73–74, 82, 90, 107, 109, 110, 114, 115, 144, 174, 197, 201
Powell, Barbara, 73–74, 235n21
Prasad, G.J.V., 230n8
Pratt, Mary Louise, 236n6
Proefriedt, William A., 63

R
racialization, 2, 11, 22–23, 46, 63–64, 80–81, 100, 111–14, 128, 152, 160, 171, 183, 185, 194, 197, 211–12
Radhakrishnan, R., 163
Rak, Julie, 14–15, 231n15, 232n18
Rao, Eleonora, 153, 155, 164
Rao, Sathya, 231n12
Ravage, M.E., 233n3
Rayson, Ann, 105, 237n9
Reed-Danahay, Deborah, 236n6
Reynolds, Bryan, 231n12
rhetoric, 9, 35–36, 49, 89, 178–79, 200–201, 218–19
Rhys, Jean, 197
Rich, Adrienne, 15, 19, 192
Ricoeur, Paul, 6, 9, 29, 34–35, 42, 43, 66–67, 125, 129–30, 131, 193
Riis, Jacob, 233n3
Ripley, William Z., 233n2
Roberts, Richard, 23, 177
Rousseau, Jean Jacques, 69, 90, 235n22
Roy, Sukhmani, 156, 157, 166, 240n14
Roy, Wendy, 235n21
Rosenzweig, Franz, 42
Russell, Catherine, 96, 98, 101

S
Salverson, Laura Goodman, 38, 41–46, 69–91, 93, 96, 97, 117, 119, 123, 126, 136, 144, 150, 235–36nn21ff.

Salz, Evelyn, 49, 65, 68, 233n1, 3, 6, 234n8, 11, 13, 235nn16–17
Sanders, Leslie, 180
San Juan, E., Jr., 239n8
Sapir-Whorf hypothesis, 140
Sarbadhikary, Krishna, 242n16
Schleiermacher, Friedrich, 42, 43, 70
Sedgwick, Ellery, 49, 50, 64, 65, 68, 233n3, 235n16
Seferis, George, 153
Senghor, Léopold, 177, 194
Sengupta, Mahasweta, 89
sexuality, 2, 5, 20, 44, 55, 72–73, 75, 90, 106, 126, 138, 146, 149, 167, 186, 188, 209–12
Shakespeare, William, 130
Shell, Marc, 224
Shields, Kathleen, 232n27
Shima, George, 112
signifying, 179, 185, 190, 197–98, 200, 205–208, 210, 219, 241–42n9
silence, 30, 40, 71, 90, 104, 105, 109–10, 113, 126, 128, 135, 136, 153, 162, 166, 180, 184–96, 214, 220
Simon, Sherry, 4, 12, 30, 126
Singer, Isaac Bashevis, 233n3
slums, 57, 58, 60–61, 63, 66, 80
Smith, Sidonie, 8, 14–15, 27, 50, 74, 147, 150, 161, 233n5, 235n18; and Julia Watson, 14, 15, 231n15, 18, 233n30
Snead, James A., 184, 219
Soliday, Mary, 44
Sollors, Werner, 49, 50, 52, 141, 163, 234n10, 239n8
Sone, Monica, 237n7
Spender, Dale, 19
Spivak, Gayatri Chakravorty, 12, 29, 33–34, 127, 176
Stachiewicz, Wanda, 237n13
Stanton, Domna, 16
Steedman, Carolyn, 231n18
Stein, Gertrude, 197
Stern, Elizabeth, 233n3, 239n9
Stich, K.P., 77, 78, 79, 80, 83, 90, 230n2, 236n25
Sturken, Marita, 110–11

subjectivity, 4–5, 7, 16–18, 22–23, 26–28, 30, 32, 37, 66, 74, 82, 89, 94, 117, 118, 123, 126, 128, 141, 147–48, 150, 151, 155–57, 163, 169, 181, 184, 186, 193, 197–200, 206–207, 210, 220, 225
Suleiman, Susan Rubin, 216
supplement, 6–7, 10, 12, 15, 30, 33, 47, 125, 155, 195, 216

T
Talib, Ismail S., 214, 241n3, 242n14
Tan, Amy, 133, 171
Temple, Bogusia, 237n10, 238n13
Thompson, Dawn, 185–86
Tostevin, Lola Lemire, 155, 163, 170, 239n13
Traill, Catharine Parr, 46
translation: as cannibalism, 32, 217–18; as commodity, 5; culture and, 11–13, 27, 30–33, 41, 77, 103, 118, 125, 136; as cultural enrichment, 78, 87–88, 90, 93, 236n28; Derrida's definition of, 4; as equivalence, 9, 11, 67, 91, 118, 125, 130, 136, 148, 176, 224, 227; Eurocentric definition of, 4, 32; feminist view of, 5–6, 10–11, 19–20, 30, 84; fidelity and betrayal, 8–9, 42, 49, 67, 88, 106, 129, 132, 153; foreignizing and domesticating, 38, 42–43, 50–52, 56–57, 61, 65, 70–71, 76–77, 86, 89–91, 122, 124, 130, 207; genealogy and, 10, 26, 39–40, 48, 77, 84, 90, 94, 97, 108, 120–21, 125, 173, 176, 186, 196, 201, 216; Godard's definition of, 19; in-betweenness of, 9, 11–12, 18, 26, 28, 30, 43, 133, 136, 148, 163–68, 169, 212; Jakobson's definition of, 3–4; linguistic hospitality of, 35, 43, 94, 126, 130, 193, 225, 227; mourning and, 95, 120, 130–31, 183, 220; narrow and broad views of, 5, 33–34; proper name and property rights in, 9–10, 37, 39, 56, 120, 197, 215, 224–26; as re/version, 176, 180, 195, 207, 212, 220; Ricoeur's definition of, 9; supplementarity of, 6–7, 20, 30, 33; as transversal movement, 12, 75

transnationality, 1, 20, 23, 31, 39, 163–64, 177, 224, 227, 232n28
transparency, 11, 14, 32, 33, 50, 52, 70–71, 76, 94, 102, 117–19, 122–24, 130, 163, 169, 214, 219, 224
trauma, 39–40, 96, 100, 110–11, 114, 115, 126, 133–34, 142–43, 152, 169, 176, 179, 183, 186, 212, 231n18
travel writing, 31, 38, 39, 161, 179, 188, 193–94
Tury, Gideon, 230n7
Tymoczko, Maria, 94, 230n5, 7, 244n29

U
Uchida, Yashiko, 237n7
Usandizaga, Aranzazu, 233n7
utopia, 20, 27, 71, 184, 187, 190–91

V
Van Herk, Aritha, 69, 126
Venuti, Lawrence, 70–71, 124
Vieira, Else Ribeiro Pires, 244n31
Visweswaran, Kamala, 93, 163–64

W
Wah, Fred, 232n19
Walcott, Derek, 182, 197
Warhol, Robyn, 230n6
Warren, Catherine E., 98
Washington, Booker T., 233n3
Washington, George, 49, 61
Wasson, Kirsten, 56, 233n5, 235n18
Watson, Julia, 14, 15
Webb, Phyllis, 153
Wegierski, Marek, 123
Weisser, Susan Ostrov, 98
West, Elizabeth J., 242n19
Wheatley, Phillis, 233n3
White, Frances E., 177
whiteness, 63–64, 80, 113, 123, 171, 185, 198, 204–205, 212, 218
Whitlock, Gillian, 15–16, 23; and Anna Poletti, 232n19
Whitman, Walt, 235n15
Wilde, Oscar, 70
Wildeman, Marlene, 17–18
Williamson, Janice, 155, 159
Winslow, Donald J., 230n2

Wolf, Doris, 194
Wong, Nellie, 114
Wong, Sau-Ling Cynthia, 48
Woodsworth, J.S., 236n25
Woolf, Virginia, 153

Y
Yamamoto, Traise, 111
Yeats, William Butler, 139

Yezierska, Anzia, 233n3, 239n9

Z
Zaborowska, Magdalena, 54–55, 146, 171, 233n5, 239n9
Zaleski, Irma, 237n11
Zamora, Lois Parkinson, 231n13
Zangwill, Israel, 51, 234n10–11, 236n27
Zierler, Wendy, 55, 234n8

Books in the Life Writing Series
Published by Wilfrid Laurier University Press

Haven't Any News: Ruby's Letters from the Fifties edited by Edna Staebler with an Afterword by Marlene Kadar • 1995 / x + 165 pp. / ISBN 0-88920-248-6

"I Want to Join Your Club": Letters from Rural Children, 1900–1920 edited by Norah L. Lewis with a Preface by Neil Sutherland • 1996 / xii + 250 pp. (30 b&w photos) / ISBN 0-88920-260-5

And Peace Never Came by Elisabeth M. Raab with Historical Notes by Marlene Kadar • 1996 / x + 196 pp. (12 b&w photos, map) / ISBN 0-88920-281-8

Dear Editor and Friends: Letters from Rural Women of the North-West, 1900–1920 edited by Norah L. Lewis • 1998 / xvi + 166 pp. (20 b&w photos) / ISBN 0-88920-287-7

The Surprise of My Life: An Autobiography by Claire Drainie Taylor with a Foreword by Marlene Kadar • 1998 / xii + 268 pp. (8 colour photos and 92 b&w photos) / ISBN 0-88920-302-4

Memoirs from Away: A New Found Land Girlhood by Helen M. Buss / Margaret Clarke • 1998 / xvi + 153 pp. / ISBN 0-88920-350-4

The Life and Letters of Annie Leake Tuttle: Working for the Best by Marilyn Färdig Whiteley • 1999 / xviii + 150 pp. / ISBN 0-88920-330-x

Marian Engel's Notebooks: "Ah, mon cahier, écoute" edited by Christl Verduyn • 1999 / viii + 576 pp. / ISBN 0-88920-333-4 cloth / ISBN 0-88920-349-0 paper

Be Good Sweet Maid: The Trials of Dorothy Joudrie by Audrey Andrews • 1999 / vi + 276 pp. / ISBN 0-88920-334-2

Working in Women's Archives: Researching Women's Private Literature and Archival Documents edited by Helen M. Buss and Marlene Kadar • 2001 / vi + 120 pp. / ISBN 0-88920-341-5

Repossessing the World: Reading Memoirs by Contemporary Women by Helen M. Buss • 2002 / xxvi + 206 pp. / ISBN 0-88920-408-x cloth / ISBN 0-88920-410-1 paper

Chasing the Comet: A Scottish-Canadian Life by Patricia Koretchuk • 2002 / xx + 244 pp. / ISBN 0-88920-407-1

The Queen of Peace Room by Magie Dominic • 2002 / xii + 115 pp. / ISBN 0-88920-417-9

China Diary: The Life of Mary Austin Endicott by Shirley Jane Endicott • 2002 / xvi + 251 pp. / ISBN 0-88920-412-8

The Curtain: Witness and Memory in Wartime Holland by Henry G. Schogt • 2003 / xii + 132 pp. / ISBN 0-88920-396-2

Teaching Places by Audrey J. Whitson • 2003 / xiii + 178 pp. / ISBN 0-88920-425-x

Through the Hitler Line by Laurence F. Wilmot, M.C. • 2003 / xvi + 152 pp. / ISBN 0-88920-448-9

Where I Come From by Vijay Agnew • 2003 / xiv + 298 pp. / ISBN 0-88920-414-4

The Water Lily Pond by Han Z. Li • 2004 / x + 254 pp. / ISBN 0-88920-431-4

The Life Writings of Mary Baker McQuesten: Victorian Matriarch edited by Mary J. Anderson • 2004 / xxii + 338 pp. / ISBN 0-88920-437-3

Seven Eggs Today: The Diaries of Mary Armstrong, 1859 and 1869 edited by Jackson W. Armstrong • 2004 / xvi + 228 pp. / ISBN 0-88920-440-3

Love and War in London: A Woman's Diary 1939–1942 by Olivia Cockett; edited by Robert W. Malcolmson • 2005 / xvi + 208 pp. / ISBN 0-88920-458-6

Incorrigible by Velma Demerson • 2004 / vi + 178 pp. / ISBN 0-88920-444-6

Auto/biography in Canada: Critical Directions edited by Julie Rak • 2005 / viii + 264 pp. / ISBN 0-88920-478-0

Tracing the Autobiographical edited by Marlene Kadar, Linda Warley, Jeanne Perreault, and Susanna Egan • 2005 / viii + 280 pp. / ISBN 0-88920-476-4

Must Write: Edna Staebler's Diaries edited by Christl Verduyn • 2005 / viii + 304 pp. / ISBN 0-88920-481-0

Pursuing Giraffe: A 1950s Adventure by Anne Innis Dagg • 2006 / xvi + 284 pp. (photos, 2 maps) / 978-0-88920-463-8

Food That Really Schmecks by Edna Staebler • 2007 / xxiv + 334 pp. / ISBN 978-0-88920-521-5

163256: A Memoir of Resistance by Michael Englishman • 2007 / xvi + 112 pp. (14 b&w photos) / ISBN 978-1-55458-009-5

The Wartime Letters of Leslie and Cecil Frost, 1915–1919 edited by R.B. Fleming • 2007 / xxxvi + 384 pp. (49 b&w photos, 5 maps) / ISBN 978-1-55458-000-2

Johanna Krause Twice Persecuted: Surviving in Nazi Germany and Communist East Germany by Carolyn Gammon and Christiane Hemker • 2007 / x + 170 pp. (58 b&w photos, 2 maps) / ISBN 978-1-55458-006-4

Watermelon Syrup: A Novel by Annie Jacobsen with Jane Finlay-Young and Di Brandt • 2007 / x + 268 pp. / ISBN 978-1-55458-005-7

Broad Is the Way: Stories from Mayerthorpe by Margaret Norquay • 2008 / x + 106 pp. (6 b&w photos) / ISBN 978-1-55458-020-0

Becoming My Mother's Daughter: A Story of Survival and Renewal by Erika Gottlieb • 2008 / x + 178 pp. (36 b&w illus., 17 colour) / ISBN 978-1-55458-030-9

Leaving Fundamentalism: Personal Stories edited by G. Elijah Dann • 2008 / xii + 234 pp. / ISBN 978-1-55458-026-2

Bearing Witness: Living with Ovarian Cancer edited by Kathryn Carter and Lauri Elit • 2009 / viii + 94 pp. / ISBN 978-1-55458-055-2

Dead Woman Pickney: A Memoir of Childhood in Jamaica by Yvonne Shorter Brown • 2010 / viii + 202 pp. / ISBN 978-1-55458-189-4

I Have a Story to Tell You by Seemah C. Berson • 2010 / xx + 288 pp. (24 b&w photos) / ISBN 978-1-55458-219-8

We All Giggled: A Bourgeois Family Memoir by Thomas O. Hueglin • 2010 / xiv + 232 pp. (20 b&w photos) / ISBN 978-1-55458-262-4

Just a Larger Family: Letters of Marie Williamson from the Canadian Home Front, 1940–1944 edited by Mary F. Williamson and Tom Sharp • 2011 / xxiv + 378 pp. (16 b&w photos) / ISBN 978-1-55458-323-2

Burdens of Proof: Faith, Doubt, and Identity in Autobiography by Susanna Egan • 2011 / x + 200 pp. / ISBN 978-1-55458-333-1

Accident of Fate: A Personal Account 1938–1945 by Imre Rochlitz with Joseph Rochlitz • 2011 / xiv + 226 pp. (50 b&w photos, 5 maps) / ISBN 978-1-55458-267-9

The Green Sofa by Natascha Würzbach, translated by Raleigh Whitinger • 2012 / xiv + 240 pp. (5 b&w photos) / ISBN 978-1-55458-334-8

Unheard Of: Memoirs of a Canadian Composer by John Beckwith • 2012 / x + 393 pp. (74 illus., 8 musical examples) / ISBN 978-1-55458-358-4

Borrowed Tongues: Life Writing, Migration, and Translation by Eva C. Karpinski • 2012 / viii + 274 pp. / ISBN 978-1-55458-357-7

Basements and Attics, Closets and Cyberspace: Explorations in Canadian Women's Archives edited by Linda M. Morra and Jessica Schagerl • forthcoming 2012 / 355 pp. / ISBN 978-1-55458-632-5

Not the Whole Story: Challenging the Single Mother Narrative edited by Lea Caragata and Judit Alcalde • forthcoming 2012 / 176 pp. / ISBN 978-1-55458-624-0